Samy Bengio   Hervé Bourlard

Machine Learning for Multimodal Interaction

First International Workshop, MLMI 2004
Martigny, Switzerland, June 21-23, 2004
Revised Selected Papers

 Springer

Volume Editors

Samy Bengio
Hervé Bourlard
IDIAP Research Institute
Rue du Simplon 4, P.O. Box 592, 1920 Martigny, Switzerland
E-mail: {bengio,bourlard}@idiap.ch

Library of Congress Control Number: 2004118425

CR Subject Classification (1998): H.5.2-3, H.5, I.2.6, I.2.10, I.2, I.7, K.4, I.4

ISSN 0302-9743
ISBN 3-540-24509-X Springer Berlin Heidelberg New York

Springer is a part of Springer Science+Business Media

springeronline.com

© Springer-Verlag Berlin Heidelberg 2005
Printed in Germany

Typesetting: Camera-ready by author, data conversion by Scientific Publishing Services, Chennai, India
Printed on acid-free paper   SPIN: 11384212   06/3142   5 4 3 2 1 0

Preface

This book contains a selection of refereed papers presented at the 1st Workshop on Machine Learning for Multimodal Interaction (MLMI 2004), held at the "Centre du Parc," Martigny, Switzerland, during June 21–23, 2004. The workshop was organized and sponsored jointly by three European projects,

- AMI, Augmented Multiparty Interaction, http://www.amiproject.org
- PASCAL, Pattern Analysis, Statistical Modeling and Computational Learning, http://www.pascal-network.org
- M4, Multi-modal Meeting Manager, http://www.m4project.org

as well as the Swiss National Centre of Competence in Research (NCCR):

- IM2: Interactive Multimodal Information Management, http://www.im2.ch

MLMI 2004 was thus sponsored by the European Commission and the Swiss National Science Foundation.

Given the multiple links between the above projects and several related research areas, it was decided to organize a joint workshop bringing together researchers from the different communities working around the common theme of advanced machine learning algorithms for processing and structuring multimodal human interaction in meetings. The motivation for creating such a forum, which could be perceived as a number of papers from different research disciplines, evolved from a real need that arose from these projects and the strong motivation of their partners for such a multidisciplinary workshop. This assessment was indeed confirmed by the success of this first MLMI workshop, which attracted more than 200 participants.

The conference program featured invited talks, full papers (subject to careful peer review, by at least three reviewers), and posters (accepted on the basis of abstracts) covering a wide range of areas related to machine learning applied to multimodal interaction—and more specifically to multimodal meeting processing, as addressed by the M4, AMI and IM2 projects. These areas included:

- human-human communication modeling
- speech and visual processing
- multimodal processing, fusion and fission
- multimodal dialog modeling
- human-human interaction modeling
- multimodal data structuring and presentation
- multimedia indexing and retrieval
- meeting structure analysis
- meeting summarizing
- multimodal meeting annotation
- machine learning applied to the above

Out of the submitted full papers, about 60% were accepted for publication in this volume, after the authors were invited to take review comments and conference feedback into account.

In this book, and following the structure of the workshop, the papers were divided into the following sections:

1. HCI and Applications
2. Structuring and Interaction
3. Multimodal Processing
4. Speech Processing
5. Dialogue Management
6. Vision and Emotion

In the spirit of MLMI 2004 and its associated projects, all the oral presentations were recorded, and synchronized with additional material (such as presentation slides) and are now available, with search facilities, at: **http://mmm.idiap.ch/mlmi04/**

Based on the success of MLMI 2004, a series of MLMI workshop is now being planned, with the goal of involving a larger community, as well as a larger number of European projects working in similar or related areas. MLMI 2005 will be organized by the University of Edinburgh and held on 11–13 July 2005, also in collaboration with the NIST (US National Institute of Standards and Technology), while MLMI 2006 will probably be held in the US, probably in conjunction with a NIST evaluation.

Finally, we take this opportunity to thank our Program Committee members for an excellent job, as well as the sponsoring projects and funding agencies. We also thank all our administrative support, especially Nancy Robyr who played a key role in the management and organization of the workshop, as well as in the follow-up of all the details resulting in this book.

December 2004   Samy Bengio
                                                                  Hervé Bourlard

Organization

General Chairs

Samy Bengio — IDIAP Research Institute, Switzerland
Hervé Bourlard — IDIAP Research Institute and EPFL, Switzerland

Program Committee

Jean Carletta — University of Edinburgh, UK
Daniel Gatica-Perez — IDIAP Research Institute, Switzerland
Phil Green — University of Sheffield, UK
Hynek Hermansky — IDIAP Research Institute, Switzerland
Jan Larsen — Technical University of Denmark
Nelson Morgan — ICSI, Berkeley, USA
Erkki Oja — Helsinki University of Technology, Finland
Barbara Peskin — ICSI, Berkeley, USA
Thierry Pun — University of Geneva, Switzerland
Steve Renals — University of Edinburgh, UK
John Shawe-Taylor — University of Southampton, UK
Jean-Philippe Thiran — EPFL Lausanne, Switzerland
Luc Van Gool — ETHZ Zurich, Switzerland
Pierre Wellner — IDIAP Research Institute, Switzerland
Steve Whittaker — University of Sheffield, UK

Sponsoring Projects and Institutions

Projects:

- Augmented Multiparty Interaction (AMI), http://www.amiproject.org
- Pattern Analysis, Statistical Modeling and Computational Learning (PASCAL), http://www.pascal-network.org
- Multi-modal Meeting Manager (M4), http://www.m4project.org
- Interactive Multimodal Information Management (IM2), http://www.im2.ch

Institutions:

- European Commission
- Swiss National Science Foundation, through the National Centres of Competence in Research (NCCR) program

Table of Contents

MLMI 2004

I HCI and Applications

II Structuring and Interaction

III   Multimodal Processing

IV   Speech Processing

V   Dialogue Management

VI   Vision and Emotion

Accessing Multimodal Meeting Data: Systems, Problems and Possibilities

Simon Tucker and Steve Whittaker

Department of Information Studies, University of Sheffield,
Regent Court, 211 Portobello Street, Sheffield, S1 4DP, UK
{s.tucker,s.whittaker}@shef.ac.uk

Abstract. As the amount of multimodal meetings data being recorded increases, so does the need for sophisticated mechanisms for accessing this data. This process is complicated by the different informational needs of users, as well as the range of data collected from meetings. This paper examines the current state of the art in meeting browsers. We examine both systems specifically designed for browsing multimodal meetings data and those designed to browse data collected from different environments, for example broadcast news and lectures. As a result of this analysis, we highlight potential directions for future research - semantic access, filtered presentation, limited display environments, browser evaluation and user requirements capture.

1 Introduction

Several large-scale projects (e.g. [1,2]) have examined the collection, analysis and browsing of multimodal meeting data. Here we provide an overview of browsing tools, where we refer to any post-hoc examination of meetings data (e.g. searching a meeting transcript or reviewing a particular discourse) as *browsing*. As a result of our analysis, we are also in a position to highlight potential areas of research for future meeting browsers.

Despite being an emerging field, there are a large number of browsers described in the literature, and therefore the first stage of summarising the field was to determine a suitable browser taxonomy. The scheme used in tthis paper is to classify browsers according to their focus of navigation or attention. The taxonomy is described in more detail in Section 2 and is summarised in Table 1.

The structure of this papers is as follows. We begin by discussing how meeting browsers are classified and continue by describing each browser, according to its classification. A summary of all the browsers is then given, as a result of which we highlight directions for future research.

2 A Meeting Browser Taxonomy

Since browsing of meetings data is still an emerging field, the classification system used here is necessarily preliminary, but achieves a segregation of the range of browsers described in the literature. Browsers are classified primarily by their *focus*,

S. Bengio and H. Bourlard (Eds.): MLMI 2004, LNCS 3361, pp. 1–11, 2005.

and secondarily by properties unique to that focus. The focus of a browser is defined to be either the main device for navigating the data, or the primary mode of presenting the meeting data to the user.

Table 1. Overview of taxonomy of meeting browsers and typical indexing elements used in each class

PERCEPTUAL	SEMANTIC
Audio	*Artefacts*
• Speaker Turns • Pause Detection • Emphasis • User determined markings	• Presented Slides • Agenda Items • Whiteboard Annotations • Notes - both personally and privately taken notes. • Documents discussed during the meeting.
• Video	• Derived Data
• Keyframes • Participant Behaviour	• ASR Transcript • Names Entities • Mode of Discourse • Emotion

Given this definition, and the range of data collected from meetings, three classes of browsers immediately present themselves. Firstly, there are browsers whose focus is largely *audio*, including both audio presentation [3] and navigation via audio [4]. Secondly, there are browsers whose focus is largely *video*; again, including both video presentation systems [5] and those where video is used for navigation [6]. The third class of browsers are focused on *artefacts* of the meetings. Meeting artefacts may be notes made during the meeting, slides presented, whiteboard annotations or documents examined in the meeting.

A fourth class of browser accounts for browsers whose focus is on *derived data forms*. Since analysis of meeting data is largely made on the nature and structure of conversation, this final class is largely concerned with browsing discourse. In this class are browsers whose focus is the automatic speech recognition (ASR) transcript and its properties [7], and those which focus on the temporal structure of discourse between participants [8].

This taxonomy is shown in Table 1 and each of the following sections describe each browser class in detail, in the order in which they were presented above. We refer to audio and video indices as *perceptual* since they focus on low-level analysis of the data. Artefacts and derived indices are referred to as *semantic* since they perform a higher-level analysis of the raw data.

2.1   Audio Browsers

This section discusses browsers whose main focus is *audio*. We separate these browsers into two main subcategories. The first subcategory consists of audio browsers with detailed visual indices; the second category is audio browsers with limited, or no visual feedback.

Both Kimber *et al.* [9] and Hindus and Schmandt [10] describe a meeting browser whose primary means of navigation is via a visual index generated from speaker segmentation. The view presented to the listener is of participant involvement in the meeting - users are able to navigate to each speaker segment and can also navigate between neighbouring speaker segments.

Degen *et al.* [3] describe an indexed audio browser designed for visually reviewing recordings made with a personal tape recorder. The tape recorders allow users to mark salient points whilst recording, the marked recordings then being digitised for review on a computer. The computer interface affords several methods of browsing the recordings. Firstly, users can randomly access any part of the recording, and can also navigate using the markings they made during the recording phase. The visual representation of the recording is of amplitude against time, displayed as a vector or colour plot. Users can also zoom in and out of this display and also have the ability to speed up playback (see the discussion surrounding SpeechSkimmer below).

A key element to these browsers is that the visual representations allow users to immediately see the structure of a meeting. This view, however, is dependent on the browsing environment allowing visual representations to be made. There are situations and devices which do not allow for this visual feedback, so that 'pure' audio browsing requires a substantially different interface.

SpeechSkimmer [4] is a system for interactive 'skimming' of recorded speech. Skimming is defined as system-controlled playback of samples of original audio. A four level skimming system is implemented, each level compressing the speech further, whilst attempting to retain salient content. The first level is unprocessed playback, the second shortens pauses, whilst the third level plays back only speech which follows significant pauses. The final level uses an emphasis detector to select salient segments of the speech to present to the listener. On top of these skimming levels is a mechanism which allows the playback speed to be altered whilst maintaining the pitch of the speaker. In this way the playback speed can be increased without a significant loss in comprehension. It should also be noted that the interface allows users to skim backwards in a recording - in this mode short segments of speech are played forwards but in reverse order.

Roy and Schmandt [11] describe a portable news reader implemented in a small, Walkman style device. The interface was designed iteratively in software, before being transferred to the hardware device. The resulting interface allowed listeners to playback a news report and to also navigate through the report using pre-defined jump locations, computed from an analysis of pause lengths in the audio. In the course of designing the device it was noted that users preferred simpler, more controlled interfaces, preferring manual skims via jumping rather than having software controlled skims. The device also implements a form of speed-up similar to that described above, with users able to select from three different playback speeds.

Because of their nature, audio browsers are largely implemented in hardware devices and so can be argued to be distinct from meeting browsers making use of multimodal data. It has been seen, however, that these browsers have overcome the limitations of just audio and are able to provide means of browsing audio using computed indices and speed-up techniques. As a complement to this, the following section describes browsers whose primary focus is video.

2.2   Video Browsers

The following class of browsers focus on *video*. Note that whilst each of these browsers have audio and video components, the main component for presentation or navigation in each case is video.

Foote *et al.* [5] describe a simple video browser with two primary modes of navigation. Firstly the user has the ability randomly access any section of the meeting, or to jump between index points which are precomputed from properties of the audio and video. The same indexing, when converted to a continuous 'confidence' measure can also be used to control the playback speed. For example, the playback speed could be related to gesture recognition so that portions of the meeting with significant gestures are played at different speeds, and index marks are made according to these significant gestures.

Girgensohn *et al.* [6] describe video interfaces centred around the use of *keyframes*. Keyframes are static images which have been automatically selected from continuous video according to some heuristic. In the video browsing system, keyframes are chosen according to an importance score, depending on the rarity and duration of each shot. Frames are then sized according to their importance (so that keyframes of higher importance are larger) and are placed linearly on the page. The resulting interface is then similar to a comic book or Japanese Manga drawings. This method can be used to produce a single summary of a full meeting and the user can playback salient portions of the meeting by selecting keyframes, or by choosing a point on a horizontal time line.

A more complex video focused meeting browser is described by Lee *et al.* [13]. A novelty for this system is that it does not require a dedicated meeting room; instead, capture is performed by a single device, encompassing a camera which captures a panoramic video of the meeting and four microphones to record audio. A real-time interface allows meeting participants to examine audio and video during the meeting, as well as making notes during the course of the meeting. The meeting is then archived and processed in preparation for browsing.

The browsing interface has a large number of navigational options. Central to the interface is the video screen, showing both the panorama and a close-up of the currently speaking participant. Users can navigate via a number of indexes, including representations of speaker transitions and visual and audio activity. There is also the opportunity to review an automatically produced transcript of the meeting, and to navigate the meeting via this transcript. A final option for navigating the meeting is a set of automatically generated keyframes. The interface also allows the user to review any notes made during the meeting and to examine any artefacts produced from the meeting.

We note that the number of browsers in this class is relatively small, mainly because video is largely supplemented with other browsing devices and is rarely solely used as a means of navigation. Furthermore, often meeting data does not contain the salient visual events that are useful for video browsing. The browsers described above, however, have shown that there is potential for making use of video as a means of browsing meeting data, although its value is not yet determined [12].

2.3   Artefact Browsers

The final browser classification based on data collected during the meeting is that of the *artefact* browser. We use the term artefact to describe any physical item recorded during a meeting which isn't audio or video. Browsers in this class fall into two subclasses: those which focus on slides presented and those which focus on notes taken by meeting participants. An important difference between this class of system and video or audio browsers is that artefacts are usually *searchable*, making it possible to both browse and search data. We will discuss each subclass in turn.

Brotherton *et al.* [14] describe a system for the visualisation of multiple media streams for the *Classroom 2000* project. The project views a classroom lecture as a multimedia authoring program, trying to extract useful information from classroom lectures to present in a suitable form to the user. The resultant interface is web-based and shows the slides used during the presentation. Slide transitions are indexed, allowing the user to jump between the segments of the lecture relating to each slide. The slides can be manually annotated both during and after the lecture and this information is also indexed. Further to the visual interface, audio segments relating to the slides can be played back.

Users can search through transcribed audio, slide text and lecturer annotations. In this way students are able to see how different topics relate to each other, as well as being able to locate specific information from a series of lectures.

Whilst the slide browsers described above have used lectures as their data source, there are slide browsers which have examined meetings data. An example of this is the TeamSpace project described in [15]. TeamSpace supports the organising, recording and reviewing of meetings; we shall, however, focus on the interface used to review archived meetings.

The interface consists of two main components. Firstly, there are two indexes - the first giving an overview of the full meeting and the second being of a detailed portion of the overview. The second main component for browsing is a tabbed pane containing annotated slides, agenda items and video displays. The slide view has an index showing each of the slides discussed in the meeting, so that users can jump to relevant portions of the meeting; furthermore, there is a larger view of the slide currently being discussed. A similar approach is taken to showing the meeting agenda, where the agenda acts as an index for the meeting and an indicator of the agenda item currently being discussed.

Cutler *et al.* [16] describe a meetings browser in which the central component is captured images from a whiteboard. The interface also contains a participant and whiteboard index, allowing users to jump to particular segments of the meeting, or to review segments which relate to specific elements of the whiteboard annotations. Furthermore, two video components are included - a panorama of all the participants and a close up view of the current speaker. In addition to these components the browser also allows the user to speed up playback, and also to skip the contributions of selected participants.

The browsers described above have focused their attention on presenting *community artefacts* - those which can be altered or viewed by all meeting participants. The final set of browsers in this class examine more private artefacts; specifically, they make use of notes made by participants as a means of indexing and browsing meetings.

Whittaker *et al.* [17] outline the *Filochat* system which combines an audio recorder with a tablet for taking notes as a means of constructing a meeting record. The tablet acted as a virtual notebook and allowed users to store several pages of notes and organise them into sections. Users can then use the notes they have taken to jump to the relevant portion of the conversation. The interface also affords the ability to manually navigate the audio by jumping forwards and backwards. The system was tested on users both in the field and in lab experiments.

The use of notes to assist recall of meetings was also investigated by Moran *et al.* [18]. The data used for the study was collected from meetings chaired by a single person, in which audio and notes taken both on a shared whiteboard and by the meeting chair were recorded and timestamped. The meeting records were then used by the meeting chair to make technical decisions on the basis of what was said at the meeting. A detailed study of how the chair used the meeting record over a large period of time was made and identified not only how the meeting record was used, but also how the chair's use of the meeting record changed over time. This analysis identified, for example, that the chair would often annotate his notes with the word "ha", meaning that something interesting had occurred and that it would be useful to revisit this section of the meeting during the review process.

The browsers described above examine browsing of artefacts, specifically slides and notes taken by participants. User notes are a powerful means of indexing meetings, since they become both a user-defined index and a means to access speech to clarify any confusing notes taken. Equally, however, a slide index allows users to clarify any confusion originating in presentations. We now discuss the final class of meeting browsers.

2.4   Discourse Browsers

The final class of meeting browsers are focused on *derived elements* of meetings, specifically components such as ASR transcripts or participant contributions. This class of browsers is loosely segregated into those which focus on the transcript, those which focus on participant contributions and those whose focus is a combination of derived and raw data. Because they present ASR transcripts, these systems, like artefact browsers, not only allow browsing but also offer the ability to search.

Whittaker *et al.* [19] describe a system, *ScanMail*, for browsing voicemail messages using a similar interface to that used to browse email. Incoming voicemail messages are passed through a speech recognizer, and the ASR transcript produced by this recognizer forms the body of the "email". The user has options to playback the message by clicking on the transcript at any point, and can also alter the playback speed. Furthermore users can search the transcripts from multiple voicemail messages in order to identify messages and segments of interest. ScanMail also extracts important entities such as phone numbers and names from the transcript. A similar system, *Scan* [20], supported browsing and search of broadcast news, including visual overviews of search results.

Rough 'n' Ready [21] is a news browser which focuses on the ASR transcript and various views derived from this transcript. The system allows the user to search for named entities such as people, locations, organizations and automatically derived topic markers. The interface also has a timeline, which allows users to view the temporal density of their search results and to navigate between the results and an automatically derived speaker index. In keeping with the ScanMail system, users can select any part of these indices or transcript elements to navigate the news reports.

Whilst these browsers have the transcript as the central focus of the interface, Bett *et al.* [22] describe a meeting browser in which the transcript is given as much prominence as a video component. The interface also contains a participant index, which indexes single or groups of speakers. In addition to these components the browser also allows the user to construct audio, video or text summaries, using text processing, for complete meetings or salient segments of the meetings. The summary is based on the transcript data and the audio and video streams are segmented accordingly to fit with the reduced transcript. The browser also supports search of a large meetings archive and indexing of discourse features and detected emotions.

The *Ferret* browser [8] also features the transcript alongside video and participant indexes. A key feature of the browser is that additional temporal annotations can be added or removed at will. For example, it is possible to add automatically derived agenda and interest indices whilst browsing a meeting. The interface is contained in a web browser, and so the transcript can be searched much like a web page, using the browser facilities. As with other browsers, users can navigate through the meeting by clicking on the transcript or by using the derived indices. The index view is customisable and can be viewed at a variety of different zoom levels.

The *Jabber-2* system described by Kazman *et al.* [23] has many similarities with the Ferret browser. Central to Jabber-2 is the temporal view, showing the involvement of each participant. Further to this participant view is a set of keywords, defined from text processing, relating to the content of the meeting currently being browsed. In addition to these indices is a stage of discourse mode recognition which constructs an overview of a meeting by plotting a graph showing the amount of involvement each participant had in each segment of the meeting. A previous study [24] described an alternate implementation of Jabber, denoted *JabPro*, which contained a video component and allowed users to search the meeting transcript to identify where in the meeting keywords occurred.

Also included in this class is a browser described by Lalanne *et al.* [7]. Here, the transcript is supplemented with audio and video controls, as well as a view of any documents currently being discussed. Furthermore, the meeting is indexed according to participants and properties of the documents and discourse occurring throughout the meeting. A key element to this interface is that every component is time synchronised, so that any changes or transitions in one component is automatically reflected in all the other components of the interface.

Since they make use of both raw and derived data, browsers in this category tend to have a more complex interface than those discussed in the previous classes. By segregating the interface into browsing and indexing components the browsers described in this class have overcome this complexity. Furthermore, this increased complexity has allowed for complex interface components, such as a search facility.

3   Summary

We have analysed browsers designed for reviewing multimodal data captured from meetings. It has been seen that these browsers can be distinguished using the focus of their presentation and navigation. Specifically, we segregated browsers into those that are focused on audio, on video, on non audio-visual artefacts, and on elements derived from this raw data (see Table 1). One observation is that a typical meetings browser consists of two main classes of components. Firstly, there are presentation elements - which are essentially realisations of the raw data; for example, audio, video and views of discussed documents. Secondly, there is an index component. This can include indexes of participant involvement, artefact changes such as slide changes, and higher-level properties of meetings such as the agenda.

It is interesting to note that development of meeting browsers has largely focused on making use of elements on the left hand side of Table 1, with elements on the right hand side being used as indices alone. The expected use of such browsers is *index centric random access* with users navigating and identifying points of interest using the indices and then reviewing that particular portion of the meeting using the display. There are, however, other procedures for accessing meeting data which become apparent once we focus on textual data and exploiting semantic information available from the right hand side of Table 1.

Below, we outline four potential areas for future research. The first two areas concern different modes of browsing meeting data, the third considers browsing with limited resources. Finally we discuss the lack of evaluation and user requirement determination in current browsers. Note that whilst the potential features have been applied to some of the browsers described above, we feel that the areas would be benefit from further research.

3.1   Search, Topic Tracking and Summarisation

By focusing on index based browsing, most browsers have ignored semantic techniques such as search, topic tracking and summarisation. The availability of transcript data generated from meetings means that search functionality is relatively simple to implement and it is surprising that it is not more widely used in current meeting browsers. As an example of a meeting browser with search, JabberPro [24] implemented a keyword searching algorithm allowing salient portions of the meeting to be identified by providing a suitable keyword. Jabber-2 [23] also supported topic tracking.

Furthermore, only a small number of the browsers discussed above made use of summarisation (most notably [4]). Whilst the availability of the ASR transcript does not make the production of a summary straightforward, it should be noted that users are able to make good use of poor transcripts [19,20] and so it is possible that user would also be able to make use of a weak summary. Summaries may not only be useful for certain meeting participants, for example minute takers, but also for controlling the meeting presentation (see below). Another area to explore is entity extraction [21,19]. All these areas involve text processing; a potentially promising area of future research is to make use of such techniques for analysing and presenting meeting data.

3.2   Filtered Presentation

A second area for future research is that of filtered presentation. In the current set of browsers it is assumed that users will want to manually review meetings by looking at indices and then browsing using these. However, there may be an advantage in using the derived indices to *control* other components rather than use them to navigate the meeting, e.g [4,5].

Consider the use of a search component in [25]. Here the user enters the search terms, and the result of the search then becomes a new index with which the user can navigate the meeting. An alternate approach to using the search results would be to play back only sections of the report which relate to the search terms. The advantage of this approach is that the browser becomes a more active tool for navigating meetings and users are able to playback areas of interest directly, rather than having to determine these areas themselves.

3.3   Limited Resource Browsing

Another common assumption made by browsers discussed in this paper is that they will be accessed solely through a computer workstation with a high resolution display. Whilst the audio browsers are naturally suited to less functional hardware, it could be advantageous to have access to a different type of browser in a limited environment.

Research in this direction should address several questions. Firstly, in relation to the previous section, studies should identify the needs of users in these environments. This, in turn, will address what sort of components the limited resource browsers will require. In this environment there will also be a problem of how to make the best use of screen space; it can be argued that textual representations would be advantageous here, since text is a relatively compact representation compared to the video or artefact views described above.

Furthermore, there are a large number of technical problems that the limited resource browsers should address, for example how the device can gain access to the relevant data. There could also be advantages in developing browsers for use during meetings - allowing an *in situ* review of the meeting to clarify current discussions.

3.4   User-Driven Development and Evaluation

Another key area addressed by a small number of the browsers discussed above, is that of measuring the *quality* of the browser and, related to this, how well the browser meets the user requirements for reviewing meeting data. The audio browsers are good examples of using user requirements to drive the design and evaluation of the browser. The NewsComm [11] audio browser went through 4 iterations of different interfaces in order to identify both what functionality users required and also how they should be able to access this functionality. Furthermore both Arons [4] and Whittaker *et al.* [19] describe lengthy user evaluation studies which examine not only how well their systems function but also evaluate the use of specific components of the systems.

It could be argued that the reason for this lack of evaluation of browsers is that, since the field is still emerging, the browsers are designed to examine the success of the underlying technologies and, therefore, evaluation of the browsers is a secondary concern to that of evaluation of the technology. Since the technology has now reached a sufficient level of maturity, however, it can be seen that robust evaluation of browsers must be considered for any new meeting browsers. With respect to this, it is promising to note that some effort is being made to be able to evaluate new browsers with respect to browsers previously developed - see [26].

4   Conclusion

This paper has examined the state of the art of meeting browsers. We segregated the field into four classes, three derived from browsers focused on data collected from meetings and the fourth being browsers whose focus is derived data. We also identified four areas for future research: semantic access, limited resource browsing, filtered presentation and rigorous development and evaluation.

References

[1] M4 Project, http://www.m4project.org/

[2] IM2 Project, http://www.im2.ch/

[3] Degen, L., Mander, R., Salomon, G.: Working With Audio: Integrating Personal Tape Recorders And Desktop Computers. In: Proceedings of CHI '92, Monterey, CA, USA (1992) 413-418

[4] Arons, B.: SpeechSkimmer: A System for Interactively Skimming Recorded Speech. ACM Transcations on Computer-Human Interaction (1997) 3-38

[5] Foote, J., Boreczky, G., Wilcox, L.: An Intelligent Media Browser Using Automatic Multimodal Analysis. In: Proceedings of ACM Multimedia, Bristol, UK (1998) 375-380

[6] Girgensohm, A., Borczky, J., Wilcox, L.: Keyframe-based User Interfaces For Digital Video. IEEE Computer (2001) 61-67

[7] Lalanne, D., Sire, S., Ingold, R., Behera, A., Mekhaldi, D., Rotz, D.: A Research Agenda For Assessing The Utility Of Document Annotations In Multimedia Databases Of Meeting Recordings. In: Proceedings of 3rd International Workshop on Multimedia Data And Document Engineering, Berlin, Germany (2003)

[8] Ferret Browser, http://mmm.idiap.ch/

[9] Kimber, D.G., Wilcox, L.D., Chen, F.R., Moran, T.P.: Speaker Segmentation For Browsing Recorded Audio. In: Proceedings of CHI '95 (1995)

[10] Hindus, D., Schmandt, C.: Ubiquitous Audio: Capturing Spontaneous Collaboration. In: Proceedings of 1992 ACM Conference on Computer-Supported Cooperative Work, Toronto, Ontario, Canada (1992) 210-217

[11] Roy, D.K., Schmandt, C.: NewsComm: A Hand-Held Interface for Interactive Access To Structured Audio. In: Proceedings of CHI '96, (1996)

[12] Christel, M.G., Smith, M.A., Taylor, C. R., Winkler, D.B.: Evolving Video Skims Into Useful Multimedia Abstractions. In: Proceedings of CHI '98, Los Angeles, CA (1998)

[13] Lee, D., Erol, B., Graham, J., Hull, Jonathan J., Murata, N.: Portable Meeting Recorder. In: Proceedings of ACM Multimedia, (2002) 493-502

[14] Brotherton, J. A., Bhalodia, J. R., Abowd, G. D.: Automated Capture, Integration and Visualization of Multiple Media Streams. In: Proceedings of The IEEE International Conference on Multimedia Computing And Systems, (1998) 54-63

[15] Geyer, W., Richter, H., Fuchs, L., Frauenhofer, T., Daijavad, S., Poltrock, S.: A Team Collaboration Space Supporting Capture And Access Of Virtual Meetings. In: Proceedings of 2001 International ACM SIGGROUP Conference On Supporting Group Work, Boulder, Colorado (2001) 188-196

[16] Cutler, R., Rui, Y., Gupta, A., Cadiz, J.J., Tashev, I., He, L., Colburn, A., Zhang, Z., Liu, Z., Silverberg, S.: Distributed Meetings: A Meeting Capture And Broadcasting System. In: Proceedings of 10th ACM International Conference on Multimedia, Juan-les-Pins, France (2002) 503-512

[17] Whittaker, S., Hyland, P., Wiley, M.: Filochat: Handwritten Notes Provide Access To Recorded Conversations. In: Proceedings of CHI '94, Boston, Massachusetts, USA (1994)

[18] Moran, Thomas P., Palen, L., Harrison, S., Chiu, P., Kimber, D., Minneman, S., Melle, W., Zellweger, P.: "I'll get that off the audio": A Case study of salvaging multimedia meeting records. In: Proceedings of CHI '97, Atlanta, Georgia (1997)

[19] Whittaker, S., Hitschberg, J., Amento, B., Stark, L., Bacchiani, M., Isenhour, P., Stead, L., Zamchick, G., Rosenberg, A.: SCANMail: A Voicemail Interface That Makes Speech Browsable, Readable and Searchable. In: Proceedings of CHI 2002, Minneapolis, Minnesota, USA (2002)

[20] Whittaker, S., Hirschberg, J., Choi, J., Hindle, D., Pereira, F., Singhal, A.: SCAN: Designing and Evaluating User Interfaces to Support Retrieval from Speech Archives. In: Proceedings of SIGIR99 Conference On Research And Development In Information Retrieval, Berkley, USA (1999) 26-33

[21] Colbath, S., Kubala, F., Liu, D., Srivastava, A.: Spoken Documents: Creating Searchable Archives From Continuous Audio. In: Proceedings of 33rd Hawaii International Conference On System Sciences, (2000)

[22] Bett, M., Gross, R., Yu, H., Zhu, X., Pan, Y., Yang, J., Waibel, A.: Multimodal Meeting Tracker. In: Proceedings of RIAO, Paris, France (2000)

[23] Kazman, R., Kominek, J.: Supporting the Retrieval Process In Multimedia Information Systems. In: Proceedings of Proceedings of the 30th Annual Hawaii International Conference On System Sciences, Hawaii (1997) 229-238

[24] Kazman, R., Al-Halimi, R., Hunt, W., Mantei, M.: Four Paradigms for Indexing Video Conferences. IEEE Multimedia 3(1) (1996) 63-73

[25] Chiu, P., Boreczky, J., Girgensohn, A., Kimber, D.: LiteMinutes: An Internet-Based System For Multimedia Meeting Minutes. In: Proceedings of 10th WWW Conference, Hong Kong (2001) 140-149

[26] Flynn, M., Wellner, P.D.: In Search of a Good BET: A Proposal for a Browser Evaluation Test. IDIAP IDIAP-COM03-11 (2004)

Browsing Recorded Meetings with Ferret

Pierre Wellner, Mike Flynn, and Maël Guillemot

IDIAP Research Institute, Martigny, Switzerland, Rue du Simplon 4,
CH-1920 Martigny, Switzerland
{Wellner, Flynn, guillemot}@idiap.ch

Abstract. Browsing for elements of interest within a recorded meeting is time-consuming. We describe work in progress on a meeting browser, which aims to support this process by displaying many types of data. These include media, transcripts and processing results such as speaker segmentations. Users interact with these visualizations to observe and control synchronized playback of the recorded meeting.

1 Introduction

Imagine that you missed a two-hour meeting with your colleagues, but that this meeting was recorded. You want to know what you missed, but you do not want to replay the entire meeting. Instead, you want to find quickly just the parts that most interest you.

A number of research projects are developing systems to capture, store, process, and retrieve recorded meeting data [2][6][7]. These recordings include not only audio from multiple microphones, but also video from multiple cameras and additional data streams such as hand-written notes and projected displays. The amount of data captured can be enormous, and making this data easily accessible and usable by humans is a challenging problem which has been approached in a number of different ways [10]. The Ferret Meeting Browser aims to provide the ability to quickly find and play back segments of interest from a meeting recording.

This paper begins by illustrating some of the observations people find of interest within meeting recordings; it describes our meeting room and some of the data streams captured from it; the Ferret meeting browser is described in detail, along with its software architecture, and we conclude with discussion on future work.

2 Observations of Interest

A first step towards the design and evaluation of a meeting browser is to determine what users are interested in finding within recording meetings. Understanding this motivates the features we choose to implement, and will help us to evaluate browser performance. The precise information that people find interesting obviously depends on the individuals, and on the specific meeting in question. So rather than ask people in general what they might look for in a meeting recording, we ask people to make specific "observations of interest" about particular meeting recordings. We can then see how much people agree or differ on events of significance within these meetings,

S. Bengio and H. Bourlard (Eds.): MLMI 2004, LNCS 3361, pp. 12–21, 2005.

and we can design and test features of our meeting browser to help locate the observations that people find interesting. An initial pilot collection of observations indicates that:

- a large majority of observations are associated with a particular meeting participant;
- most observations of interest are about spoken content;
- substantial agreement between observers on their selection of significant events and where they occur.

We do not yet have measures for these patterns, but we can use them to illustrate how a browser can help find the typical observations made in a meeting. Two example observations, on a meeting that discussed movies were:

- "Alice knew the actors well."
- "Bob prefers the movie Terminator 2 over Terminator 1."

In the sections below, we will see how features of our meeting room and browser can help to find observations like these.

3 The IDIAP Smart Meeting Room

The IDIAP smart meeting room is an ordinary conference room with a table, chairs, whiteboard, and computer projection screen. In addition, it is also equipped with 24 microphones, which are configured as lapel microphones, as the ears of a binaural manikin, and as a pair of 8-channel tabletop microphone arrays (see *Fig. 1*).

The room also has three video cameras and equipment for capturing time-stamped whiteboard strokes, Anoto pen strokes [3], and the computer-projected images. All recorded data is precisely synchronized so that every microphone, pen-stroke, and video sample can be associated with simultaneously captured samples from other media streams. Further details about this room and its equipment are described in [9].

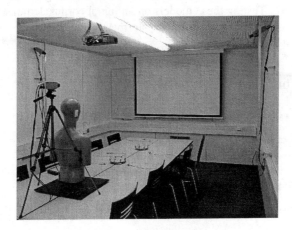

Fig. 1. IDIAP smart meeting room

4 Captured Media Streams

Initial observations make clear that knowing *who* is talking in a meeting is very important to viewers, and to support this, a tabletop microphone array has been built (see *Figure 2*). This microphone array is capable of tracking the directions from which speech is coming around the table, and can detect which participants are speaking at any time.

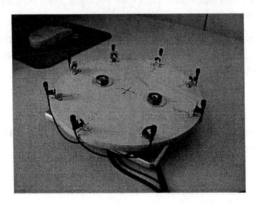

Fig. 2. Tabletop Microphone Array

   Processed output from the microphone array shows the direction of sound sources and energy levels from four different speaker locations [4]. This output can be used in our browser to show when each participant speaks, and also some aspects of global meeting structure, such as when discussions occurred, or when a monologue was interrupted by a question.

   Some of these meeting actions can be detected automatically. In experiments described in [8], audio and visual features for each participant are extracted from the raw data, and the interaction of participants is modeled using Hidden Markov Model based approaches. Testing these models on an initial corpus demonstrated the ability of the system to recognize a set of simple meeting actions such as presentations, monologues and discussion.

5 Ferret from User's Perspective

The Ferret browser is typically used in four stages:

1. Meeting selection, where one meeting is chosen from many;
2. Initial choice of interval data streams to be visualized.
3. Interactive browsing and playback of the recording.
4. Addition and removal of data visualizations.

These are discussed in the following sub-sections.

5.1 Meeting Selection

The user first chooses a meeting to browse. *Figure 3* below illustrates an example of a browser to navigate within a set of meetings, showing summary information and pictures of which people participated at a particular meeting, as well as a selection of additional data available to browse.

At this time, Ferret does not provide an inter-meeting search facility for querying across a large set of meeting recordings. It focuses primarily on browsing within a single meeting recording, assuming that the meeting was selected through some other means, such as this simple hierarchical list.

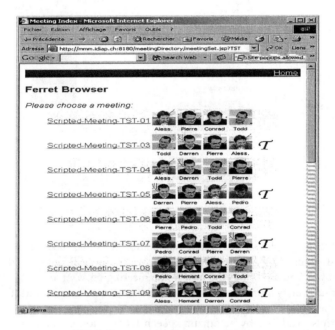

Fig. 3. Inter-meeting browser prototype

5.2 Initial Choice of Data

Once users have selected a meeting to browse, they select which particular data streams are of interest by clicking on checkboxes of available interval data streams. *Figure 4* below shows an example for one meeting.

This web page displays the available annotation files and media files. Once a user has selected which XML streams, HTML transcripts or ASR output is desired, pushing the "Browse" button brings the user to the meeting browser.

In order to verify our example observations, a user might select the speaker segmentations, to see when each person speaks, and the transcript (if available). Note that transcripts produced by automatic speech recognition contain many errors, and may not be directly applicable.

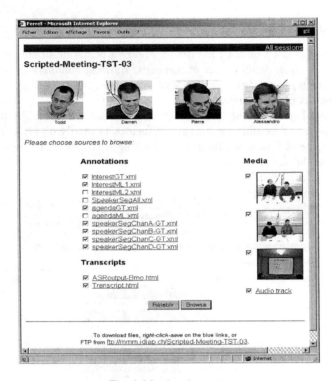

Fig. 4. Meeting data page

This web page displays the available annotation files and media files. Once a user has selected which XML streams, HTML transcripts or ASR output is desired, pushing the "Browse" button brings the user to the meeting browser.

In order to verify our example observations, a user might select the speaker segmentations, to see when each person speaks, and the transcript (if available). Note that transcripts produced by automatic speech recognition contain many errors, and may not be directly applicable.

5.3 Interactive Browsing and Playback

The upper part of the graphical user interface illustrated in *Figure 5* below contains a media player for synchronized playback of audio and video. This allows viewing and listening what happened at particular moment of the meeting from multiple angles as with a multi-TV system. The VCR controls (play, pause, sound adjustment, time display) are on the left pane.

The lower part of the interface shows graphical representations of interval data streams in a vertical, scrollable timeline.

A large number of processed interval data streams can be made available to assist with browsing of the meetings. Ferret allows users to select any combination of available data streams as described in the previous section and display them alongside each other for inspection and comparison.

Interval data can include speaker turn intervals, meeting actions, level of interest representation, or textual transcripts. Clicking on elements in the timeline controls playback in the media player and scrolls the textual transcript. And clicking on the transcript also scrolls the timeline and controls media playback.

The user can zoom into particular parts of interest by means of the zoom buttons on the left. By zooming out, the user gets an overview of the meeting in terms of who talked the most, what meeting actions etc. Crosses at the top of each stream allow for deleting streams, while the add button in the control panel permits adding a new XML or HTML annotation stream to be visualized.

To illustrate how this browser can be used, imagine someone who wants to verify the truth of one of the typical statements shown above, e.g. "Bob prefers the movie Terminator 2 over Terminator 1."

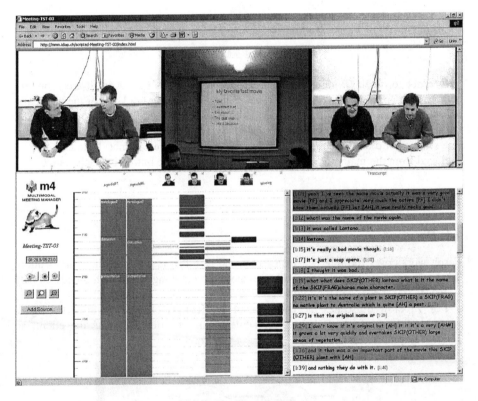

Fig. 5. The Ferret browser

To find where this is discussed in the meeting, a user can invoke the browser's "Find" function in the transcript window, and enter keywords such as "prefer" or "terminator," which would scroll the browser down to the section in the transcript where these words occur. If the words are not visible, e.g. because of speech recognition errors, then the user can see the parts of the meeting where Bob is speaking, and click only on those parts to find the parts where Bob is talking.

5.4   Addition and Removal of Data

To supplement the data presented initially, users may add data of their own choosing
to the display. This data does not need to be on any special server – but it must be
accessible by the Internet. This feature is used by researchers who are testing new
segmentation or recognition algorithms and want to see how their results look alongside other data, or want to check the accuracy of their results against playback of the
media.

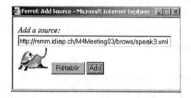

Fig. 6. The Add Source dialog box

In order to display a new data source, the user presses the "Add Source" button,
and a dialog appears, illustrated in *Figure 6* above. Entering the URL of the new data,
and pressing the "Add" button, the data is displayed alongside the previously selected
data. In effect, the Ferret browser acts as a "shopping basket" into which many dispa-
rate sources of data may be loaded from any server on the Internet. Data can also be
removed from the main display by pressing the small close button by each source.

6   Architecture

6.1   Overview

Ferret works over the Internet, using a normal web browser as the client application.
The main meeting corpus also resides on the Internet, along with much processed data
– such as transcripts and recognition results.

Fig. 7 below illustrates the client-server architecture. The left side of the figure
represents the content of the server, while the right side represents the client, an
Internet Explorer web browser.

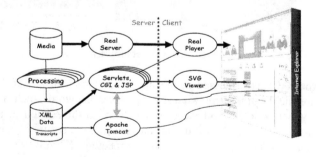

Fig. 7. Ferret Architecture

6.2 Framework

A set of JSP-generated frames is used to produce the overall frame structure of the Ferret browser. Each JSP-generated page provides one of the many frames in the display, and is used to create the embedding of plug-ins for video and graphics. In turn, each embedded plug-in is given the URL of data to display.

6.3 Graphical Display

A free plug-in, the SVG Viewer [1] allows complex graphics to be displayed and dynamically updated. This is used to display the meeting segmentations graphically, with interaction and dynamic updates of the graphics.

The URL passed by the Ferret framework to the graphics plug-in, invokes a Java servlet. The servlet generates the graphical content from the XML sources, dynamically. Running under the Apache Tomcat servlet container, it reads a list of XML data URLs to display. The servlet fetches each in turn, parses the XML content and generates SVG. Finally, the SVG is streamed back to the graphics plug-in in the browser for display.

6.4 Media Display

The media resides on the mmm.idiap.ch media server, which contains AVI, RM videos, WAV and RM audio files. It is streamed to the Internet by RealServer and displayed in a browser through the free RealPlayer plug-in (available from www.real.com). RealPlayer facilitates the playback of streamed media, over the Internet, synchronising multiple sources.

The URL passed by the Ferret framework to the media plug-in, invokes a CGI program that dynamically generates SMIL to send back to the plug-in. SMIL is a standard language for presentation of multiple media sources. It allows multiple sources to be played in parallel, or in sequence (or any combination) with time off-sets. The video plug-in reads the SMIL and then begins to fetch each media source at the appropriate moment.

6.5 Data Stream Management with Cookies

The list of data to display is obtained from cookies kept by the client browser – no session information is kept in Ferret. Every client request to the server is accompanied by the current set of cookies, each giving one source to browse. Cookies are largely managed at the client, by JavaScript functions associated with the various browser forms, including the "Add Source" dialog, and the source-closing buttons.

6.6 Controls

A simple control frame contains player controls, zoom buttons and the "Add Source" button, described below.

The zoom buttons reload the graphics frame with a new zoom parameter. The list of sources to display is not disturbed, since this is stored as cookies. Therefore, exactly the same set of sources is re-displayed at the new zoom setting. The control panel itself is re-loaded, as new settings for the zoom buttons must be supplied.

The "Add Source" button either creates a new "Add Source" dialog window, or brings any existing one to the front. Entering a URL and pressing the "Add" button creates a new cookie (holding the new URL) and forces a re-load of the graphics frame. The graphics are re-generated, now with the new source included.

In addition to the data currently displayed by Ferret, we are in the process of adding additional streams such as pen and whiteboard strokes, and representations of continuous data, such as energy levels or head positions.

6.7 Browser Evaluation Test

The evaluation of meeting browsers is typically subjective, making it impossible to compare browsers and browsing techniques objectively. It can also be difficult to know when a browser is truly effective in helping users find the information they are interested in, rather than simply finding the information the experimenter believes is important.

To evaluate Ferret (and other meeting browsers), we are developing a test that aims to be:

1. an objective measure of browser effectiveness based on user performance rather than judgement;
2. independent of experimenter perception of the browsing task;
3. able to produce directly comparable numeric scores, automatically; and
4. replicable, through a publicly accessible web site.

The design of this test is discussed in [5], and depends on the collection of "observations of interest" made by people who view the meetings. These observations are subsequently used to generate test questions about the meeting which subjects must try to answer using a browser, and resulting in a numeric score that can be used to compare alternate browser designs.

7 Summary and Conclusion

We describe work in progress on the Ferret meeting browser, which can display a number of user-selected processed interval data streams, and transcripts generated from meeting recordings. These displays are interactively used to control synchronized media playback of the recorded audio and video.

The aim of this work is to make it easy and quick for users to find information of interest within meeting recordings. Future versions of Ferret (and other meeting browsers we develop) will be objectively compared, in order to learn which of the interaction techniques and data visualization methods we have implemented are of most value to the task of browsing recorded meetings.

A working version of Ferret is available online at http://mmm.idiap.ch along with a collection of short meetings that can be browsed with it. Additional meeting recordings and data are available to project partners.

Acknowledgements

The Authors thank our colleagues at IDIAP for their collaboration in building the systems used in this paper. This work was partly supported by: the European Union

6th FWP IST Integrated Project AMI (Augmented Multi-party Interaction, FP6-506811, publication AMI-17); the Swiss National Science Foundation, through the National Centre of Competence in Research (NCCR) on "Interactive Multimodal Information Management (IM2)"; the European project "M4: MultiModal Meeting Manager", through the Swiss Federal Office for Education and Science (OFES).

References

[1] Adobe SVG viewer http://www.adobe.com

[2] AMI project http://www.amiproject.org

[3] Anoto http://www.anoto.com

[4] G. Lathoud and I. McCowan. *Location Based Speaker Segmentation*, in "Proceedings of the 2003 IEEE International Conference on Acoustics, Speech, and Signal Processing (ICASSP-03)", 2003.

[5] M. Flynn and P. Wellner, In Search of a good BET: A proposal for a Browser Evaluation Test, IDIAP-COM 03-11, September 2003.

[6] IM2 project http://www.im2.ch

[7] M4 project http://www.m4project.org

[8] I. McCowan, S. Bengio, D. Gatica-Perez, G. Lathoud, F. Monay, D. Moore, P. Wellner, and H. Bourlard. *Modeling Human Interaction in Meetings* in "Proceedings of International Conference on Acoustics, Speech and Signal Processing", 2003.

[9] D. Moore. *The IDIAP Smart Meeting Room.* IDIAP-COM 01-07, November 2002.

[10] Simon Tucker, Steve Whittaker, *Accessing Multimodal Meeting Data: Systems, Problems and Possibilities* Multimodal Interaction and Related Machine Learning Algorithms Workshop, June 2004.

Meeting Modelling in the Context of Multimodal Research

Dennis Reidsma, Rutger Rienks, and Nataša Jovanović

University of Twente, Dept. of Computer Science, HMI Group,
P.O. Box 217, 7500 AE Enschede, the Netherlands
{dennisr, rienks, natasa}@ewi.utwente.nl *

Abstract. This paper presents a framework for corpus based multi-modal research. Part of this framework is applied in the context of *meeting modelling*. A generic model for different aspects of meetings is discussed. This model leads to a layered description of meetings where each layer adds a level of interpretation for distinct aspects based on information provided by lower layers. This model should provide a starting point for selecting annotation schemes for layers of the meeting and for defining a hierarchy between individual layers.

1 Introduction

Meetings are an important part of daily life. They are a complex interplay of interaction between participants with each other and their environment, and contain a broad spectrum of multimodal information [1]. The interactions can be (automatically) analyzed to gain knowledge about multimodal human-human interaction. There is also a need for applications that support meetings in several ways. For example, an increasing number of meetings involves remote participation, where effectiveness of the meetings depends on support from the remote conferencing application [2]. Furthermore, people often want access to material from past events. Good summarization and browsing tools are indispensable for this. Simulation tools provide a method for validation of models underlying the technology.

This paper starts by presenting a framework for corpus based research on multimodal human-human interaction which interrelates aspects such as those described above. Part of the framework is subsequently elaborated for meetings.

The work presented in this paper is carried out in the context of the AMI project. Other projects that work on the same subjects are for example the Meeting Room project at Carnegie Mellon University [3], the M4 project [4] and the NIST Meeting Room Project [5].

---

* This work was partly supported by the European Union 6th FWP IST Integrated Project AMI (Augmented Multi-party Interaction, FP6-506811, publication AMI-13). For more information see http://www.amiproject.org/

S. Bengio and H. Bourland (Eds.): MLMI 2004, LNCS 3361, pp. 22–35, 2005.

The structure of this paper is as follows. Section 2 describes a general framework for research on multimodal human-human interaction that will be used to position our work. The main part of the paper is presented in Sections 3 and 4, where the annotation and modelling parts of the framework are tailored for the meeting domain. The resulting model will be discussed extensively. The paper ends with a discussion of several issues related to annotations of corpora 5.

2   A General Framework for Corpus Based Research on Human-Human Interaction

This section discusses our view on research on human-human interaction, of which Figure 1 shows a schematic representation. Based on a corpus of interaction recordings (Box I), manual or automatic recognition processes create layers of annotation (Box II). These annotations are used by the different tools (Box IV). As discussed above, research in social sciences (Box V) contributes to development of techniques and tools, but also makes use of the information provided by them. As will be discussed below, models and theories of human interaction (Box III) are of major importance in this context. The rest of this section discusses the different boxes in more detail. After that the remainder of the article will elaborate on the boxes II and III.

2.1   Box I: Corpus

Research on multimodal interaction often uses a corpus of audio and video recordings. In general, a corpus should be representative of the domain, be large

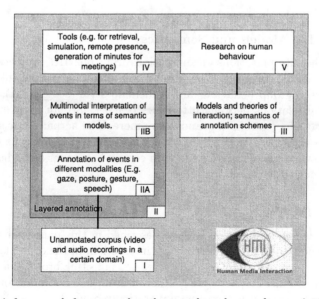

Fig. 1. A framework for corpus based research on human-human interaction

enough to do relevant research and be accessible. Many projects use smart rooms to record data. These smart rooms are equipped with a range of sensors (visual, aural and other types) that allow, often detailed, capturing of the interactions in the room. Examples of existing corpora containing meeting recordings are those used in the Meeting Room project at Carnegie Mellon University [3], in the The Meeting Recorder Project at ICSI [6] and in the M4 project [4].

2.2 Box II: Layered Annotation

The box for layered annotation is divided into two sub boxes. This division reflects the difference between direct annotation of objective events and interpretation of these events on a semantic level, or *form* and *function*. Consider e.g. the situation where a user raises his or her hand. In box IIA this is detected and annotated as an event HAND-RAISING. In box IIB this event might be interpreted as e.g. a request for a dialogue turn or as a vote in a voting situation, based on analysis of speech transcripts. The semantic models which underly the interpretations in box IIB belong to box III and are discussed below.

Box IIA This box involves (semi) automatic recognition of events in interaction recordings. Techniques such as computer vision or speech processing are used to obtain representations of the interactions in an efficient way.

Box IIB On this level fusion techniques are applied on the annotations from box IIA to align them and to interpret them in terms of semantic models from box III. This leads to annotations that are semantically oriented, such as description of argumentative structures, intentions of users and other aspects that support more sophisticated processing of the data.

2.3 Box III: Models and Semantics

To enable the interpretations of annotations from box IIB, we need models of human interaction. There is a large variety of examples: models of the dependences between group behaviour and leadership style (see e.g. [7]), a model of the rhetorical relations between utterances (see e.g. [8]), an agent model incorporating emotions (see e.g. [9]) and many more. The actual models depend on the research objectives or the application. Research on the corpus can provide insights into what people may intend with certain behaviour and what types and patterns of behaviour exist.

2.4 Box IV: Tools

Research of human interaction such as described in this paper will also lead to the development tools for supporting this interaction. In the context of meetings, some of these tools are useful for end users (e.g. a meeting browser, a minute generator, a remote meeting assistant), others will mostly be useful for supporting the annotation process (e.g. custom annotation modules).

Simulation tools can be used for testing hypotheses about certain aspects of human interaction based on these explanatory models in order to validate the models. See for example the work of Carletta et al. [10] where certain mechanisms for turn taking in small group discussions are examined through simulating the resulting floor patterns and comparing them with patterns observed in real life.

Virtual simulation using avatars is another current topic at the University of Twente [11, 12]. One type of virtual simulation may involve virtual replay of a meeting from specific viewpoints such as the viewing perspective of one participant. This could give the impression of watching the meeting through his or her eyes, especially if the participant's head orientation is included in the viewpoint. This might give researchers a unique perspective on the behaviour of meeting participants. This type of simulation can also be used for summarization purposes, creating one virtual meeting that contains the main events of several related meetings in a coherent fashion.

Remote presence tools that allow manipulation of the environment and the representation of participants, adding or exaggerating aspects of behaviour, enable experiments for research on human behaviour in specific (virtual) circumstances. Bodychat by Vilhjálmsson and Cassell [13] provides a good example of simulated nonverbal behaviour in a virtual multi-user environment.

2.5 Box V: Human Behaviour

Research on human behaviour, for example social psychology, provides an insight into human interaction patterns and their components. This in turn is a basis for automatic analysis of this interaction and the retrieval of components.

On the other hand, analysis of interactions opens possibilities for research of human behaviour. In the first place the corpus can be analyzed to discover regularities in human behaviour and construct corresponding models and hypotheses. In the second place the annotations can be used to test and evaluate these models, for example using simulations (see e.g. [10, 14]).

Work that can be placed in the context of this box is for example that of McGrath [15] (group dynamics and collaborative tasks), Carletta et al. [14, 10] (models of group behaviour) and Shi et al. [16] (gaze, attention and meeting dynamics).

3   Meeting Modelling: Overview

The framework in Figure 1 enables us to obtain a structured view on any work that is carried out in the field of multimodal human-human interaction research. In this section we extend the framework for the meeting domain by instantiating the boxes IIA and IIB from the generic framework in a way that covers the meeting domain. Furthermore we will discuss issues related to the semantic models for box III underlying the higher level annotations of box IIB.

Marchand-Maillet [17] described a first approach of meeting modelling.

3.1   Box IIA and IIB for the Meeting Domain

Figure 2 shows the proposed meeting model. The bottom level of the model corresponds to box IIA in Figure 1. Box IIB is divided into three levels, containing labelling of events with an interpretation on the lowest level, evolving state descriptions on the second level and global meeting parts on the highest level.

On the first level, single or combined events from box IIA are labelled with an interpretation. For instance a posture can be SITTING, a gesture or utterance may be an acknowledgement, etc.

The second level of interpretation consists of different types of incremental states that evolve during a meeting. Each occurrence of an event on the first level adds to one or more of these states. The physical state of a meeting (the setting), for example, is dependent on non-communicative actions of the participants (walking, moving objects, etc). These two levels together constitute an extensive *discourse state* of the meeting.

The topmost level of interpretation is the highest level of semantic interpretation of distinct meeting parts (e.g. a sequence of agenda items or meeting activities).

Clark defines a joint *activity* as an activity with more than one participant that serves a common goal [18]. A joint activity consists of joint subactivities and joint *actions*. A joint action consists of a group of people coordinating with each other in executing a step in the process of achieving the common goal of the joint activity. Each person can have his or her own *role* in that joint action.

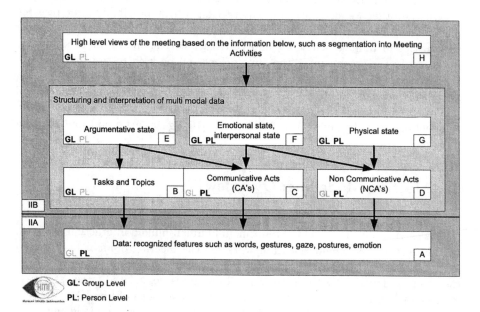

Fig. 2. Box IIA and IIB tailored to the meeting domain

Meeting activities are joint activities in this sense. One of the goals of the AMI and M4 projects is to find these kinds of group events in order to detect meeting structures (see e.g. [19]). To detect these highest level components a combination of the first and second level of interpreted information is needed.

Consider for example a situation with one person standing in front of the whiteboard. This person is the only one who is talking. He or she points at the projector screen every now and then. The argumentative structure of the communication is very simple (not many counterarguments and few conflicting statements). This evidence suggests that at the highest level this meeting segment can be interpreted as a 'presentation'. Other possibilities can be 'discussion', 'break' and 'brainstorm'. See [20] for a possible list of meeting activities. Note that in other publications these meeting activities are called *meeting acts* or *meeting actions*. To avoid confusion with the low level meeting actions this paper will employ the term *meeting activity* for the high level activities.

4   Meeting Modelling in More Detail

This section will explain the boxes at each level in Figure 2 in more detail. For each box is indicated whether the components from that box belong to the personal or the group level of the meeting. Non-communicative acts such as MOVING A COFFEE MUG for instance can only occur at a personal level, where as the argumentative state will always be at a group level.

The arrows depict the dependencies between the different boxes: The set of arrows leaving a box represent the input for the recognition and interpretation algorithms that construct the data in that box. The evolution of the argumentative state is dependent on the communicative acts and tasks and topics at a certain segment in the meeting. Vice versa, different communicative acts have a different impact on the argumentative structure that is being constructed by the recognition modules.

4.1   The First Level

Box A: Unimodal Events
The bottom level of the model is the level with the basic, uncombined, uninterpreted events from different modalities. Since this level pertains to *uninterpreted* events there is no reference to complicated interpretation models for this box. It contains unimodal events such as words, non-word sounds, gestures, postures, gaze direction, etc. on a personal level. Events such as the light falling out, falling chairs or the beamer malfunctioning are also included here.

4.2   The Second Level

The second level of the model contains the boxes B, C and D. Box B concerns *topics* and *tasks*. In box C and D we find the joint and autonomous actions as defined by Clark [18]. Some of these actions have a communicative intent (verbal or non-verbal) and can be annotated as Communicative Acts (box C). The other meeting actions, without communicative intent, are called Non-Communicative Acts (box D).

Box B: Topics, Tasks

Topic and task are closely entwined views on a meeting segment. The question "what is the segment about?" may as well be answered with a task description (e.g. "brainstorming") as with a topic (e.g. "the shape of the appliance that is being designed in this meeting"), but each answer is incomplete, if the other answer is not taken into consideration as well. Tasks and topics can exist both on a person and on group level. They can be part of a hierarchy of subtasks and subtopics. Both may be related to agenda points. A task can be evaluated in terms of its progress. As background knowledge for this box, the meeting agenda gives an indication of several tasks and topics that will appear in the meeting.

Box C: Communicative Acts

A communicative act (CA) is a joint action with communicative intent, i.e. through which a person makes others understand what he or she means. CAs may be verbal or non-verbal or a combination of these. Examples of CAs are asking a question, answering and giving a suggestion. The following aspects are relevant for modelling CAs.

1. Function: the type of CA, see the examples above
2. Agent: the participant performing the CA
3. Addressee: the participant(s) to whom the CA is directed
4. Target: in case of some non-verbal CAs such as pointing there may be a target
5. Relation to other CAs (e.g. question/answer combinations)

A concrete choice for an annotation scheme for CAs is based on the functional aspect and might be based on an adaptation of some dialogue act annotation scheme such as MRDA [21], SWBD-DAMSL [22] or the IPA of Bales [23].

The boxes B and C have been drawn together as we expect a close relation between these boxes. We expect that for various tasks carried out during the meeting there will be specific sets of CAs occurring more frequently for this task than for any other task. We also expect that for every type of CA there will be a set of tasks (within a meeting) where these CAs will appear with a higher frequency than in the other tasks.

We conducted some first experiments to test this hypotheses. The results tentatively confirm our expectations. Five meetings have been annotated with communicative act types, topics, temporal and personal aspects of topics and tasks. Analysis of the results shows a clear relation between certain aspects of the topic and task on one side and the most frequently used CAs on the other side. Some first conclusions from those experiments are the following. Meeting segments about topics dealing with future events contain significantly more action motivators (command, commitment, offer, etc.) than segments about topics dealing with past or present or atemporal events. Segments dealing with topics that directly relate to the speaker or the whole group as opposed to topics about something entirely external also contain significantly more action motivators.

Box D: Non-Communicative Acts
NCAs are much like CAs, but there is no communicative intent and therefore no addressee. Examples are manipulation of objects or walking to a different location.

4.3   The Third Level

On the third level we distinguish three different components: the physical, the emotional and the argumentative states. All of these non overlapping components can be created out of the level two components.

Box E: Argumentative State
For effective summarization and structuring of meeting content the argumentations posed in the meeting should be interpreted and structured. An argumentative state consists of several aspects. In the first place there is the logical *argument structure* describing the relations between statements, evidence, support arguments and counterarguments. Much work has been done in extension of the IBIS system of Kunz and Rittel [8].

In the second place there is the *argument discourse*. This discourse concerns the order and manner in which argumentations are introduced. Pallotta and Hatem describe both argument structure and discourse in one formalism [24]. How people select and introduce their arguments depends on the goals during the current task of both the group and the individuals [25].

Communicative Acts can introduce positions, arguments etc. but can also aim at discussion *control* rather than discussion *content*. For example, the sentence "We will discuss this later in the meeting" does not change the logical argument structure but is certainly relevant to understanding the decision process from a rhetorical perspective.

Another rhetorical technique to reach one's goals in a discussion concerns the use of *emotional* arguments. In its simplest form this could, for example, be the purely emotional rejection of a statement using the expression "I don't feel it that way", which, although it contains no *logical* argument, can influence the outcome of the discussion. Carofiglio and De Rosis [26] state that argumentation knowledge and emotion should be combined to select the most promising strategy to reach one's goals.

Information about previous meetings might, as background knowledge, be relevant for understanding some of the argument structures.

Box F: Emotional state
The second box on this level depicts the emotional state of the meeting on group level and personal level. Aspects such as the mood of the meeting, the emotional state of the individuals or the attitudes of people with respect to each other (in-

terpersonal state) will be modelled here. They can be derived from NCAs (e.g. yawning, posture) as well as CAs (explicitly stating your attitude, or a certain choice of CAs which may signal a specific emotion). People can be indifferent, angry, cooperative, positive, afraid at all times during the meeting.

Background information in this box could be personality, relative status, interpersonal attitudes and meeting roles.

Box G: Physical state
The physical state of a meeting consists of the meeting objects, participants and their locations. Changes to this state follow from observed non-communicative acts.

4.4   The Fourth Level

Box H: High level segmentation
On this level a meeting is segmented into meeting activities, joint activities that are specific for meetings (cf introduction). A subjective approach to define meeting activities would be to use "common sense segmenting". A meeting then consists of a sequence of "typical components" that make up the meeting. A model (cf. introduction) can be developed that explains why certain activities are the highest level components in meetings and how they are related.

Higher level statistical models can be trained to classify combinations of occurrences from lower level components as specific types of higher level components. A recognition module would use such a model to detect the occurrence of e.g. a presentation activity when observing a pattern of certain NCAs, CAs and physical state combined with certain argumentative structures in the data. The training can be done using machine learning techniques like Hidden Markov Models [19] or Dynamic Bayesian Networks, looking for statistical correlations.

This level requires a lexicon of meeting activity types. An example of such a lexicon can be found in [20]. An approach to obtain such a lexicon is the use of unsupervised clustering techniques on the lower level annotation elements, as mentioned in [27]. The resulting clusters can be indicative of possible meeting activity types.

5   Annotations

As meetings can be structured in layers and we wish to label or annotate chunks of data in accordance with these layers, there is a need for an annotation language that supports these structures. An annotation format can be seen as an instantiation of a model. A model describes how the annotation should look like, which annotation structures are possible and what these structures mean. This implies, however, that if the model changes, the annotations are influenced as well and vice versa.

The choice of annotation schemas and structures for the separate boxes should in most applications be inspired by explanatory models of humans interaction and the application goals. Different models or different uses of the models may lead to distinct annotation schemas for the information in the boxes.

5.1   Manual Annotations

The annotations discussed above are not necessarily automatically produced: corpus based work always involves a large amount of manual annotation work as well. There are several reasons for creating manual annotations of corpus material. In the first place ground truth knowledge is needed in order to evaluate new techniques for automatic annotation. In the second place high quality annotations are needed to do social psychology research on the corpus data. As long as the quality of the automatic annotation results is not high enough, only manual annotations provide the quality of information to analyze certain aspects of human behaviour.

It is a well known problem that manual annotation of human interaction is extremely expensive in terms of effort. Annotating a stretch of video with not-too-complicated aspects may easily take ten times the duration of that video. Shriberg et al. report an efficiency of 18xRT (18 times the duration of the video is spent on annotating) on annotation of Dialog Acts boundaries, types and adjacency pairs on meeting recordings [28]. Simple manual transcription of speech usually takes 10xRT. For more complicated speech transcription such as prosody 100-200xRT has been reported in Syrdal et al. [29]. The cost of syntactic annotation of text (PoS tagging and annotating syntactic structure and labels for nodes and edges) may run to an average of 50 seconds per sentence with an average sentence length of 17.5 tokens (cf. Brants et al. [30], which describes syntactic annotation of a German newspaper corpus). As a final example, Lin et al. [31] report an annotation efficiency of 6.8xRT for annotating MPEG-7 metadata on video using the VideoAnnEx tool. The annotation described there consists of correction of shot boundaries, selecting salient regions in shots and assigning semantic labels from a controlled lexicon. It may be obvious that more complex annotation of video will further increase the cost.

The type of research for which the framework described in this paper is developed requires not one or two annotation types on the data but a rich set of different annotations. It is therefore an important task to cut down the time needed to annotate multimodal data. This section discusses a few approaches to this problem.

5.2   Efficient Interfaces for Manual Annotation

In the first place, whenever manual annotation is inevitable, the efficiency of creating this annotation is heavily dependent on the user interface of the annotation tool. Different aspects (dialogue act labelling, hand gestures, head orientation) are best annotated with different strategies. Figure 3 shows an example of such a specifically targeted strategy, an annotation module for head orientation. The figure shows the video of a person whose head orientations are to be annotated. A coffee mug is used as a proxy for his head. A flock-of-birds 6 DOF position and orientation sensor is attached to the side of the mug, keeping track of its orientation. Rotating the mug in response to head movements in the video results in a real-time annotation of the head orientation of the person in the video. A small 3D display of a virtual head follows the mug for verification of the annotation quality. For fragments with fast head movements the video speed can be slowed down. On those fragments an efficiency ratio of 1:2 per annotated person can be achieved.

Fig. 3. Realtime annotation of head orientation

5.3   Semi-Automatic Annotation

Apart from interface improvements in order to increase the annotation efficiency, tools are developed to perform annotations automatically. Although many of these efforts result in low-quality annotations, some automatic annotation procedures can provide support for for manual annotation. These kinds of semi-automatic annotation techniques are already applied for audio transcriptions and video segmentation (e.g. manual correction of automatically detected boundaries). Manual correction of automatic annotations is much faster than complete manual annotation [29].

For example, the labelling of hand gestures can be facilitated with a semi-automatic procedure. Gesture labelling schema's such as that of McNeill [32] describe gestures using attributes such as hand shape, symmetry, category of gesture and the relative location of the gesture with respect to the subject's body. McNeill uses the gesture space of Pedelty (see figure 4) to distinguish gesture locations. There are reliable automatic recognition procedures for hand and face tracking under the right conditions (see e.g. [33]). Therefore the annotation environment can reliably fill in the relative location attributes. Furthermore the information contained in this tracking data can give an indication of which gesture type occurred, allowing the annotation environment to give a default suggestion for that attribute. Syrdal et al. show that, at least in some cases, default suggestions can speed up manual labelling without introducing much bias in the annotation [29].

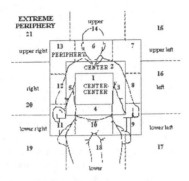

Fig. 4. The gesture space of Pedelty, 1987

5.4   Integrating Annotations

The annotations should be stored in a suitable data format, supported by a powerful API toolkit. Such a toolkit should meet several requirements. It should support development of custom annotation modules such as described above. Different layers of annotation should be easy to integrate. Transformation of annotations from other formats into the desired format should be supported. The data formats should allow explicit expression of the layered structure of the annotations and their derivational relations. There are many publications dealing with these issues, the reader is referred to [34] for more information.

We chose to work with the layered stand-off annotation format from The University of Edinburgh, the Nite XML Toolkit [35]. The layered structure of the annotations described before is very easy to map on a data model in this toolkit. It enables each of the component classes from the various layers to be supplied with their own models and annotation schemas. Higher level annotations can relate to or be dependent on lower level annotations.

6   Conclusions

This paper presents a view on corpus based research in the domain of human-human interaction in general. Various kinds of research can be positioned in this framework, relating them to each other. Part of the framework is elaborated for meetings. Different aspects of meeting modelling are discussed. Annotations are an important aspect of corpus based research. Continuing focus on development of efficient annotation tools and schemas is needed, where the underlying models should guide the development.

References

1. Armstrong, S., et al, A.C.: Natural language queries on natural language data: a database of meeting dialogues. In: Proc. of NLP and Information Systems-NLDB'03. (2003) 14–27
2. Vertegaal, R.: Who is looking at whom. PhD thesis, University of Twente (1998)
3. http://www.is.cs.cmu.edu/meeting_room/.
4. http://www.m4project.org/.
5. http://www.nist.gov/speech/test_beds/mr_proj/.
6. http://www.icsi.berkeley.edu/Speech/mr/.
7. Hersey, P., Blanchard, K.: Management of Organizational Behavior: Utilizing Human Resources. Prentice Hall (1988)
8. Kunz, W., Rittel, H.W.J.: Issues as elements of information systems. Working Paper WP-131, Univ. Stuttgart, Inst. Fuer Grundlagen der Planung (1970)
9. Pelachaud, C., Bilvi, M.: Computational model of believable conversational agents. Communication in MAS: background, current trends and future (2003)
10. Padilha, E., Carletta, J.: Nonverbal behaviours improving a simulation of small group discussion. In: Proc. 1st Nordic Symp. on Multimodal Comm. (2003) 93–105
11. Nijholt, A.: Meetings, gatherings and events in smart environments. In: Proc. ACM SIGGRAPH VRCAI2004. (2004) to appear.
12. Nijholt, A.: Where computers disappear, virtual humans appear. Computers and Graphics 28 (2004) to appear.
13. Vilhjalmsson, H., Cassell, J.: Bodychat: Autonomous communicative behaviors in avatars. In: Proc. of the 2nd Annual ACM Int. Conf. on Autonomous Agents. (1998)
14. Carletta, J., Anderson, A., Garrod, S.: Seeing eye to eye: an account of grounding and understanding in work groups. Cognitive Studies: Bulletin of the Japanese Cognitive Science Society 9(1) (2002) 1–20
15. McGrath, J.: Groups: Interaction and Performance. Prentice Hall (1984)
16. Shi, Y., Rose, R.T., Quek, F., McNeill, D.: Gaze, attention, and meeting dynamics. In: ICASSP2004 Meeting Recognition Workshop. (2004) to appear.
17. Marchand-Maillet, S.: Meeting record modelling for enhanced browsing. Technical Report 03.01, Computer Vision and Multimedia Laboratory, University of Geneva (2003)
18. Clark, H.: Using language. Cambridge University Press (1996)
19. McCowan, I., Bengio, S., Gatica-Perez, D., Lathoud, G.: Automatic analysis of multimodal group actions in meetings. Technical Report IDIAP-RR 03-27, IDIAP (2003)
20. Jovanovic, N.: Recognition of meeting actions using information obtained from different modalities. Report TR-CTIT-03-48, CTIT (2003)
21. Dhillon, R., Bhagat, S., Carvey, H., Shriberg, E.: Meeting recorder project: Dialogue act labeling guide. Technical report, ICSI Speech Group, Berkeley, USA (2003)
22. Jurafsky, D., Shriberg, E., Biaska, D.: Switchboard SWBD-DAMSL shallow-discourse-function annotation (coders manual, draft 13). Technical report, Univ. of Colorado, Inst. of Cognitive Science (1997)
23. Bales, R.F.: Interaction Process Analysis. Addison-Wesley (1951)
24. Pallotta, V., Hatem, G.: Argumentative segmentation and annotation guidelines. Technical report (2003)
25. Gilbert, M.A.: Goals in argumentation. In: Proc. of the conf. on Formal and Applied Practical Reasoning. (1996)

26. Carofiglio, V., de Rosis, F.: Combining logical with emotional reasoning in natural argumentation. In: 3rd Workshop on Affective and Attitude User Modeling. (2003)
27. Dong Zhang, Daniel Gatica-Perez, S.B.I.M., Lathoud, G.: Multimodal Group Action Clustering in Meetings. In: ACM 2nd International Workshop on Video Surveillance & Sensor Networks in conjunction with 12th ACM International Conference on Multimedia. (2004) IDIAP-RR 04-24.
28. Shriberg, E., Dhillon, R., et al., S.B.: The icsi meeting recorder dialog act (mrda) corpus. In: Proc. HLT-NAACL SIGDIAL Workshop. (2004) to appear.
29. Syrdal, A.K., Hirschberg, J., McGory, J., Beckman, M.: Automatic tobi prediction and alignment to speed manual labelling of prosody. Speech communication **33** (2001) 135–151
30. Brants, T., Skut, W., Uszkoreit, H.: 5. In: Syntactic annotation of a German newspaper corpus. Kluwer, Dordrecht (NL) (2003)
31. Lin, C.Y., Tseng, B.L., Smith, J.R.: Video collaborative annotation forum: Establishing ground-truth labels on large multimedia datasets. In: Proc of the TRECVID2003. (2003)
32. McNeill, D.: Hand and Mind: What gestures reveal about thought. University of Chicago Press (1995)
33. Brethes, L., Menezes, P., Lerasle, F., Hayet, J.: Face tracking and hand gesture recognition for human-robot interaction. In: Proc. of the International Conference on Robotics and Automation. (2004)
34. http://www.ldc.upenn.edu/annotation/.
35. Carletta, J., Evert, S., Heid, U., Kilgour, J., Robertson, J., Voormann, H.: The NITE XML toolkit: flexible annotation for multi-modal language data. Behavior Research Methods, Instruments, and Computers **35(3)** (2003) 353–363

Artificial Companions

Yorick Wilks

University of Sheffield

What will an artificial Companion be like? Who will need them and how much good or harm will they do? Will they change our lives and social habits in the radical way technologies have in the past: just think of trains, phones and television? Will they force changes in the law so that things that are not people will be liable for damages; up till now, it is the case that if a machine goes wrong, it is always the maker or the programmer, or their company, which is at fault. Above all, how many people, with no knowledge of technology at all, such as the old and very young, will want to go about, or sit at home, with a companion that may look like a furry handbag on the sofa, or a rucksack on the back, but which will keep track of their lives by conversation, and be their interface to the rather elusive mysteries we now think of as the Internet or Web.

One thing we can be quite sure of is that artificial Companions are coming. In a small way they have already arrived and millions of people have already met them. The Japanese toys Tamagochi (literally little eggs) were a brief craze in the West that saw sensible people worrying that they had not played with their Tamagochi for a few hours and it might have begun to pine, where pining meant sad eyes and icons on a tiny screen, and playing with it meant pushing a feed button several times! The extraordinary thing about the Tamagochi (and later the US Furby) phenomenon was that people who knew better began to feel guilt about their behaviour towards a small cheap and simple toy that could not even speak.

The brief history of those toys said a great deal about people and their ability to create and transfer their affections, despite their knowledge of what is really going on inside their object. This phenomenon is almost certainly a sign of what is to come and of how easily people will find it to identify with and care for automata that can talk and appear to remember who they are talking to. This chapter is about what it will be like when those objects are available: since most of the basic technologies such as speech recognition and simple machine reasoning and memory are already in place, this will not be long. Simple robot home helps are already available in Japan but we only have to look at them and their hard plastic exteriors and their few tinny phrases about starting the dishwasher to realise that this is almost certainly not how a Companion should be.

The technologies needed for a Companion are very near to a real trial model; some people think that Artificial Intelligence (AI) is a failed project after nearly fifty years, but that is it not true at all: it is simply everywhere. It is in the computers on 200-ton planes that land automatically in dark and fog and which we trust with our lives; it is in chess programs like IBM's Big Blue that have beaten the world's champion, and it is in the machine translation programs that offer to translate for you any page of an Italian or Japanese newspaper on the web.

S. Bengio and H. Bourlard (Eds.): MLMI 2004, LNCS 3361, pp. 36–45, 2005.
© Springer-Verlag Berlin Heidelberg 2005

And where AI certainly is present, is in the computer technologies of speech and language: in those machine translation programs and in the typewriters that type from your dictation, and in the programs on the phone that recognise where you want to buy a train ticket to. But this is not a chapter about computer technology any more than it is about robots, nor is it about philosophy. Companions are not at all about fooling us because they will not pretend to be human at all: imagine the following scenario, which will become the principal one, running through this paper. An old person sits on a sofa, and beside them is a large furry handbag, which we shall call a Senior Companion; it is easy to carry about, but much of the day it just sits there and chats. Given the experience of Tamagochi, and the easily ascertained fact that old people with pets survive far better than those without, we will expect this to be an essential lifespan and health improving objective to own.

Nor is it hard to see why this Companion that chats in an interesting way would become an essential possession for the growing elderly population of the EU and the US, the most rapidly growing segment of the population, but one relatively well provided with funds.

Other Companions are just as plausible as this one, in particular the Junior Companion for children, that would most likely take the form of a backpack, a small and hard to remove backpack that always knew where the child was but the Senior Companion will be our focus, not because of its obvious social relevance and benefit, possibly even at a low level of function that could be easily built with what is now available in laboratories, but because of the particular fit between what a Companion is and old people's needs.

Common sense tells us that no matter what we read in the way of official encouragement, a large proportion of today's old people are effectively excluded from information technology, the web, the internet and some mobile phones because "they cannot learn to cope with the buttons". This can be because of their generation or because of losses of skill with age: there are talking books in abundance now but many, otherwise intelligent, old people cannot manipulate a tape recorder or a mobile phone, which has too many small controls for them with unwanted functionalities. All this is pretty obvious and well known and yet there is little thought as to how our growing body of old people can have access to at least some of the benefits of information technology without the ability to operate a PC or even a mobile phone.

After all, their needs are real, not just to have someone to talk to, but to deal with correspondence from public bodies, such as councils and utility companies demanding payment, with the need to set up times to be visited by nurses or relatives by phone, how to be sure they have taken the pills, when keeping any kind of diary may have become difficult, as well as deciding what foods to order, even when a delivery service is available via the net but is impossibly difficult in practice for them to make use of.

In all these situations, one can see how a Companion that could talk and understand and also gain access to the web, to email and a mobile phone could become an essential mental prosthesis for an old person, one that any responsible society would have to support. But there are also aspects of this which are beyond just getting information, such as having the newspapers blown up on the TV screen till the print was big enough to be read, and dealing with affairs, like pay bills from a bank account.

It is reliably reported that many old people spend much of their day sorting and looking over photographs of themselves and their families, along with places they have lived and visited. This will obviously increase as time goes on and everyone begins to have access to digitised photos and videos throughout their lives. One can see this as an attempt to establish the narrative of one's life: what drives the most literate segment of the population to write autobiographies (for the children) even when, objectively speaking, they may have lived lives with little to report. But think of what will be needed if a huge volume of material is to be sorted. A related notion of "memories for life" has been developed and recently been declared a major challenge for future UK computing and we shall discuss this whole matter again later.

One can see what we are discussing, then, as democratising the art of autobiography which was about Chaps, as Benchley readers will remember, whereas the art of Geography was about Maps. And this will mean far more than simply providing ways in which people with limited manipulative skills can massage photos and videos into some kind of order on a big glossy screen: it will require some guiding intelligence to provide and amplify a narrative that imposes a time order. Lives have a natural time order, but this is sometimes very difficult to impose and to recover for the liver; even those with no noticeable problems from aging find it very hard to be sure in what order two major life events actually happened: "I know I married Lily before Susan but in which marriage did my father die?"

The frivolous example is to illustrate, and we shall see something of how it is actually done later on, how an artificial agent might assist in bringing events whether in text or pictures, into some single coherent order or at least some partial orders so that one knew some things were before others, even if there were some events (e.g. Teddy's and Joan's marriages) that we could not order with certainty. This is, the kind of thing today's computers can be surprisingly good at, but it is a very complex and abstract notion, that of the time ordering of events, which can be simple (I know James was born before Ronnie) or only partial in some situations (I know my brother's children were born after my marriage and before my wife died, but in what order did they come?)

These may seem odd or contrived but do represent real problems at the border of memory and reasoning for many people, especially with age.

Another reason why this notion of ordering life narratives is so important, for a Senior Companion and elsewhere, is that it is also a way of separating different but similar lives from each other on the web, and these two notions are closely related as we shall show. This is jumping ahead a little, but many people know the experience of searching for, say, "George Bush" in Texas with Google on the web and finding there are about 25 of them who merit some attention from Google. Since two of them have been US Presidents, they cannot be distinguished from each other by name and job alone, and one must then use life events, dates of birth and so on to separate them. To put the whole thing simply, distinguishing closely related or confusingly named people on the web requires something like a coherent life line of some of the events in their lives, which is the same notion we have been discussing for imposing coherence on the, possibly muddled, whole life memories of old people.

We have talked of Companions as specialised computers that could talk and assist needy groups of people such as the old. That help will almost certainly require helping organise their lives and memories but also interacting with the electronic world outside for them. That may be as simple as using the web to find a supermarket's home delivery service for groceries. More interestingly, it may involve using the web to find out what has happened to their old school friends and workmates, something millions already use the web for. But, as we saw, we shall need some notion of time lines and the coherence of lives on the web to sort of the right friends and schoolmates from the thousands of other people with the same names.

So, the reasoning technologies we shall need to organise the life of the Companion's owner may turn out to be very same technologies we have not really shown this yet, just said it to locate other individuals on the web and select them out from all the personal information about the world's population that fills up the web, since the web is now not just for describing the famous but covers potentially everyone. Two of my friends and colleagues who are professors of computer science have some difficulty distinguishing, and maintaining a difference, between themselves on the web and, in one case, a famous pornography supplier in Dallas, and in another case a reasonably well known disc-jockey in Houston.

These problems will soon become not just quirky but the norm for everyone, and what I shall want to argue later is that the kind of computer agency we shall need in a Companion, and possibly a Companion that deals with the web for us, if we are old or maybe just lazy, is in fact closely related to the kind of agency we shall need to deal with the web in any case as it becomes more complex. To put this very simply: the web will become unusable for non-experts unless we have human-like agents to manage its complexity for us. The web itself must develop more human-like characteristics at its peripheries to survive as a usable resource and technology: just locating individual on the web when a majority of the EU and US populations have a web presence, will become far more difficult and time consuming that it is now. If this is right, Companions will be needed by everyone, not simply the old, the young and the otherwise handicapped. It is going to be impossible to conceive of the web without some kind of a human face.

The notion of a Companion developed so far is anything but superhuman; it is vital to stress this because some of the public rhetoric about what companionable computers will be like has come from films such as 2001, whose computer HAL is superhuman in knowledge and reasoning. He is a very dangerous Companion, and prepared to be deceptive to get what he wants, which may be not at all what we want. Seymour Papert at MIT always argued that it was a total misconception that AI would ever try to model the superhuman, and that its mission just like AI-pioneer John McCarthy's emphasis on the importance of common sense reasoning was to capture the shorthand of reasoning, the tricks that people actually use to cope with everyday life. Only then would we understand the machines we have built and trained and avoid them becoming too clever or too dangerous. This same issue was very much behind Asimov's Laws of Robotics, which we shall discuss later, and which set out high-level principles that no robot should ever break so as to bring harm to humans.

The difficulty here is fairly obvious: if a robot were clever enough it would find a way of justifying (to itself) an unpleasant outcome for someone, perfectly consistently with acceptable overall principles. One say clever enough but doing that has also been a distinctively, human characteristic throughout history: one thinks of all those burned for the good of their own souls and all those sacrificed so that others might live. In the latter case, we are probably grateful for those lost in what were really medical experiments such as the early heart transplants even though they were never called that.

It will not be possible to ignore all these questions when presenting Companions in more detail, and in particular the issue of where responsibility and blame may lie when a Companion acts as a person's agent and something goes wrong. At the moment, Anglo-American law has no real notion of any responsible entity except a human, if we exclude Acts of God in insurance policies. The only possible exception here is dogs, which occupy a special place in Anglo-Saxon law and seem to have certain rights and attributions of character separate from their owners. If one keeps a tiger, one is totally responsible for whatever damage it does, because it is ferae naturae, a wild beast. Dogs, however, seem to occupy a strange middle ground as responsible agents, and an owner may not be responsible unless the dog is known to be of bad character. We shall return to this later and argue that we may have here a narrow window through which we may begin to introduce notions of responsible machine agency, different from that of the owners and manufacturers of machines at the present time.

It is easy to see the need for something like this: suppose a Companion told one's grandmother that it was warm outside and, when she went out into the freezing garden on the basis of this news, she caught and chill and became very ill. In such a circumstance one might well want to blame someone or something and would not be happy to be told that Companions could not accept blame and that, if one read the small print on the Companion box, one would see that the company had declined all blame and had got one to sign a document saying so. All this may seem fanciful, and even acceptable if one's grandmother recovered and one had the company give the Companion a small tweak so it never happened again.

This last story makes no sense at the moment, and indeed the Companion might point out with reason, when the maintenance doctor called round, that it had read the outside temperature electronically and could show that it was a moderate reading and the blame should fall on the building maintenance staff, if anywhere. These issues will return later but what is obvious already is that Companions must be prepared to show exactly why they said the things they said and offered the advice they did.

A Companion's memory of what it has said and done may be important but will be used only rarely one hopes; though it may be necessary for it to repeat its advice at intervals with a recalcitrant user: (You still haven't taken your pills. Come on, take them now and I'll tell you a joke you haven't heard before). James Allen is already said to have modelled a talking companionable pill for the old!

What may become a very important feature of Senior Companions is putting coherence into the memories of their owners: we mentioned this earlier as a way of sorting an organising memories and sorting fragments of text and old photographs, but there is another aspect to this which is not so much for the user as for their relatives later on. One can reasonably suppose that years of talking with an elderly user, and helping them organise their memories, will mean that the Companion also has access to a life-story of the user that is has built up from those hours of conversation. The user might not want to hear any of this played back but it could be used as a body of facts and assumptions to help organise the user's life as well as text and images. But what should now happen to this biographical account that the Companion has, and which could exist in several forms: e.g. a document the Companion could print or a collage of things said by the user and Companion put together coherently from recorded pieces, or even a single autobiographical account in the Companion's version of the user's own voice. This is not at all far-fetched: there are speech generation packages now available that can train to imitate a particular person's voice very accurately with plenty of training time, and time is exactly what the Companion and user would have.

I would suggest that memoirs like these, produced over a long period by the Companion, are exactly what the user's relatives will want after the user is gone, something more helpful and less gruesome than the tiny video clips one can now find and run at the touch of a button on some Italian tombstones. The need for these is now greater than it was, as people live farther from their parents when old and see them less. Many people have wished they had spent more time discussing a parent's earlier memories before their deaths how one's parents had met and fallen in love, for example, but then suddenly it is too late to ask, or unobtainable because of shyness on the part of parent or child. This kind of limited memoir is a an important role a Companion might come to play in society; experience may well show that old people will reveal memories and anecdotes to a Companion they would perhaps not feel able to tell their close relatives. Indeed, there is a long tradition in AI of arguing that people may sometimes prefer machines to people in certain roles: AI-pioneer Donald Michie always claimed that drivers always preferred traffic lights (or "robots" as they are called in some parts of the world) to policemen on traffic duty.

The possibility of a Companion constructing and storing a biography for its owner raises in one form the major issue of identity: is the Companion to be distinguished from the owner whose life it knows so well and whose voice it will almost certainly be able to imitate. And this may be just another version of the old joke about pets getting like their owners, since we have chosen to describe the Senior Companion as a kind of pet. Other forms of identity will also be touched on later, in particular the identity of the Companion as an agent for the owner, and its similarity and distinctness from the owner, while on the other hand functioning as a web agent in the world of electronic information. We have not yet properly introduced the notion of a web agent it is, very roughly, an intelligent package of software that one can encounter on the Internet and which will give expert advice. It is now expected that web agents will have to make deals and transactions of all sorts with each other and learn to trust each other, as they already do in a rudimentary sense in the world of banking where agents in their thousands clinch money transactions between financial institutions. The kind visible to a use, but still rudimentary, are those which will search the whole web to find the cheapest source of, say, a particular camera.

All this is for later and elsewhere, but these two issues of identity in an artificial world will also draw upon other ways in which identity has become an issue for internet users and which are relatively well known. The first, known to all newspaper readers, is that of chat room users who pretend to be what they are not; normally this is quite innocent pretence, and little more than hiding behind a pseudonym during conversations and sometimes pretending to be a different kind of person, often of the opposite sex. In that sense, the Victorian game of sex-pretending, on which Turing based his famous imitation game for computers, has come back as a widely played reality. The problems only arise, and they are very real, when impressionable people, usually children, are lured into meetings with people who have been encountered under false pretences.

The other issue of identity, which is a standard problem for web searchers, is finding too many people under the same name with a Google search and trying to find the right one, or even how many there are, a topic we already touched on above. It is a much researched problem at the moment how to sort out exactly how many people there are in the pages retrieved by, Google for the same name. One can see the pressing interest here, in that many scientists now rate how famous they are by how many Google hits their name gets, compared to their competitors. But how can they be sure all those retrieved are really themselves? A quite well known British computing professor has a very long list indeed, which is boosted by a mid-Western disc jockey with the same name!

The George Bush example, mentioned earlier, suggests that the best way must require something like a rule that looks at dates, on the assumption that two people with the same name are very unlikely to have the same date of birth. And other rules will almost certainly deal with aspects of people such as their occupations, which will, however, come up against the unusual but very real cases like Vanbrugh, the 18th C playwright, and his separation from the 18th C architect of Blenheim Palace of the same name who, amazingly enough, were one and the same person, hard though it would be for most rules (and people) to accept.

There is a further kind of complication in that, even if we could sort out muddled identities of these kinds, given enough information, there is the fact that in some cases people do not agree on how many objects or people there are under discussion, so that it becomes a matter of conflict or, as you might say, individual belief, how many people are being talked about. In the case of Vanbrugh we can imagine a strained conversation between a person sure they were two similarly named individuals and someone else who knew they were not. It is, as one could put it, very difficult but just possible for people to communicate who do not agree on what things there are in the world, on the ontology, to use a word in its original sense that is now normally used to mean something quite different. Later we shall look at methods of analysis and descriptions of knowledge that might allow people to reason with others, or their Companions, when they disagreed in this way about what there is out there. How should a Companion discuss relatives when it was sure Jack was Ethel's auntie, and its owner even said that the day before, but is now convinced they are quite different people? This is a deep matter to which we shall return later.

Problems of identity will arise both in the context of representing individuals in a Companion's world, which is very much based on that of its user, one the Companion seeks to learn, and also in the wider world of information, which for convenience we will often identify with what can be found on the Web or Internet. It is quite normal now to hear people speak of "virtual worlds" in connection with the Web and Internet, although it is usually unclear exactly what they have in mind. The only obvious place where virtual worlds belong there naturally is in computer games, whose interaction with the Web we will also need to discuss later, certainly in the case of Companions for the young, who spend more time in games worlds than the rest of the population.

The general interest here is in the interaction of these considerations with identity; having a verifiable identity is part of what it means to be a human being, or at least a modern human being. If a Companion is to have human-like characteristics, one will want to explore how its identity can have human-like features, as opposed to machine-like features where identity is usually a trivial matter: a car is identified uniquely simply by the sum of the numbers stamped on its chassis and its engine and there is no interesting issue about that outside the world of car fraud.

If a Companion is to be an interface to the web, say, for a user who is technologically incompetent yet who must conform to the standards of identity that society requires and imposes, then the Companion will have to understand identity to some degree and possibly be able to manipulate slightly different forms of it. In the US and UK, identity is currently established by a range of items with numbers, from passports through credit cards to health, driving licence and tax numbers (some with associated passwords or PINs), with the Social Security number having a definite primacy in the US. In most EU countries there is a single ID number based, of which the clearest is on the life-long single Personnummer in Sweden. States prefer a citizen to be identified by a single number and in the UK there is currently strong pressure for something closer to the Swedish model, although UK law has, at the moment, no clear definition of identity (with legally registered unique names and addresses, as in most of the EU) and there is no legal problem in the UK with having a number of identities simultaneously and bank accounts for each (as a famous case brought, and lost, by the Post Office showed some years ago) so long as there is no intention to defraud.

All this is important since identity checks are the basis of all Web transactions and if a Companion is to deal with an old person's affairs it will need something approaching a power of attorney or at least an understanding of how identity is established in Web transactions, as well as a method for establishing that its owner approves of what it is doing in individual transactions, in case of later disputes (e.g. by angry relatives after an old person's money has been spent). Neil Birch has recently described a scenario in which security of identity can be achieved with out the imposition of unique identity, which security-minded authorities would certainly resist but may be very important to someone who feels that they have a right to buy something on the Internet revealing only, say, their age but not who they actually are.

All these issues are the subjects of active research programs, but what I am introducing here is the possibility that a Companion, as a new kind of artefact among us, may focus our minds on a set of intellectual and practical issues in a new way, even though some of them are very traditional issues indeed.

How does this rather airy vision connect to the general state of R & D in speech recognition and natural language processing at the time of writing?

My own hunch is that most of the components needed for a minimally interesting Companion are already available; certainly the Companion is not particularly vulnerable to one major current technical weakness, namely the imperfect recognition rate of available ASR systems. This, of course, is because a Companion is by definition dedicated to a user and so the issue of user-independent ASR does not initially arise.

However, the Companion is not merely an application wholly neutral between current disputes about how best to advance speech and language systems, in part because it will surely need a great deal of representation of human knowledge and belief and therefore the Companion's development would seem to need overall approaches and architectures that allow such representations and, ultimately, their derivation from data by machine learning.

One could describe the current debate over methodology, very crudely, by drawing an analogy with the situation in the late 1980's when symbolic NLP was invaded by an empirical and statistical methodology driven by recent successes in speech processing. The shock troops of that invasion were the IBM team under Jelinek which developed a wholly novel statistical approach to machine translation (MT), one that was not ultimately successful (see Wilks 1994 for a discussion) but did better than anyone in conventional, symbolic, MT initially expected, and set in train a revolution in methodology in NLP as a whole.

Although the IBM team began without any attention to the symbolic content of linguistic MT, they were forced, by their inability to beat conventional MT systems in DARPA competitions, to take on board notions such as lexicons, morphology and grammar, but, of course, they imported them in forms such they could be learned in their turn and that fact was the ultimate triumph of their revolution.

The present situation in dialogue modelling is in some ways a replay, at a lower level, of that titanic struggle. The introduction into ASR of so called "language models" which are usually no more than corpus bi-gram statistics to aid recognition of words by their likely neighbours-----have caused some, like Young (2002) to suggest that simple extensions to ASR methods could solve all the problems of language dialogue modelling.

Young describes a complete dialogue system seen as what he calls a Partially Observable Markov process, of which subcomponents can be observed in turn with intermediate variables and named:

- Speech understanding
- Semantic decoding
- Dialogue act detection
- Dialogue management and control
- Speech generation

Such titles are close to conventional for an NLP researcher, e.g. when he intends the third module as something that can also recognise what we may call the *function* of an utterance, such as being a command to do something and not a pleasantry. Such terms have been the basis of NLP dialogue pragmatics for some thirty years, and the interesting issue here is whether Young's Partially Observable Markov Decision Process, are a good level at which to describe such phenomena, implying as it does that the classic ASR machine learning methodology can capture the full functionality of a dialogue system, when its internal structures cannot be fully observed, even in the sense that the waves, the phones and written English words can be. The analogy with Jelinek's MT project holds only at its later, revised stage, when it was proposed to take over the classic structures of NLP, but recapitulate them by statistical induction. This is, in a sense exactly Young's proposal for the classic linguistic structures associated with dialogue parsing and control with the additional assumption, not made earlier by Jelinek, that such modular structures can be learned even when there are no distinctive and observable input-output pairs for the module that would count as data by any classic definition, since they cannot be word strings but symbolic formalisms like those that classic dialogue managers manipulate.

The intellectual question of whether the methodology of speech research, tried, tested and successful as it is, can move in and take over the methodologies of language research may seem to many a completely arcane issue, like ancient trade union disputes in shipbuilding, say, as to who bored the holes and who held the drills. But, as with those earlier labour struggles, they seem quite important to the people involved in them and here, unlike shipbuilding, we have a clash of expertise but no external common-sense to come in and give a sensible decision.

Jelinek's original MT strategy was non/anti-linguistic with no intermediate representations hypothesized, whereas Young assumes roughly the same intermediate objects as linguists but in very simplified forms. So, for example, he suggests methods for learning to attach Dialogue Acts to utterances but by methods that make no reference to linguistic methods for this (since Samuels et al. 1998) and, paradoxically, Young's equations do not make the Dialogue Acts depend on the words in the utterance, as all linguistic methods do.

His overall aim is to obtain training data for all of them so the whole process becomes a single throughput Markov model, and Young concedes this model may only be for simple domains, such as, in his example, a pizza ordering system.

All parties in this dispute, if it is one, concede the key role of machine learning, and all are equally aware that structures and formalisms designed at one level can ultimately be represented in virtual machines of less power but more efficiency. In that sense, the primal dispute between Chomsky and Skinner about the nature of the human language machine was quite pointless, since Chomsky's transformational grammars could be represented, in any concrete and finite case, such as a human being, as a finite state machine.

All that being so, researchers have firm predilections as to the kinds of design within which they believe functions and capacities can best be represented, and, in the present case, it is hard to see how the natural clusterings of states that form a topic can be represented in finite state systems, let alone the human ability to return in conversation to a previously suspended topic, all matters that can be represented and processed naturally in well understood virtual machines above the level of finite state matrices (see Wilks et al. 2004).

There is no suggestion that a proper or adequate discussion of Young's views has been given here, only a plea that machine learning must be possible over more linguistically adequate structures than finite state matrices if we are to be able to represent, in a perspicuous manner, the sorts of belief, intention and control structures that complex dialogue modelling will need; it cannot be enough to always limit ourselves to the simples applications on the grounds, as Young puts it, that "the typical system S will typically be intractably large and must be approximated".

References

1. Wilks, Y., Webb, N., Setzer, A., Hepple, M., and Catizone, R. (2004) Machine Learning approaches to human dialogue modelling. In Kuppervelt, Smith (eds.) Current and New Directions in Discourse and Dialogue, Kluwer, Berlin.
2. Young, S. (2002) "Talking to machines"statistically speaking, Proc. ICSOS'02.
3. Samuel, K., Carberry, S., and Vijay-Shankar, R. (1998) Dialogue Act Tagging with Transformation-Based Learning. In Proc. COLING98, Montreal.
4. Wilks, Y. (1994) Stone Soup and the French Room: the empiricist-rationalist debate about machine translation. Reprinted in Zampolli, Calzolari and Palmer (eds.) Current Issues in Computational Linguistics: in honor of Don Walker. Kluwer: Berlin

Zakim – A Multimodal Software System for Large-Scale Teleconferencing

Max Froumentin

World Wide Web Consortium – mf@w3.org

Abstract. This paper describes Zakim, a multimodal teleconference system used at the World Wide Web Consortium (W3C). The main requirement that differentiates Zakim from other resarch projects was that the system had to be robust and be universally accessible, as W3C teleconferences run around the clock and are accessed by hundreds of people weekly. The Internet Relay Chat was chosen as the control protocol for the telephone bridge, allowing for easy access to a majority participants. The second part of the paper describes how this system has dramatically improved the way teleconferences are run.

1   Introduction

This paper describes Zakim, a multimodal teleconference system used at the World Wide Web Consortium [1]. While the technology presented here does not introduce advanced research work, the it has been developed with robustness in mind, as it is used almost round-the-clock by several hundred people. The context and requirements are introduced first, followed by a description of the system's features. Lastly we describe how the structure of W3C teleconferences has been modified by the use of Zakim, and discuss some issues and possible improvements.

2   Context

The World Wide Web Consortium (W3C) gathers experts both from industry and academia, to work on developing the architecture of the Web. This mostly consists in writing documents: specifications (e.g. HTML, CSS), guidelines or technical reports, which once finalised can be used by software developers to write browsers or by webmasters to design sites, among other usages.

Specifications published by the W3C are written by Working Groups. There are about 50 such groups, each of which comprising between 10 and 90 people. Groups communicate through four means: a mailing list (archived on the web), the group's web site, teleconferences (with up to 50 people attending), and face-to-face meetings. Typically a group will hold one or two one-hour teleconferences every week, hold quarterly face-to-face meetings, and exchange 20 to 150 emails a month. Telephone and face-to-face discussions are lead by the group's *chair*,

S. Bengio and H. Bourlard (Eds.): MLMI 2004, LNCS 3361, pp. 46–55, 2005.

and are recorded by a *scribe* who is in charge of sending meeting minutes to the group's mailing list (scribes rotate among the group's membership).

One basic principle of W3C groups is to record as much of the discussion as possible on the web, whether they occurred on the mailing list, in teleconferences or at face-to-face meetings.

Running meetings for almost 10 years has empirically made people aware of issues that are well-known to researchers in CSCW, but which we detail below to highlight those that are addressed by the architecture described here:

- Mailing list discussions can be very verbose, as well as quite inefficient, especially when it comes to making decisions.
- Face-to-face meetings are much more time-efficient, but because of the distributed nature of the W3C membership, their frequency is necessarily limited.
- Teleconferences are next best to face-to-face meetings, but the lack of visual cues (who is speaking, who would like to speak and in what order, etc.) and the occasionally poor sound quality (preventing accurate minuting) can be detrimental to efficiency.

Zakim has mostly improved the situation described by the third point above, although it will be mentioned that means other than teleconferences are influenced by the design as well.

3   The Zakim Telephone Bridge and Its Interfaces

The W3C runs its own teleconference system (*bridge*), which is usually active 12 hours a day on average, with up to 9 simultaneous teleconferences. The Zakim[1] bridge is a customized Compunetix Contex conferencing system [2]. To the core teleconference system has been added a few software components, as well as interfaces between them, described below.

3.1   Components

The Telephone Bridge. The functionalities of the bridge itself, upon which all the software described below builds are simple. The bridge can hold several teleconferences simultaneously, it has a programmable schedule that stores all the teleconferences, their time, duration and maximum number of participants. Each teleconference is identified by a pass-code, that the participants dial in through DTMF, after calling the bridge's phone number.

The bridge also retrieves and makes available Automatic Number Identification data (ANI, more familiarly known as caller-ID) when available, and can also react to DTMF tones. The original interface, proprietary software provided

---

[1] The name Zakim originates from the way W3C names the various teleconference bridges it uses, after the names of the vehicle bridges that cross the Charles River in Boston.

by the bridge vendor, lets the operator monitor the activity of each line (noise or voice), and allows various operations such as muting or unmuting a participant, call a number or disconnect a line.

IRC. The *Internet Relay Chat* [3] is a internet protocol for real-time forum systems. It was chosen by W3C mostly because of the fact that it is an open protocol, and is thus implemented by many pieces of software on nearly all existing operating systems. W3C runs its own IRC server, and people connecting to it can create discussion forums as they require. In particular, Working Groups often have their own discussion channels, usually active during telephone or face-to-face meetings, but which can remain permanently open for casual off-meeting chats. IRC is a text only protocol, and a simple client might display part of a conversation as:

```
<John> what's the agenda of today's meeting?
<Mary> http://www.w3.org/2003/05/12-foo-wg-meeting.html
<John> thanks Mary.
```

By itself, IRC already helps teleconferences in several ways: participants can exchange information such as URLs which would otherwise be difficult and error-prone to spell out on the phone, as in the example above. During discussions, parts of proposed text for a specification can also be copied and refined, without having to be read multiple times on the phone. Finally, the scribe can take minutes directly on the channel, which provides a way for other people to follow the discussion as well as giving them an opportunity to correct or complete the notes that were taken.

```
<Al-scribe> John: I see two solutions to this problem
<Al-scribe> John: one is to remove section 1.
<John> I actually said 'section 2', Al.
<Al-scribe> Sorry, thanks for the correction, John.
```

The Web. The Web is W3C's means of archiving documents: draft specifications, meeting minutes, miscellaneous notes and memos, etc.

Scribes are responsible for making meeting minutes available on the W3C's site. There are no particular rules that scribes have to follow, either in the way minutes are synthesized (from litteral transcript to short synthesis of the decisions made) or how they are published on the web (possibilities include: sending the IRC text log directly to the mailing list's web archive, or publishing a properly formatted HTML page, with colour codes for speakers, separations of comments made on IRC or on the phone, etc.) This lack of coherence in style was never deemed critical, since a consequence of publishing minutes on the web is that they can be corrected or superceded in place if the group decides to.

The web site can also be used to display and send commands to the bridge, as described below.

3.2   Interfaces

Interfaces between the bridge, IRC and the web have been developed in order to make the complete system more efficient than if the components were used separately.

IRC/Bridge: Zakim-bot. *Zakim-bot* is a software component that was developed to allow users to send commands to the bridge using IRC. The interface is a *bot*, a software-controlled IRC pseudo-user that responds to specific commands and can write in channels when some events occur. For example:

```
<scribe> John: one solution is to remove section 1.
<Zakim>  +Mike
<John>   Zakim, who's on the call?
<Zakim>  On the phone I see John, Mike, Mary (muted),
         Alexei
<Alexei> Zakim, mute me
<Zakim>  Alexei should now be muted
```

Zakim-bot warns when a participant connects to the teleconference (second line above) or when one hangs up – callers are recognised through caller-ID lookup. The bot also warns when a teleconference starts. Other features are accessible through commands, as shown on the third line above: people present on the bridge, as well as people whose line is muted.

Teleconference control commands include displaying the list of all the teleconferences scheduled at this time, or associating a meeting to the IRC channel Zakim-bot is in (the bot can be in multiple channels for simultaneous teleconferences):

```
<John>   Zakim, list teleconferences
<Zakim>  I see VB_VBWG(ssml)12:00PM, XML_QueryWG()12:00PM
         active.
<John>   Zakim, this is VBWG
<Zakim>  ok, John
<John>   Zakim, what's the passcode?
<Zakim>  the conference code is 8294, John
<Zakim>  +John
```

As shown above, Zakim-bot also accepts commands to retrieve the pass-code is for a given meeting, and can also be told to disconnect a participant, or to ask who is currently speaking:

```
<John>   Zakim, who's speaking?
<Zakim>  John, listening for 10 seconds I heard sound from
         the following: Mary (10%), Robert (45%)
```

Another functionality that Zakim-bot provides is floor control. Although this feature is not directly connected to bridge functionality, it has proven very useful for palliating the lack of visual information and to prevent speaker collisions and interruptions. The bot maintains a queue of speakers, which people on IRC can add themselves to, or leave:

```
<John>      queue+ to ask if we should remove section 1
<Zakim>     I see Mary, John on the speaker queue
<Bob-chair> ack John
<Zakim>     John, you wanted to ask if we should remove
            section 1
<Zakim>     I see Mary on the speaker queue
<Al-scribe> John: Yes, I really think we should remove
            the section
...
<Bob-chair> queue?
<Zakim>     I see Mary on the speaker queue
```

With the meeting chair monitoring the queue by asking Zakim-bot, people who wish to actively participate to the meeting can do so without having to interrupt the current speaker.

Yet another functionality is agenda management. Similarly to the speaker queue, Zakim maintains a list of agenda topics which the chair can go through, possibly adding or removing items:

```
<John> agenda+ recommending changing section 3
* Zakim notes agendum 5 added
<John> agenda?
* Zakim sees 5 items remaining on the agenda:
* Zakim 4. solving issue #42
* Zakim 5. recommending changing section 3 [from John]
...
<Bob-chair> Zakim, take up agendum 5
<Zakim> agendum 5. "recommending changing section 3"
        taken [from John]
```

Again this functionality makes it easier to track what is happening on the teleconference and helps produce accurate meeting minutes.

Finally, Zakim-bot accepts commends from privileged users to set up ad-hoc teleconferences which are not in the normal schedule. If enough resources are available on the bridge at the requested time and for the requested number of participants, the bot will schedule the requested teleconference.

IRC/Web: RRSAgent. *RRSAgent* is another IRC bot that automatically publishes the log of the current channel on the web, updating the page regularly. It chooses the URL automatically according to a given scheme, and also lets the participants set the access controls of the page (some W3C meeting records are member-restricted or staff-restricted). For instance:

```
<John> RRSAgent, record
* RRSAgent is logging to
           http://www.w3.org/2004/03/18-vbwg-irc
...
<John> RRSAgent, please make log member-visible
<RRSAgent> I have made the request, John
```

Bridge/Web Interface. IRC is a linear medium and the only way for a participant to know information such as who is on the call, is to ask Zakim-bot explicitly. If many people on the call request the information at different times, this can add a lot to the IRC channel, which can be detrimental to the readability of the meeting record. Therefore a dynamic web page is more adapted to this task, as it can be accessed individually[2]. Such a page exists on the W3C's site and displays the names of participants to all the running teleconferences in real time (Fig. 1).

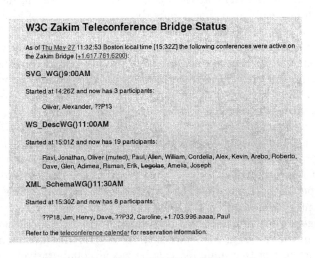

Fig. 1. Screenshot of Zakim's Web monitor

Another web form also provides a way to have the bridge dial out to a number among a list. One could imagine the speaking queue and agenda be displayed similarly on the web, but this has not been implemented so far.

Phone/Bridge Interface. In situations where the user cannot connect to IRC or to the web (e.g. if the user is attending the teleconference with their mobile phone), the Zakim interface can also recognise DTMF sequences as commands: 61# is used for muting, 60# for unmuting, one can adds themself to the speaker

---

[2] Note that commands can also be sent to Zakim-bot in a private IRC chat, avoiding interference with the group's channel.

queue by dialing 41#, or be removed with 40#. The result of these commands are reflected on IRC:

```
...
* Zakim hears Susan's hand up...
```

4   Results

4.1   How Meeting Efficiency has Increased

As the functionality presented above shows, many casual teleconference operations that would have had to be managed by hand are now handled by the bridge and its interfaces. In fact, meeting administration is now almost entirely detached from the contents of the meeting. All the participants (not only the operator, as was originally available) can now enquire and operate bridge controls without interfering with the teleconference. This has dramatically reduced the time some parts of the meetings previously took, such as the roll call formerly carried through by the chair at the beginning of each meeting: now the list is provided automatically, and thus avoids the lengthy process of asking who is on the call. Another formerly inconvenience that Zakim has remedied is line noise: often some connections are burdensome, either because the participant is in a noisy environment, or because the line itself produces static or echoes. The 'offending' participant or line are sometimes hard to determine, as people are not always aware of the effect problems on their side cause. Zakim makes it easier to detect noisy lines through the "who is speaking?" command and allows other users to mute them.

The queue management mechanism has also improved efficiency, not only because it provides equal opportunity for participants to express themselves on the teleconference, but also because time is no longer lost by interruptions on the call by people notifying that they would like to say something.

RRSAgent provides automatic publishing of the IRC log of the meeting, while the agenda feature of Zakim-bot adds information to the log about the progression of the meeting. As is outlined above, IRC discussions has two main benefits. The first is that minutes can be taken collaboratively, people other than the scribe can complete the record, or take over when the scribe themself is speaking. This usually greatly improves the quality of meeting records, and this use of IRC has thus been successfully generalised to face-to-face meetings. The other benefit is the accessibility IRC provides: because notes are taken in near real-time, people who have trouble listening to the teleconference, often because they are not native English speakers, can follow the meeting much more easily.

4.2   Problems and Improvements

Although Zakim has made working group meetings easier, some problems remain. This section summarises them, as well as lists planned improvements.

Shortcomings and Limitations. The first category of limitations, making it difficult to make the meetings as efficient and comfortable as participants would hope, comes from the phone system itself, as well as the teleconference bridge hardware and interface. Line noise originates independently of the teleconference bridge, and while one could envisage noise recognition and cancelling algorithms applied within the bridge, it is a difficult system to implement and necessitates dedicated hardware to process the signal in real-time.

Similarly, DTMF tones can be heard on the bridge, and since some telephones send them at a somewhat high volume, they can end up being a nuisance if too many people use them. This is why the set of DTMF commands has been deliberately kept small. However DTMF tone cancelling could also be achieved with techniques similar as above. The bridge vendor has announced they will work on an upgrade to the bridge's firmware that would mute all DTMF from the teleconferences. This would then allow the implementation of more DTMF commands without the current drawback.

Another issue originating either from the phone system or privacy concerns is with the ANI: some calls, often going through relays in different countries do not provide phone number information. Or, it can happen that the the participant is not calling from a registered number. Another problematic situation is when callers are behind a corporate switchboard (PBX). It then becomes difficult to know who is on the call, and also to map the list of people on the bridge to the list of people on IRC. In those cases, it has to be done manually:

```
<Zakim> +??P14
<John> Zakim, P14 is me
<Zakim> +John, got it
```

Zakim also has a DTMF sequence permitting callers to provide a personal identifier: callers can dial a personal code which the bridge can detect to associate that caller's Zakim identifier to the phone line they are dialing from.

A limitation, this time coming from IRC as well as the web, is the lack of real-time monitoring of the lines, in order to detect who is speaking or which line is making noise. While the bridge's original interface shows the information in real time, Zakim-bot only displays it after listening to the line a few seconds. It is imaginable that Zakim-bot would just dump the information on IRC as fast as it samples the line noise, but it would quickly drown the IRC channel with hundreds of lines of text. This necessary sampling over a few seconds has the consequence that it is hard to identify a speaker if more than one person has been speaking, or to identify a noisy line if a buzz is intermittent.

Yet another category of problem that occurs with this setup originates from the participants: discipline, for one, becomes more critical than usual, as people are expected to respect the speaker order. The chair, in particular, has the additional duty of keeping the speaker queue managed by Zakim-bot synchronous with the way the actual meeting is happening. People who for some reason cannot use IRC (coreporate firewalls being the most common cause) might also feel frustrated as some aspects of how the meeting is run, visible on IRC, could escape them.

Moreover there is often a tendency to see the meeting discussions split: conversations arising from a side comment that someone typed on IRC can diverge from the main telephone conversation, leading to confusion about what to record of the meeting, and in what order. Here also, this behaviour can be a concern if not all participants use IRC.

Reciprocally it has happened that people attended a meeting only through IRC. This has proven to be quite inconvenient as, even though they could follow the meeting, the time delay between phone conversation and their record on IRC made it very difficult for them to react to a statement, as the meeting may have moved on quickly.

Improvements. Other technical shortcomings of Zakim are presumably easier to address and a few of them are under study either by the maintainers of the system or by individual working groups.

The linear nature of IRC makes it difficult to perform some tasks that are idiosyncratic to the activity of a working group. As mentioned above, portions of specifications being discussed can be copied on the channel so that the participants can review and correct them. However those sections must remain short, and IRC does not provide a view of the effect of the changes in the whole specification – in particular people are not necessarily up to date with the location of the text in the document. One way to palliate this deficiency is to have the document's editor amend the text as decided and, as often as possible, publish it on the web during the meeting. While W3C provides this facility and makes it simple, it suffers from delays inherent to the W3C web site, mostly caused by mirroring the site. Using a real-time CSCW system would possibly overcome this limitation as well as allow simultaneous editing of the document. An example of such a system is SubEthaEdit [4], a distributed document editing tool, which would seem quite valuable to the type of work done at W3C. Nevertheless it remains to be tested if such systems are able to scale to up to 50 participants.

A similar well-known problem is that of the distributed white-board, which many research project and commercial products already address. Unfortunately the lack of a common and open protocol, resulting in too few cross-platform implementations has prevented its use so far. The scalability concern mentioned above applies here as well.

Video conferencing has also been investigated, without a definite outcome yet: technical difficulties (choice of protocol, bandwidth required) compared to the apparent lack of obvious benefits has made it a secondary improvement. However, ongoing testing is being performed and may lead to production use for some meetings in the future.

Recording the audio channel of the meetings is also not considered critical, given that the burden of storing and accessing the recordings as well as annotating the sound segments and correlating them with the written record does not appear very advantageous over the current architecture. However, ongoing research such as that carried out by EU project AMI [5] could provide interesting solutions.

Voice recognition for bridge commands seems a facility that, even if it appears feasible, would probably not provide many advantages over the existing system. While accessibility would be increased for participants not on IRC or who cannot use DTMF, it might add to the confusion as bridge commands are intermixed with meeting discussions. Voice recognition for automatically recording the meeting minutes is a much farther goal, especially because of the unreliable voice quality of some callers, as well as the necessity to synthesize minutes, as opposed to the limited usefulness of a literal transcript.

5 Conclusion

This paper introduced the Zakim teleconference bridge used at the World Wide Web Consortium. While academic research describes much more advanced multimodal meeting systems, the requirement that the system be robust as well as accessible to the greatest possible number of participants, has made the feature set seemingly limited, compared to today's advanced experiments. However it has radically changed the way W3C holds meetings, improving time efficiency as well as accessibility for most participants, and provides valuable insight into large-scale augmented distributed meetings.

Acknowledgements

Work on this article was supported by EU FP6 projects MWeb and AMI. Development of Zakim-bot was supported in part by funding from US Defense Advanced Research Projects Agency (DARPA) and Air Force Research Laboratory, Air Force Materiel Command, USAF, under agreement number F30602-00-2-0593, "Semantic Web Development". The views are those of the authors, and do not represent the views of the funding agencies.

The author would like to acknowledge Ralph Swick, of W3C, for developing the software presented in this paper. RRSAgent is based on an irc logger tool written by Dave Beckett of Institute for Learning, Research and Technology, UK.

References

1. World Wide Web Consortium (http://www.w3.org/Consortium/)
2. Compunetix Contex teleconference system (http://www.compunetix.com/ix/csd/prod/index-sp.html)
3. J. Oikarinen, D. Reed. *Internet Relay Chat Protocol.* IETF RFC1459. 1993 (ftp://ftp.rfc-editor.org/in-notes/rfc1459.txt)
4. SubEthaEdit - collaborative editor (http://www.codingmonkeys.de/subethaedit/)
5. Augmented Multi-party Interaction - EU IST FP6 Project - (http://www.amiproject.org/)

Towards Computer Understanding of Human Interactions

Iain McCowan, Daniel Gatica-Perez, Samy Bengio,
Darren Moore, and Hervé Bourlard

IDIAP Research Institute,
P.O. Box 592, CH-1920, Martigny,
Switzerland
{mccowan, gatica, bengio, moore, bourlard}@idiap.ch
http://www.idiap.ch/

Abstract. People meet in order to interact - disseminating information, making decisions, and creating new ideas. Automatic analysis of meetings is therefore important from two points of view: extracting the information they contain, and understanding human interaction processes. Based on this view, this article presents an approach in which relevant information content of a meeting is identified from a variety of audio and visual sensor inputs and statistical models of interacting people. We present a framework for computer observation and understanding of interacting people, and discuss particular tasks within this framework, issues in the meeting context, and particular algorithms that we have adopted. We also comment on current developments and the future challenges in automatic meeting analysis.[1]

1   Introduction

The domain of human-computer interaction aims to help humans interact more naturally with computers. A related emerging domain of research instead views the computer as a tool to assist or understand human interactions : putting computers in the human interaction loop [1]. Humans naturally interact with other humans, communicating and generating valuable information. The most natural interface for entering this information into a computing system would therefore be for the computer to extract it directly from observing the human interactions.

The automatic analysis of human interaction is a rich research area. There is growing interest in the automatic understanding of group behaviour, where the interactions are defined by individuals playing and exchanging both similar and complementary roles (e.g. a handshake, a dancing couple, or a children's game)

---

[1] This article is an updated version of one that originally appeared in *Proceedings of the European Symposium on Ambient Intelligence*, Springer Lecture Notes in Computer Science, November 2003.

S. Bengio and H. Bourlard (Eds.): MLMI 2004, LNCS 3361, pp. 56–75, 2005.
© Springer-Verlag Berlin Heidelberg 2005

[2, 3, 4, 5, 6]. Most of the previous work has relied on visual information and statistical models, and studied three specific scenarios: surveillance in outdoor scenes [5, 6], workplaces [3, 4], and indoor group entertainment [2]. Beyond the use of visual information, dialogue modelling [7, 8] analyses the structure of interactions in conversations.

While it has only recently become an application domain for computing research, observation of human interactions is not a new field of study - it has been actively researched for over fifty years by a branch of social psychologists [9, 10, 11]. For example, research has analysed turn-taking patterns in group discussions [12, 13, 14], giving insight into issues such as interpersonal trust, cognitive load in interactions, and patterns of dominance and influence [11]. Research has also shown that interactions are fundamentally multimodal, with participants coordinating speaking turns using a variety of cues, such as gaze, speech back-channels, changes in posture, etc. [12, 13, 15]. In general, visual information can help disambiguate audio information [16], and when the modalities are discrepant, participants appear to be more influenced by visual than by audio cues [11, 17].

Motivated therefore by a desire to move towards more natural human-machine interfaces, and building upon findings of social psychologists regarding the mechanisms and significance of human interactions, this article presents an observational framework for computer understanding of human interactions, focussing on small group meetings as a particular instance.

Meetings contain many complex interactions between people, and so automatic meeting analysis presents a challenging case study. Speech is the predominant modality for communication in meetings, and speech-based processing techniques, including speech recognition, speaker identification, topic detection, and dialogue modelling, are being actively researched in the meeting context [18, 8, 19, 20]. Visual processing, such as tracking people and their focus of attention, has also been examined in [1, 21]. Beyond this work, a place for analysis of text, gestures, and facial expressions, as well as many other audio, visual and multimodal processing tasks can be identified within the meeting scenario. While important advances have been made, to date most approaches to automatic meeting analysis have been limited to the application of known technologies to extract information from individual participants (e.g. speech, gaze, identity, etc). Intuitively, the true information of meetings is created from interactions between participants, and true understanding of meetings can only emerge from considering their group nature.

The remainder of this article is organised as follows. Section 2 describes a multi-sensor meeting room that we have installed to enable our research. A framework for computer understanding of human interactions is outlined in Section 3, along with some specific issues and algorithms related to the meeting context. Finally, some perspective on future directions in automatic meeting analysis is given in Section 4, followed by concluding remarks in Section 5.

2   A Multi-sensor Meeting Room

As mentioned above, interactions between people in meetings are generally multi-modal in nature. While the *audio* modality is the most obvious source of information in discussions, studies have shown that significant information is conveyed in the *visual* modality, through expressions, gaze, gestures and posture [12, 13, 15]. In meetings, the *textual* modality is also important, with presentation slides, whiteboard activity, and shared paper documents providing detailed information.

To facilitate research into automatic meeting analysis, a meeting room at IDIAP has been equipped with multi-media acquisition facilities for recording meetings with up to 4 participants. Audio information is captured from both headset and lapel microphones on each participant, a tabletop microphone array, and a binaural manikin. Video information is collected using seven cameras. Four cameras are positioned in the centre of the meeting table, providing close-up facial views of each participant with sufficient resolution for tasks such as face identification and audio-visual speech recognition. The three remaining cameras acquire wider angle frontal views of the participants and a view of the entire meeting room scene. Unique presentation slides are captured at native VGA resolutions from the monitoring output of a data projector, whiteboard activity is recorded using transmitting pens and a receiver attached to a standard whiteboard, and participants' notes are acquired using a digital pen capture system. The acquisition of all modalities is completely synchronised and all data streams are accurately time-stamped.

Meeting recording efforts at IDIAP have occurred at various stages in the evolution of the meeting room acquisition capabilities. An initial audio-visual corpus of approximately sixty, five-minute, four-person scripted meetings was acquired using three wide-angle cameras, per-participant lapel microphones and a microphone array. Subsequent recordings focussed on the recording of less

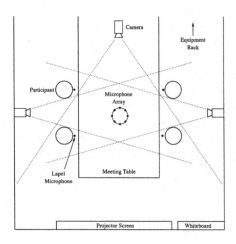

Fig. 1. Meeting recording configuration

constrained and more naturally occurring meeting scenarios and used the same A/V sensor configuration together with slide and whiteboard capture capabilities. The meeting room configuration used for these recordings is illustrated in Figure 1. The resulting meeting recordings have been annotated to differing degrees, and all raw and meta- data is available for online public distribution through a MultiModal Media file server at `mmm.idiap.ch`. A new round of meeting recordings has been recently launched using the full multimodal acquisition capabilities. This round of recordings (in conjunction with recordings from two partner sites) aims to collect 100 hours of annotated meeting data to satisfy the multimodal meeting data needs of the AMI research consortium[2].

3   Multimodal Processing

We propose a framework for computer understanding of human interactions that involves the following basic steps in a processing loop :

```
1. locate and track participants
2. for each located participant
   (a) enhance their audio and visual streams
   (b) identify them
   (c) recognise their individual actions
3. recognise group actions
```

The first step is necessary to determine the number and location of participants. For each person present, we then extract a dedicated enhanced audio and visual stream by focussing on their tracked location. Audio-visual (speech and face) speaker identification techniques can then be applied to determine who the participant is. Individual actions, such as speech activity, gestures or speech words may also be measured or recognised from the audio and visual streams. The ultimate goal of this analysis is then to be able to recognise actions belonging to the group as a whole, by modelling the interactions of the individuals.

Specific issues and algorithms for implementing a number of these steps for the case of meeting analysis are presented in the following sub-sections. A primary focus of our research is the multimodal nature of human interactions in meetings, and this is reflected in the choice of tasks we have included. Naturally, there are many other processing tasks involved in understanding meetings, such as speech recognition and dialogue modelling, that are not covered here.

3.1   Audio-Visual Speaker Tracking

The Problem in the Global View. Locating and tracking speakers represents an important first step towards automatic understanding of human interactions. As mentioned previously, speaker turn patterns convey a rich amount of

---

[2] http://www.amiproject.org/

information about the behaviour of a group and its individual members [10, 13]. Furthermore, experimental evidence has highlighted the role that non-verbal behaviour (gaze, facial expressions, and body postures) plays in interactions [13]. Recognising such rich multimodal behaviour first requires reliable localisation and tracking of people.

Challenges in the Meeting Context. The separate use of audio and video as cues for tracking are classic problems in signal processing and computer vision. However, sound and visual information are jointly generated when people speak, and provide complementary advantages. While initialisation and recovery from failures can be addressed with audio, precise object localisation is better suited to visual processing.

Long-term, reliable tracking of multiple people in meetings is challenging. Meeting rooms pose a number of issues for audio processing, such as reverberation and multiple concurrent speakers, as well as for visual processing, including clutter and variations of illumination. However, the main challenge arises from the behaviour of multiple participants resulting in changes of appearance and pose for each person, and considerable (self-)occlusion. At the same time, meetings in a multi-sensor room present some advantages that ease the location and tracking tasks. Actions usually unfold in specific areas (meeting table, whiteboard, and projector screen), which constrains the group dynamics in the physical space. In addition, the availability of multiple cameras with overlapping fields of view can be exploited to build more reliable person models, and deal with the occlusion problems.

Our Approach. We are developing principled methods for speaker tracking, fusing information coming from multiple microphones and uncalibrated cameras [22], based on *Sequential Monte Carlo* (SMC) methods, also known as *particle filters* (PFs) [23]. For a state-space model, a PF recursively approximates the conditional distribution of states given observations using a dynamical model and random sampling by (i) generating candidate configurations from the dynamics (*prediction*), and (ii) measuring their likelihood (*updating*), in a process that amounts to random search in a configuration space.

The state-space formulation is general. As an option, it can be defined over only one person, implying that the tracker should lock onto the current speaker at each instant. More generally, the state-space could be defined over all the people present in the scene. In this joint representation, both the location and the speaking status of each participant should be tracked all the time.

Our work is guided by inherent features of AV data, taking advantage of the fact that data fusion can be introduced in both stages of the PF algorithm. First, audio is a strong cue to model discontinuities that clearly violate usual assumptions in dynamics (including speaker turns across cameras), and (re)initialisation. Its use for prediction thus brings benefits to modelling real situations. Second, audio can be inaccurate at times, but provides a good initial localisation guess that can be enhanced by visual information. Third, although audio might be imprecise, and visual calibration can be erroneous due to distortion in wide-angle cameras, the joint occurrence of AV information in the constrained physical space in meetings tends to be more consistent, and can be learned from data.

Our methodology exploits the complementary features of the AV modalities. In the first place, we use a 2-D approach in which human heads are visually represented by their silhouette in the image plane, and modelled as elements of a *shape-space*, allowing for the description of a head template and a set of valid geometric transformations (motion). In the second place, we employ *mixed-state* space representations, where in addition to the continuous subspace that represents head motion, we also include discrete components. In a multi-camera setup, a discrete variable can indicate the specific camera plane in which a speaker is present, thus helping define a generative model for camera switching. For a multi-object state space, discrete variables are additionally used to indicate the speaking/non-speaking status of each participant. In the third place, we asymmetrically handle audio and video in the PF formulation. Audio localisation information in 3-D space is first estimated by an algorithm that reliably detects speaker changes with low latency, while maintaining good estimation accuracy. Audio and skin-color blob information are then used for prediction, and introduced in the PF via *importance sampling*, a technique which guides the search process of the PF towards regions of the state space likely to contain the true configurations. Additionally, audio, color, and shape information are jointly used to compute the likelihood of candidate configurations. Finally, we use an AV calibration procedure to relate audio estimates in 3-D and visual information in 2-D. The procedure uses easily generated training data, and does not require precise geometric calibration of cameras and microphones [22].

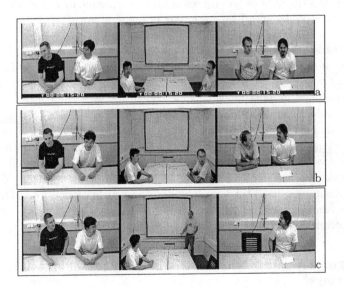

Fig. 2. Single-object speaker tracker in the meeting room. The tracker locks onto one speaker

Table 1. Single-object AV speaker tracking results. For full details of techniques and experimental conditions, see [22]

error type	modality	cam$_1$	cam$_2$	cam$_3$	global
$\epsilon_k (\times 10^{-2})$	AV	1.91	0.31	25.00	11.27
$\epsilon_{(T^x, T^y)}$	AV	1.88	1.69	0.40	1.00
	A	11.39	11.86	10.60	11.20

When applied to the single-object state-space, the particle filtering framework results in a method that can initialise and track a moving speaker, and switch between multiple people across cameras with low delay, while tolerating visual clutter. An example for the setup of Figure 1 is shown in Figure 2, for a two-minute sequence, using 500 particles. Given a ground-truth of speaker segments, which consists of the camera index and the approximate speaker's head centroid in the corresponding image plane for each speaker segment, Table 1 shows that the percentage of error on the estimated camera indices ϵ_k is quite small for the close-view cameras, but larger for the wide-view case. Additionally, the median localisation error in the image plane $\epsilon_{(T^x, T^y)}$ (in pixels) remains within a few pixels, and is smaller than the error obtained using only the audio modality, thus justifying a multimodal approach. Other AV tracking examples for single- and multi-camera set-ups can be found at www.idiap.ch/~gatica.

An example of the joint multi-object tracking system is shown in Fig. 3 for the case of non-overlapped views, using 1000 particles. The four participants are simultaneously tracked, and their speaking status is inferred at each time. In practice, the multi-object tracker significantly requires more computational resources given the joint object representation. Refinements of the approach, and the evaluation of the algorithms are part of current work.

Open Problems. Although the current approaches are useful in their current form, there is much room for improvement. In the following we identify three specific lines of research. We will extend the multi-object tracker to a multi-camera scenario with overlapping fields of view, which involves the consistent labelling of tracked objects across cameras. In the second place, a joint state-space representation for multi-object tracking significantly increases the dimensionality of the state space, which calls for efficient inference mechanisms in the resulting statistical model. We have made some progress in this direction [24]. The third line of research is the joint formulation of tracking and recognition. We are conducting research on head trackers that simultaneously estimate head orientation (a simple form of recognition), which is in turn a strong cue for detection of focus of attention, and useful for higher-level recognisers [25].

3.2   Speech Segmentation and Enhancement Using Microphone Arrays

The Problem in the Global View. Having located and tracked each person, it is next necessary to acquire an enhanced dedicated audio channel of their

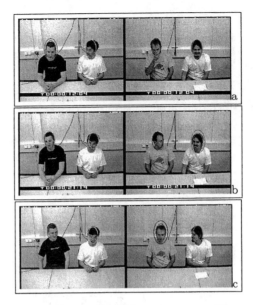

Fig. 3. Multi-object speaker tracker in the meeting room. The speaking status is inferred for each participant, a speaker is shown with a double ellipse

speech. Speech is the predominant communication modality, and thus a rich source of information, in many human interactions.

Most state-of-the-art speech and speaker recognition systems rely on close-talking head-set microphones for speech acquisition, as they naturally provide a higher signal-to-noise ratio (SNR) than single distant microphones. This mode of acquisition may be acceptable for applications such as dictation, however as technology heads towards more pervasive applications, less constraining solutions are required. *Microphone arrays* present a promising alternative to close-talking microphones, as they allow for signal-independent enhancement, localisation and tracking of speakers, and non-intrusive hands-free operation. For these reasons, microphone arrays are being increasingly used for speech acquisition in such applications [26, 27].

Challenges in the Meeting Context. Meetings present a number of interesting challenges for microphone array research. A primary issue is the design of the *array geometry* : how many microphones should be used, and where should they be placed in the room? Naturally a geometry giving high spatial resolution uniformly across a room is desirable for best performance and lowest constraint on the users, however this requires prohibitively large numbers of microphones, and complex installation [28]. For these reasons, more practical solutions with smaller numbers of microphones need to be researched to address computational and economical considerations.

A second challenge in the meeting context is the natural occurrence of overlapping speech. In [29] it was identified that around 10-15% of words, or 50% of speech segments, in a meeting contain a degree of overlapping speech. These overlapped segments are problematic for speaker segmentation, and speech and speaker recognition. For instance, an absolute increase in word error rate of between 15-30% has been observed on overlap speech segments using close-talking microphones [29, 8].

Our Approach. While it is clear that a large microphone array with many elements would give the best spatial selectivity for localisation and enhancement, for microphone arrays to be employed in practical applications, hardware cost (microphones, processing and memory requirements) must be reduced. For this reason, we focus on the use of small microphone arrays, which can be a viable solution when assumptions can be made about the absolute and relative locations of participants.

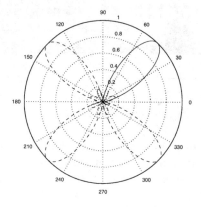

Fig. 4. Microphone array directivity patterns at 1000 Hz (speaker 1 direction in bold)

As shown in Figure 1, the particular array geometry we have chosen is an 8-element circular array (of radius 10cm) placed at the centre of the meeting table. This geometry and placement was selected based on the assumption that a meeting generally consists of small groups of people seated and talking face to face in well-defined regions. Each array is designed to cater for a small group of up to 4 people. In larger meetings, multiple (potentially interacting) small array modules are positioned along the table, where each module is responsible for the people in its local region. The circular geometry was selected as it gives uniform spatial selectivity between people sitting around it, leading to good general performance in separating overlapping speech. This is important for meetings where background noise is generally low, and so overlapping speech is the primary noise source. To illustrate, Figure 4 shows the theoretical *directivity pattern* (array gain as a function of direction) for the array at 1000 Hz for 4 speakers separated by 90 degrees. Having the array on the table also means it is placed in close proximity to participants, leading to naturally high signal levels compared to background noise caused by distant sources.

Given accurate tracking of the speaker locations in the room, the next task is to determine segments of continuous speech from a given speaker location.

Speaker segmentation in meetings is problematic for traditional techniques based on simple energy or spectral features, as a significant amount of cross-talk from other speakers exists even on close-talking microphones [30, 31]. In [32, 33] we presented a *location-based segmentation* technique that is capable of providing a smooth speech/silence segmentation for a specified location in a room. As it is based on speech location features from the microphone array, rather than standard spectral features, this location-based segmentation has the important benefit of being able to accurately handle multiple concurrent speakers (identifying which locations are active at any given time). In [34], this segmentation algorithm was integrated with automatic speaker tracking and tested on a set of 17 short (5 minute) meetings recorded in the room described in Section 2. Results of these experiments are summarised in Table 2. Results are in terms of the common precision (PRC), recall (RCL) and F measures ($F = \frac{2 \times PRC \times RCL}{PRC + RCL}$). The location-based technique is compared to a baseline energy-based approach using lapel microphones. The results show that, while the location-based approach yields comparable overall segmentation accuracy, it achieves a significant improvement during periods of overlapping speech (recall increasing from 66% to 85%, precision from 47% to 55%). Full experimental details and discussion can be found in [34].

Table 2. Segmentation results on 17 meetings. The location-based approach uses distant microphones only. Values are percentages, results on overlaps only are indicated in brackets. Table reproduced from [34]

Metric	Location-based	Lapel baseline
PRC	79.7 (55.4)	84.3 (46.6)
RCL	94.6 (84.8)	93.3 (66.4)
F	86.5 (67.0)	88.6 (54.7)

Once the location of the speakers is known along with their speech activity segmentation, we can then apply microphone array *beamforming* techniques to enhance their speech, attenuating background noise and conflicting speech sources. Beamforming consists of filtering and combining the individual microphone signals in such a way as to enhance signals coming from a particular location. For beamforming filters, we adopt standard *superdirective* filters, which are calculated to maximise the array gain for the desired direction [35]. In addition, we apply a *Wiener post-filter* to the beamformer output to further reduce the broadband noise energy. The post-filter is estimated from the auto- and cross-spectral densities of the microphone array inputs, and is formulated assuming a diffuse background noise field [36]. This post-filter leads to significant improvements in terms of SNR and speech recognition performance in office background noise [36].

To assess the effectiveness of the beamformer in improving eventual speech recognition performance, a multi-microphone corpus was recorded for experimentation and public distribution. The database was collected by outputting

Table 3. Word error rate results for speech recorded on a close-talking lapel microphone, a microphone placed in the centre of the meeting table, and the output of a microphone array beamformer. For full details of techniques and experimental conditions, see [37]

Simultaneous Speakers	Lapel	Centre	Array
1	7.01	10.06	7.00
2	24.43	57.56	19.31
3	35.25	73.55	26.64

utterances from the Numbers corpus (telephone quality speech, 30-word vocabulary) on one or more loudspeakers, and recording the resulting sound field using a microphone array and various lapel and table-top microphones. The goal of this work was to compare relative speech recognition performance using different microphone configurations in various noise situations, and thus a small vocabulary corpus was considered appropriate. Initial results on this corpus (MONC: Multi-channel Overlapping Numbers Corpus, available from the Center for Spoken Language Understanding at OGI) were presented in [37], and are reproduced in Table 3. These results show that the array processing significantly improves over a single distant microphone (centre), and also over a close-talking lapel microphone in situations where there is significant overlapping speech between speakers.

Open Problems. While microphone array speech processing techniques are already relatively mature, a number of open issues remain in this context. One of these is the need to focus on algorithms that handle multiple concurrent, moving, speakers. While work cited in this paper indicates progress in this direction, there remains a need for testing of multi-speaker localisation, tracking and beamforming in real applications, such as large vocabulary speech recognition in meetings. Another interesting research direction is the use of multiple interacting small microphone array modules to cover arbitrary areas, instead of using a single larger array.

3.3   Audio-Visual Person Identification

The Problem in the Global View. Identifying participants is important for understanding human interactions. When prior knowledge about the participants is available (such as their preferred way of communicating, topics of interests, levels of language, relative hierarchical levels in a given context, etc), knowing the participants' identities would imply knowing this prior information, which could in turn be used to better tune the algorithms used to analyse the interaction. Fortunately, *biometric authentication* [38], which is the general problem of authenticating or identifying a person using his or her behavioural and physiological characteristics such as the face or the voice, is a growing research domain which has already shown useful results, especially when using more than one of these characteristics, as we propose to do here.

Challenges in the Meeting Context. In order to perform AV identification during a meeting, we need to extract reliably the basic modalities. For the face, we require a face localisation algorithm that is robust to the kind of images available from a video stream (relatively low-quality and low-resolution), robust to the participants' varying head poses, and able to cope with more than one face per image. This could be done using our AV tracking system described in Section 3.1. For the voice, taking into account that several microphones are available in the meeting room, the first challenge is to separate all audio sources and attribute each speech segment to its corresponding participant. Again, this could be done using our speaker segmentation and enhancement techniques, described in Section 3.2. Afterward, classical face and speaker verification algorithms could be applied, followed by a fusion step, which provides robustness to the failure of one or the other modality. Finally, an identification procedure could be applied.

Our Approach. Our identification system is based on an AV biometric verification system. Assuming that we are able to obtain reliable speech segments and localised faces from the meeting raw data, we can then apply our state-of-the-art verification system, which is based on a *speaker verification* system, a *face verification* system, and a *fusion* module.

Our speaker verification system first starts by extracting useful features from the raw speech data: we extract 16 Mel scale Frequency Cepstral Coefficient (MFCC) features every 10 ms, as well as their first temporal derivative, plus the first derivative of the log energy of the signal. Then, a silence detector based on an unsupervised 2-Gaussian system is used to remove all silence frames. Finally, the verification system itself is based on the modelling of one Gaussian Mixture Model (GMM) for each individual, adapted using *Maximum A Posteriori* (MAP) techniques from a *World Model* trained by *Expectation-Maximisation* on a large set of prior data. The score for a given access is obtained as the logarithm of the ratio between the likelihood of the data given the individual model and the likelihood given the world model. This system obtains state-of-the-art performance on several benchmark verification databases [39].

Our face verification system is comprised of two main parts: an automatic face locator and a local feature probabilistic classifier. To locate faces, a fast cascade of boosted Haar-like features is applied to the integral image to detect potential faces [40], followed by post-processing using a Multi-Layer Perceptron [41] to provide the final localized face. The probabilistic classifier uses DCTmod2 features [42] and models faces using pseudo-2D Hidden Markov Models (HMMs) [43]. In DCTmod2 feature extraction, each given face is analyzed on a block by block basis; from each block a subset of Discrete Cosine Transform (DCT) coefficients is obtained; coefficients which are most affected by illumination direction changes are replaced with their respective horizontal and vertical deltas, computed as differences between coefficients from neighbouring blocks. For the pseudo-2D HMM topology, we use a top-to-bottom main HMM with each state being modeled by a left-to-right HMM. Parameters for each client model are obtained via Maximum *a Posteriori* (MAP) adaptation of a generic face HMM; the generic face HMM is in turn trained using the Expectation Max-

Table 4. Verification performance on the English subset of the BANCA database, protocol P, in terms of HTER (the lower, the better)

Voice	Face	Fusion
4.7%	20.9%	2.8%

imization algorithm, on a large generic dataset. As for the speech system, a score for a given face is found by taking the logarithm of the ratio between the likelihood of the face belonging to the true client and the likelihood of the face belonging to the impostor model.

Our fusion algorithm is based on Multi-layer Perceptrons (experiments with Support Vector Machines give similar performances). The fusion model takes as input the log likelihood scores coming from both the face and the speaker verification systems, and combines them non-linearly in order to obtain a unified and more robust overall score. Optionally, confidence values could also be computed on both the voice and face scores, which then enhance the quality of the fusion model [44].

Finally, in order to identify the correct individual, the whole verification system is run over all previously stored individual models, and the model corresponding to the highest obtained score over a pre-defined threshold (in order to account for unknown individuals) identifies the target individual.

While we currently do not have results in the context of meetings, we did apply them on several benchmark databases and always obtained state-of-the-art performance. For instance, Table 4 shows the performance of our models on the difficult but realistic audio-visual BANCA database [45], using protocol P of the English subset, and measured in terms of *half total error rate* (HTER), which is the average of the rates of false acceptances and false rejections.

We can see from this Table that speaker verification is in general more robust than face verification, and that fusing both of them still increases the overall performance. We note that this face verification system ranked first in a recent international competition on this corpus [46].

Open Problems. Assuming that speaker segmentation and face tracking have given perfect segmentation, for a given meeting, we will have potentially several minutes of speech and face data per individual. In general, a classical verification system only requires a few face images and less than one minute of speech data to attain acceptable performance. However, the environment is unconstrained, the meeting data may be noisy for different reasons - the individual may not always look at the camera and speak loudly and intelligibly. In this case, rather than using all available data to identify a person, a better solution could be to be more strict on the selection of faces and speaker segments in order to keep only the best *candidates* for identification. Hence, we should try to remove highly noisy or overlapping speech segments, badly tracked face images and faces that are not in a good frontal pose and good lighting condition.

3.4 Group Action Recognition

The Problem in the Global View. The ultimate goal of automatic analysis of human interactions is to recognise the group actions. As discussed previously, the true information of meetings is created from interactions between participants playing and exchanging roles. In this view, an important goal of automatic meeting analysis is the segmentation of meetings into high-level agenda items which reflect the action of the group as a whole, rather than just the behaviour of individuals (e.g. discussions and presentations, or even higher level notions, like planning, negotiating, and making decisions).

Challenges in the Meeting Context. Recognition of group actions in meetings entails several important problems for which no satisfactory solutions currently exist. These include (1) devising tractable multi-stream sequence models, where each stream could arise from either a modality (AV) or a participant; (2) modelling asynchronicity between participants' behaviour; (3) extracting features for recognition that are robust to variations in human characteristics and behaviour; (4) designing sequence models that can integrate language features (e.g. keywords or dialog acts) with non-verbal features (e.g. emotion as captured from audio and video); and (5) developing models for recognition of actions that are part of a hierarchy.

One potentially simplifying advantage to recognise group actions in meetings is that participants usually have some influence on each other's behaviour. For example, a dominant speaker grabbing the floor often makes the other participants go silent, and a presentation will draw most participants' attention in the same direction. The recognition of some group actions can be therefore benefit from the occurrence of these multiple similar individual behaviours.

Our Approach. We have addressed meeting group action recognition as the recognition of a continuous, non-overlapping, sequence of lexical entries, analogous to observational approaches in social psychology for analysis of group interaction [10], and to speech or continuous gesture recognition [47, 48]. Continuous recognition generates action-based meeting segmentations that can be directly used for browsing. Furthermore, the definition of multiple lexica would provide alternative semantic views of a meeting. Note that in reality, most group actions are characterised by soft (natural) transitions, and specifying their boundaries beyond a certain level of precision has little meaning.

In particular, we have modelled meeting actions based on a set of multimodal turn-taking events. Speaking turns are mainly characterised by audio information, but significant information is also present in non-verbal cues like gaze and posture changes [13], which can also help disambiguate audio information [16]. The specific actions include monologues (one participant speaks continuously without interruption), discussions (all participants engage in a discussion), presentations (one participant at front of room makes a presentation using the projector screen), white-boards (one participant at front of room talks and uses the white-board), and group note-taking (all participants write notes).

Fig. 5. Simple meeting browser interface, showing recognised meeting actions

In a first approach [49], we used a number of Hidden Markov Model (HMM) variants to recognise the group actions by direct modelling of low-level features. The models investigated included early integration HMMs [47], multi-stream HMMs [50], asynchronous HMMs [51], and coupled HMMs [52]. Features were extracted from both audio and visual modalities, and included speech activity, pitch, energy, speaking rate, and head and hand location and motion features. For experiments, we used the meeting corpus described in Section 2. Meetings followed a loose script to ensure an adequate amount of examples of all actions, and to facilitate annotation for training and testing, but otherwise the individual and group behaviour is natural.

A detailed account of the experiments and results can be found in [49], but we repeat the summarised findings here:

1. The best system achieves an action error rate (equivalent to word error rate in ASR) of 8.9%.
2. There is benefit in a multi-modal approach to modelling group actions in meetings.
3. It is important to model the correlation between the behaviour of different participants.
4. There is no significant asynchrony between audio and visual modalities for these actions (at least within the resolution of the investigated frame rate).
5. There is evidence of asynchrony between participants acting within the group actions.

These findings appeal to the intuition that individuals act in a group through both audio and visual cues which can have a causal effect on the behaviour of other group members.

More recently, a two-layer HMM framework was proposed in [53]. The first layer HMM (individual-level) recognises a small set of individual actions for each participant (speaking, writing, idle) using the same set of low-level audio-visual features described above. The results of these first layer HMMs are concatenated and modelled by a second layer HMM (group-level), which then attempts to recognise the group actions. For an augmented set of group actions (discussion, monologue, monologue + note-taking, note-taking, presentation, presentation + note-taking, white-board and white-board + note-taking), the two-layer system achieved an action error rate of only 15.1%, compared with a 23.7% error rate on the same task using the best single-layer HMM system (equivalent to those proposed in [49]: the higher error rate is due to the increased lexicon size). Full experimental details can be found in [53].

An example of the application of the action recognition results for meeting browsing is shown in Figure 5.

Open Problems. The experience gained from our results confirms the importance of modelling the interactions between individuals, as well as the advantage of a multimodal approach for recognition. We believe there is much scope for work towards the recognition of different sets of high-level meeting actions, including other multimodal turn-taking events, actions based on participants' mood or level of interest, and multimodal actions motivated by traditional dialogue acts. To achieve this goal, ongoing and future work will investigate richer feature sets, and appropriate models for the interactions of participants. Another task will be to incorporate prior information in the recognition system, based on the participant identities and models of their personal behaviour. We also plan to collect a larger meeting corpus, and work on the development of more flexible assessment methodologies.

4   Future Directions

From the framework outlined in the beginning of Section 3, while much room clearly remains for new techniques and improvements on existing ones, we can see that steps 1-2(c) are reasonably well understood by the state-of-the-art. In contrast, we are far from making similar claims regarding step 3, recognition of group actions.

The first major goal in computer understanding of group actions, is to clearly identify lexica of such actions that may be recognised. A simple lexicon based on multimodal turn-taking events was discussed in Section 3.4, however there is a need to progress towards recognition of higher level concepts, such as decisions, planning, and disagreements. In this regard, the social psychology literature represents an important source of information for studies on the tasks and processes that arise from human interactions, as was discussed in [49].

Having identified relevant group actions, a further research task is then to select appropriate features for these actions to be recognised. At this moment, features are intuitively selected by hand, which has obvious limitations. Approaches for feature selection could arise from two areas. The first one is human. We require a deeper understanding of human behaviour. Existing work in psychology could provide cues for feature selection towards, for example, multimodal recognition of emotion [54]. The second one is computational. Developments in machine learning applied to problems in vision and signal processing point to various directions [40].

Finally, to recognise the group actions, there is a need to propose models capable of representing the interactions between individuals in a group (see e.g. [55, 5, 49]). Some particular issues are the need to model multiple data streams, asynchronicity between streams, hierarchies of data and events (e.g. building on [53]), as well as features of different nature (e.g. discrete or continuous).

5   Conclusion

This article has discussed a framework for computer understanding of human interactions. A variety of multimodal sensors are used to observe a group and extract useful information from their interactions. By processing the sensor inputs, participants are located, tracked, and identified, and their individual actions recognised. Finally, the actions of the group as a whole may be recognised by modelling the interactions of the individuals.

While initial work in this direction has already shown promising progress and yielded useful results, it is clear that many research challenges remain if we are to advance towards true computer understanding of human interactions.

Acknowledgements

The authors would like to acknowledge our colleagues at IDIAP involved in the research described in this article, in particular Guillaume Lathoud, Dong Zhang, Norman Poh, Johnny Mariéthoz, Sebastien Marcel, Conrad Sanderson, Olivier Masson, Pierre Wellner, Mark Barnard, Kevin Smith, Sileye Ba, Jean Marc Odobez and Florent Monay.

This work was supported by the Swiss National Science Foundation through the National Centre of Competence in Research (NCCR) on "Interactive Multimodal Information Management (IM2)". The work was also funded by the European project "M4: MultiModal Meeting Manager", through the Swiss Federal Office for Education and Science (OFES).

References

1. Waibel, A., Schultz, T., Bett, M., Malkin, R., Rogina, I., Stiefelhagen, R., Yang, J.: SMaRT:the Smart Meeting Room Task at ISL. In: Proc. IEEE ICASSP 2003. (2003)

2. Bobick, A., Intille, S., Davis, J., Baird, F., Pinhanez, C., Campbell, L., Ivanov, Y., Schutte, A., Wilson, A.: The KidsRoom: A Perceptually-Based Interactive and Immersive Story Environment. PRESENCE: Teleoperators and Virtual Environments **8** (1999)
3. Johnson, N., Galata, A., Hogg, D.: The acquisition and use of interaction behaviour models. In: Proc. IEEE Int. Conference on Computer Vision and Pattern Recognition. (1998)
4. Jebara, T., Pentland, A.: Action reaction learning: Automatic visual analysis and synthesis of interactive behaviour. In: Proc. International Conference on Vision Systems. (1999)
5. Oliver, N., Rosario, B., Pentland, A.: A bayesian computer vision system for modeling human interactions. IEEE Transactions on Pattern Analysis and Machine Intelligence **22** (2000)
6. Hongeng, S., Nevatia, R.: Multi-agent event recognition. In: Proc. IEEE Int. Conference on Computer Vision, Vancouver (2001)
7. Carletta, J., Isard, A., Isard, S., Kowtko, J., Doherty-Sneddon, G., Anderson, A.: The coding of dialogue structure in a corpus. In Andernach, J., van de Burgt, S., van der Hoeven, G., eds.: Proceedings of the Twente Workshop on Language Technology: Corpus-based approaches to dialogue modelling. Universiteit Twente (1995)
8. Morgan, N., Baron, D., Edwards, J., Ellis, D., Gelbart, D., Janin, A., Pfau, T., Shriberg, E., Stolcke, A.: The meeting project at ICSI. In: Proc. of the Human Language Technology Conference, San Diego, CA (2001)
9. Bales, R.F.: Interaction Process Analysis: A method for the study of small groups. Addison-Wesley (1951)
10. McGrath, J.E.: Groups: Interaction and Performance. Prentice-Hall (1984)
11. McGrath, J., Kravitz, D.: Group research. Annual Review of Psychology **33** (1982) 195–230
12. Padilha, E., Carletta, J.C.: A simulation of small group discussion. In: EDILOG. (2002)
13. Parker, K.C.H.: Speaking turns in small group interaction: A context-sensitive event sequence model. Journal of Personality and Social Psychology **54** (1988) 965–971
14. Fay, N., Garrod, S., Carletta, J.: Group discussion as interactive dialogue or serial monologue: The influence of group size. Psychological Science **11** (2000) 487–492
15. Novick, D., Hansen, B., Ward, K.: Coordinating turn-taking with gaze. In: Proceedings of the 1996 International Conference on Spoken Language Processing (ICSLP-96). (1996)
16. Krauss, R., Garlock, C., Bricker, P., McMahon, L.: The role of audible and visible back-channel responses in interpersonal communication. Journal of Personality and Social Psychology **35** (1977) 523–529
17. DePaulo, B., Rosenthal, R., Eisenstat, R., Rogers, P., Finkelstein, S.: Decoding discrepant nonverbal cues. Journal of Personality and Social Psychology **36** (1978) 313–323
18. Kubala, F.: Rough'n'ready: a meeting recorder and browser. ACM Computing Surveys **31** (1999)
19. Waibel, A., Bett, M., Metze, F., Ries, K., Schaaf, T., Schultz, T., Soltau, H., Yu, H., Zechner, K.: Advances in automatic meeting record creation and access. In: Proc. IEEE ICASSP, Salt Lake City, UT (2001)
20. Renals, S., Ellis, D.: Audio information access from meeting rooms. In: Proc. IEEE ICASSP 2003. (2003)

21. Cutler, R., Rui, Y., Gupta, A., Cadiz, J., Tashev, I., He, L., Colburn, A., Zhang, Z., Liu, Z., Silverberg, S.: Distributed meetings: A meeting capture and broadcasting system. In: Proc. ACM Multimedia Conference. (2002)
22. Gatica-Perez, D., Lathoud, G., McCowan, I., Odobez, J.M.: A mixed-state i-particle filter for multi-camera speaker tracking. In: Proceedings of WOMTEC. (2003)
23. Doucet, A., de Freitas, N., Gordon, N.: Sequential Monte Carlo Methods in Practice. Springer-Verlag (2001)
24. Smith, K., Gatica-Perez, D.: Order matters: a distributed sampling method for multi-object tracking. In: IDIAP Research Report IDIAP-RR-04-25, Martigny (2004)
25. Ba, S., Odobez, J.M.: A probabilistic framework for joint head tracking and pose estimation. In: Proc. ICPR, Cambridge (2004)
26. Cutler, R.: The distributed meetings system. In: Proceedings of IEEE ICASSP 2003. (2003)
27. Stanford, V., Garofolo, J., , Michel, M.: The nist smart space and meeting room projects: Signals, acquisition, annotation, and metrics. In: Proceedings of IEEE ICASSP 2003. (2003)
28. Silverman, H., Patterson, W., Flanagan, J., Rabinkin, D.: A digital processing system for source location and sound capture by large microphone arrays. In: Proceedings of ICASSP 97. (1997)
29. Shriberg, E., Stolcke, A., Baron, D.: Observations on overlap: findings and implications for automatic processing of multi-party conversation. In: Proceedings of Eurospeech 2001. Volume 2. (2001) 1359–1362
30. Pfau, T., Ellis, D., Stolcke, A.: Multispeaker speech activity detection for the ICSI meeting recorder. In: Proceedings of ASRU-01. (2001)
31. Kemp, T., Schmidt, M., Westphal, M., Waibel, A.: Strategies for automatic segmentation of audio data. In: Proceedings of ICASSP-2000. (2000)
32. Lathoud, G., McCowan, I.: Location based speaker segmentation. In: Proceedings of the International Conference on Acoustics, Speech and Signal Processing. (2003)
33. Lathoud, G., McCowan, I., Moore, D.: Segmenting multiple concurrent speakers using microphone arrays. In: Proceedings of Eurospeech 2003. (2003)
34. Lathoud, G., Odobez, J.M., McCowan, I.: Unsupervised location-based segmentation of multi-party speech. In: Proceedings of the 2004 ICASSP-NIST Meeting Recognition Workshop. (2004)
35. Bitzer, J., Simmer, K.U.: Superdirective microphone arrays. In Brandstein, M., Ward, D., eds.: Microphone Arrays. Springer (2001) 19–38
36. McCowan, I., Bourlard, H.: Microphone array post-filter based on noise field coherence. To appear in IEEE Transactions on Speech and Audio Processing (2003)
37. Moore, D., McCowan, I.: Microphone array speech recognition: Experiments on overlapping speech in meetings. In: Proceedings of the International Conference on Acoustics, Speech and Signal Processing. (2003)
38. Jain, A., Bolle, R., Pankanti, S.: Biometrics: Person Identification in Networked Society. Kluwer Publications (1999)
39. Mariéthoz, J., Bengio, S.: A comparative study of adaptation methods for speaker verification. In: Proceedings of the International Conference on Spoken Language Processing, ICSLP. (2002)
40. Viola, P., Jones, M.: Rapid object detection using a boosted cascade of simple features. In: Proc. IEEE Int. Conf. on Computer Vision (CVPR), Kawaii (2001)
41. Rowley, H., Baluja, S., Kanade, T.: Neural network-based face detection. IEEE Tran. Pattern Analysis and Machine Intelligence **20(1)** (1998) 23–38

42. Sanderson, C., Paliwal, K.: Fast features for face authentication under illumination direction changes. Pattern Recognition Letters **24** (2003) 2409–2419
43. Cardinaux, F., Sanderson, C., Bengio, S.: Face verification using adapted generative models. In: Proc. Int. Conf. Automatic Face and Gesture Recognition (AFGR), Seoul, Korea. (2004)
44. Bengio, S., Marcel, C., Marcel, S., Mariéthoz, J.: Confidence measures for multimodal identity verification. Information Fusion **3** (2002) 267–276
45. Bailly-Baillière, E., Bengio, S., Bimbot, F., Hamouz, M., Kittler, J., Mariéthoz, J., Matas, J., Messer, K., Popovici, V., Porée, F., Ruiz, B., Thiran, J.P.: The BANCA database and evaluation protocol. In: 4th International Conference on Audio- and Video-Based Biometric Person Authentication, AVBPA, Springer-Verlag (2003) 625–638
46. Messer, K., Kittler, J., Sadeghi, M., Hamouz, M., Kostyn, A., Marcel, S., Bengio, S., Cardinaux, F., Sanderson, C., Poh, N., Rodriguez, Y., Kryszczuk, K., Czyz, J., Vandendorpe, L., Ng, J., Cheung, H., Tang, B.: Face authentication competition on the BANCA database. In: International Conference on Biometric Authentication, ICBA. (2004)
47. Rabiner, L.R., Juang, B.H.: Fundamentals of Speech Recognition. Prentice-Hall (1993)
48. Starner, T., Pentland, A.: Visual recognition of american sign language using HMMs. In: Proc. Int. Work. on Auto. Face and Gesture Recognition, Zurich (1995)
49. McCowan, I., Gatica-Perez, D., Bengio, S., Lathoud, G.: Automatic analysis of multimodal group actions in meetings. Technical Report RR 03-27, IDIAP (2003)
50. Dupont, S., Luettin, J.: Audio-visual speech modeling for continuous speech recognition. IEEE Transactions on Multimedia **2** (2000) 141–151
51. Bengio, S.: An asynchronous hidden markov model for audio-visual speech recognition. In Becker, S., Thrun, S., Obermayer, K., eds.: Advances in Neural Information Processing Systems, NIPS 15, MIT Press (2003)
52. Brand, M.: Coupled hidden markov models for modeling interacting processes. TR 405, MIT Media Lab Vision and Modeling (1996)
53. Zhang, D., Gatica-Perez, D., Bengio, S., McCowan, I., Lathoud, G.: Modeling individual and group actions in meetings: a two-layer hmm framework. In: Proc. IEEE CVPR Workshop on Event Mining, Washington, DC (2004)
54. De Gelder, B., Vroomen, J.: The perception of emotions by ear and by eye. Cognition and Emotion **14** (2002) 289–311
55. Basu, S., Choudhury, T., Clarkson, B., Pentland, A.: Learning human interactions with the influence model. Technical Report 539, MIT Media Laboratory (2001)

Multistream Dynamic Bayesian Network for Meeting Segmentation

Alfred Dielmann and Steve Renals*

Centre for Speech Technology Research,
University of Edinburgh,
Edinburgh EH8 9LW, UK
{a.dielmann, s.renals}@ed.ac.uk

Abstract. This paper investigates the automatic analysis and segmentation of meetings. A meeting is analysed in terms of individual behaviours and group interactions, in order to decompose each meeting in a sequence of relevant phases, named meeting actions. Three feature families are extracted from multimodal recordings: prosody from individual lapel microphone signals, speaker activity from microphone array data and lexical features from textual transcripts. A statistical approach is then used to relate low-level features with a set of abstract categories. In order to provide a flexible and powerful framework, we have employed a dynamic Bayesian network based model, characterized by multiple stream processing and flexible state duration modelling. Experimental results demonstrate the strength of this system, providing a meeting action error rate of 9%.

1 Introduction

Group meetings are part of many professional activities. Meetings are not only useful to plan work or to solve problems, but also to share knowledge between people and to promote good interpersonal relations. Since a large amount of information is generated during a meeting, automated systems to preserve and access meeting contents could prove to be invaluable [1].

Meetings may be successfully recorded using multiple cameras, microphones and other specialised multimodal recording equipment. However, without additional processing, the semantic content and the meeting structure remains locked into a number of distinct multimodal data streams. We are interested in the development of models able to discover meeting structure automatically through the analysis of such multimodal data. Our current work is mainly focused on the automatic segmentation of meetings into a set of actions or phases (*meeting actions*). Following Mc Cowan et al [2], we have defined a meeting as a sequence of basic group social actions, such as monologue, discussion and presentation.

Multiparty meetings are a good example of an interactive situation in which participants show both an individual behaviour and a joint group behaviour. We are interested

---

* Supported by EU IST project M4 (IST–2001–34485).

S. Bengio and H. Bourlard (Eds.): MLMI 2004, LNCS 3361, pp. 76–86, 2005.

in the automatic recognition of meeting actions which involve the whole group and are independent from who is attending the meeting. Thus we need to identify the set of clues in both individual and group behaviours, and to highlight repetitive patterns in the communicative process. These may then be integrated into the abstract concept of meeting actions.

In this work we have been mainly concerned with multichannel audio data streams, from which we extracted a variety of features relating to prosody, speaker activity and lexical content. In section 2 we outline the IDIAP M4 Meetings Corpus used in this work. In section 3 we outline the feature sets that we have used to characterize multiparty meeting interactions, and we present some introductory results, achieved using these feature families and a simple hidden Markov model. We have modelled these data streams using multistream dynamic Bayesian networks (DBNs). We review DBNs and their graphical formalism in section 4, introducing the basic multistream DBN model, describing an extended and enhanced version and outlining how inference is performed. In section 5 we describe a set of meeting segmentation experiments on the IDIAP corpus, using these DBN models.

2   M4 Meetings Data Collection

Our experiments have been performed using the M4 corpus of 53 short meetings, recorded at IDIAP[1] using an instrumented meeting room [2]. These meetings all involved four participants, and were recorded using four lapel microphones (one for each participant) and an eight element circular microphone array placed on the table between the participants. In addition to the audio, video data was captured using three fixed cameras, and all recording tracks were time-synchronized. The recording conditions were realistic and without any constraint over factors such as noise, reverberation, cross-talk and visual occlusion.

The four participants in each meeting were chosen randomly from two independent sets of 8 people. Each meeting had a duration of about five minutes, resulting in a corpus of about four hours of multichannel audio/video recordings. For each meeting the sequence (and approximate timing) of meeting actions was defined in advance, with the meeting actions drawn from a dictionary containing the following: monologue (one for each participant), discussion, note taking, presentation, presentation at the white-board, consensus and disagreement. The dictionary of meeting actions was exhaustive and the individual actions were mutually exclusive, hence each meeting could be described by a sequence of non-overlapping group actions. On average, discussion and monologue were the most frequent actions, and also had the longest average duration. The mean number of actions per meeting was five.

These meetings are scripted at the level of the sequence of meeting actions, and are somewhat naïve from a social psychology viewpoint. However the acoustic and visual behaviours are natural and spontaneous, and this corpus provides a good resource for experiments to model higher level behaviours in terms of lower level signals.

---

[1] This corpus is publicly available from http://mmm.idiap.ch/

3   Features

The human communicative process behind a meeting is usually spread over a wide set of modalities, such as speech, gesture, handwriting and body movement. Not all modalities carry the same importance: for example, speech may be regarded as the most informative one. For this reason, we have based our initial efforts on speech and audio modalities, in particular features based on prosody, speaker activity and the lexical transcription. We are currently investigating the incorporation of streams based on video features to the models described in this paper.

3.1   Prosody

Prosodic features were extracted from the four audio channels associated with individual lapel microphones. We computed three feature streams:

- Baseline pitch: based on a rough intonation contour estimate, obtained using the ESPS pitch extraction algorithm, then denoised with a histogram filter and a median filter, and stylised with using a piecewise linear interpolation [3];
- Rate of speech: an estimate of the syllabic rate of speech using the multiple rate (MRATE) estimator [4]
- Energy: root mean square value of the signal energy.

These acoustic features appeared as four feature sets (one per channel) with three features each, or as a 12-dimensional feature vector. In order to cope with the high level of cross-talk between audio channels, each feature set was forced to zero if the corresponding speaker was not active. Individual speaker activities were evaluated using a speaker localization process applied to the eight-channel microphone array. The whole prosodic feature set highlights the currently active speakers, and may indicate the level of engagement in the conversation for each participant.

3.2   Speaker Activity Features

Microphone arrays can be used to simulate steerable directional microphones, enabling the estimation of sound source directions (*localization*) and the algorithmic steering of the array to improve sensitivity in a given direction (*beamforming*). In the M4 data collection, meeting participants tend to occupy only a restricted set of spatial regions i (their seats $i = 1, ..., 4$, a presentation space $i = 5$, and the whiteboard area $i = 6$). We predefine these spatial regions and collect sound source activations from each region, to give an estimate of speaker activity in that region [5]. For example a high sound activity $L_3(t)$, from the region around seat 3, means that the participant number 3 is probably speaking. Information about speaker activities taking was extracted, building up a 216-dimensional feature vector, whose elements corresponded to the 6^3 possible products of "sound activities" $L_i(t)$ evaluated at the 6 most probable speaker locations, during the most recent three frames [6]:

$$S_{ijk}(t) = L_i(t) \cdot L_j(t-1) \cdot L_k(t-2)   \forall i, j, k \in [1, 6]$$

A speaker activity feature vector at time t thus gives a local sample of the speaker interaction pattern in the meeting at around time t.

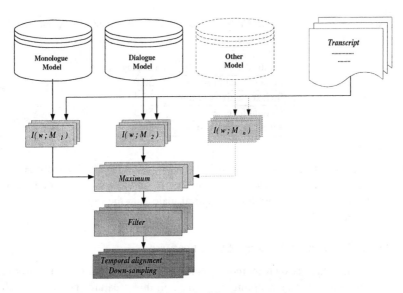

Fig. 1. Overview of the lexical feature generation process

3.3   Lexical Features

In addition to the paralinguistic features outlined above, we also used a set of lexical features extracted from the word-level transcription. A transcript is available for each speaker, resulting in a sequence of words. In these initial experiments, we have used human generated transcriptions, however work in progress is employing speech recognition output. [2]

In this work we have used lexical features to discriminate between monologues and discussion. Our approach (outlined in figure 1) is based on unigram language models with a multinomial distribution over words used to model the monologue class M_1 and the discussion or dialogue class M_2; this approach could be extended easily to the other meeting actions. The sequence of words (from the transcript under test) is compared with each model M_k, and each word w is classified as a member of the class $\tilde{k}$ which provides the highest mutual information $I(w; M_k)$:

$$\tilde{k}(w) = \arg\max_{k \in K} \{I(w; M_k)\}$$

The sequence of symbols $\tilde{k}$ is very noisy, and the true classification output is hidden by a cloud of mis-classified words. To address this drawback we compute a smoothed version of $\tilde{k}$, that uses only the most frequent symbols. This is achieved by computing the relative symbol frequencies of $\tilde{k}$ across a sliding window of 24 words, and taking only symbols with higher frequency. After filtering in this way, these lexical features may be used to

---

[2] The M4 corpus is a challenging speech recognition task, due to its conversational nature, the high percentage of non-native accents, and the degraded acoustic quality arising from the fact that head-mounted microphones were not used.

Table 1. Accuracy (%) of a simple HMM based meeting action recognizer using only one feature set at a time, or all 3 sets together. Higher values means better performances

Feature	Accuracy
Prosodic features	50.0
Speaker activity features	65.4
Lexical features	58.3
All 3 feature groups	**70.5**

label monologues and discussions, taken from unseen hand labelled transcriptions, with an accuracy of 93.6% (correct classified words). The resulting symbol sequence is then translated from the discrete word level temporal scale, into the same frame rate used for the prosodic and speaker activity features.

3.4   Some Experimental Results About Features

Each feature class has its own temporal scale and its individual sampling frequency. In order to share a common sampling frequency, all three features groups were down-sampled to a sampling frequency of 2Hz.

To compare the different feature families, we used a baseline hidden Markov model (HMM) approach to segment the meetings into sequences of meeting actions. Each meeting action was modelled using an 11-state HMM, and we experimented with observations consisting of each one of the feature streams, and all features combined. We used the 30 meeting training set for these experiments, using a leave-one-out cross validation procedure. The results are shown in table 1. Considering the models trained on each the three feature streams independently, it is clear that the speaker activity features result in the most accurate classifier (65% of actions correctly recognized), with the prosodic features resulting in a model with only 50% of actions correctly classified. The lexical features, which offer 93% correct classification between monologue and discussion result in an HMM with an overall accuracy of 58% when all actions are considered (monologues and discussions cover about the 60% of the meeting corpus). When all these features are merged into a single feature vector, the number of correctly recognized actions rises to 70%, indicating that the different feature families supply non-redundant information that the HMM can exploit.

4   Dynamic Bayesian Networks

Bayesian Networks (BNs) are directed acyclic graphical models, in which the network topology represents statistical relationships among variables [7]. In the BN graphical formalism, nodes represent random variables, and arcs represent conditional dependencies. Thus directed arcs between nodes depict the influence from each variable to the others, and the lack of direct and indirect connections represents a conditional independence relationship between variables. The generalization of BNs to dynamic processes are usually referred as Dynamic Bayesian Networks (DBNs) [8, 9]. In a DBN the time flow is discretized, and a static BN is assigned to each temporal slice. Variables of different time-slices are connected through directed arcs, which explicitly represent the time flow in terms of conditional dependences. DBNs are a powerful mathematical formalism, able to group together a large variety of statistical models such as HMMs, hierarchical HMMs, input-output HMMs, factorial HMMs, and Kalman filters [10].

4.1   Multi Stream DBN Model

The DBN formalism allows the construction and development of a variety of models, starting from a simple HMM and extending to more sophisticated models, with richer hidden state. Among the many advantages provided by the adoption of a DBN formalism, one benefit is the unequalled flexibility in the model internal state factorization. With a small effort, DBNs are able to factorize the internal hidden state, organizing it in a set of interconnected and specialised hidden variables.

Our model (figure 2) exploits this principle in two ways: decomposing meeting actions into smaller logical units, and modelling the three feature streams independently. We assume that a meeting action can be decomposed into a sequence of small units: meeting subactions. In accordance with this assumption the state space is decomposed into two levels of resolution: meeting actions (nodes A) and meeting subactions (nodes S^F). Note that the decomposition of meeting actions into meeting subactions is done automatically through the training process. These synthetic subactions do not necessarily have a clear human interpretation.

Feature sets derived from different modalities are usually governed by different laws, have different characteristic time-scales and highlight different aspects of the communicative process. Starting from this hypothesis we further subdivided the model state space according to the nature of features that are processed, modelling each feature stream independently—a multistream approach. The resulting model has an independent substate node S^F for each feature class F (prosodic features, speaker activities, and lexical features), and integrates the information carried by each feature stream at

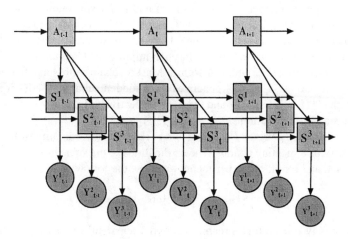

Fig. 2. Multistream DBN model; square nodes represent discrete hidden variables and circles must be intend as continuous observations

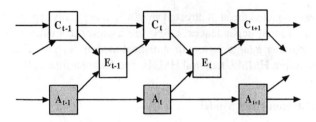

Fig. 3. Counter structure

a 'higher level of the model structure (arcs between A and S^F, $F = [1,3]$). The joint distribution for a sequence of T temporal slices is:

$$P(A_{1:T}, S_{1:T}^1, S_{1:T}^2, S_{1:T}^3, Y_{1:T}^1, Y_{1:T}^2, Y_{1:T}^3) =$$

$$P(A_1) \cdot \prod_{F=1}^{3} \{P(S_1^F \mid A_1) \cdot P(Y_1^F \mid S_1^F)\} \cdot \prod_{t=2}^{T} \{P(A_t \mid A_{t-1}) \cdot$$

$$\cdot \prod_{F=1}^{3} \{P(S_t^F \mid S_{t-1}^F, A_t) \cdot P(Y_t^F \mid S_t^F)\}\} \quad (1)$$

Each substate node S^F, $F = [1,3]$ follows an independent Markov chain, but the substate transition matrix and an initial state distribution are functions of the action variable state $A_t = k$:

$$\tilde{A}_k^F(i,j) = P(S_t^F = j \mid S_{t-1}^F = i, A_t = k) \quad (2)$$

$$\tilde{\pi}_k^F(j) = P(S_1^F = j \mid A_1 = k) \quad (3)$$

where $\tilde{A}_k^F(i,j)$ is an element of the transition matrix for subaction S_t^F given that the meeting action variable ($A_t = k$) is in state k, and $\tilde{\pi}_k^F(j)$ is the initial substate distribution for the stream F, given k as initial action ($A_1 = k$). The discrete substates S^F generate the continuous observation vectors Y^F through mixtures of Gaussians.

The sequence of action nodes A form a Markov chain with subaction nodes S^F, $F = 1, 2, 3$ as parents. Hence A generates three hidden subaction sequences S^1, S^2, S^3 through $\tilde{A}_k^1(i,j)$, $\tilde{A}_k^2(i,j)$ and $\tilde{A}_k^3(i,j)$ respectively. Like any ordinary Markov chain A has an associated transition matrix $P(A_t = j \mid A_{t-1} = i) = A(i,j)$ and an initial state probability vector $P(A_1 = i) = \pi(i)$. A has a cardinality of 8, since there is a dictionary of 8 meeting actions. The cardinalities of the subaction nodes are part of parameter set, and for all our experiments we chose the following values:

$$|S^1| = 6, \ |S^2| = 6, \ |S^3| = 2 \quad (4)$$

Considering only one feature stream, our model apparently looks like a hierarchical HMM, but here A is free to change independently of the state of S^F: there is no feedback from S^F to A enabling state transitions of A only when S^F is in a terminal state [11, 12].

4.2   Counter Structure

In an HMM, the probability of remaining in a given state decreases following an inverse exponential distribution [13]. This distribution is not well-matched to the behaviour of meeting action durations. Rather than adopting ad hoc solutions, such as action transition penalties, we preferred to improve the flexibility of state duration modelling, by enhancing the existing model with a counter structure (figure 3). This additional structure is composed of a Markov chain of counter nodes C, and a set of binary enabler variables E. The counter variable C, being ideally incremented during each action transition, attempts to model the expected number of recognized actions. The binary enabler variable E ($E_t = 1$ only if $A_t \neq A_{t-1}$ and therefore $C_t = C_{t-1} + 1$) forms an interface between the action variables A and counter nodes C, thus reducing the model's dimension. The joint distribution for the "counter structure" alone, computed for a sequence of T temporal slices is:

$$P(C_{1:T}, E_{1:T}, A_{1:T}) = P(C_1) \cdot P(E_1) \cdot P(A_1) \cdot$$
$$\cdot \prod_{t=2}^{T} \{ P(C_t \mid C_{t-1}, E_{t-1}) \cdot P(E_t \mid C_t, A_t) \cdot P(A_t \mid A_{t-1}) \} \quad (5)$$

The whole joint distribution of a multi stream model enhanced with a counter structure (figures 2 and 3 combined) is given by the product of (1) with

$$P(C_1) \cdot P(E_1) \cdot \prod_{t=2}^{T} \{ P(C_t \mid C_{t-1}, E_{t-1}) \cdot P(E_t \mid C_t, A_t) \}$$

Note that now action variables A generate, not only a sequence of subaction nodes S^j, but also a sequence of hidden enabler nodes E.

The state transition probability for the counter variable C is given by:

$$P(C_t = j \mid C_{t-1} = i, E_{t-1} = f) = \begin{cases} j = i+1 \text{ if } f = 1 \\ j = i \quad \text{if } f = 0 \end{cases} \quad (6)$$

this means that C can be incremented only if the enabler variable E was high ($E_{t-1} = 1$) during the previous temporal slice $t-1$. $D_{j,k}(f)$ represents the state transition probability for the enabler variable E_t given that the action variable A is in state k and the counter C in state j:

$$P(E_t = f \mid C_t = j, A_t = k) = D_{j,k}(f) \quad (7)$$

If $A_t = k$ is the jth recognised "meeting action", the probability to start evaluating the $(j+1)^{th}$ action and therefore to activate E ($E_t = 0, E_{t+1} = 1$), is modelled by $D_{j,k}(f)$. Initial state probabilities of C and E are respectively set to: $P(C_1 = 0) = 1$ and $P(E_1 = 0) = 1$, stating that *action* transitions are not allowed at the initial frame $t = 0$.

4.3   Inference

Statistical inference, which may be regarded as the estimation of a conditional distribution, is an essential step both for testing purposes (making predictions based on the model) and for model training (learning about the parameters of the model).

As mentioned in section 4, each directed acyclic graph (DAG) associated with a BN encodes a set of conditional independence properties. Joint probability distributions can be factorised, exploiting conditional independence statements provided by the graph. For example, consider a chain of four variables X,B,A,Y in which: X is the only parent of B, B is the only parent of A and A is the only parent of Y. The computation of $P(Y \mid X) = \sum_{A,B} P(Y, A, B \mid X)$ can be simplified by taking into account conditional independences:

$$P(Y, A, B \mid X) = P(Y \mid A)P(A \mid B)P(B \mid X) .$$

Therefore $P(Y \mid X)$ could be evaluated with less operations through:

$$P(Y \mid X) = \sum_A P(Y \mid A) \sum_B P(A \mid B)P(B \mid X) .$$

An efficient factorization of this type is at the core of every inference algorithm for graphical models, such as the junction-tree (JT) algorithm [14, 7].

Some graph manipulations [7, 15, 8] are needed to transform the original DAG into an equivalent form, suitable for the exact inference JT algorithm. The first step called *moralization* converts the DAG into an undirected graph, removing the directions of arcs and joining unconnected parents. The second step *triangulation* ensures the decomposability of the graph, by numbering each node A in decreasing order and adding arcs between all the pairs of A's neighbours characterized by a lower ordering number. A joint distribution that can be factorized on the original graph can also be factored on the larger triangulated graph. The final step is the construction of a junction tree from the triangulated (hence, decomposable) graph. The junction tree is a tree of cliques made with nodes from the original graph, satisfying some properties [15] such as the *running intersection property* and the *immediate resolution property*. The JT algorithm provides exact inference, exploiting as efficiently as possible the conditional independence contained into the original graph. Frequently, exact inference is not a feasible approach, due to model complexity and practical temporal constraints. In such cases approximate inference approaches, such as Monte Carlo sampling and variational techniques have been successfully applied [8].

There are several software packages that possess the functionalities required to work with graphical models. In this work we have used the Graphical Models ToolKit (GMTK) [16].

5   Experiments

Experimental evaluations were performed on 30 fully transcribed meetings, part of the corpus described in section 2. Performances were evaluated using a leave-one-out cross-validation procedure, in which the system was trained using 29 meetings and tested on the remaining one, iterating this procedure 30 times. The annotation of meeting actions is rather subjective, and their boundaries must be considered to be approximate. We adopted the Action Error Rate (AER) metric that privileges the recognition of the correct action sequence, rather than the precise temporal alignment of recognised symbols. Like the

Table 2. Performances (%) for: a simple HMM, our multistream approach, and the multistream model enhanced with a "counter structure"; using: (A) prosody and speaker activities or (B) prosody, speaker activities and lexical feature

Model	Corr.	Sub.	Del.	Ins.	AER
(A) HMM	64.1	14.7	21.2	21.2	57.1
(B) HMM	70.5	10.3	19.2	14.7	44.2
(A) multistream	84.6	9.0	6.4	1.3	16.7
(B) multistream	91.7	4.5	3.8	2.6	10.9
(A) multistream + counter	86.5	6.4	7.1	1.3	14.7
(B) multistream + counter	92.9	5.1	1.9	1.9	9.0

Word Error Rate metric used in speech recognition, the AER is obtained by summing the insertion, deletion and substitution errors when aligned against the reference sequence. Table 2 shows some experimental results achieved using six experimental configurations. These configurations are obtained evaluating three models: a hidden Markov model, a basic multistream approach and the counter enhanced variant. Two features sets were used. Feature set (A) contains prosodic features and speaker activities. Feature set (B) extends (A) with the addiction of lexical features. Therefore multistream based models applied to the feature set (A) are evaluated using a double-stream model with only sub-actions S^1 and S^2. Multistream models associated with (B) have an additional Markov chain composed by substates S^3 and observable binary lexical features Y^3. During both the experiments with a simple HMM, all features families have been merged in advance into a single feature vector (*early integration*). As anticipated in section 3.4 a simple HMM has poor performances, independently from the feature set used: 57% AER using two feature families and an improvement to 44% using lexical features as well. The adoption of a multistream based approach reduces the AER to less than 20%, and another small improvement is granted by the counter structure. Independently of the feature set, a counter structure leads to a better insertions/deletions ratio, enabling the model to fit better the experimental data and to have a further improvement in AER. Enhancing the feature set with lexical features, improves the percentage of correctly recognized actions by about 6%, independently of the adopted model (HMM, multistream, counter enhanced multistream). Therefore we reached our best results (9% AER and 92% correct) using the most elaborate DBN model with the most comprehensive feature set.

6   Conclusion

In this paper, we have presented a framework for automatic segmentation of meetings into a sequence of meeting actions. These actions or phases are result of the participants' interactions and involve multiple modalities. Starting from individual and environmental audio recordings, some relevant acoustic features were extracted. A set of prosodic features was evaluated over individual lapel microphone signals, and the dynamics of speaker activity were highlighted using a microphone array based sound direction estimation process. A lexically based monologue/ discussion discriminator was developed using textual transcriptions. All these three features streams were individually tested, and then integrated using a specialized DBN model. This model included the individual processing of different feature families (multistream approach), and a simple mechanism to improve action duration modelling (counter structure). The resulting system, tested with the M4 meeting corpus, attained an accuracy of 92% correct, with an action error rate of 9%. The chosen DBN framework seems to be a flexible and promising approach to the meeting segmentation and structuring task. Further multimodal features will be soon integrated into this scalable model. Ongoing work concerns some video related features, and an extended lexical meeting actions discriminator is being investigated.

References

1. R. Kazman, R. Al Halimi, W. Hunt, and M. Mantei. Four paradigms for indexing video conferences. *IEEE Multimedia*, 3(1), 1996.
2. I. McCowan, S. Bengio, D. Gatica-Perez, G. Lathoud, F. Monay, D. Moore, P. Wellner, and H. Bourlard. Modelling human interaction in meetings. *Proc. IEEE ICASSP*, 2003.
3. K. Sonmez, E. Shriberg, L. Heck, and M. Weintraub. Modelling dynamic prosodic variation for speaker verification. *Proc. ICSLP*, pages 3189–3192, 1998.
4. N. Morgan and E. Fosler-Lussier. Combining multiple estimators of speaking rate. *Proc. IEEE ICASSP*, pages 729–732, 1998.
5. I. McCowan, D. Gatica-Perez, S. Bengio, and G. Lathoud. Automatic analysis of multimodal group actions in meetings. *IDIAP RR 03-27*, May 2003. Submitted to IEEE Transactions of Pattern Analysis and Machine Intelligence.
6. A. Dielmann and S. Renals. Dynamic Bayesian networks for meeting structuring. *Proc. IEEE ICASSP*, pages 629–632, 2004.
7. R. G. Cowell, A. P. Dawid, S. L. Lauritzen, and D. J. Spiegelhalter. *Probabilistic Networks and Expert Systems*. Springer, 1999.
8. K. Murphy. *Dynamic Bayesian Networks: Representation, Inference and Learning*. PhD thesis, UC Berkeley, 2002.
9. J. Bilmes. Graphical models and automatic speech recognition. *Mathematical Foundations of Speech and Language Processing*, 2003.
10. P. Smyth, D. Heckerman, and M. I. Jordan. Probabilistic independence networks for hidden Markov probability models. *Neural Computation*, 9(2):227–269, 1997.
11. S. Fine, Y. Singer, and N. Tishby. The hierarchical hidden Markov model: Analysis and applications. *Machine Learning*, 32(1):41–62, 1998.
12. A. Divakaran L. Xie, S.-F. Chang and H. Sun. Unsupervised discovery of multilevel statistical video structures using hierarchical hidden Markov models. *Proc. IEEE ICME, Baltimore*, 2003.
13. L. R. Rabiner. A tutorial on hidden Markov models and selected applications in speech recognition. *Proc. of the IEEE*, 2(77):257—286, 1989.
14. F. V. Jensen. *An Introduction to Bayesian Networks*. Springer, 1996.
15. G. Zweig. *Speech Recognition with Dynamic Bayesian Networks*. PhD thesis, UC Berkeley, 1998.
16. J. Bilmes and G. Zweig. The Graphical Model ToolKit: an open source software system for speech and time-series processing. *Proc. IEEE ICASSP*, Jun. 2002.

Using Static Documents as Structured and Thematic Interfaces to Multimedia Meeting Archives

Denis Lalanne[1], Rolf Ingold[1], Didier von Rotz[2], Ardhendu Behera[1],
Dalila Mekhaldi[1], and Andrei Popescu-Belis[3]

[1] University of Fribourg, Faculty of Science,
DIUF/DIVA, 3, ch. du Musée,
CH-1700 Fribourg, Switzerland
{denis.lalanne, rolf.ingold, ardhendu.behera,
dalila.mekaldi}@unifr.ch
[2] Ecole d'ingénieurs et d'architectes de Fribourg,
Bd de Pérolles 80 - CP 32,
CH-1705 Fribourg, Switzerland
didier.vonrotz@eif.ch
[3] University of Geneva,
School of Translation and Interpreting (ETI),
TIM/ISSCO, 40, bd. du Pont d'Arve,
CH-1211 Geneva 4, Switzerland
andrei.popescu-belis@issco.unige.ch

Abstract. Static documents play a central role in multimodal applications such as meeting recording and browsing. They provide a variety of structures, in particular thematic, for segmenting meetings, structures that are often hard to extract from audio and video. In this article, we present four steps for creating a strong link between static documents and multimedia meeting archives. First, a document-centric meeting environment is introduced. Then, a document analysis tool is presented, which builds a multi-layered representation of documents and creates indexes that are further on used by document/speech and document/video alignment methods. Finally, a document-based browsing system, integrating the various alignment results, is described along with a preliminary user evaluation.

1 Introduction

There is a significant research trend on recording and analyzing meetings, mostly in order to advance the research on multimodal content analysis and on multimedia information retrieval, which are key features for designing future communication systems. Many research projects aim at archiving meeting recordings in suitable forms for later browsing and retrieval [1, 2, 3, 4, 5, 6]. However, most of these projects do not take into account the printed documents that are often an important part of the information available during a meeting.

S. Bengio and H. Bourlard (Eds.): MLMI 2004, LNCS 3361, pp. 87–100, 2005.

Printed documents have been for centuries the predominant medium of remote communication between humans. With the recent advances in multimedia and multimodal applications, new means, such as audio and video, are appearing for exchanging information. These advances strengthen the role of printed documents, which co-exist in the physical world and the digital one. Documents are highly thematic and structured, relatively easy to index and retrieve, and thus can provide natural and thematic means for accessing and browsing efficiently large multimedia meeting corpora. For that reason, it is essential to find links between documents and multimodal annotations of meeting data such as audio and video.

Two groups of meeting room systems emerge from a quick overview [7]. The first group is focused on document related annotations such as handwriting and slide analysis: Microsoft [4], FXPal [3], eClass [2], DSTC [5] and Cornell [6]. These meeting browser interfaces are based on visualizations of the slide changes time line, and of the notes taken by participants. In these interfaces, slides and notes are used as quick visual indexes for locating relevant meeting events and for triggering their playback. The second group of systems is based on speech related annotations such as the spoken word transcript: ISL [1] and eClass [2]. These meeting browser interfaces are based on keyword search in the transcripts. In that context, higher-level annotations such as speech acts or thematic episodes can also be used to display quick indexes of selected meeting parts. The document-centric and the speech-centric applications correspond respectively to the visual and to the verbal communication modalities (or channels) of a meeting. Since these channels are really integrated, we propose to create links between them and include them in meeting archives and related user-interfaces. Further, we suggest considering both the visual and the verbal links with documents in order to fully align them with temporal data.

In this article we present four steps for bridging the gap between documents and multimedia meeting data: document-centric meeting environment (Section 2), document recognition and indexing (Section 3), document alignment using various techniques (Sections 4, 5 and 6), and document-enabled multimedia meeting browsing system (Section 7).

2   Document-Centric Meeting Recording

A document-centric meeting room has been installed at the University of Fribourg to record different types of meetings (Figure 1). The room records several modalities related to documents, either projected or laying on the meeting table, and related to the participants' discussion. The room is currently equipped with 14 firewire webcams (8 close-ups, 6 overviews), 8 microphones, a video projector, a projection screen and a camera for capturing slides. It implements a distributed and scalable architecture remotely controlled (6 capture boxes with one master PC). All the capture boxes are synchronized. The meeting capture application controls all cameras and microphones devices in the meeting room. It enables not only basic operations like starting and stopping the recordings, but

Fig. 1. Fribourg document-centric meeting recording environment is equipped with standard webcams and microphones for each participant and captures the document projected and standing on the meeting table

it also enables to automate post-processing, compression and file transfers to the server. It stands on the master PC and allows to control and to visualize all the slave's processing. Further, a user-friendly control interface has been developed that allows to select which devices to use (cameras, microphones, etc), to register the participants around the table, ant to select frame rate, resolution, etc. Post-processing, compression, file transfer, generation of the global descriptors and a SMIL presentation (including all the audio and video streams) are all automated and controllable through this interface. In the future, the meeting room will be enhanced for real-time interactions with documents, either projected or laying on the meeting table.

Several document-centric meeting scenarios have been considered (press reviews, lectures, reading clubs, personal presentations, etc.). In total, 22 press-reviews, 4 job interviews and 4 student presentations have been recorded, then manually transcribed and annotated. Further, all the meeting documents have been indexed and structured in a canonical representation containing text, and physical and logical structures. In the press-review scenario, participants discuss in French the front page and the contents of one or more French-speaking news-papers. The meetings last for about 15 minutes each. Documents' structures have been manually encoded in XML. Further, each meeting is accompanied by an XML-encoded global descriptor, coming alone with audio and video files for each participant, and both the PDF and image form of all the documents.

3   Document Analysis

Documents play an important role in everyday communication. With the ever-increasing use of the Web, a growing number of documents are published and accessed on-line. Unfortunately, document structures are not often considered, which considerably weaken users' browsing and searching experience. There are many levels of abstraction in a document, conveyed by its various structures: thematic, physical, logical, relational or even temporal. In most of the search engines and information retrieval systems, this multi-layered structure is not taken into account; documents are indexed in the best case according to their thematic structure or simply represented as a bag of words. The form of the documents, i.e. their layout and logical structures, is underestimated and could carry important clues about how the document is organized. We believe that document structure extraction will drastically improve documents indexing and retrieval, as well as linking with other media.

We have chosen to analyze PDF documents mainly because PDF has become the common format for exchanging printable documents and because it preserves the display format. The use of PDF is frequently limited to displaying and printing, regardless of the improvements it could bring to search and retrieval. We believe that the extraction from documents of both layout and logical structure will enrich PDF indexing and linking with other media. In particular, in the present application, the document structures allow the linking of PDF documents with the speech transcript. We recently proposed a novel approach that merges low-level extraction methods applied on PDF files with layout analysis of a synthetically generated TIFF image [8].

In the field of document analysis, image segmentation aims at zoning a given document image into homogenous regions that have meaningful properties, e.g. text, image, graphics, etc. Our segmentation algorithm first extracts threads, frames and text lines, then separates image and text zones, and finally merges lines into homogeneous blocs. The algorithm's input is the TIFF image generated from the PDF file, while the output is an XML file, which describes the segmentation results for the document components mentioned above. In parallel, the various objects contained in the PDF file, including text, images, and graphics, are extracted. The PDF file is first disambiguated; the different representations are then homogenized, and the cleaned PDF is parsed into a unique tree, which can be then transformed either into an XML document, e.g. in SVG. Finally, the objects extracted from the PDF document are matched with the result of the layout analysis in order to construct a structured XML representation of the PDF document. For example the text is matched with the physical blocks in order to create associations between the two [8].

In order to produce a proper ground-truth for our press reviews, documents have been segmented manually [9]. The PDF documents corresponding to the newspapers' front pages discussed in the recorded meetings have been first converted automatically to text and then logically structured in XML along with information about the layout structure, i.e. the bounding boxes of each logical block, topological positions, fonts, etc. For instance, a Newspaper front page bears the newspaper's Name, the Date, one MasterArticle, zero, one or more Highlights, one or more Articles, etc. Each Article has a Title, Authors, a Content, etc.

4   Temporal Document Alignments

In order to browse multimedia corpuses through static documents, it is first necessary to build links between those documents, which are non-temporal, and other media, which are generally temporal. We call "document temporal alignment" the operation of extracting the relationships between a document excerpt, at variable granularity levels, and the meeting presentation time. Document temporal alignment create links between document extracts and the time intervals in which they were in: (a) the speech focus, (b) the visual focus and/or into (c) the gestural focus of a meeting. It is thus possible to align document extracts with audio and video extracts, and by extension with any annotation of audio and/or video and/or gesture. There are three modalities related to documents that we use for further temporal alignment:

1. **Speech**: documents' content is matched with speech transcripts' content, which holds timestamps for each speaker turn and speech utterance.
2. **Video**: electronic documents are matched with extracted frames from the meeting's documents videos (e.g. slides projected) in order to extract time stamps associated with visible state changes.
3. **Gesture**: gestural interactions with documents are captured and analyzed (e.g. pointing a document), in order to find out when and which specific document part was in gestural focus.

Both document/video and document/gesture alignment are video-based and bridge the gap between document excerpts and video extracts. These approaches take advantage of the observable events related to documents that are visible during meetings, such as projected documents or documents standing on the meeting table. Documents' intra-events (slide changes, animations, zooming, scrolling, etc.) are handled by the document/video alignment, whereas documents' extra-events (e.g. pointing a projected document with a laser-beam, finger-pointing of documents laying on a table, pen-based gestural interactions on a TabletPC, etc.) are handled by the document/gesture alignment, in order to find out when and which specific document part was in gestural focus.

In the next two sections, the advancement of our work on document/speech and document video alignments is presented. Document/gesture has not yet been handled; the technique we envision to use to solve this alignment combines two established domains: gestural interaction and document analysis. The gestural analysis leads to high-level annotations on gests (such as pointing, circling, underlying, etc.) with their associated timestamps. Document analysis techniques provide methods for extracting the logical structure from electronic documents, as described in Section 3, which will greatly help to determine which document block has been pointed, circled or underlined. Gestural interactions with documents have been rarely tackled and should lead to new document related annotations and also to real-time prototypes that bring back old technologies such as paper documents to the digital world [10, 11]. In general, this document/gesture alignment will help answering two questions:

1. When was a document pointed to?
2. Which document or document part was pointed to?

5   Document/Speech Alignment

In document/speech alignment, textual content is matched with speech transcript in order to detect citation/paraphrase, reference and thematic alignments. Citation alignments are pure lexicographic matches between terms in documents and terms in the speech transcription. Paraphrase is an oral rewording of a written sentence. Reference alignments establish links between documents and structured dialogs through the references that are made to documents in speech transcript (e.g. "the article about Iraq"). Finally, thematic alignments are similarity matches between documents' units (sentences, logical blocks, etc.) and speech transcript's units (utterances, turns, etc.). This document/speech alignment will help answering two questions:

1. When was a document discussed? Or referenced?
2. What was said about a document part?

5.1   Document/Speech Thematic Alignment

A reliable thematic alignment has been implemented, using various state-of-the-art metrics (cosine, Jaccard, Dice) and considering document and speech units as bags of weighted words. After suppression of stop-words and proper stemming, document elements' content is compared with speech transcript units' content. Recall and precision are relatively high when matching speech utterances with document logical blocks. Using cosine metric, recall is 0.84 and precision is 0.77, which are encouraging results. And when matching speech turns with logical blocks, recall stays at 0.84 and precision rises to 0.85.

On the other hand, utterance-to-sentence alignment is less precise but is more promising since it does not require to extract the logical structure from documents. Indeed, PDF documents are automatically converted in their textual form, further segmented in sentences, and finally matched with the speech utterances. In this case, using Jaccard metric, recall is 0.83, and precision is 0.76. We believe that these simple automatic alignments can help both structuring documents and the transcription of the meeting dialogs.

Most of the meetings tested were relatively stereotyped; newspapers' articles were presented rather than discussed. In few meetings, participants were not following closely the articles' content, arguing more about the daily news (an average of 55 speaker turns for 94 utterances: ratio $> 1/2$), compared to more stereotyped meetings (average 20 speaker turns for 60 utterances: ratio $1/3$). This gives a good indication of how well perform our method in realistic meetings. In this case, recall and precision values decrease drastically for utterances/sentences alignment (recall 0.74 and precision 0.66) and remain stable for utterances/document logical blocs alignment. More results and details can be found in [9].

Thematic units have been considered neither for documents nor for speech transcript, mainly because the results of thematic structure segmentation, using state-of-the-art methods, were not satisfactory. For this reason, a combined thematic segmentation of both documents and speech transcripts, benefiting from the alignment results, has been implemented. The idea of this method was to detect the most connected regions in the bipolar alignment graph, using clustering techniques and to project the denser clusters on each axis, corresponding respectively to meeting documents and the speech transcript. A recent evaluation has shown that our bi-modal thematic segmentation method outperforms standard mono-modal segmentation methods, which tends to prove that combining modalities improves considerably segmentation scores and that documents greatly help structuring meetings [12].

5.2   Alignment Based on References to Documents

During meetings, speakers often refer to a document or to parts of it. To solve these references to documents, it is necessary to find links between each spoken referring expression (RE) and the corresponding document element. For example, if a participant says: "I do not agree with the title of our latest report", then "our latest report" refers to a document that can be retrieved from the file repository, and "the title of our latest report" refers to its title, a textual zone that can be retrieved from the respective document.

We have implemented an algorithm inspired from work on anaphora resolution, which attempts to solve these references [13]. Anaphors, such as pronouns, are expressions that point back to previously introduced discourse entities. The algorithm keeps track of the *current document* and the *current article* while scanning the meeting transcript for referring expressions, in chronological order. The algorithm monitors document changes by detecting mentions of the newspapers' names in the referring expressions. To detect the change (or not) of the current article, the algorithm recognizes a set of phrases that are most likely anaphors, such as "the article", "this article", "it", "the author" (in fact their equivalents in French). If the current RE is an anaphor, then its referent is simply the current article. If it is not an anaphor (i.e. if it introduces a new referent), then a matching procedure is applied to select the best matching article from the current document. This procedure matches the RE, with its right context (i.e. the words uttered after the RE), against the articles, for which titles, authors, and full content are considered separately. The referent of the RE is the article that scores the most matches.

The first results using this algorithm on a 14-meeting subset with 322 annotated REs are encouraging. The identification of the document referred to by each RE is 98% accurate – or more correctly, considering only meetings that involve two documents or more, 93%, still a high score. The highest accuracy for document elements (specified by their ID) is 64%. This should be compared with baseline scores of simplistic heuristics such as "all REs refer to the front page" (16% accuracy) or "all REs refer to the MasterArticle" (18% accuracy). Moreover, if the anaphors are not considered for resolution, i.e. if the RE-article matching is attempted for all REs, then the score drops to 54%, which shows the present relevance of anaphora spotting. On the other hand, if the surrounding context of REs is not considered, the score drops to 27%.

In the near future, we are planning to combine citations, references and thematic alignments, since they are complementary and should be considered within a common framework, so that they can be consolidated and compared. Further on, their fusion will enable a robust document-to-speech alignment.

6   Document/Video Alignment

This video-based document alignment method bridges the gap between document excerpts and video extracts. The approach takes advantage of the observable events related to documents that are visible during meetings, such as projected documents or documents standing on the meeting table. Our method first detects the scene changes (e.g. slide changes) and extracts a document image for each stable period in the webcam's video stream. Then, it associates a visual signature to each extracted low-resolution document image, and finally it matches the signature, in order to identify it and enrich it with textual content, with the PDF form of electronic documents stored in a repository. This method attempts therefore to answer three questions:

1. When was a document in the visible focus?
2. Which document or document part was it?
3. What was the textual content of this document?

6.1   Slide Change Detection

Instead of trying to detect slide changes, our method identifies slide stabilities, i.e. periods during which a unique document image is displayed. Our algorithm follows two steps: first it detects unstable periods, and then it looks for the exact position of the slide change.

Frames are extracted from the video, low pass filtered for noise reduction and finally adaptively thresholded to produce binary images. The first frame image F_S of the video is compared with the frame image F_E standing 2 seconds after. The two frames are considered similar if the ratio of common black pixels overcomes a specific threshold. If they are similar, F_S and F_E are moved half a second after and compared again, and so on until dissimilarity is detected. If they are dissimilar, a queue containing all the frames starting from F_S and finishing in F_E is built. The first frame is compared with the rest of the frames in the queue. Because of the webcam auto-focusing, the dissimilarity distance gradually stabilizes after a slide change. Further, just after a slide change, the new slide image risks to be overlapped with the previous one, due to the fade-in/fade-out transition and to the relatively high movie capture frame rate. For this reason, we consider that the exact slide change position stands in between the queue's minimal and maximal dissimilarity values. An evaluation on 30 slideshows and roughly 1000 slide changes has shown that our method performs better than state-of-the-art techniques (recall 0.83, precision 0.82) [14].

6.2   Identification of Visible Documents

For each stable period, determined by the previous slide change detection method, a stable image is extracted. The extracted image is further compared with the original document images in the database, in order to identify it. The slide identification method we have implemented has two stages.

First, a hierarchically structured visual signature is extracted, containing global features and zones (textual, images, bullets, etc.), for both images extracted from the video and images of the original PDF document. The extraction is based on document image analysis methods such as the Run Length Smearing Algorithm, connected components, projection profiles, etc.

Second, a multi-level comparison of the visual signatures takes place, following their hierarchies. The highest-level features are first compared; all the images in the database, which similarity overcomes a prefixed threshold, are kept. The comparison continues on the resulting subset of images with lower-level features. When all the feature levels have been compared, i.e. when the matching reaches the leaves, the best images are kept (on a global basis, i.e. a weighted combination of all the features) and the comparison restarts at the root of the visual signature hierarchy with a more restrictive threshold.

A major advantage of this method is that it does not require any classification technique. It is fast, mainly because the visual signature hierarchy guides the search towards fruitful solution spaces. Further, by alternating feature-specific matching with global distance comparison, it guaranties that no good solutions are avoided. A recent evaluation has shown that this simple method performs well for slideshows having a homogeneous background, without complex textures (recall 0.54 and precision 0.91)[15].

In the near future, we plan to improve this identification method by considering the color information in order to identify the various background patterns. Finally, we plan to evaluate the performance of our visual signature for identifying low-resolution documents, using or not color information, and to evaluate the performance of our matching techniques on slideshow repositories of various sizes.

6.3   Document Content Extraction and Video Annotation

Both the visual signature and the output of the tool presented in section 3 are in XML. The two XML files are matched in order to extract the textual content of the slides images by considering the textual bounding boxes. The procedure does not require any OCR.

Finally, the slide video is annotated with the extracted data and stored in an XML file. Once the slide change detection is completed, the start and end time of each slide and the corresponding meeting id, are stored in the annotation file. Once the slide image is identified, the original document, in the meeting repository, is attached using XPath. Finally, after the content extraction, the textual content is added.

7   A Document-Centric Multimedia Browsing Interface

Current researches in image and video analysis are willing to automatically create indexes and pictorial video summaries to help users browse through multimedia corpuses [16]. However, those methods are often based on low-level visual features and lack semantic information. Other research projects use language understanding techniques or text caption derived from OCR, in order to create more powerful indexes and search mechanisms [17]. Our assumption is that in a large proportion of multimedia applications (e.g. lectures, meetings, news, etc.), classical printable documents play a central role in the thematic structure of discussions. Further, we believe printable documents could provide a natural and thematic mean for browsing and searching through large multimedia repository.

Our prototype of document-centric multimedia meeting browser is illustrated in figure 2 and then on figure 3. First of all, figure 2 presents our cross-meeting browser, allowing a thematic search and browsing on a multimedia archive. All the newspaper articles, stored in the press reviews archive, are plotted on the visualization according to user request (e.g. "Bush, Irak, Sharon, etc."). The most

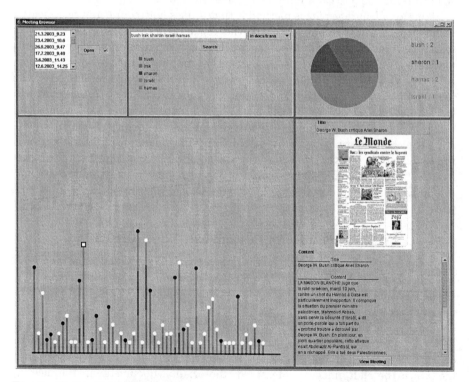

Fig. 2. All the documents relevant to a query, i.e. a set of keywords, are visualized. Clicking on one article of a newspaper retrieves the related multimedia data and opens the document-centric meeting browser displayed at the time the article was discussed or projected (cf. fig. 3)

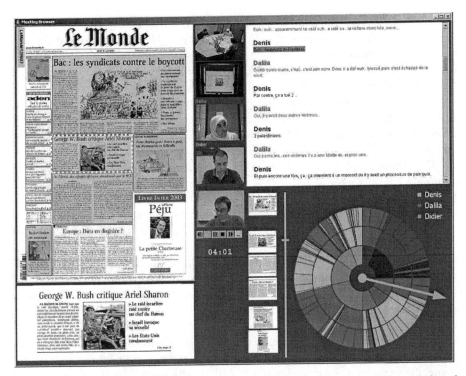

Fig. 3. The document-centric meeting browser. This prototype has been developed in Java (using Batik and JMF). All the components (documents discussed and documents projected, audio/video, transcription, visualizations) are synchronized through the meeting time, thanks to the document alignments

relevant articles are returned by the system and organized spatially according to the user keywords; the higher is an article, represented as a white circle, on the visualization, the more it contains user keywords and thus answers the user request. Further, the relative participation of each keyword is represented using histograms. The horizontal axis represents the date of the meeting in which the article was projected or discussed. This way, the visualization also indicates the evolution of a theme throughout the time. On the same visualization, the speech transcript for each meeting, represented as a black circle, is plotted following the same visualization rules. In fact, this cross-meeting browser allows visualizing quickly an important number of meetings, and favours a thematic browsing of the meeting archive, using not only the meetings speech transcript but also the content of the documents, discussed or projected during the meetings, as entry points to the meeting archive.

When the user selects an article, the corresponding meeting recordings are opened at the time when the article was discussed or projected. On figure 3, our intra-meeting browser is presented; it is composed of the following components: the documents in focus on the left, on top documents discussed and under documents projected, the audio/video clips in the middle, the structured transcription of the meeting dialogs on the right part, and finally the chronograph visualization on the bottom-right of the interface. All the representations are synchronized, meaning they all have the same time reference, and clicking on one of them causes all the components to visualize their content at the same time. For instance, clicking on a journal article positions audio/video clips at the time when it was discussed, positions the speech transcription at the same time, and displays the document that was projected. These visual links directly illustrate the document/speech and document/video alignments presented above in the article.

The chronograph visualization at the bottom-right of figure 3 represents the complete meeting's duration. It is a visual overview of the overall meeting and can serve as a control bar. Each layer stands for a different temporal annotation: speaker turns, utterances, document blocks and slides projected. Other annotations can be displayed depending on the meeting type (topics, silences, dialog acts, pen-strokes for handwritten notes, gesture, etc.). Those temporal annotations are currently stored in the form of XML files, which hold timestamps for each state change (i.e. new speaker, new topic, slide change, etc.) and spatial information for documents. For example, the speech transcript contains speaker turns, divided in speech utterances, with their corresponding start and end times.

Furthermore, the chronograph visualization is interactive; users can click on any pie slice of a circle layer in order to access a specific moment of the meeting, a specific topic or a specific document article, thanks to the document/speech alignment. On the document side, clicking on an article places the audio/video sequences at the moment when the content of this document block is being discussed and it highlights the most related articles in other documents. This is a direct illustration of document/speech and document/document alignments. The chronograph or other similar visualizations reveal some potential relationships between sets of annotations, synergies or conflicts, and can bring to light new methods in order improve the automatic generation of annotations.

At the time of writing, 22 meetings, of roughly 15 minutes each, have been integrated in our meeting browser, both at the cross-meetings and intra-meeting levels. Based on those data, a preliminary user evaluation of this document-centric browser has been performed on 8 users. The goal was to measure the usefulness of document alignments for browsing and searching through a multimedia meeting archive. Users' performance in answering questions, both uni-modal and multimodal schemas (e.g. "Which articles from the New York Times have been discussed by Denis?"), have been measured on both qualitative and quantitative basis (e.g. task duration, number of clicks, satisfaction, etc.).

Users browsing meetings using document alignments solved 76% of the questions and users browsing meetings without the document alignments solved 66% of the questions. The performance difference becomes particularly significant for multi-modal questions, i.e. requiring information both from the speech transcript and from document discussed or projected. In this case, around 70% of the questions were solved when users were benefiting from the alignments and only half of the questions were solved without the alignments.

8   Conclusion

This article proposes four steps for bridging the gap between static documents and multimedia meeting data. A document analysis tool first builds a multi-layered representation of documents and creates indexes that are further used by document alignment methods. In particular, document/speech and document/video alignment methods have been presented along with preliminary evaluations. Finally, a document-enabled browsing system, taking advantage of the integration of the four steps, has been described.

The work presented in this article has demonstrated that considering electronic documents used during meetings as an additional modality improves significantly the usefulness of recorded meetings. On the one hand, it brings in additional information useful for the thematic analysis and automatic structuring of a meeting; on the other hand, at the browser level, when linked with other media, documents provide a natural user interface for navigating efficiently through multimedia meeting archives.

Acknowledgments

We would like to thank the University of Applied Sciences of Fribourg for helping to set up the capture environment, and Maurizio Rigamonti and Karim Hadjar who greatly contributed to the advancement of the electronic document analysis tool.

References

1. Bett, M., Gross, R., Yu, H., Zhu, X., Pan, Y., Yang, J., Waibel, A.: Multimodal meeting tracker. In: Conference on Content-Based Multimedia Information Access, RIAO 2000, Paris, France (2000)
2. Brotherton, J.A., Bhalodia, J.R., Abowd, G.D.: Automated capture, integration, and visualization of multiple media streams. In: IEEE International Conference on Multimedia Computing and Systems. (1998) 54
3. Chiu, P., Kapuskar, A., Reitmeier, S., Wilcox, L.: Room with a rear view: meeting capture in a multimedia conference room. In: IEEE Multimedia. Volume 7:4. (2000) 48–54
4. Cutler, R., Rui, Y., Gupta, A., Cadiz, J., Tashev, I., He, L.w., Colburn, A., Zhang, Z., Liu, Z., Silverberg, S.: Distributed meetings: a meeting capture and broadcasting system. In: 10th ACM International Conference on Multimedia, Juan les Pins, France (2002) 503–512
5. Hunter, J., Little, S.: Building and indexing a distributed multimedia presentation archive using SMIL. In: 5th European Conference on Research and Advanced Technology for Digital Libraries. (2001) 415–428
6. Mukhopadhyay, S., Smith, B.: Passive capture and structuring of lectures. In: 7th ACM International Conference on Multimedia, Orlando, FL, USA (1999) 477–487
7. Lalanne, D., Sire, S., Ingold, R., Behera, A., Mekhaldi, D., von Rotz, D.: A research agenda for assessing the utility of document annotations in multimedia databases of meeting recordings. In: 3rd Workshop on Multimedia Data and Document Engineering, Berlin, Germany (2003)

8. Hadjar, K., Rigamonti, M., Lalanne, D., Ingold, R.: Xed: a new tool for extracting hidden structures from electronic documents. In: International Workshop on Document Image Analysis for Libraries, Palo Alto, CA, USA (2004) 212–224
9. Lalanne, D., Mekhaldi, D., Ingold, R.: Talking about documents: revealing a missing link to multimedia meeting archives. In: Document Recognition and Retrieval XI, IS&T/SPIE's International Symposium on Electronic Imaging 2004, San Jose, CA (2000) 82–91
10. Klemmer, S.R., Graham, J., Wolff, G.J., Landay, J.A.: Books with voices: paper transcripts as a physical interface to oral histories. In: Conference on Human Factors in Computing Systems, CHI 2003, Ft. Lauderdale, FL, USA (2003) 89–96
11. Wellner, P.: Interacting with paper on the digitaldesk. In: Communications of the ACM. Volume 36:7. (1993) 86–96
12. Mekhaldi, D., Lalanne, D., Ingold, R.: Thematic segmentation of meetings throught document/speech alignment. In: 12th ACM International Conference on Multimedia, New York, NY, USA (2004)
13. Popescu-Belis, A., Lalanne, D.: Reference resolution over a restricted domain: References to documents. In: ACL 2004 Workshop on Reference Resolution and its Applications, Barcelona, Spain (2004) 71–78
14. Behera, A., Lalanne, D., Ingold, R.: Looking at projected documents: Event detection & document identification. In: IEEE International Conference on Multimedia and Expo, ICME 2004, Taiwan (2004)
15. Behera, A., Lalanne, D., Ingold, R.: Visual signature based identification of low-resolution document images. In: ACM Symposium on Document Engineering, Milwaukee, WI, USA (2004)
16. Uchihashi, S., Foote, J., Girgensohn, A., Boreczky, J.: Video manga: generating semantically meaningful video summaries. In: 7th ACM International Conference on Multimedia, Orlando, FL, USA (1999) 383–392
17. Smith, M.A., Kanade, T.: Video skimming and characterization through the combination of image and language understanding techniques. In: International Workshop on Content-Based Access of Image and Video Databases, CAIVD 1998, Bombay, India (1998) 61–70

An Integrated Framework for the Management of Video Collection

Nicolas Moënne-Loccoz*, Bruno Janvier,
Stéphane Marchand-Maillet, and Eric Bruno

Viper group - CVMlab - University of Geneva,
Computer Science Department - 24 rue du General Dufour 1211,
Geneva 4 Switzerland
Nicolas.Moenne-Loccoz@cui.unige.ch

Abstract. Video document retrieval is now an active part of the domain of multimedia retrieval. However, unlike for other media, the management of a collection of video documents adds the problem of efficiently handling an overwhelming volume of temporal data. Challenges include balancing efficient content modeling and storage against fast access at various levels. In this paper, we detail the framework we have built to accommodate our developments in content-based multimedia retrieval. We show that not only our framework facilitates the developments of processing and indexing algorithms but it also opens the way to several other possibilities such as rapid interface prototyping or retrieval algorithms benchmarking. In this respect, we discuss our developments in relation to wider contexts such as MPEG-7 and The TREC Video Track.

1 Motivations

Video data processing has for long been of high interest for the developments of compression and efficient transmission algorithms. In parallel, the domain of content-based multimedia retrieval has developed, initially from text retrieval, then for images and now addressing video content retrieval. Whereas in text and image retrieval, the volume of data and associated access techniques are well under control, this is largely not the case for video collection management. Not only video data volume may rapidly grow complex and huge but it also requires efficient access techniques associated to the temporal aspect of the data.

Efforts in video content modeling such as MPEG-7 are providing a base for the solution to the problem of handling large amount of temporal data. MPEG-7 formalizes the definition of temporal points associated with any relevant information along the multimedia stream. This way, every local or global descriptor may be associated with a temporal reference point or interval within a multimedia document.

* This work is funded by EU-IST project M4 (www.m4project.org) and the Swiss NCCR IM2 (Interactive Multimodal Information Management).

S. Bengio and H. Bourlard (Eds.): MLMI 2004, LNCS 3361, pp. 101–110, 2005.

In this paper, we present the framework we have constructed for the management of our video document collection. Rather than presenting a temporal document model alone, our ultimate goal is to develop content characterization and indexing algorithms for the management of large video collections. When addressing such problems, one rapidly faces the need for a favorable context on which to base these developments and also that permit rapid and objective evaluation of research findings. ¿From an extensible multimedia document model, we have built a database framework comprising all needed reference information of raw video documents. Efficient access to the original is ensured by a generic accessor called OVAL that we have embedded within several prototyping platforms. This way, we are combining the benefits of a classical DBMS for rapid access to indexed description data with the efficient random access capabilities of our platform.

In section 2, we review the model we propose for a multimedia documents and associated description data. In section 3, we detail how we may create the required data associated with each video document. Section 4 presents access techniques that we have created to and from this data repository. In section 5, we show how our framework has been used to develop and evaluate novel video content characterization and indexing algorithms. Throughout the paper, we briefly discuss the relation between our developments and common efforts with in particular the TRECVid Retrieval Evaluation challenge.

2   Temporal Document Modeling

The design of our framework is centered around the concept of temporal information. We consider that any part of our data store can be associated with a temporal stamp. The data itself may be located within either of the three layers depicted in figure 2. Namely, we follow a hierarchical scheme able to embed heterogeneous data such as an audio-visual (AV) stream (video) associated with metadata and a set of keyframes (still pictures), themselves described by textual annotations.

More formally, our scheme comprises:

- **Document Information** : global information about each document including meta-information and raw-data information. (Subsets of the *creation information, media information* and *usage information* of the MPEG-7 standard)
- **Document structure** : the temporal decomposition of video documents that comes from the temporal segments covered by the description data.
- **Document description** : the set of description data that is either automatically extracted (*feature-based*) or entered manually by human operators. (*semantic annotation*)

2.1   Modeling the Temporal Dimension

The key part of our model is the temporal decomposition of each document. We take the temporal dimension as a feature common to all modalities (visual,

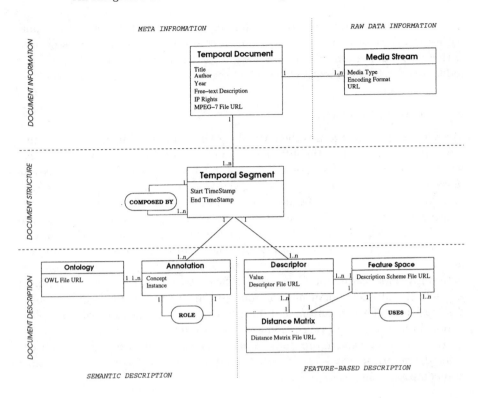

Fig. 1. Conceptual Model of a Video corpus representation

audio, textual) and exploit this property to create relations between pieces of information. By contrast, any other possible decomposition such as that proposed by the MPEG-7 standard would become an extra information attached to a particular information stream (eg, the spatial decomposition of a keyframe).

The notion of a *temporal segment* is therefore the central building block for our model. It is initially defined as a continuous temporal interval over the multimedia stream S:

$$I_a^b(S) = [a, b], \forall\, a, b \text{ s.t } 1 \leq a \leq b \leq T_S \tag{1}$$

where T_S is the total length of the stream. In the most general case, a temporal segment may also be an arbitrary composition of such intervals.

$$I_{(a_k)}^{(b_k)}(S) = \bigcup_k I_{a_k}^{b_k}, k = 1, \cdots, n \tag{2}$$

Any temporal pattern may therefore be defined within our scheme. The aim is to create logical temporal entities with which to associate combined multimedia information. Since no absolute temporal reference may be used, the definition makes sense only in association to a particular document (as identified by its *document information*).

The converse is also true. To be valid, any piece of information should come with a temporal reference. In particular, a complete document S is associated with $I_1^{Ts}(S)$ and any partition of S with a partition of that interval. Thus, our model readily copes concurrent temporal segmentations of a given document.

2.2   Description Spaces

Temporal segments organize the data along the temporal dimension. We define a further classification of the information contained in the *document description* layer (the temporal information) into main categories. We define the *asserted description* as the description that is given from an external knowledge source and the *deduced description* as being a description inferred or computed from the multimedia stream itself. Typically, the asserted description may be provided by a human operator annotating the document in question and therefore be located at a rather high semantic level. The deduced description is computed automatically and corresponds to the document features extracted from the data itself. This distinction places us in a favorable context for the development and test of multimedia information processing algorithms. For example, deduced description will form an automated characterization that the asserted description may help in evaluating (see section 5 for an example).

In order to implement our data model, the distinction to consider is between *semantic description* and *feature-based description*, which corresponds to distinct and complementary storage modes.

Semantic Description. We normalize external knowledge by the use of an **ontology**. The semantic description therefore lists the set of instances of concepts (as defined by the ontology) that occur within the given temporal segment. This scheme allows us to use generic multimedia annotation frameworks such as that given by the Semantic Web (see [4] for a more detailed proposition). As a complement, associations between instances may be created, according to their possible *roles*, as defined by the ontology. Note that our proposed model is directly able to represent different semantic descriptions, using different ontologies.

Clearly, tradeoffs are to be determined between the complexity of the ontology used and the level of description needed. An important factor to take into account is also the complexity of the annotation, strongly related to the size of the ontology at hand. In our research-oriented scheme however, the semantic description plays a crucial role. It provides a semantic organization of the content that may be used for high-level querying and browsing the collection, and for training or evaluation of classification or recognition algorithms.

Feature-Based Description. The main goal of our framework is to store, organize and create relations between automatically computed features. These are seen as a description deduced on a particular temporal segment. A feature-based description (or simply, a descriptor) of a multimedia content is defined in relation to a feature space. In the general case, a descriptor attached to a temporal segment corresponds to a set of points or a trajectory within that feature space. Further, as some descriptors may be computed from other descriptors (e.g. shape descriptor computed on a spatial segmentation), feature spaces may be related through a *uses* relationship. Here again, our model closely matches the underlying architecture of the feature extraction procedures used.

For the sake of simplicity, simple descriptors are represented by their values. In the most complex case, we use external files storing these values. Descriptors may also be seen as pre-computations over several temporal segments. In this case, for fast access, distance matrices are also stored, representing the structure of the feature space for a given document collection.

Our framework therefore provides an efficient way to store output of multimedia stream content analysis algorithms for evaluation or comparison purposes. The co-existence of both levels of description within an unified repository makes it easy to define evaluation or supervised training procedures. Further, as a complement to the semantic description, the feature-based representation of the temporal segments opens the way to construct query and browsing mechanisms.

3   Entering the Data

We have mapped our model onto a database schema. Our database currently handles more than 60GB of video data coming from the two corpora gathered by the MPEG-7 and the TREC Video Retrieval Evaluation (2003) communities. This heterogeneous set of videos contains many genres, including sport, sitcom series, variety program, TV news and documentaries. It illustrates typical TV broadcast by the variety of its content and is widely used as a benchmark for video analysis and indexing tasks.

We have processed the raw documents, in order to extract low-level information about their temporal structure (shot detection), their activity content (camera displacement, regions of activity, event) and their global color distribution. The speech transcripts extracted by Automatic Speech Recognition (ASR) at LIMSI laboratory [2] and all data made available on the TRECVid data are also stored in the database. These descriptors, associated to pre-computed distance matrix, provide us various viewpoints on the raw documents according to their intrinsic audio-visual properties. In parallel with these automatic processes, we have manually annotated part of the collection, not only to enrich the description, but also to efficiently evaluate our algorithms.

3.1   Semantic Annotations

The database is enriched with semantic descriptions of the documents. These annotations rely on an ontology based on the lexicon of the TRECVid Collaborative Annotation Forum [5] (figure 2). This ontology is centered around the concept of a video shot. It is widely acknowledge that shots form essential semantic elements of a video stream. However, within our data model, shots are a particular case of temporal segments. Thus, others ontologies may be used based for example on the concept of *scene* (set of visually correlated shots) or

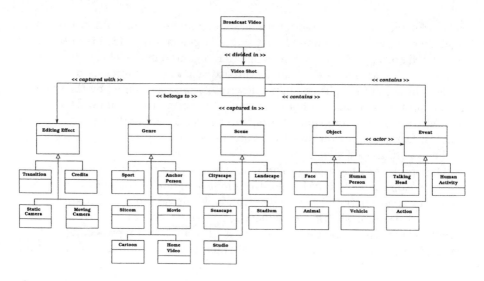

Fig. 2. Ontology for semantic annotation of video documents

story (set of semantically correlated shots). This simple ontology creates annotations that provide us sufficient information for easy access to our database content and corresponds well to the documents features we wish to characterize automatically (eg, editing effects, human face, *etc*).

3.2   Data Processing

As already mentioned, our goal is to facilitate multimedia data processing and organize the storage and access of the data and its associated description. Here, we detail raw data processing that leads to storing data descriptions within our framework. In section 5, we give the example of a complete application based on our framework.

Temporal Partitioning. Since the temporal structure of multimedia documents is central to our framework, the first step we take is to achieve temporal segmentation of multimedia streams. This approach is compatible with the fact of considering a video shot as a temporal unit for subsequent processing.

An automatic algorithm for video temporal segmentation based on the minimization of an information-based criterion has been developed [3]. It offers very good detection performance for abrupt as well as smooth transitions between shots. The algorithm proceeds according to the following steps.

The video content is first abstracted by a color dissimilarity profile using classic color histogram and the Jeffrey divergence. The complexity of further processing is then reduced by easily detecting non-ambiguous events such as hard transitions and sequences of still-frames. An information-based segmentation is performed using a minimum message length criterion and a Dynamic

Table 1. Performances of the shot boundaries detection algorithm

Performances	Our algorithm	Hardcut detection alone
Recall	86.2	67.6
Precision	77.2	78.8

Programming algorithm. This parameter-free algorithm uses information theoretic arguments to find the partitioning which agrees with the Occam's razor principle : the simplest model that explains data is the one to be preferred.

At this stage, we obtain temporal segments whose definition is not guaranteed to match that of a shot. Since we see this level of decomposition as containing useful information, it is stored within our database. However, to remain compatible with other studies, a final merging algorithm uses statistical hypothesis testing to group together segments that are unlikely to form different shots.

As a first example of evaluation facilitated by our framework, table 1 presents the results of an experience using 70 videos of the TRECVid corpus and the evaluation framework of [7]. We used 35 hours of news programs and the ground truth provided by the TRECVid community.

From these results, we have built confidence in our algorithm and used its results for the processing of streams where ground-truth was not available.

Event-Based Feature Space. We present a final example of processing exploiting our framework and illustrating its capabilities to facilitate event-based collection-wide access to multimedia information [1].

In an unsupervised context, we apply nonlinear temporal modeling of wavelet-based motion features directly estimated from the image sequence within a shot. Based on SVM-regression, this nonlinear model is able to learn the behavior of the motion descriptors along the temporal dimension and to capture useful information about the dynamic content of the shot. An inter-shot similarity measure based on this activity characterization is then applied to documents within our repository. The similarity measure is defined as a quadratic error between models. We are therefore able to compute similarity matrix at the collection level that we store within our repository. In section 5, we show how to construct and evaluate a complete application based on these computations.

4   Exploring the Database

We now have a data repository that stores structured temporal audio-visual data enriched with low-level and semantic data. Basic access is given by our DBMS. The underlying model opens access to data using a document reference and a given temporal point within it. From there, any information related to that temporal point may be extracted. Subsequent links with other temporal points may be defined, based on the various notions of similarity we have created.

4.1   Assessing Data

Our storage scheme enables easy access to any part of a document from a reference to that document, along with a temporal segment. We have developed a suitable software framework, called OVAL (Object-based Video Access Library [6]) that permits random access of data on AV streams. Typically, OVAL offers a common API on AV streams so as to emancipate from the actual type of storage used for that particular stream (advantages of particular storage modes may however still be accessed, such as motion vector within a MPEG-2 stream). One advantage of OVAL on other data access libraries is that its abstraction enables generic VCR-like operations and also adds random access facility to data streams. For example, using OVAL a keyframe in a video stream is retrieved on-line by the sequence of open, goto and extract operations, thus avoiding duplication of data that may become obsolete. OVAL includes index pre-computation and buffering facilities so as to make the use of these operations as efficient as possible.

OVAL is written in C++ and wrapped into a MATLAB MEX mechanism to allow for easy video and audio frame access within MATLAB. A Java JNI extension of OVAL is also proposed.

4.2   Querying Documents

OVAL and our DBMS now form our base for query audio-visual data. ¿From this setup, we have constructed a global access framework that makes transparent data access at various levels and from different modes.

Documents may first be queried explicitly by attributes known to be present within their associated description (eg comprised within the ontology used in the case of annotations). Attributes here may either be textual or by values of features. In that sense, a document fully matches or not the query.

Similarity queries are also available. Similarity derives from ongoing studies described in sections 3 and 5. Currently, we may combine several access techniques including textual matching of descriptions (directly supported by the DBMS), content-based visual similarity to similarity based on motion pattern, handled by external prototypes of indexing engines.

5   Example Applications

Finally, we see, as an appliclation, a situation where having an efficient data access and storage framework is crucial for objective systematic evaluation of our algorithms.

We have mentioned in section 3.2 the evaluation of our temporal partitioning procedure against external ground-truth. We have also evaluated the above video retrieval application by testing its ability to discriminate events within videos. Using the ontology defined in 3.1, we have defined three types of generic event classes:

Fig. 3. Precision-Recall graph for three events. Horizontal lines represent the percentage of each label in the database (numerical values are given in titles)

- **Action** corresponds to high activity events, such as sport and dance sequences.
- **Human activity** corresponds to events representing human or crowd walking or doing large gestures.
- **Talking head** corresponds to close-up view on talking people, such as anchor scenes in news, dialog scenes in sitcom.

More than 800 video shots have been manually annotated by one of these three labels, or the label *null* when shots do not contain any of these three events (30% of the documents). Each document was then used as base for a query by similarity over the whole set of documents. Resulting Precision-Recall graphs averaged over each of the three above classes are presented in figure 3.

6   Conclusion

We are advocating the use of an advanced data storage and retrieval framework for the development and evaluation of multimedia processing algorithms. We have based the development of our framework around the temporal properties of the data to be stored. Within our data model, raw data, annotations and extracted features coexist and may even overlap along the temporal dimension. Although not explicitly using any standard, we remain fully compatible with alternative description schemes such as MPEG-7 while not being constrained by their syntax or structure.

We have presented an application that we have based on our framework. We believe that the use of such a framework is unavoidable for the development of video indexing and retrieval applications. We further showed that the very same framework may also serve for the evaluation. Duality between development and evaluation is made evident using an incremental annotation scheme whereby ground-truth is incrementally built for subsequent processing or objective systematic evaluation. Further developments will address the test and extension of our models to handle richer multimedia data. We are also ready to accommodate and process new data coming from forthcoming TRECVid 2004.

References

1. Eric Bruno and Stéphane Marchand-Maillet. Nonlinear temporal modeling for motion-based video overviewing. In *Proceedings of the European Conference on Content-based Multimedia Indexing, CBMI'03*, September 2003.
2. J.L. Gauvain, L. Lamel, and G. Adda. The limsi broadcast news transcription system. *Speech Communication*, 37(1-2):89–108, 2002.
3. Bruno Janvier, Eric Bruno, Stéphane Marchand-Maillet, and Thierry Pun. Information-theoretic framework for the joint temporal partioning and representation of video data. In *Proceedings of the European Conference on Content-based Multimedia Indexing, CBMI'03*, September 2003.
4. Carlo Jelmini and Stéphane Marchand-Maillet. DEVA: an extensible ontology-based annotation model for visual document collections. In R. Schettini and S. Santini Eds, editors, *Proceedings of SPIE Photonics West, Electronic Imaging 2002, Internet Imaging IV*, Santa Clara, CA, USA, 2003.
5. Ching-Yung Lin, Belle L. Tseng, and John R. Smith. Video collaborative annotation forum: Establishing ground-truth labels on large multimedia datasets. In *Proceedings of the TRECVID 2003 Workshop*, 2003.
6. Nicolas Moënne-Loccoz. OVAL: an object-based video access library to facilitate the developement of content-based video retrieval systems. Technical report, Viper group - University of Geneva, 2004.
7. R. Ruiloba, P. Joly, S. Marchand-Maillet, and Georges Quenot. Towards a standard protocol for the evaluation of video-to-shots segmentation algorithms. In *International Workshop in Content-Based Multimedia Indexing (CBMI)*, 1999.

The NITE XML Toolkit Meets the ICSI Meeting Corpus: Import, Annotation, and Browsing*

Jean Carletta and Jonathan Kilgour

University of Edinburgh, HCRC Language Technology Group,
2 Buccleuch Place, Edinburgh EH8 9LW, Scotland, UK
{jeanc, jonathan}@inf.ed.ac.uk

Abstract. The NITE XML Toolkit (NXT) provides library support for working with multimodal language corpora. We describe work in progress to explore its potential for the AMI project by applying it to the ICSI Meeting Corpus. We discuss converting existing data into the NXT data format; using NXT's query facility to explore the corpus; hand-annotation and automatic indexing; and the integration of data obtained by applying NXT-external processes such as parsers. Finally, we describe use of NXT as a meeting browser itself, and how it can be used to integrate other browser components.

1 Introduction

The AMI project is developing meeting browsing technology. This requires multimodal data to be captured and annotated for a wide range of properties that are of use to the browser, reflecting not just low level properties like who is speaking, gesturing, or standing up when, but also properties that are less easy to read directly off signal, such as when the group has reached a decision and what the decision was. Here the intention is to hand-annotate the information required and then to use that to derive similar annotation automatically, either via statistical modelling, symbolic processing based on the understanding of the data that the hand-annotation affords, or a combination of the two. Finally, the automatically derived annotations must be made accessible to the browser. Data annotation and search are therefore central to the browsing technology.

In this paper, we describe work in progress to explore the possible uses of the NITE XML Toolkit [1, 2] within the AMI project. NXT, although it is relatively new, has been successfully deployed to annotate and search a range of data sets, and many of the uses relate to AMI concerns. Although the main concern for its users is to publish their core research, there are some reports about how NXT contributed to the work that are in the public domain [3, 4]. Taken together, the existing uses suggest that NXT could be helpful for AMI work not just in NXT's core areas of hand-annotation and data exploration, but for other purposes as

---

* This work was carried out under funding from the European Commission (AMI, FP6-506811).

S. Bengio and H. Bourlard (Eds.): MLMI 2004, LNCS 3361, pp. 111–121, 2005.

well. During the initial stages of the project, several partners are prototyping their methods using the ICSI Meeting Corpus, which differs from the proposed AMI data in several ways (not least in being audio-only) but has the advantage of being available now. We discuss converting the existing data into the NXT data format; using NXT's query facility to explore the corpus; hand-annotation and automatic indexing; and the integration of data obtained by applying NXT-external processes such as parsers. Finally, we describe use of NXT as a meeting browser itself, and how it can be used to integrate other browser components.

2   The ICSI Meeting Corpus

The ICSI Meeting Corpus [5], available from the Linguistic Data Consortium (catalog number LDC2004S02) is a corpus of meetings recorded at the International Computer Science Institute in Berkeley. The data set consists of 75 natural meetings from ICSI's own research groups, recorded using both close-talking and far field microphones. Transcription is also available (LDC2004T04) and is given in XML files, one per meeting, where the meeting is divided into timestamped segments that contain the words as textual content. Segments change at utterance boundaries (that is, whenever there is a major pause for one speaker) and otherwise whenever the transcribers found it convenient to insert a timestamp. There is sometimes an intermediate tag between the words and their containing segments in order to indicate some quality of importance to speech recognition, such as emphasis. Such tags are also used to indicate places where the transcriber was uncertain of the correct transcription, where foreign language phrases are used and where pronounciation diverges significantly from normal or expected pronounciation variations. There are also the usual tags interspersed among the words, familiar from the Text Encoding Initiative [6], for indicating the placement of things like pauses and nonvocal and vocal sounds, and for transcriber comments. The textual transcription itself also contains punctuation, including left- and right-handed quotation marks. This includes the use of hyphens to punctuate the moment of interruption in disfluencies, and underscores occur after capitalized letters to indicate that the letter name has been pronounced. Otherwise mixed case and punctuation in the transcription are used at the transcriber's discretion and tend to mirror written English.

In addition to this base data, several sites have annotated it for various types of information, with more types of annotation planned. So far, we have worked with two of the existing annotations. The first of these is dialogue act annotation using the MRDA tagset [7]. The basic dialogue act annotation gives start and end times, speaker, and the words for each tag. The SRI speech recognizer has been used to produce a forced alignment of the words in each act, and so the dialogue act annotation also contains the start and end times for each word. Meanwhile, hot spot annotation [8] simply gives start and end times for sections of the meeting during which the participants were unusually animated. Both the dialogue act and hot spot annotation are distributed separately from the main corpus, the former in a comma-separated value format and the latter in a tab-delimited format.

3 The NITE XML Toolkit

The core of NXT consists of two types of functionality: routines that load, access, manipulate, and save data according to a particular data model; and an engine that evaluates queries expressed in NXT's Query Language (NQL). Several groups plan library support with similar functionality, of which the Atlas project is perhaps the closest in style [9]. The furthest developed of these is the Annotation Graph Toolkit (AGTK) [10]. NXT differs from AGTK in two ways. First, its data model and query language are oriented towards those users who build descriptive analyses of heavily cross-annotated multimodal corpora in preparation for defining appropriate statistical models, and therefore it allows easy access to an expressive range of data relationships, at the expense of processing speed. Second, it supplements the data and query facilities with library routines for building displays and interfaces based on Java Swing. The libraries include a default top level interface that allows one to choose an observation (in this case, a meeting) and a tool to run on it from those registered in the corpus metadata; audio and video players; a search interface for running queries and displaying the results; basic display layouts such as text areas and trees that synchronize with the data and with the media and search facilities; and standard utilities for things like opening an observation and saving some annotation. These libraries are intended to make it possible to build tailored end user tools at low cost. There is also a default data display that is never as good as a tailored one but at least allows any corpus in the correct format to be viewed and searched without further programming.

4 Conversion to NXT Data Format

The first step in testing NXT on the ICSI Meeting Corpus was to transform the data into NXT's stand-off XML storage format. NXT represents the data for one meeting as a related set of XML files, with a "metadata" file that expresses information about the structure and location of the files. For corpora such as this one that contain timing information, NXT stores data for each participant separately. This is because the data in one NXT file must follow a strict temporal order, but speech from different speakers can overlap. Relationships among files are represented using stand-off links that reference individual elements using a filename and id; in one of the possible link syntaxes ranges can be expressed, with the meaning that the relationship holds from the first to the last element in the range. Figure 1 gives an extract across the files for words, dialogue acts, and speech quality tags for one agent in one meeting in order to show that both the links and the individual files are quite simple in structure.

4.1 Orthography

Since the orthography was already in an XML format, up-translation was relatively easy. We first divided the orthographically transcribed segments from the original by speaker. Although we wished to preserve the original segmentation,

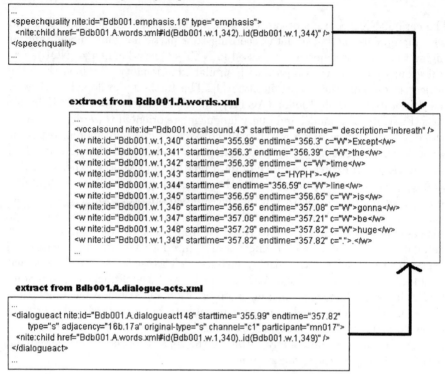

extract from Bdb001.A.speech-quality.xml

```
...
<speechquality nite:id="Bdb001.emphasis.16" type="emphasis">
  <nite:child href="Bdb001.A.words.xml#id(Bdb001.w.1,342)..id(Bdb001.w.1,344)" />
</speechquality>
...
```

extract from Bdb001.A.words.xml

```
...
<vocalsound nite:id="Bdb001.vocalsound.43" starttime="" endtime="" description="inbreath" />
<w nite:id="Bdb001.w.1,340" starttime="355.99" endtime="356.3" c="W">Except</w>
<w nite:id="Bdb001.w.1,341" starttime="356.3" endtime="356.39" c="W">the</w>
<w nite:id="Bdb001.w.1,342" starttime="356.39" endtime="" c="W">time</w>
<w nite:id="Bdb001.w.1,343" starttime="" endtime="" c="HYPH">-</w>
<w nite:id="Bdb001.w.1,344" starttime="" endtime="356.59" c="W">line</w>
<w nite:id="Bdb001.w.1,345" starttime="356.59" endtime="356.65" c="W">is</w>
<w nite:id="Bdb001.w.1,346" starttime="356.65" endtime="357.08" c="W">gonna</w>
<w nite:id="Bdb001.w.1,347" starttime="357.08" endtime="357.21" c="W">be</w>
<w nite:id="Bdb001.w.1,348" starttime="357.29" endtime="357.82" c="W">huge</w>
<w nite:id="Bdb001.w.1,349" starttime="357.82" endtime="357.82" c=".">.</w>
...
```

extract from Bdb001.A.dialogue-acts.xml

```
...
<dialogueact nite:id="Bdb001.A.dialogueact148" starttime="355.99" endtime="357.82"
      type="s" adjacency="16b.17a" original-type="s" channel="c1" participant="mn017">
  <nite:child href="Bdb001.A.words.xml#id(Bdb001.w.1,340)..id(Bdb001.w.1,349)" />
</dialogueact>
...
```

Fig. 1. Example file and link structure

it was felt that most new annotations should point either directly to words or to new, more theoretically motivated segments. For this reason, the old segments were pulled out into a separate file that applications could load or fail to load at will. Words are represented in their own flat file along with other transcription elements such as silences and anchors that represent the placement of disfluencies. In the original, speech quality tags (such as those for emphasis) came between segments and transcription elements; this is inconvenient for many kinds of processing because these tags only occur sporadically. For this reason, we pulled these tags out into a separate file that points to words independently of the original containing segments.

NXT's references between files are based on XML element IDs. This means that in order to have the segments and speech quality tags reference words, we needed to tokenize the transcription. In order to do this we altered a pre-existing tokenization algorithm [11] to take into account some of the conventions of the ICSI transcription. Our tokenization attempts to encode the information given by syntactic conventions used in the ICSI data in a systematic way. For example we aim to provide a word token containing the string "ICSI" whether or not the letters are pronounced separately or they are pronounced together as

"Icksy". Information about the pronounciation is encoded in an attribute value. Our tokenization is designed to split words into the minimal units that might be required should we wish to apply natural language processing the data, so for example hyphenated words are normally split into their constituent parts with a "HYPH" token between them.

4.2   Dialogue Acts and Hot Spots

Although the file format for the dialogue act annotation is simple, up-translation was nontrivial because we needed to transfer the dialogue acts onto the top of the newly tokenized orthography, preserving both the timestamping from the former and the non-word content from the latter. This was made more complex by the fact that the dialogue acts did not cover all of the spoken words, in particular where the transcription was not taken from close-talking microphones, and in some relatively rare cases where the forced alignment between transcript and audio signals failed. There is one part of the ICSI meeting data that is routinely transcribed but deliberately does not form a part of the dialogue acts: the "Digits Task" where meeting participants read out strings of digits. For an individual speaker, words in the orthography and in the acts came in the same order, but this was the only property the input data guaranteed. The algorithm that we devised traversed the two inputs in parallel, running through the orthography until it found a match for the words to the next act. It then considered the left and right context up to the immediately preceding and following words in order to decide whether or not to assimilate non- word content into the move. In the left context, we assimilated any preceding left-handed quotation mark. In the right context, content was assimilated up until the last punctuation (excluding left-handed quotation marks) before the following word.

We have one side comment about the process of developing a strategy for translating the dialogue act annotation: it was easier to know what to do once we understood what the data contained, and NXT was itself useful for this purpose. Our first step in the translation process was to transform the dialogue act annotation into a rival segmentation and transcription in NXT format and load both it and the original into a simple NXT display. This allowed us compare the versions visually; where the alignment was not obvious we were able to use the search highlighting to find which segments overlapped which dialogue acts. We could also search, e.g., for segments that did not overlap with any dialogue act and for words from the orthography that did not match any words with compatible timings from the dialogue acts.

The hot spot annotation was trivial to translate because it only consists of tags with start and end times that are independent of any other data. We transformed it into a separate XML file containing a flat list of tags.

5   Hand Annotation

One of the strengths of NXT's library-based approach to GUI support is that it allows new tools that support new kinds of hand-annotation to be built. Our

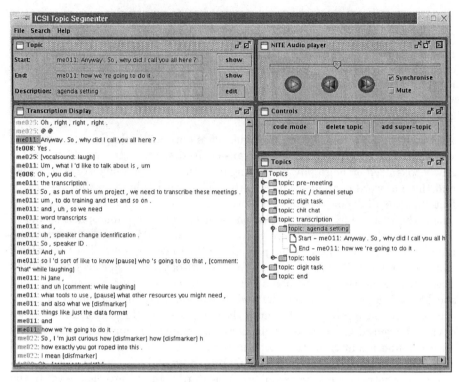

Fig. 2. A tool for hierarchical topic segmentation built using NXT

current priorities for this data set are a kind of hierarchical topic segmentation and a variant of Bales' Interaction Process Analysis [12, 13]. A preliminary screenshot for the former is shown in figure 2. NXT has been used for a range of other annotations that may also be of interest on this data, including coreference, named entities, the linking of gestures to deictic language, and an n-way classification of utterances by the type of information they contain in preparation for argument-based summarization.

Although NXT's libraries have some facilities for editing annotation times, they are designed primarily for adding structural information, such as that required for linguistic annotation, over the top of some existing time- stamped segmentation of the data, such as orthographic or gestural transcription. Thus we expect time-aligned data to be constructed using some other tool as input to NXT. This could include transcription tools like The Transcriber [14], time-aligned coding tools such as The Observer [15], Anvil [16], or TASX [17], or automatic derivation from signal.

6   Automatic Annotation

NXT provides a facility for automatic indexing based on query language matches for queries expressed in NQL. This is primarily for caching intermediate results of complicated queries that will be needed again, although it is also useful for adding theoretically motivated constructs to the data. For instance, one project has employed this facility in order to identify "markables", or the sorts of entities which contribute to information structure and to coreferential relationships, based on prior syntactic annotation [3]. This facility may be of use within AMI, especially for positing higher level structures from annotations that are closer to signal. Simple queries in NQL express variable bindings for n-tuples of objects, optionally constrained by type, and give a set of conditions on the n-tuples combined with boolean operators. The defined operators for the condition tests allow full access to the timing and structural relationships of the data. A complex query facility passes variable bindings from one query to another for filtering, returning a tree structure. To give the flavour of the query language, consider the following example.

```
($a w):(TEXT($a) ~ /th.*/)::
    ($s speechquality):($s ∧ $a) && ($s@type="emphasis")
```

On this data set, this query finds instances of words starting with "th", and then for each finds instances of speech quality tags of type emphasis that dominate the word, discarding any words that are not dominated by at least one such tag in the process. The query returns a tree structured index into the data with words at the first level down from the root and the emphasis tags below them. Return values can be saved in NXT format, in which case they can be co-loaded with the data set itself. In general, queries provide a very flexible mechanism for data processing.

NQL has its limits, both in terms of what can be expressed in it and the speed at which queries are applied, and it will of course be convenient to add annotation by other means. Because NXT stores data in a standard format and because it divides an entire data set into several files that are in themselves quite simple, this is relatively easy to do. Some natural language processing tools, such as those available from [18] for part of speech tagging and chunking, work natively on XML data. Many useful annotations, such as word counts and durations for segments, can be added using a simple XSLT stylesheet. It is often useful to supplement this approach with fsgmatch, an XML transduction mechanism that provides good support for regular expressions, and xmlperl, a stylesheet language that has access to perl programming statements. Both of these are also available from [18]. Recourse to non-XML processes requires translation to and from the required format, although it is sometimes possible within xmlperl to set up communication with the external process so that the stylesheet transforms information into the right format, streams it externally, accepts the output back, and reintegrates it. Another useful technique is passing XML ids through the external process as an extra field so that output can be spliced into the original XML data. However an annotation has been added, the metadata must be modified to reflect the change, a process that in distributed data annotation requires careful management.

Because of the way in which NXT breaks up a data set into files, it is often possible to send single files for external processing. For when this is not the case, we are currently developing a number of utilities that create new XML documents with tree structures that draw elements from across a data set using the stand-off pointers and that explode a tree back into the correct component structures, complete with any modifications.

7   Browser Component Integration

NXT widgets have two useful properties built in: registration with a central clock that allows a set of signal and data displays to synchronize with each other, and the highlighting of query results on a data display. These two properties are exactly what is needed for a meeting browser, since together they allow users to navigate around the meeting by time or by properties of interest, albeit ones currently expressed in a rather formal language. Figure 3 shows the screenshot of a very simple NXT-based browser. When the user evaluates a query and selects part of the result, the corresponding part of the data display is highlighted in grey. As one plays the audio signal, the data corresponding to the current time is highlighted in green. It is possible to play extracts corresponding to particular annotations, although due to limitations in the libraries underlying the current NXT implementation, the start and end times of the extracts are approximate. Whatever kinds of annotations a data set contains, a browser can be built for them. An Edinburgh student project, for instance, has used NXT to compare a meeting transcription with extractive summaries derived from it using several different approaches.

Anything can be an NXT data display with time and search highlighting as long as it implements the interfaces that NXT widgets themselves use to provide these properties. This raises the interesting prospect that integrating a new component into a meeting browser could be a matter of implementing these interfaces – that is, that AMI meeting browsers could themselves be NXT applications.

One AMI project partner has gone partway to proving that the most important part of this approach, time synchronization, will work by demonstrating NXT with a radically different kind of display than the text-based ones that come in the interface library. The demonstration is of coding head orientation by manipulating a coffee cup instrumented with a "flock-of-birds" motion sensor, where the cup's handle is a convenient stand-in for the nose. An on-screen display based on the Java 3D graphics libraries provides feedback whilst coding or for replay. As the video plays, the coder captures and writes new annotations for head orientation every frame. The partner reports that implementing the TimeHandler interface that makes the system work was simple to do [19].

Performance will be an issue with this approach if NXT is used unadulterated, especially when the browser is used to look at a series of meetings. Streaming data in a radically non-tree-structured data model such as NXT's is still a research issue, and NXT's design is predicated on the assumption that graphical

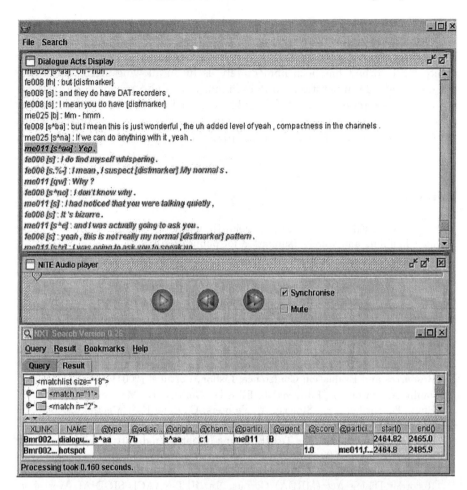

Fig. 3. A simple NXT-based meeting browser that places one dialogue act per line and shows hotspots italicized and in red, with a user search highlighting one dialogue act by speaker me011 during a hotspot

user interfaces will only be required for a limited amount of data at a time. We believe this difficulty can be overcome by loading the individual XML files that make up an NXT data set incrementally and building external indices into the data model for the properties of most importance to the browser. Integrating non-Java components is theoretically possible but has not yet been attempted, nor has the interface that enables search highlighting been implemented for anything apart from textual displays. Thus this approach to brower component integration looks promising, but proving that it is useful requires future work.

8 Conclusions

Translating the basic ICSI Meeting Corpus plus other existing annotations for it into NXT format has been immediately useful in allowing us to understand the data and add annotations to it by hand. It has also provoked an interesting thought exercise in how NXT could be used for some kinds of automatic annotation that are necessary for browsing meetings, as well as providing the mechanism by which different meeting browser components could be integrated.

References

1. Carletta, J., Kilgour, J., Evert, S., Heid, U., Chen, Y.: The NITE XML Toolkit: data handling and search. (submitted for publication)
2. Carletta, J., Evert, S., Heid, U., Kilgour, J., Robertson, J., Voormann, H.: The NITE XML Toolkit: flexible annotation for multi-modal language data. Behavior Research Methods, Instruments, and Computers **35** (2003) 353–363
3. Carletta, J., Dingare, S., Nissim, M., Nikitina, T.: Using the NITE XML Toolkit on the Switchboard Corpus to study syntactic choice: a case study. In: Fourth Language Resources and Evaluation Conference, Lisbon, Portugal (2004)
4. Heid, U., Voormann, H., Milde, J.T., Gut, U., Erk, K., Pad, S.: Querying both time-aligned and hierarchical corpora with NXT Search. In: Fourth Language Resources and Evaluation Conference, Lisbon, Portugal (2004)
5. Janin, A., Baron, D., Edwards, J., Ellis, D., Gelbart, D., Morgan, N., Peskin, B., Pfau, T., Shriberg, E., Stolcke, A., Wooters, C.: The ICSI Meeting Corpus. In: ICASSP, Hong Kong (2003)
6. TEI Consortium: TEI: The Text Encoding Initiative (n.d.) http://www.tei-c.org/; accessed 26 May, 2003.
7. Shriberg, E., Dhillon, R., Bhagat, S., Ang, J., Carvey, H.: The ICSI Meeting Recorder Dialog Act (MRDA) Corpus. In: HLT-NAACL SIGDIAL Workshop, Boston (2004)
8. Wrede, B., Shriberg, E.: Spotting "hot spots" in meetings: Human judgements and prosodic cues. In: EUROSPEECH, Geneva (2003)
9. National Institute of Standards, Technology: ATLAS Project (2000) http://www.nist.gov/speech/atlas/; last update 6 Feb 2003; accessed 1 Mar 2004.
10. Linguistic Data Consortium: AGTK: Annotation Graph Toolkit (n.d.) http://agtk.sourceforge.net/; accessed 1 Mar 2004.
11. Grover, C., Matheson, C., Mikheev, A., Moens, M.: LT TTT - a flexible tokenisation tool. In: Second International Conference on Language Resources and Evaluation (LREC 2000). Volume 2. (2000) 1147–1154
12. Bales, R.F.: Social Interaction Systems: Theory and Measurement. Transaction Publishers (1999)
13. Bales, R.F.: Interaction Process Analysis: A method for the study of small groups. Addison-Wesley, Cambridge, MA (1951)
14. Barras, C., Geoffrois, E., Wu, Z., Liberman, M.: Transcriber: development and use of a tool for assisting speech corpora production. Speech Communication **33** (2000) special issue, Speech Annotation and Corpus Tools.

15. Noldus, L., Trienes, R., Hendriksen, A., Jansen, H., Jansen, R.: The Observer Video-Pro: new software for the collection, management, and presentation of time-structured data from videotapes and digital media files. Behavior Research Methods, Instruments & Computers **32** (2000) 197–206
16. Kipp, M.:   Anvil - a generic annotation tool for multimodal dialogue.   In: Seventh European Conference on Speech Communication and Technology (EUROSPEECH), Aalborg (2001) 1367–1370
17. Milde, J.T., Gut, U.: The TASX-environment: an XML-based corpus database for time aligned language data. In Bird, S., Buneman, P., Liberman, M., eds.: Proceedings of the IRCS Workshop on Linguistic Databases. University of Pennsylvania, Philadelphia (2001) 174–180 Anvil look-alike; open source.
18. University of Edinburgh Language Technology Group: LTG Software (n.d.) http://www.ltg.ed.ac.uk/software/; accessed 1 Mar 2004.
19. Reidsma, D. personal communication, (2004) 11 March.

S-SEER: Selective Perception in a Multimodal Office Activity Recognition System[*],[**]

Nuria Oliver and Eric Horvitz

Adaptive Systems & Interaction,
Microsoft Research Redmond,
WA USA
{nuria, horvitz}@microsoft.com

Abstract. The computation required for sensing and processing perceptual information can impose significant burdens on personal computer systems. We explore several policies for selective perception in SEER, a multimodal system for recognizing office activity that relies on a cascade of Hidden Markov Models (HMMs) named Layered Hidden Markov Model (LHMMs). We use LHMMs to diagnose states of a user's activity based on real-time streams of evidence from video, audio and computer (keyboard and mouse) interactions. We review our efforts to employ expected-value-of-information (EVI) to limit sensing and analysis in a context-sensitive manner. We discuss an implementation of a greedy EVI analysis and compare the results of using this analysis with a heuristic sensing policy that makes observations at different frequencies. Both policies are then compared to a random perception policy, where sensors are selected at random. Finally, we discuss the sensitivity of ideal perceptual actions to preferences encoded in utility models about information value and the cost of sensing.

1 Introduction

Investigators have long pursued the dream of building systems with the ability to perform automatic recognition of human behavior and intentions from observations. Successful recognition of human behavior enables compelling services and applications, including the provision of appropriate help and assistance, automated visual surveillance and multimodal user interfaces —user interfaces that allow human-computer interaction via perceptual channels such as acoustical and visual analyses. Such systems can employ representations of a user's *context* and reason about the most appropriate control and services in different settings. There has been progress on multiple fronts in recognizing human

---

[*] @ACM,2003. This is a minor revision of the work published in the 5th International Conference on Multimodal Interfaces, 2003, pp. 36–43. http://doi.acm.org/10.1145/958432.958442.

[**] @ELSEVIER,2004. Parts of the paper have been reprinted from "Layered Representations for Learning and Inferring Office Activity from Multiple Sensory Channels", published in the Computer Vision and Image Understanding Journal, Volume 96, N. 2, 2004, pp. 163–180, Oliver et al.

S. Bengio and H. Bourlard (Eds.): MLMI 2004, LNCS 3361, pp. 122–135, 2005.
© Springer-Verlag Berlin Heidelberg 2005

behavior and intentions. However, challenges remain for developing machinery that can provide rich, human-centric notions of context in a tractable manner.

We address in this paper the computational burden associated with perceptual analysis. Computation for visual and acoustical analyses has typically required a large portion, if not nearly all, of the total computational resources of personal computers that make use of such perceptual inferences. Thus, we have pursued principled strategies for limiting in an automated manner the computational load of perceptual systems.

For a testbed, we have considered the allocation of perceptual resources in SEER, a multimodal, probabilistic reasoning system that provides real-time interpretations of human activity in and around an office [1]. We have explored different strategies for sensor selection and sensor data processing in SEER. The result is a new system named S-SEER, or *Selective* SEER.

This paper is organized as follows: We first provide background on multimodal systems and principles for guiding perception in these systems in Section 2. In Section 3 we describe the challenge of understanding human activity in an office setting and review the perceptual inputs that are used. We also provide background on the legacy SEER system, focusing on our work to extend a single-layer implementation of HMMs into a more effective cascade of HMMs, that we refer to as Layered Hidden Markov Models (LHMMs). Section 4 describes the three selective perception strategies that we have studied in experiments: EVI-based, rate-based and random-based perception. In Section 5 we review the implementation of S-SEER. Experimental results with the use of S-SEER are presented in Section 6. Finally, we summarize our work in Section 7.

2   Prior Related Work

Human Activity Recognition. Most of the prior work on leveraging perceptual information to recognize human activities has centered on the identification of a specific type of activity in a particular scenario. Many of these techniques are targeted at recognizing single events, *e.g.*, "waving the hand" or "sitting on a chair". Over the past few years, there has been increasing work on methods for identifying more complex patterns of human behavior, including patterns extending over increasingly long periods of time. A significant portion of work in this arena has harnessed Hidden Markov Models (HMMs) [2] and extensions. Starner and Pentland in [3] use HMMs for recognizing hand movements used to relay symbols in American Sign Language. More complex models, such as Parameterized-HMMs [4], Entropic-HMMs [5], Variable-length HMMs [6], Coupled-HMMs [7], structured HMMs [8] and context-free grammars [9] have been used to recognize more complex activities such as the interaction between two people or cars on a freeway.

Moving beyond the HMM representation and solution paradigm, researchers have investigated more general temporal dependency models, such as dynamic Bayesian networks. Dynamic Bayesian networks have been adopted by several researchers for the modeling and recognition of human activities [10, 11, 12, 13, 14, 15].

We have explored the use of a layering of probabilistic models at different levels of temporal abstraction. We have shown that this representation allows a system to learn and recognize in real-time common situations in office settings [1]. Although the methods have performed well, a great deal of perceptual processing has been required by the system, consuming most of the resources available by personal computers. We have thus been motivated to explore strategies for selecting on-the-fly the most informative features, starting with the integration of decision-theoretic approaches to information value for guiding perception.

Principles for Guiding Perception. Decision theory centers on representations and principles for deciding among alternative courses of action under uncertainty. At the heart of decision theory are the axioms of utility, desiderata about preferences under uncertainty. The axioms imply the Principle of Maximum Expected Utility (MEU), which asserts that the best action to take is the one associated with the highest expected utility. The engineering discipline of Decision Analysis has developed a rich set of tools, methods and practices on top of the theoretical foundations of Decision Theory. Expected Value of Information (EVI) refers to the expected value of making observations under uncertainty, taking into consideration the probability distribution over values that would be seen should an observation be made. In practice, EVI computations can be used to identify MEU decisions with regards to information gathering actions.

The connection between decision theory and perception received some attention by AI researchers studying computer vision tasks in the mid-70's, but interest faded for nearly a decade. Decision theory was used to model the behavior of vision modules [16], to score plans of perceptual actions [17] and plans involving physical manipulation with the option of performing simple visual tests [18]. This early work introduced decision-theoretic techniques to the perceptual computing community.

Following this early research, was a second wave of interest in applying decision theory in perceptual applications in the early 90's, largely for computer vision systems [19] and in particular in the area of active vision search tasks [20].

3   Toward Robust Context Sensing

Before focusing on the control of perceptual actions, let us discuss in more detail the domain and original SEER office-awareness prototype. We shall turn to selective perception for HMM-centric multimodal systems in Section 4.

A key challenge in inferring human-centric notions of context from multiple sensors is the fusion of low-level streams of raw sensor data—for example, acoustic and visual cues—into higher-level assessments of activity. We have developed a probabilistic representation based on a tiered formulation of dynamic graphical models that we refer to as Layered Hidden Markov Models (LHMMs) [1]. For recognizing office situations, we have explored the challenge of fusing information from the following sensors:

1. Binaural microphones: Two mini-microphones (20 − 16000 Hz, SNR 58 dB) capture ambient audio information and are used for sound classification and localization. The audio signal is sampled at 44100 KHz.

2. Camera: A video signal is obtained via a standard Firewire camera, sampled at 30 f.p.s, that is used to determine the number of persons present in the scene.

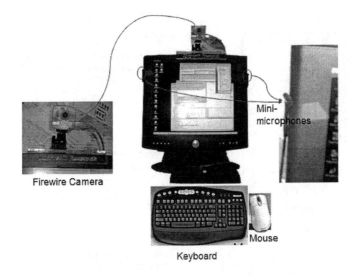

Fig. 1. Hardware utilized in the SEER system

3. **Keyboard and mouse:** SEER keeps a history of keyboard and mouse activities during the past 1, 5 and 60 seconds.

Figure 1 illustrates the hardware configuration used in the SEER system.

3.1   Hidden Markov Models (HMMs)

In early work on SEER we explored the use of single-layer hidden Markov models (HMMs) to reason about an overall office situation. Graphically, HMMs are often depicted "rolled-out in time". We found that a single-layer HMM approach generated a large parameter space, requiring substantial amounts of training data for a particular office or user. The single-layer model did not perform well: the typical classification accuracies were not high enough for a real application. Also, when the system was moved to a new office, copious retraining was typically necessary to adapt the model to the specifics of the signals and/or user in the new setting. Thus, we sought a representation that would be robust to typical variations within office environments, such as changes of lighting and acoustics, and models that would allow the system to perform well when transferred to new office spaces with minimal tuning through retraining.

3.2   Layered Hidden Markov Models (LHMMs)

We converged on the use of a multilayer representation that reasons in parallel at multiple temporal granularities, by capturing different levels of temporal detail. We formulated a layered HMM (LHMM) representation that had the ability to decompose the parameter space in a manner that reduced the training and tuning requirements. In LHMMs, each layer of the architecture is connected to the next layer via its inferential results. The representation segments the

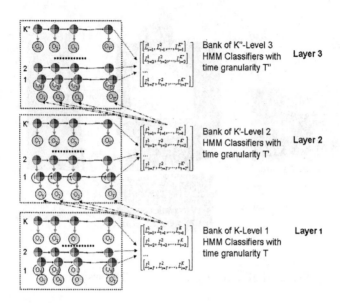

Fig. 2. Graphical representation of LHMMs with 3 different levels of temporal granularity

problem into distinct layers that operate at different temporal granularities[1] —allowing for temporal abstractions from pointwise observations at particular times into explanations over varying temporal intervals. LHMMs can be regarded as a cascade of HMMs. The structure of a three-layer LHMM is displayed in Figure 2.

The layered formulation of LHMMs makes it feasible to decouple different levels of analysis for training and inference. As we review in [1], each level of the hierarchy is trained independently, with different feature vectors and time granularities. In consequence, the lowest, signal-analysis layer, that is most sensitive to variations in the environment, can be retrained, while leaving the higher-level layers unchanged. Figure 2 highlights how we decompose the problem into layers with increasing time granularity.

4   Selective Perception Policies

Although the legacy SEER system performs well, it consumes a large portion of the available CPU time to process video and audio sensor information to

---

[1] The "time granularity" in this context corresponds to the window size or vector length of the observation sequences in the HMMs.

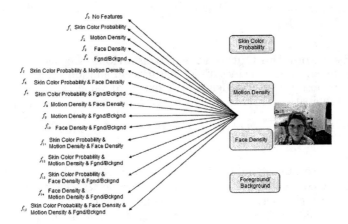

Fig. 3. Possible feature combinations for the vision sensor

make inferences. We integrated into SEER several methods for selecting features dynamically.

4.1 EVI for Selective Perception

We focused our efforts on implementing a principled, decision-theoretic approach for guiding perception. Thus, we worked to apply *expected value of information* (EVI) to determine dynamically which features to extract from sensors in different contexts.

We compute the expected value of information for a perceptual system by considering the value of eliminating uncertainty about the state of the set of features $f_k, k = 1...K$, under consideration. For example, as illustrated in Figure 3, the features associated with the vision sensor (camera) are motion density, face density, foreground density and skin color density in the image[2]. There are $K = 16$ possible combinations of these features and we wish the system to determine in real-time which combination of features to compute, depending on the context[3].

Perceptual Decisions Grounded in Models of Utility. We wish to guide the sensing actions with a consideration of their influence on the global expected utility of the system's performance under uncertainty. Thus, we need to endow the perceptual system with knowledge about the value of action in the world. In our initial work, we encoded utility as the cost of misdiagnosis by the system. We assess utilities, $U(M_i, M_j)$, as the value of asserting that the real-world activity

---

[2] By "density" we mean the number of pixels in the image that, for example, have motion above a certain threshold, divided by the total number of pixels in the image.

[3] In the following we will refer to features instead of sensors, because one can compute different features for each sensor input –e.g. skin density, face density, motion density, etc, for the camera sensor.

M_i is M_j. In any context, a maximal utility is associated with the accurate assessment of M_j as M_j.

Uncertainty About the Outcome of Observations. Let us take $f_k^m, m = 1...M$ to denote all possible values of the feature combination f_k, and E to refer to all previous observational evidence. The expected value (EV) of computing the feature combination f_k is,

$$EV(f_k) = \sum_m P(f_k^m|E) \max_i \sum_j P(M_j|E, f_k^m) U(M_i, M_j) \tag{1}$$

As we are uncertain about the value that the system will observe when it evaluates f_k, we consider the change in expected value associated with the system's overall output, given the current probability distribution of the different values m that would be obtained if the features in f_k would in fact be computed, $P(f_k^m|E)$.

The expected value (EVI) of evaluating a feature combination f_k is the difference between the expected utility of the system's best action when observing the features in f_k and not observing them, minus the cost of sensing and computing such features, $cost(f_k)$. If the net expected value is positive, then it is worth collecting the information and therefore computing the features.

$$EVI(f_k) = EV(f_k) - \max_i \sum_j P(M_j|E) U(M_i, M_j) - cost(f_k) \tag{2}$$

where $cost(f_k)$ is in our case the computational cost associated with computing feature combination f_k. Perceptual systems normally incur significant cost with the *computation* of the features from the sensors. Thus, we trade the information value of observations with the cost due to the analysis required to make the observations. Note that all the terms in Equation 2 should have the same units. Traditionally, EVI approaches convert all the terms to dollars. In our case, we use a scale factor for the $cost(f_k)$.

EVI in HMMs Our probabilistic modules are HMMs, with one HMM per class. In the case of HMMs, with continuous observation sequences $\{O_1, ..., O_t, O_{t+1}\}$ and an observation space of M dimensions (after discretization[4]), the EVI of features f_k is given by:

$$EVI \propto \sum_{m=1}^{M} \sum_n [\sum_s \alpha_t^n(s) \sum_l a_{sl}^n b_l^n(O_{t+1}^{f_k^m})] P(M_n)$$
$$\max_i \sum_j U(M_i, M_j) p(M_j) - \max_i \sum_j U(M_i, M_j) p(M_j) - cost(O_{t+1}^{f_k})$$

where $\alpha_t^n(s)$ is the alpha or forward variable at time t and state s in the standard Baum-Welch algorithm [21], a_{sl}^n is the transition probability of going from state s to state l, and $b_l^n(O_{t+1}^{f_k^m})$ is the probability of observing $O_{t+1}^{f_k^m}$ in state l, all of them in model M_n.

---

[4] In S-SEER M is typically 10.

The computational overhead added to carry out the EVI analysis is –in the discrete case– $O(M * F * N^2 * J)$, where M is the maximum cardinality of the features, F is the number of feature combinations, N is the maximum number of states in the HMMs and J is the number of HMMs.

4.2   Alternative Perception Policies

In order to better understand the properties of the EVI approach, we have developed alternative methods for selective perception. We explored, in a second selective perception policy, a heuristic, rate-based approach. This policy consists of defining an observational frequency and duty cycle (*i.e.* amount of time during which the feature is computed) for each feature f. With this approach, each feature f is computed periodically. The period between observations and the duty cycle of the observation is determined by means of cross-validation on a validation set of real-time data.

For another baseline policy, we developed a simple random-selection method, where features are selected randomly for use on a frame-by-frame basis. In this case, the average computational cost of the system is constant, independent of the current sensed activity, and lower than the cost of computing all of the features all the time.

5   Implementation of S-SEER

S-SEER operates the same way as its predecessor, SEER, except in the availability of several selection perception policies. Figure 4 illustrates S-SEER's architecture. For clarity, we shall include a brief summary of the core system and move onto the details of experiments with selective perception in Section 6.

5.1   Core Learning and Inference

SEER consists of a two-level LHMM architecture with three processing layers. For a more detailed description we direct the reader to [1].

The raw sensor signals are preprocessed to obtain feature vectors (*i.e.* observations) for the first layer of HMMs.

With respect to the audio analysis, Linear Predictive Coding coefficients [2] are computed. Feature selection is applied to these coefficients via principal component analysis. The number of features is selected such that at least 95% of the variability in the data is maintained, which is typically achieved with no more than 7 features. We also extract other higher-level features from the audio signal such as its energy, the mean and variance of the fundamental frequency over a time window, and the zero crossing rate [2]. The source of the sound is localized using the Time Delay of Arrival (TDOA) method.

Four features are extracted from the video signal: the density of skin color in the image (obtained by discriminating between skin and non-skin models, consisting of histograms in YUV color space), the density of motion in the image (obtained by image differences), the density of foreground pixels in the image (obtained by background subtraction, after having learned the background), and

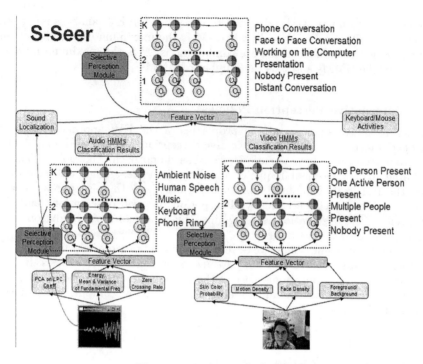

Fig. 4. Architecture of S-SEER

the density of face pixels in the image (obtained by means of a real-time face detector).

Finally, a history of the last 1, 5 and 60 seconds of mouse and keyboard activities is logged.

First Level HMMs. The first level of HMMs includes two banks of distinct HMMs for classifying the audio and video feature vectors. The structure for each of these HMMs is determined by means of cross-validation on a validation set of real-time data. On the audio side, we train one HMM for each of the following office sounds: *human speech, music, silence, ambient noise, phone ringing*, and the sounds of *keyboard typing*. In our architecture, all the HMMs are run in parallel. At each instant, the model with the highest likelihood is selected and the data −*e.g.* sound in the case of the audio HMMs− is classified correspondingly. We will refer to this kind of HMMs as *discriminative* HMMs. The video signals are classified using another bank of discriminative HMMs that implement a person detector. At this level, the system detects whether *nobody, one person (semi-static), one active person, or multiple people* are present in the office.

Each bank of HMMs can use any of the previously defined selective perception strategies to determine which features to use. For example, a typical scenario is one where the system uses EVI analysis to select in real-time the motion and skin density features when there is *one active person* in the office, and skin density and face detection when there are *multiple people* present.

Second Level HMMs. The inferential results[5] from this layer (*i.e.* the outputs of the audio and video classifiers), the derivative of the sound localization component, and the history of keyboard and mouse activities constitute a feature vector that is passed to the next (third) and highest layer of analysis. This layer handles concepts with longer temporal extent. Such concepts include the user's typical activities in or near an office. In particular, the activities modeled are: (1) *Phone conversation*; (2) *Presentation*; (3) *Face-to-face conversation*; (4) *User present, engaged in some other activity;* (5) *Distant conversation* (outside the field of view); (6) *Nobody present.* Some of these activities can be used in a variety of ways in services, such as those that identify a person's availability.

The models at this level are also discriminative HMMs and they can also use selective perception policies to determine which inputs from the previous layer to use.

5.2   Performance of SEER

We have tested S-SEER in multiple offices, with different users and respective environments for several weeks. In our tests, we have found that the high-level layers of S-SEER are relatively robust to changes in the environment. In all the cases, when we moved S-SEER from one office to another, we obtained nearly perfect performance *without* the need for retraining the higher levels of the hierarchy. Only some of the lowest-level models required re-training to tune their parameters to the new conditions (such as different ambient noise, background image, and illumination) . The fundamental decomposability of the learning and inference of LHMMs makes it possible to reuse prior training of the higher-level models, allowing for the selective retraining of layers that are less robust to the variations present in different instances of similar environments. We direct the reader to [1] for a detailed description of the experiments comparing HMMs and LHMMs for office activity recognition as well as a review of an evaluation of the recognition accuracy of the system.

6   Experiments with Selective Perception

We performed a comparative evaluation of the S-SEER system when executing the EVI, rate-based, and random selective perception algorithms when applied at the highest level of the Layered HMMs architecture. Therefore, in the experiments that follow the selective perception policies will select any combination of four possible sensors: vision, audio, keyboard and mouse activities and sound localization.

6.1   Studies of Accuracy and Computation

In an initial set of studies, we considered diagnostic accuracy and the computational cost incurred by the system. The results are displayed in Tables 1 and 2. We use the abbreviations: PC=Phone Conversation; FFC=Face to Face Conversation; P=Presentation; O=Other Activity; NP=Nobody Present; DC=Distant Conversation.

---

[5] See [1] for a detailed description of how we use these inferential results.

Table 1. Average accuracies and computational costs for S-SEER with and without different selective perception strategies

Recognition Accuracy (%)					Computational Costs (% of CPU time)			
	Nothing	EVI	Rate-based	Random		Nothing	EVI	Rate-based	Random
PC	100	100	29.7	78	PC	61.22	44.5	37.7	47.5
FFC	100	100	86.9	90.2	FFC	67.07	56.5	38.5	53.4
P	100	97.8	100	91.2	P	49.80	20.88	35.9	53.3
O	100	100	100	96.7	O	59	19.6	37.8	48.9
NP	100	98.9	100	100	NP	44.33	35.7	39.4	41.9
DC	100	100	100	100	DC	44.54	23.27	33.9	46.1
	(a)					(b)			

Observations that can be noted from our experiements are: (1) At times the system does not use any features at all, as S-SEER is confident enough about the situation, and it selectively turns the features on only when necessary; (2) the system guided by EVI tends to have longer switching time (*i.e.* the time that it takes to the system to realize that a new activity is taking place) than when using all the features all the time. We found that the EVI computations trigger the use of features again only after the likelihoods of hypotheses have sufficiently decreased, *i.e.* none of the models is a good explanation of the data; (3) in most of our experiments, S-SEER never turned the *sound localization* feature on, due to its high computational cost versus the relatively low informational value this acoustical feature provides.

Tables 1 (a) and (b) compare the average recognition accuracy and average computational cost (measured as % of CPU usage) when testing S-SEER on 600 sequences of office activity (100 sequences/activity) with and without (first column, labeled "Nothing") selective perception. Note how S-SEER with selective perception achieved as high a level of accuracy as when evaluating all the features all the time, but with a significant reduction on the CPU usage. Given S-SEER's –without selective perception– perfect accuracy, one could think that the task is too easy for the model and that is the reason why the selective perception policies have reasonable accuracies as well. We would like to emphasize that the results reflected on the table correspond to a particular test set. In a real scenario, S-SEER's accuracy is on average 95% or higher, leaving still some room for improvement. We are also exploring more challenging scenarios for S-SEER, both in terms of the number of activities to classify from and their complexity.

6.2   Richer Utility and Cost Models

The EVI-based approach experiments previously reported correspond to using an identity matrix as the system's utility model $U(M_i, M_j)$ and a measure of cost $cost(f_k)$, proportional to the percentage of CPU usage. However, we can assess more detailed models that capture a user's preferences about different misdiagnoses in various usage contexts and about latencies associated with computation for perception.

Models of the Cost of Misdiagnosis. As an example, one can assess in dollars the cost to a user of misclassifying M_i as M_j, $i, j = 1...N$ in a specific setting. In one assessment technique, for each actual office activity M_i, we seek the dollar amounts that users would be willing to pay to avoid having the activity misdiagnosed as M_j by an automated system, for all $N-1$ possible misdiagnoses.

Models of the Cost of Perceptual Analysis. In determining a real world measure of the expected value of computation, we also need to consider the deeper semantics of the computational costs associated with perceptual analysis. To make cost-benefit tradeoffs, we map the computational cost and the utility to the same currency. Thus, we can assess cost in terms of dollars that a user would be willing to pay to avoid latencies associated with a computer loaded with perceptual tasks.

We can introduce key contextual considerations into a cost-model. For example, we can condition cost models on the specific software application that has focus at any moment. We can also consider settings where a user is not explicitly interacting with a computer (or is not relying on the background execution of primary applications), versus cases where a user is interacting with a primary application, and thus, at risk of experiencing costly latencies.

We compared the impact of an activity-dependent cost model in the EVI-based perception approach. We run S-SEER on 900 sequences of office activity (150 seq/activity) with a fixed cost model (*i.e.* the computational cost) and an activity-dependent cost model. In the latter case, the cost of evaluating the features was penalized when the user was interacting with the computer (*e.g. Presentation, Person Present-Other Activity*), and it was reduced when there was no interaction (*e.g. Nobody Present, Distant Conversation Overheard*).

Table 2. Impact of a variable cost model in EVI-based selective perception as measured in percentage of time that a particular feature was "ON"

	PC	FFC	P	O	NP	DC		PC	FFC	P	O	NP	DC
Video	86.7	65.3	10	10	78.7	47.3	Video	78	48.7	2	1.3	86	100
Audio	86.7	65.3	10	10	78.7	47.3	Audio	78	40.7	2	1.3	86	100
Sound Loc	0	0	0	0	0	0	Sound Loc	14.7	0	2	1.3	86	100
Kb/Mouse	100	100	27.3	63.3	80.7	100	Kb/Mouse	100	100	53.3	63.3	88	100
Accuracy (%)	100	100	97.8	100	98.9	100	Accuracy (%)	82.27	100	97.7	87.02	98.47	100

(a) Constant Cost   (b) Variable Cost

Table 2 summarizes our findings. It contains the percentage of time per activity that a particular feature was active both with constant costs and activity-dependent costs. Note how the system selects less frequently computationally expensive features (such as video and audio classification) when there is a person interacting with the computer (third and fourth columns in the table) while it uses them more frequently when there is nobody in front of the computer (last two columns in the table). Finally, the last row of each section of the table corresponds to the average accuracy of each approach.

Volatility and Persistence of the Observed Data. We can extend our analysis by learning and harnessing inferences about the persistence versus volatility of observational states of the world. Rather than consider findings unobserved at a particular time slice if the corresponding sensory analyses have not been immediately performed, the growing error for each sensor (or feature computation), based on the previous evaluation of that sensor (or feature) and the time since the finding was last observed, is learned. The probability distribution of how each feature's uncertainty grows over time can be learned and then captured by functions of time. For example, the probability distribution of the skin color feature used in face detection that had been earlier directly observed in a previous time slice can be modeled by learning *via* training data. As faces do not disappear instantaneously –at least typically, approximations can be modeled and leveraged based on previously examined states. After learning distributions that capture a probabilistic model of the dynamics of the volatility versus persistence of observations, such distributions can be substituted and integrated over, or sampled from, in lieu of assuming "not observed" at each step. Thus, such probabilistic modeling of persistence can be leveraged in the computation of the expected value of information to guide the allocation of resources in perceptual systems.

We are currently working on learning the uncertainties for each sensor (feature) from data and applying this approach to our EVI analysis.

7   Summary

We have reviewed our efforts to endow a computationally intensive perceptual system for office activity recognition with selective perception policies. We have explored and compared the use of different selective perception policies for guiding perception in our models, emphasizing the balance between computation and recognition accuracy. In particular, we have compared *EVI-based* perception and *rate-based* perception techniques to a system evaluating all features all of the time all and a random feature selection approach. We have carried out experiments probing the performance of LHMMs in S-SEER, a multi-modal, real-time system for recognizing typical office activities.

Although the EVI analysis adds computational overhead to the system, we have shown that a utility-directed information-gathering policy can significantly reduce the computational cost of the system by selectively activating features, depending on the situation. When comparing the EVI analysis to the rate-based and random approaches, we found that EVI provides the best balance between computational cost and recognition accuracy. We believe that this approach can be used to enhance multimodal interaction in a variety of domains.

We have found that selective perception policies can significantly reduce the computation required by a multimodal behavior-recognition system. Selective perception policies show promise for enhancing the design and operation of multimodal systems–especially for systems that consume a great percentage of available computation on perceptual tasks.

References

1. Oliver, N., Horvitz, E., Garg, A.: Layered representations for human activity recognition. In: Proc. of Int. Conf. on Multimodal Interfaces. (2002) 3–8
2. Rabiner, L., Huang, B.: Fundamentals of Speech Recognition. (1993)

3. Starner, T., Pentland, A.: Real-time american sign language recognition from video using hidden markov models. In: Proceed. of SCV'95. (1995) 265–270

4. Wilson, A., Bobick, A.: Recognition and interpretation of parametric gesture. In: Proc. of International Conference on Computer Vision, ICCV'98. (1998) 329–336

5. Brand, M., Kettnaker, V.: Discovery and segmentation of activities in video. IEEE Transactions on Pattern Analysis and Machine Intelligence **22(8)** (2000)

6. Galata, A., Johnson, N., Hogg, D.: Learning variable length markov models of behaviour. International Journal on Computer Vision, IJCV (2001) 398–413

7. Brand, M., Oliver, N., Pentland, A.: Coupled hidden markov models for complex action recognition. In: Proc. of CVPR97. (1996) 994–999

8. S. Hongeng, F.B., Nevatia, R.: Representation and optimal recognition of human activities. In: Proc. of the IEEE Conference on Computer Vision and Pattern Recognition, CVPR'00. (2000)

9. Ivanov, Y., Bobick, A.: Recognition of visual activities and interactions by stochastic parsing. IEEE Trans. on Pattern Analysis and Machine Intelligence, TPAMI **22(8)** (2000) 852–872

10. Madabhushi, A., Aggarwal, J.: A bayesian approach to human activity recognition. In: In Proc. of the 2nd International Workshop on Visual Surveillance. (1999) 25–30

11. Hoey, J.: Hierarchical unsupervised learning of facial expression categories. In: Proc. ICCV Workshop on Detection and Recognition of Events in Video, Vancouver, Canada (2001)

12. Fernyhough, J., Cohn, A., Hogg, D.: Building qualitative event models automatically from visual input. In: ICCV'98. (1998) 350–355

13. Buxton, H., Gong, S.: Advanced Visual Surveillance using Bayesian Networks. In: International Conference on Computer Vision, Cambridge, Massachusetts (1995) 111–123

14. Intille, S.S., Bobick, A.F.: A framework for recognizing multi-agent action from visual evidence. In: AAAI/IAAI'99. (1999) 518–525

15. Forbes, J., Huang, T., Kanazawa, K., Russell, S.: The batmobile: Towards a bayesian automated taxi. In: Proc. Fourteenth International Joint Conference on Artificial Intelligence, IJCAI'95. (1995)

16. Bolles, R.: Verification vision for programmable assembly. In: Proc. IJCAI'77. (1977) 569–575

17. Garvey, J.: Perceptual strategies for purposive vision. Technical Report 117, SRI International (1976)

18. Feldman, J., Sproull, R.: Decision theory and artificial intelligence ii: The hungry monkey. Cognitive Science **1** (1977) 158–192

19. Wu, H., Cameron, A.: A bayesian decision theoretic approach for adaptive goal-directed sensing. ICCV **90** (1990) 563–567

20. Rimey, R.D.: Control of selective perception using bayes nets and decision theory. Technical Report TR468 (1993)

21. Rabiner, L.R.: A tutorial on hidden Markov models and selected applications in speech recognition. Proceed. of the IEEE **77** (1989) 257–286

Mapping from Speech to Images Using Continuous State Space Models

Tue Lehn-Schiøler, Lars Kai Hansen, and Jan Larsen*

The Technical University of Denmark,
Informatics and Mathematical Modelling,
Richard Petersens Plads, Bld. 321
{tls, lkh, jl}@imm.dtu.dk
www.imm.dtu.dk

Abstract. In this paper a system that transforms speech waveforms to animated faces are proposed. The system relies on continuous state space models to perform the mapping, this makes it possible to ensure video with no sudden jumps and allows continuous control of the parameters in 'face space'.

The performance of the system is critically dependent on the number of hidden variables, with too few variables the model cannot represent data, and with too many overfitting is noticed.

Simulations are performed on recordings of 3-5 sec. video sequences with sentences from the Timit database. From a subjective point of view the model is able to construct an image sequence from an unknown noisy speech sequence even though the number of training examples are limited.

1 Introduction

The motivation for transforming a speech signal into lip movements is at least threefold. Firstly, the language synchronization of movies often leaves the actors mouth moving while there is silence or the other way around, this looks rather unnatural. If it was possible to manipulate the face of the actor to match the actual speech it would be much more pleasant to view synchronized movies (and a lot easier to make cartoons). Secondly, even with increasing bandwidth sending images via the cell phone is quite expensive, therefore, a system that allows single images to be sent and models the face in between would be useful. The technique will also make it possible for hearing impaired people to lip read over the phone. If the person in the other end does not have a camera on her phone, a model image can be used to display the facial movements. Thirdly, when producing agents on a computer (like Windows Office Mr. clips) it would make

---

* The work is supported by the European Commission through the sixth framework IST Network of Excellence: Pattern Analysis, Statistical Modelling and Computational Learning (PASCAL), contract no. 506778.

S. Bengio and H. Bourlard (Eds.): MLMI 2004, LNCS 3361, pp. 136–145, 2005.

communication more plausible if the agent could interact with lip movements corresponding to the (automatically generated) speech.

Lewis [1] provides an early overview paper about state of the art lip-sync in 1991. He concludes that using loudness to control the jaw is not a useful approach since sounds made with closed mouth can be just as loud as open mouth sounds. He also notes that the spectrum matching method used by MIT in the early 1980's has severe problems due to the formants independence of pitch. In this method the shape of the mouth is determined from the frequency content of the speech. The problem is illustrated by the fact that the mouth shape is the same when a sound e.g. an 'a' is spoken with a high or a deep voice. Final he mentions that it is possible to automatically generate speech from text and in this way gain control of what phoneme to visualize. In his view the speech synthesis in 1991 was not of sufficient quality to sound natural, and although progress has been made in the field automatic generated speech is still far from perfect. The suggestion in [1] is to extract phonemes using a Linear Prediction speech model and then map the phonemes to keyframes given by a lip reading chart.

The idea of extracting phonemes or similar high-level features from the speech signal before performing the mapping to the mouth position has been widely used in the lip-sync community. Goldenthal [2] suggested a system called "Face Me!". He extracts phonemes using Statistical Trajectory Modeling. Each phoneme is then associated with a mouth position (keyframe). In Mike Talk [3], phonemes are generated from text and then mapped onto keyframes, however, in this system trajectories linking all possible keyframes are calculated in advance thus making the video more seamless. In "Video rewrite" [4] phonemes are again extracted from the speech, in this case using Hidden Markov Models. Each triphone (three consecutive phonemes) has a mouth sequence associated with it. The sequences are selected from training data, if the triphone does not have a matching mouth sequence in the training data, the closest available sequence is selected. Once the sequence of mouth movements has been determined, the mouth is mapped back to a background face of the speaker. Other authors have proposed methods based on modeling of phonemes by correlational HMM's [5] or neural networks [6].

Methods where speech is mapped directly to facial movement are not quite as popular as phoneme based methods. However, in 'Picture my voice' [7], a time dependent neural network, maps directly from 11×13 Mel Frequency Cepstral Coefficients (MFCC) as inputto 37 facial control parameters. The training output is provided by a phoneme to animation mapping but the trained network does not make use of the phoneme representation. Also Brand [8] has proposed a method based on (entropic) HMM's where speech is mapped directly to images. Methods that do not rely on phoneme extraction has the advantage that they can be trained to work on all languages, and that they are able to map non-speech sounds like yawning or laughing.

There are certain inherent difficulties in mapping from speech to mouth positions an analysis of these can be found in [9]. The most profound is the confusion between visual and auditive information. The mouth position of sounds like /b/,/p/ and /m/ or /k/,/n/ and /g/ can not be distinguished even though the sounds can. Similarly the sounds of /m/ and /n/ or /b/ and /v/ are very similar even though the mouth position is completely different. This is perhaps best illustrated by the famous experiment by McGurk [10]. Thus, when mapping from speech to facial movements, one cannot hope to get a perfect result simply because it is very difficult to distinguish whether a "ba" or a "ga" was spoken.

2   Feature Extraction

Many different approaches have been taken for extraction of sound features. If the sound is generated directly from text [3], phonemes can be extracted directly and there is no need to process the sound track. However, when a direct mapping is performed one can choose from a variety of features. A non-complete list of possibilities include Perceptual Linear Prediction or J-Rasta-PLP as in [11, 8], Harmonics of Discrete Fourier Transform as in [12], Linear Prediction Coefficients as in [1] or Mel Frequency Cepstral Coefficients [2, 7, 6]. In this work

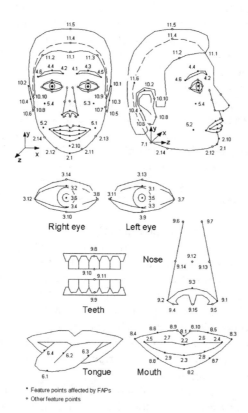

Fig. 1. Facial feature points (from www.research.att.com/projects/AnimatedHead)

Fig. 2. Image with automatically extracted feature points. The facial feature points used are selected from the MPEG-4 standard (Fig. 1), points from main groups 2,3,4,8,10 and 11 are used

the sound is split into 25 blocks per second (the same as the image frame rate) and 13 MFCC features are extracted from each block.

To extract features from the images an Active Appearance model (AAM) [13] is used. The use of this model for lipreading has previously been studied by Mathews et al. [14]. In this work the implementation by Mikkel B. Stegman [15] is used. For the extraction a suitable subset of images in the training set is selected and annotated with points according to the MPEG-4 facial animation standard (Fig. 1). Using these annotations a 14-parameter model of the face is created. Thus, with 14 parameters it is possible to create a photo realistic image of any facial expression seen in the training set. Once the AAM is created the model is used to track the lip movements in the image sequences, at each point the 14 parameters are picked up. In Fig. 2 the result of the tracking is shown for a single representative image.

3   Model

Unlike most other approaches the mapping in this work is performed by a continuous state space model and not a Hidden Markov Model or a Neural Network. The reasoning behind this choice is that it should be possible to change the parameters controlling the face continuously (unlike in HMM) and yet make certain that all transitions happen smoothly (unlike NN's). Currently an experimental comparison of the performance of HMM's and the continuous state space models is investigated.

In this work the system is assumed to be linear and Gaussian and hence the Kalman Filter can be used [16]. This assumption is most likely not correct and other models like particle filtering and Markov Chain Monte Carlo are considered. However, as it will be shown below, even with the simplification the model produces useful results.

The model is set up as follows:

$$\boldsymbol{x}_k = \boldsymbol{A}\boldsymbol{x}_{k-1} + \boldsymbol{n}_k^x \tag{1}$$

$$\boldsymbol{y}_k = \boldsymbol{B}\boldsymbol{x}_k + \boldsymbol{n}_k^y \tag{2}$$

$$\boldsymbol{z}_k = \boldsymbol{C}\boldsymbol{x}_k + \boldsymbol{n}_k^z \tag{3}$$

In this setting $\boldsymbol{z}_k$ is the image features at time k, $\boldsymbol{y}_k$ is the sound features and $\boldsymbol{x}_k$ is a hidden variable without physical meaning, but it can be thought of as some kind of brain activity controlling what is said. Each equation has i.i.d. Gaussian noise component $\boldsymbol{n}$ added to it.

During training both sound and image features are known, and the two observation equations can be collected in one.

$$\begin{pmatrix} \boldsymbol{y}_k \\ \boldsymbol{z}_k \end{pmatrix} = \begin{pmatrix} \boldsymbol{B} \\ \boldsymbol{C} \end{pmatrix} \boldsymbol{x}_k + \begin{pmatrix} \boldsymbol{n}_k^y \\ \boldsymbol{n}_k^z \end{pmatrix} \tag{4}$$

By using the EM algorithm [17, 18] on the training data, all parameters $\{\boldsymbol{A}, \boldsymbol{B}, \boldsymbol{C}, \boldsymbol{\Sigma}^x, \boldsymbol{\Sigma}^y, \boldsymbol{\Sigma}^z\}$ can be found. $\boldsymbol{\Sigma}$'s are the diagonal covariance matrices of the noise components.

When a new sound sequence arrives Kalman filtering (or smoothing) can be applied to equations (1,2) to obtain the hidden state $\boldsymbol{x}$. Given $\boldsymbol{x}$ the corresponding image features can be obtained by multiplication, $\boldsymbol{y}_k = \boldsymbol{C}\boldsymbol{x}_k$. If the intermediate smoothing variables are available the variance on $\boldsymbol{y}_k$ can also be calculated.

4   Results

The data used is taken from the vidtimit database [19]. The database contains recordings of large number of people each uttering ten different sentences while facing the camera. The sound recordings are degraded by fan-noise from the recording pc. In this work a single female speaker is selected, thus 10 different sentences are used, nine for training and one for testing.

To find the dimension of the hidden state ($\boldsymbol{x}$), the optimal parameters ($\{\boldsymbol{A}, \boldsymbol{B}, \boldsymbol{C}, \boldsymbol{\Sigma}\}$) where found for varying dimensions. For each model the likelihood on the test sequence was calculated, the result is shown in Fig. 3.

With few dimensions the model is not rich enough to capture the dynamics of the image sequence. This is illustrated by the spectrogram of a hidden variable which represent the dynamics of the hidden space, as shown in Fig. 4(c). It is noted that only low frequency components are present. As the hidden space gets larger it becomes possible to model more of the dynamics present in the image. The spectrogram of a representative hidden variable when using a 25 dimensional hidden space (Fig. 4(d)) has a structure very similar to what is found in one of the image features (Fig. 4(a)). When increasing the hidden units to 70, the model degrees of freedom becomes large and over fitting becomes possible. Fig. 4(e) and Fig. 4(f) show the spectrogram of two hidden variables and it is seen that the states specializes. In 4(e) high frequencies are dominant, and the other seemingly displays a structure, which resembles the dynamics of the sound features as seen in Fig. 4(b). This is not relevant due to the slower dynamics of the facial expressions. These specializations are furthermore specific to the training set and do not generalize according to Fig. 3. It should be noted that training a large model is difficult, both in terms of computations and convergence. With this analysis in mind a model with 25 hidden units is selected.

The test likelihood provides a measure of the quality of the model in feature space and provides a way of comparing models. This also allows comparison between this model and a similar Hidden Markov Model approach. However, it does not measure the quality of the final image sequence. No precise metric exist for evaluation of synthesized lip sequences. The distance between facial points in the true and the predicted image would be one way, another way would be to measure the distance between the predicted feature vector and the feature vector extracted from the true image. However, the ultimate evaluation of faces can be only provided by human interpretation. Unfortunately it is difficult to get an objective measure this way. One possibility would be to get a hearing impaired person to lipread the generated sequence, another to let people try to guess which sequence was real and which was computer generated. Unfortunately, such test are time and labor demanding and it has not been possible to perform them in this study.

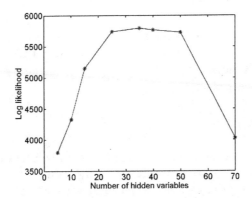

Fig. 3. The likelihood evaluated on the test data. With few hidden variables (dimesions in x space) the model is not rich enough. With too many parameters overfitting is experienced. An optimum is found in the range 25-40 hidden variables

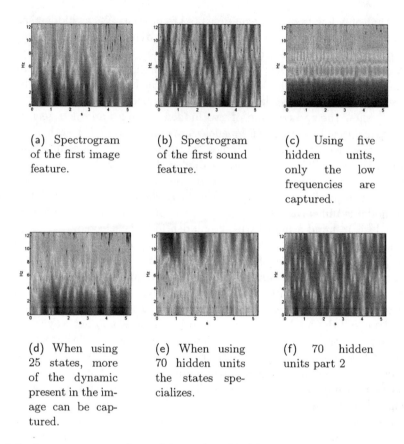

(a) Spectrogram of the first image feature.

(b) Spectrogram of the first sound feature.

(c) Using five hidden units, only the low frequencies are captured.

(d) When using 25 states, more of the dynamic present in the image can be captured.

(e) When using 70 hidden units the states specializes.

(f) 70 hidden units part 2

Fig. 4. In the spectrograms of one of the predicted hidden states of on the test sequence, the effect of varying the size of the state space can be seen. Spectrograms of the first sound and image features are provided for comparison

In Fig. 5 snapshots from the sequence are provided for visual inspection, the entire sequence is available at http://www.imm.dtu.dk/~tls/code/facedemo.php, where other demos can also be found.

5   Conclusion

A speech to face mapping system relying on continuous state space models is proposed. The system makes it possible to easily train a unique face model that can be used to transform speech into facial movements. The training set must contain all sounds and corresponding face gestures, but there are no language or phonetic requirements to what the model can handle.

Surprisingly little attention has previously been paid to the training of state space models. In this paper it is shown that the Kalman filter is able overfit

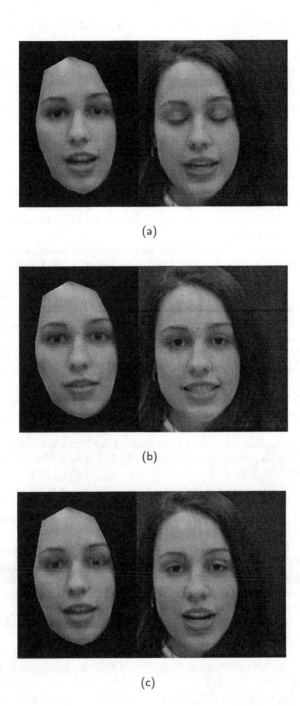

Fig. 5. Characteristic images taken from the test sequence. The predicted face is to the left and the true face to the right

when the number of parameters are too large, similar effects are expected for the Hidden Markov Model.

All though preliminary, the results are promising. Future experiments will show how the Kalman model and other instances of continuous state space models compares to Hidden Markov Model type systems.

References

1. Lewis, J.P.: Automated lip-sync: Background and techniques. J. Visualization and Computer Animation 2 (1991)
2. Goldenthal, W., Waters, K., Jean-Manuel, T.V., Glickman, O.: Driving synthetic mouth gestures: Phonetic recognition for faceme! In: Proc. Eurospeech '97, Rhodes, Greece (1997) 1995–1998
3. Ezzat, T., Poggio, T.: Mike talk: a talking facial display based on morphing visemes. Proc. Computer Animation IEEE Computer Society (1998) 96–102
4. Bregler, C., Covell, M., Slaney, M.: Video rewrite: driving visual speech with audio. In: Proceedings of the 24th annual conference on Computer graphics and interactive techniques, ACM Press/Addison-Wesley Publishing Co. (1997) 353–360
5. Williams, J.J., Katsaggelos, A.K.: An hmm-based speech-to-video synthesizer. IEEE Transactions on Neural Networks 13 (2002)
6. Hong, P., Wen, Z., Huang, T.S.: Speech driven face animation. In Pandzic, I.S., Forchheimer, R., eds.: MPEG-4 Facial Animation: The Standard, Implementation and Applications. Wiley, Europe (2002)
7. Massaro, D.W., Beskow, J., Cohen, M.M., Fry, C.L., Rodriguez, T.: Picture my voice: Audio to visual speech synthesis using artificial neural networks. Proc. AVSP 99 (1999)
8. Brand, M.: Voice puppetry. In: Proceedings of the 26th annual conference on Computer graphics and interactive techniques, ACM Press/Addison-Wesley Publishing Co. (1999) 21–28
9. Lavagetto, F.: Converting speech into lip movements: A multimedia telephone for hard of hearing people. IEEE Trans. on Rehabilitation Engineering 3 (1995)
10. McGurk, H., MacDonald, J.W.: Hearing lips and seeing voices. Nature 264 (1976) 746–748
11. Dupont, S., Luettin, J.: Audio-visual speech modelling for continuous speech recognition. IEEE Transactions on Multimedia (2000)
12. McAllister, D.F., Rodman, R.D., Bitzer, D.L., Freeman, A.S.: Speaker independence in automated lip-sync for audio-video communication. Comput. Netw. ISDN Syst. 30 (1998) 1975–1980
13. Cootes, T., Edwards, G., Taylor, C.: Active appearance models. Proc. European Conference on Computer Vision 2 (1998) 484–498
14. Matthews, I., Cootes, T., Bangham, J., Cox, S., Harvey, R.: Extraction of visual features for lipreading. Pattern Analysis and Machine Intelligence, IEEE Transactions on 24 (2002) 198 –213
15. Stegmann, M.B., Ersbøll, B.K., Larsen, R.: FAME - a flexible appearance modelling environment. IEEE Transactions on Medical Imaging 22 (2003) 1319–1331
16. Kalman, R.E.: A new approach to linear filtering and prediction problems. Transactions of the ASME–Journal of Basic Engineering 82 (1960) 35–45

17. Dempster, A.P., Laird, N.M., Rubin, D.B.: Maximum likelihood from incomplete data via the EM algorithm. JRSSB **39** (1977) 1–38
18. Ghahramani, Z., Hinton, G.: Parameter estimation for linear dynamical systems. Technical report (1996) University of Toronto, CRG-TR-96-2.
19. Sanderson, C., Paliwal, K.K.: Polynomial features for robust face authentication. Proceedings of International Conference on Image Processing **3** (2002) 997–1000

An Online Algorithm for Hierarchical Phoneme Classification

Ofer Dekel, Joseph Keshet, and Yoram Singer

School of Computer Science and Engineering,
The Hebrew University, Jerusalem, 91904, Israel
{oferd, jkeshet, singer}@cs.huji.ac.il

Abstract. We present an algorithmic framework for phoneme classification where the set of phonemes is organized in a predefined hierarchical structure. This structure is encoded via a rooted tree which induces a metric over the set of phonemes. Our approach combines techniques from large margin kernel methods and Bayesian analysis. Extending the notion of large margin to hierarchical classification, we associate a prototype with each individual phoneme and with each phonetic group which corresponds to a node in the tree. We then formulate the learning task as an optimization problem with margin constraints over the phoneme set. In the spirit of Bayesian methods, we impose similarity requirements between the prototypes corresponding to adjacent phonemes in the phonetic hierarchy. We describe a new online algorithm for solving the hierarchical classification problem and provide worst-case loss analysis for the algorithm. We demonstrate the merits of our approach by applying the algorithm to synthetic data and as well as speech data.

1 Introduction

Phonemes classification is the task of deciding what is the phonetic identity of a (typically short) speech utterance. Work in speech recognition and in particular phoneme classification typically imposes the assumption that different classification errors are of the same importance. However, since the set of phoneme are embedded in a hierarchical structure some errors are likely to be more tolerable than others. For example, it seems less severe to classify an utterance as the phoneme /oy/ (as in *boy*) instead of /ow/ (as in *boat*), than predicting /w/ (as in *way*) instead of /ow/. Furthermore, often we cannot extended a high-confidence prediction for a given utterance, while still being able to accurately identify the phonetic group of the utterance. In this paper we propose and analyze a hierarchal model for classification that imposes a notion of "severity" of prediction errors which is in accordance with a pre-defined hierarchical structure.

Phonetic theory of spoken speech embeds the set of phonemes of western languages in a phonetic hierarchy where the phonemes constitute the leaves of the tree while broad phonetic groups, such as vowels and consonants, correspond to internal vertices. Such phonetic trees were described in [1, 2]. Motivated by this phonetic structure we propose a hierarchical model (depicted in Fig. 1)

S. Bengio and H. Bourlard (Eds.): MLMI 2004, LNCS 3361, pp. 146–158, 2005.
© Springer-Verlag Berlin Heidelberg 2005

that incorporates the notion of the similarity (and analogously dissimilarity) between the phonemes and between phonetic groups and employs this notion in the learning procedure we describe and analyze below.

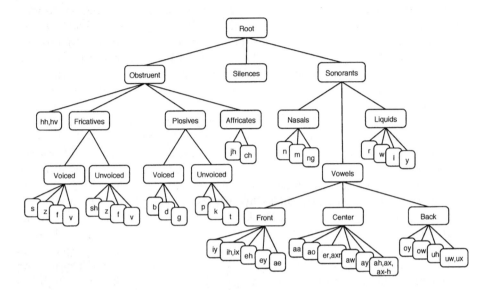

Fig. 1. The phonetic tree of American English

Most of the previous work on phoneme classification sidestepped the hierarchical phonetic structure (see for instance, [3, 4]). Salomon [5] used a hierarchical clustering algorithm for phoneme classification. His algorithm generates a binary tree which is then used for constructing a phonetic classifier that employs multiple binary support vector machines (SVM). However, this construction was designed for efficiency reasons rather than for capturing the hierarchical phonetic structure. The problem of hierarchical classification in machine learning, in particular hierarchical document classification, was addressed by numerous researchers (see for instance [6, 7, 8, 9]). Most previous work on hierarchical classification decoupled the problem into independent classification problems by assigning and training a classifier at each internal vertex in the hierarchy. To incorporate the semantics relayed by the hierarchical structure, few researchers imposed statistical similarity constraints between the probabilistic models for adjacent vertices in the hierarchy (e.g. [7]). In probabilistic settings, statistical similarities can be enforced using techniques such as back-off estimates [10] and shrinkage [7].

A significant amount of recent work on classification problems, both binary and multiclass, has been devoted to the theory and application of large margin classifiers. See for instance the book of Vapnik [11] and the references therein. In this paper, we describe, analyze, and apply a large margin approach to hierarchical classification which is in the spirit of statistical approaches. As in large margin methods, we associate a vector in a high dimensional space with each phoneme or phoneme group in the hierarchy. We call this vector the *prototype* of the phoneme or the phoneme group, and classify feature vectors according to their similarity to the various prototypes. We relax the requirements of correct classification to large margin constraints and attempt to find prototypes that comply with these constraints. In the spirit of Bayesian methods, we impose similarity requirements between the prototypes corresponding to adjacent phonemes in the hierarchy. The result is an algorithmic solution that may tolerate minor mistakes, such as predicting a sibling of the correct phoneme, but avoids gross errors, such as predicting a vertex in a completely different part of the tree.

Speech corpora typically contain a very large number of examples. To cope with large amounts of data we devise an online algorithm that is both memory efficient and simple to implement. Our algorithmic solution builds on the pioneering work of Warmuth and colleagues. In particular, we generalize and fuse ideas from [12, 13, 14]. These papers discuss online learning of large-margin classifiers. On each round, the online hypothesis is updated such that it complies with margin constraints imposed by the example observed on this round. Along with the margin constraints, the update is required to keep the new classifier fairly close to the previous one. We show that this idea can also be exploited in our setting, resulting in a simple online update which can be used in conjunction with kernel functions. Furthermore, using methods for converting online to batch learning (e.g. [15]), we show that the online algorithm can be used to devise a batch algorithm with good empirical performance.

The paper is organized as follows. In Sec. 2 we formally describe the hierarchical phoneme classification problem and establish our notation. Sec. 3 constitutes the algorithmic core of the paper. In this section we describe an online algorithm for hierarchical phoneme classification and prove a worst case bound on its performance. In Sec. 4 we briefly describe a conversion of the online algorithm into a well performing batch algorithm. In Sec. 5 we conclude the paper with a series of experiments on synthetic data and on speech data.

2   Problem Setting

Let $\mathcal{X} \subseteq \mathbb{R}^n$ be an acoustic features domain and let $\mathcal{Y}$ be a set of phonemes and phoneme groups. In the hierarchical classification setting $\mathcal{Y}$ plays a double role: first, as in traditional multiclass problems, it encompasses the set of phonemes, namely each feature vector in $\mathcal{X}$ is associated with a phoneme $v \in \mathcal{Y}$. Second, $\mathcal{Y}$ defines a set of vertices, i.e., the phonemes and the phoneme groups, arranged in a rooted tree $\mathcal{T}$. We denote $k = |\mathcal{Y}|$, for concreteness we assume that $\mathcal{Y} = \{0, \ldots, k-1\}$ and let 0 be the root of $\mathcal{T}$.

For any pair of phonemes $u, v \in \mathcal{Y}$, let $\gamma(u, v)$ denote their distance in the tree. That is, $\gamma(u, v)$ is defined to be the number of edges along the (unique) path from u to v in $\mathcal{T}$. The distance function $\gamma(\cdot, \cdot)$ is in fact a metric over $\mathcal{Y}$ since it is a non-negative function, $\gamma(v, v) = 0$, $\gamma(u, v) = \gamma(v, u)$ and the triangle inequality always holds with equality. As stated above, different classification errors incur different levels of penalty, and in our model this penalty is defined by the tree distance $\gamma(u, v)$. We therefore say that the *tree induced error* incurred by predicting the phoneme or the phoneme group v when the correct phoneme is u is $\gamma(u, v)$.

We receive a training set $S = \{(\mathbf{x}_i, y_i)\}_{i=1}^m$ of feature vector-phoneme pairs, where each $\mathbf{x}_i \in \mathcal{X}$ and each $y_i \in \mathcal{Y}$. Our goal is to learn a classification function $f : \mathcal{X} \to \mathcal{Y}$ which attains a small tree induced error. We focus on classifiers that are of the following form: each phoneme $v \in \mathcal{Y}$ has a matching prototype $\mathbf{W}^v \in \mathbb{R}^n$, where $\mathbf{W}^0$ is fixed to be the zero vector and every other prototype can be any vector in $\mathbb{R}^n$. The classifier f makes its predictions according to the following rule,

$$f(\mathbf{x}) = \operatorname*{argmax}_{v \in \mathcal{Y}} \mathbf{W}^v \cdot \mathbf{x} . \tag{1}$$

The task of learning f is reduced to learning $\mathbf{W}^1, \ldots, \mathbf{W}^{k-1}$.

For every phoneme or phoneme group other than the tree root $v \in \{\mathcal{Y} \setminus 0\}$, we denote by $\mathcal{A}(v)$ the parent of v in the tree. Put another way, $\mathcal{A}(v)$ is the vertex adjacent to v which is closer to the tree root 0. We also define $\mathcal{A}^{(i)}(v)$ to be the ith ancestor of v (if such an ancestor exists). Formally, $\mathcal{A}^{(i)}(v)$ is defined recursively as follows,

$$\mathcal{A}^{(0)}(v) = v \quad \text{and} \quad \mathcal{A}^{(i)}(v) = \mathcal{A}(\mathcal{A}^{(i-1)}(v)) .$$

For each phoneme or phoneme group $v \in \mathcal{Y}$, define $\mathcal{P}(v)$ to be the set of phoneme groups along the path from 0 (the tree root) to v,

$$\mathcal{P}(v) = \left\{ u \in \mathcal{Y} : \exists i \ u = \mathcal{A}^{(i)}(v) \right\} .$$

For technical reasons discussed shortly, we prefer not to deal directly with the set of prototypes $\mathbf{W}^0, \ldots, \mathbf{W}^{k-1}$ but rather with the difference between each prototype and the prototype of its parent. Formally, define $\mathbf{w}^0$ to be the zero vector in $\mathbb{R}^n$ and for each phoneme or phoneme group $v \in \mathcal{Y} \setminus 0$, let $\mathbf{w}^v = \mathbf{W}^v - \mathbf{W}^{\mathcal{A}(v)}$. Each prototype now decomposes to the sum

$$\mathbf{W}^v = \sum_{u \in \mathcal{P}(v)} \mathbf{w}^u . \tag{2}$$

The classifier f can be defined in two equivalent ways: by setting $\{\mathbf{W}^v\}_{v \in \mathcal{Y}}$ and using Eq. (1), or by setting $\{\mathbf{w}^v\}_{v \in \mathcal{Y}}$ and using Eq. (2) in conjunction with Eq. (1). Throughout this paper, we often use $\{\mathbf{w}^v\}_{v \in \mathcal{Y}}$ as a synonym for the classification function f. As a design choice, our algorithms require that adjacent vertices in the phonetic tree have similar prototypes. The benefit of representing each prototype $\{\mathbf{W}^v\}_{v \in \mathcal{Y}}$ as a sum of vectors from $\{\mathbf{w}^v\}_{v \in \mathcal{Y}}$ is that adjacent prototypes $\mathbf{W}^v$ and $\mathbf{W}^{\mathcal{A}(v)}$ can be kept close by simply keeping $\mathbf{w}^v = \mathbf{W}^v - \mathbf{W}^{\mathcal{A}(v)}$ small. Sec. 3 and Sec. 4 address the task of learning the set $\{\mathbf{w}^v\}_{v \in \mathcal{Y}}$ from supervised data.

3 An Online Algorithm

In this section we derive and analyze an efficient online learning algorithm for the hierarchical phoneme classification problem. In online settings, learning takes place in rounds. On round i, a feature vector, denoted $\mathbf{x}_i$, is presented to the learning algorithm. The algorithm maintains a set of prototypes which is constantly updated in accordance with the quality of its predictions. We denote the set of prototypes used to extend the prediction on round i by $\{\mathbf{w}_i^v\}_{v \in \mathcal{Y}}$. Therefore, the predicted phoneme or phoneme group of the algorithm for $\mathbf{x}_i$ is,

$$\hat{y}_i = \operatorname*{argmax}_{v \in \mathcal{Y}} \mathbf{W}_i^v \cdot \mathbf{x}_i = \operatorname*{argmax}_{v \in \mathcal{Y}} \sum_{u \in \mathcal{P}(v)} \mathbf{w}_i^u \cdot \mathbf{x}_i .$$

Then, the correct phoneme y_i is revealed and the algorithm suffers an instantaneous error. The error that we employ in this paper is the tree induced error. Using the notation above, the error on round i equals $\gamma(y_i, \hat{y}_i)$.

Our analysis, as well as the motivation for the online update that we derive below, assumes that there exists a set of prototypes $\{\boldsymbol{\omega}^v\}_{v \in \mathcal{Y}}$ such that for every feature vector-phoneme pair $(\mathbf{x}_i, y_i)$ and every $r \neq y_i$ it holds that,

$$\sum_{v \in \mathcal{P}(y_i)} \boldsymbol{\omega}^v \cdot \mathbf{x}_i - \sum_{u \in \mathcal{P}(r)} \boldsymbol{\omega}^u \cdot \mathbf{x}_i \geq \sqrt{\gamma(y_i, r)} . \tag{3}$$

The above difference between the projection onto the prototype corresponding to the correct phoneme and any other prototype is a generalization of the notion of margin employed by multiclass problems in machine learning literature [16]. Put informally, we require that the margin between the correct and each of the incorrect phonemes and phoneme groups be at least the square-root of the tree-based distance between them. The goal of the algorithm is to find a set of prototypes which fulfills the margin requirement of Eq. (3) while incurring a minimal tree-induced error until such a set is found. However, the tree-induced error is a combinatorial quantity and is thus difficult to minimize directly. We instead use a construction commonly used in large margin classifiers and employ the the the convex hinge-loss function

$$\ell\left(\{\mathbf{w}_i^v\}, \mathbf{x}_i, y_i\right) = \left[\sum_{v \in \mathcal{P}(\hat{y}_i)} \mathbf{w}_i^v \cdot \mathbf{x}_i - \sum_{v \in \mathcal{P}(y_i)} \mathbf{w}_i^v \cdot \mathbf{x}_i + \sqrt{\gamma(y_i, \hat{y}_i)} \right]_+ , \tag{4}$$

where $[z]_+ = \max\{z, 0\}$. In the sequel we show that $\ell^2\left(\{\mathbf{w}_i^v\}, \mathbf{x}_i, y_i\right)$ upper bounds $\gamma(y_i, \hat{y}_i)$ and use this fact to attain a bound on $\sum_{i=1}^m \gamma(y_i, \hat{y}_i)$.

The online algorithm belongs to the family of *conservative* online algorithms, which update their classification rules only on rounds on which prediction mistakes are made. Let us therefore assume that there was a prediction mistake on round i. We would like to modify the set of vectors $\{\mathbf{w}_i^v\}$ so as to satisfy the margin constraints imposed by the ith example. One possible approach is to simply find a set of vectors that solves the constraints in Eq. (3) (Such a set must exist since we assume that there exists a set $\{\omega_i^v\}$ which satisfies the margin requirements for *all* of the examples.) There are however two caveats in such a greedy approach. The first is that by setting the new set of prototypes to be an arbitrary solution to the constraints imposed by the most recent example we are in danger of forgetting what has been learned thus far. The second, rather technical, complicating factor is that there is no simple analytical solution to Eq. (3). We therefore introduce a simple constrained optimization problem. The objective function of this optimization problem ensures that the new set $\{\mathbf{w}_{i+1}^v\}$ is kept close to the current set while the constraints ensure that the margin requirement for the pair $(y_i, \hat{y}_i)$ is fulfilled by the new vectors. Formally, the new set of vectors is the solution to the following problem,

$$\min_{\{\mathbf{w}^v\}} \quad \frac{1}{2} \sum_{v \in \mathcal{Y}} \|\mathbf{w}^v - \mathbf{w}_i^v\|^2 \tag{5}$$

$$\text{s.t.} \quad \sum_{v \in \mathcal{P}(y_i)} \mathbf{w}^v \cdot \mathbf{x}_i - \sum_{u \in \mathcal{P}(\hat{y}_i)} \mathbf{w}^u \cdot \mathbf{x}_i \geq \sqrt{\gamma(y_i, \hat{y}_i)} .$$

First, note that any vector $\mathbf{w}^v$ corresponding to a vertex v that does not belong to neither $\mathcal{P}(y_i)$ nor $\mathcal{P}(\hat{y}_i)$ does not change due to the objective function in Eq. (5), hence, $\mathbf{w}_{i+1}^v = \mathbf{w}_i^v$. Second, note that if $v \in \mathcal{P}(y_i) \cap \mathcal{P}(\hat{y}_i)$ then the contribution of the $\mathbf{w}^v$ cancels out. Thus, for this case as well we get that $\mathbf{w}_{i+1}^v = \mathbf{w}_i^v$. In summary, the vectors that we need to actually update correspond to the vertices in the set $\mathcal{P}(y_i) \Delta \mathcal{P}(\hat{y}_i)$ where Δ designates the symmetric difference of sets (see also Fig. 2).

To find the solution to Eq. (5) we introduce a Lagrange multiplier α_i, and formulate the optimization problem in the form of a Lagrangian. We set the derivative of the Lagrangian w.r.t. $\{\mathbf{w}^v\}$ to zero and get,

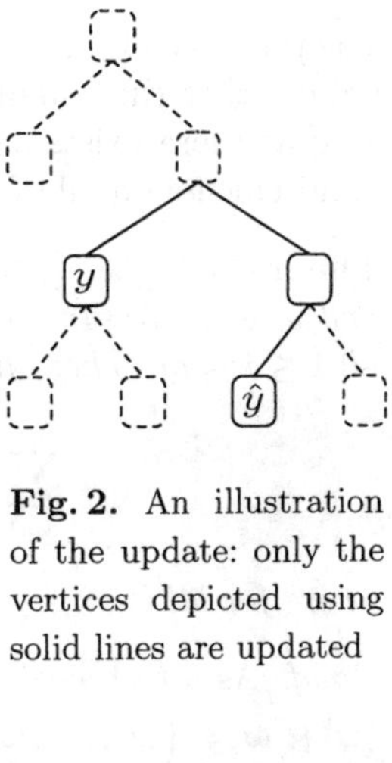

Fig. 2. An illustration of the update: only the vertices depicted using solid lines are updated

$$\mathbf{w}_{i+1}^v = \mathbf{w}_i^v + \alpha_i \mathbf{x}_i \quad v \in \mathcal{P}(y_i) \backslash \mathcal{P}(\hat{y}_i) \tag{6}$$

$$\mathbf{w}_{i+1}^v = \mathbf{w}_i^v - \alpha_i \mathbf{x}_i \quad v \in \mathcal{P}(\hat{y}_i) \backslash \mathcal{P}(y_i) . \tag{7}$$

Since at the optimum the constraint of Eq. (5) is binding we get that,

$$\sum_{v \in \mathcal{P}(y_i)} (\mathbf{w}_i^v + \alpha_i \mathbf{x}_i) \cdot \mathbf{x}_i = \sum_{v \in \mathcal{P}(\hat{y}_i)} (\mathbf{w}_i^v - \alpha_i \mathbf{x}_i) \cdot \mathbf{x}_i + \sqrt{\gamma(y_i, \hat{y}_i)}.$$

Rearranging terms in the above equation and using the definition of the loss from Eq. (4) we get that,

$$\alpha_i \|\mathbf{x}_i\|^2 |\mathcal{P}(y_i) \Delta \mathcal{P}(\hat{y}_i)| = \ell(\{\mathbf{w}_i^v\}, x_i, y_i) .$$

Finally, noting that the cardinality of $\mathcal{P}(y_i) \Delta \mathcal{P}(\hat{y}_i)$ is equal to $\gamma(y_i, \hat{y}_i)$ we get that,

$$\alpha_i = \frac{\ell(\{\mathbf{w}_i^v\}, \mathbf{x}_i, y_i)}{\gamma(y_i, \hat{y}_i) \|\mathbf{x}_i\|^2} \tag{8}$$

INITIALIZE: $\forall v \in \mathcal{Y} : \mathbf{w}_v^1 = \mathbf{0}$
FOR $t = 1, 2, \ldots, m$
- Receive acoustic feature vector $\mathbf{x}_i$
- Predict phoneme or phoneme group:

$$\hat{y}_i = \arg \max_{v \in \mathcal{Y}} \sum_{u \in \mathcal{P}(v)} \mathbf{w}_i^u \cdot \mathbf{x}_i$$

- Receive the correct phoneme y_i
- Suffer loss: $\ell \left(\{\mathbf{w}_i^v\}, \mathbf{x}_i, y_i \right)$ [see Eq. (4)]
- Update:

$$\mathbf{w}_{i+1}^v = \mathbf{w}_i^v + \alpha_i \mathbf{x}_i \quad v \in \mathcal{P}(y_i) \backslash \mathcal{P}(\hat{y}_i)$$
$$\mathbf{w}_{i+1}^v = \mathbf{w}_i^v - \alpha_i \mathbf{x}_i \quad v \in \mathcal{P}(\hat{y}_i) \backslash \mathcal{P}(y_i)$$

where
$$\alpha_i = \frac{\ell \left(\{\mathbf{w}_i^v\}, \mathbf{x}_i, y_i \right)}{\gamma(y_i, \hat{y}_i) \|\mathbf{x}_i\|^2}$$

Fig. 3. Online hierarchical phoneme classification algorithm

The pseudo code of the online algorithm is given in Fig. 3. The following theorem implies that the cumulative loss suffered by the online algorithm is bounded as long as there exists a hierarchical phoneme classifier which fulfills the margin requirements on all of the examples.

Theorem 1. *Let* $\{(\mathbf{x}_i, y_i)\}_{i=1}^m$ *be a sequence of examples where* $\mathbf{x}_i \in \mathcal{X} \subseteq \mathbb{R}^n$ *and* $y_i \in \mathcal{Y}$. *Assume there exists a set* $\{\boldsymbol{\omega}^v : \forall v \in \mathcal{Y}\}$ *that satisfies Eq. (3) for all* $1 \leq i \leq m$. *Then, the following bound holds,*

$$\sum_{i=1}^m \ell^2 \left(\{\mathbf{w}_i^v\}, \mathbf{x}_i, y_i \right) \leq \sum_{v \in \mathcal{Y}} \|\boldsymbol{\omega}^v\|^2 \, \gamma_{max} \, R^2$$

where for all i, $\|\mathbf{x}_i\| \leq R$ *and* $\gamma(y_i, \hat{y}_i) \leq \gamma_{max}$.

Proof. As a technical tool, we denote by $\bar{\boldsymbol{\omega}}$ the concatenation of the vectors in $\{\boldsymbol{\omega}^v\}$, $\bar{\boldsymbol{\omega}} = \left(\boldsymbol{\omega}^0, \ldots, \boldsymbol{\omega}^{k-1} \right)$ and similarly $\bar{\mathbf{w}}_i = \left(\mathbf{w}_i^0, \ldots, \mathbf{w}_i^{k-1} \right)$ for $i \geq 1$. We denote by δ_i the difference between the squared distance $\bar{\mathbf{w}}_i$ from $\bar{\boldsymbol{\omega}}$ and the squared distance of $\bar{\mathbf{w}}_{i+1}$ from $\bar{\boldsymbol{\omega}}$,

$$\delta_i = \|\bar{\mathbf{w}}_i - \bar{\boldsymbol{\omega}}\|^2 - \|\bar{\mathbf{w}}_{i+1} - \bar{\boldsymbol{\omega}}\|^2 \ .$$

We now derive upper and lower bounds on $\sum_{i=1}^m \delta_i$. First, note that by summing over i we obtain,

$$\sum_{i=1}^m \delta_i = \sum_{i=1}^m \|\bar{\mathbf{w}}_i - \bar{\boldsymbol{\omega}}\|^2 - \|\bar{\mathbf{w}}_{i+1} - \bar{\boldsymbol{\omega}}\|^2$$
$$= \|\bar{\mathbf{w}}_1 - \bar{\boldsymbol{\omega}}\|^2 - \|\bar{\mathbf{w}}_m - \bar{\boldsymbol{\omega}}\|^2 \leq \|\bar{\mathbf{w}}_1 - \bar{\boldsymbol{\omega}}\|^2 \ .$$

Our initialization sets $\bar{\mathbf{w}}_1 = \mathbf{0}$ and thus we get,

$$\sum_{i=1}^{m} \delta_i \leq \|\bar{\omega}\|^2 = \sum_{v \in \mathcal{Y}} \|\omega^v\|^2 . \tag{9}$$

This provides the upper bound on $\sum_i \delta_i$. We next derive a lower bound on each δ_i. The minimizer of the problem defined by Eq. (5) is obtained by projecting $\{\mathbf{w}_i^v\}$ onto the linear constraint corresponding to our margin requirement. The result is a new set $\{\mathbf{w}_{i+1}^v\}$ which in the above notation can be written as the vector $\bar{\mathbf{w}}_{i+1}$. A well known result (see for instance [17], Thm. 2.4.1) states that this vector satisfies the following inequality,

$$\|\bar{\mathbf{w}}_i - \bar{\omega}\|^2 - \|\bar{\mathbf{w}}_{i+1} - \bar{\omega}\|^2 \geq \|\bar{\mathbf{w}}_i - \bar{\mathbf{w}}_{i+1}\|^2 .$$

Hence, we get that $\delta_i \geq \|\bar{\mathbf{w}}_i - \bar{\mathbf{w}}_{i+1}\|^2$. We can now take into account that $\mathbf{w}_i^v$ is updated if and only if $v \in \mathcal{P}(y_i) \Delta \mathcal{P}(\hat{y}_i)$ to get that,

$$\|\bar{\mathbf{w}}_i - \bar{\mathbf{w}}_{i+1}\|^2 = \sum_{v \in \mathcal{Y}} \|\mathbf{w}_i^v - \mathbf{w}_{i+1}^v\|^2$$

$$= \sum_{v \in \mathcal{P}(y_i) \Delta \mathcal{P}(\hat{y}_i)} \|\mathbf{w}_i^v - \mathbf{w}_{i+1}^v\|^2 .$$

Plugging Eqs. (6-7) into the above equation, we get

$$\sum_{v \in \mathcal{P}(y_i) \Delta \mathcal{P}(\hat{y}_i)} \|\mathbf{w}_i^v - \mathbf{w}_{i+1}^v\|^2 = \sum_{v \in \mathcal{P}(y_i) \Delta \mathcal{P}(\hat{y}_i)} \alpha_i^2 \|x_i\|^2$$

$$= |\mathcal{P}(y_i) \Delta \mathcal{P}(\hat{y}_i)| \, \alpha_i^2 \|x_i\|^2$$

$$= \gamma(y_i, \hat{y}_i) \, \alpha_i^2 \|x_i\|^2 .$$

We now use the definition of α_i from Eq. (8) to obtain a lower bound on δ_i,

$$\delta_i \geq \frac{\ell^2 \left(\{\mathbf{w}_i^v\}, \mathbf{x}_i, y_i\right)}{\gamma(y_i, \hat{y}_i) \|\mathbf{x}_i\|^2} .$$

Using the assumptions $\|\mathbf{x}_i\| \leq R$ and $\gamma(y_i, \hat{y}_i) \leq \gamma_{max}$ we can further bound δ_i and write,

$$\delta_i \geq \frac{\ell^2 \left(\{\mathbf{w}_i^v\}, \mathbf{x}_i, y_i\right)}{\gamma_{max} R^2} .$$

Now, summing over all i and comparing the lower bound given above with the upper bound of Eq. (9) we get,

$$\frac{\sum_{t=1}^{m} \ell^2 \left(\{\mathbf{w}_i^v\}, \mathbf{x}_i, y_i\right)}{\gamma_{max} R^2} \leq \sum_{t=1}^{m} \delta_i \leq \sum_{v \in \mathcal{Y}} \|\omega^v\|^2 .$$

Multiplying both sides of the inequality above by $\gamma_{max} R^2$ gives the desired bound. □

The loss bound of Thm. 1 can be straightforwardly translated into a bound on the tree-induced error as follows. Note that whenever a prediction error occurs $(y_i \neq \hat{y}_i)$, then $\sum_{v \in \mathcal{P}(\hat{y}_i)} \mathbf{w}_i^v \cdot \mathbf{x}_i \geq \sum_{v \in \mathcal{P}(y_i)} \mathbf{w}_i^v \cdot \mathbf{x}_i$. Thus, the hinge-loss defined by Eq. (4) is greater than $\sqrt{\gamma(y_i, \hat{y}_i)}$. Since we suffer a loss only on rounds were prediction errors were made, we get the following corollary.

Corollary 1. *Under the conditions of Thm. 1 the following bound on the cumulative tree-induced error holds,*

$$\sum_{t=1}^{m} \gamma(y_i, \hat{y}_i) \leq \sum_{v \in \mathcal{Y}} \|\boldsymbol{\omega}^v\|^2 \, \gamma_{max} \, R^2 \ . \tag{10}$$

To conclude the algorithmic part of the paper, we note that Mercer kernels can be easily incorporated into our algorithm. First, rewrite the update as $\mathbf{w}_{i+1}^v = \mathbf{w}_i^v + \alpha_i^v \mathbf{x}_i$ where,

$$\alpha_i^v = \begin{cases} \alpha_i & v \in \mathcal{P}(y_i) \backslash \mathcal{P}(\hat{y}_i) \\ -\alpha_i & v \in \mathcal{P}(\hat{y}_i) \backslash \mathcal{P}(y_i) \\ 0 & \text{otherwise} \end{cases} \ .$$

Using this notation, the resulting hierarchical classifier can be rewritten as,

$$f(\mathbf{x}) = \underset{v \in \mathcal{Y}}{\operatorname{argmax}} \sum_{u \in \mathcal{P}(v)} \mathbf{w}_i^u \cdot \mathbf{x}_i \tag{11}$$

$$= \underset{v \in \mathcal{Y}}{\operatorname{argmax}} \sum_{u \in \mathcal{P}(v)} \sum_{i=1}^{m} \alpha_i^u \mathbf{x}_i \cdot \mathbf{x} \ . \tag{12}$$

We can replace the inner-products in Eq. (12) with a general kernel operator $K(\cdot, \cdot)$ that satisfies Mercer's conditions [11]. It remains to show that α_i^v can be computed based on kernel operations whenever $\alpha_i^v \neq 0$. To see this, note that we can rewrite α_i from Eq. (8) as

$$\alpha_i = \frac{\left[\sum_{v \in \mathcal{P}(\hat{y}_i)} \sum_{j<i} \alpha_j^v K(\mathbf{x}_j, \mathbf{x}_i) - \sum_{v \in \mathcal{P}(y_i)} \sum_{j<i} \alpha_j^v K(\mathbf{x}_j, \mathbf{x}_i) + \gamma(y_i, \hat{y}_i) \right]_+}{\gamma(y_i, \hat{y}_i) \, K(\mathbf{x}_i, \mathbf{x}_i)} \ . \tag{13}$$

4   A Batch Conversion

In the previous section we presented an online algorithm for hierarchical phoneme classification. Often, the entire training set $S = \{(\mathbf{x}_i, y_i)\}_{i=1}^{m}$ is available to the learning algorithm in advance, the batch setting is more natural. As before, the performance of a classifier f on a given example $(\mathbf{x}, y)$ is evaluated with respect to the tree-induced error $\gamma(y, f(\mathbf{x}))$. In contrast to online learning, where no assumptions are made on the distribution of examples, in batch settings it is assumed that the examples are independently sampled from a distribution $\mathcal{D}$

over $\mathcal{X} \times \mathcal{Y}$. Therefore, our goal is to use S to obtain a hierarchical classifier f which attains a low *expected* tree-induced error, $\mathbb{E}_{(\mathbf{x},y)\sim\mathcal{D}}\left[\gamma(y, f(\mathbf{x}))\right]$, where expectation is taken over the random selection of examples from $\mathcal{D}$.

Perhaps the simplest idea is to use the online algorithm of Sec. 3 as a batch algorithm by applying it to the training set S in some arbitrary order and defining f to be the last classifier obtained by this process. The resulting classifier is the one defined by the vector set $\{\mathbf{w}^v_{m+1}\}_{v\in\mathcal{Y}}$. In practice, this idea works reasonably well, as demonstrated by our experiments (Sec. 5). However, a slight modification of this idea yields a significantly better classifier with an accompanying bound on expected tree-induced error. For every $v \in \mathcal{Y}$, define $\mathbf{w}^v = \frac{1}{m+1}\sum_{i=1}^{m+1}\mathbf{w}^v_i$, where $\{\mathbf{w}^v_i | 1 \le i \le m+1, \ v \in \mathcal{Y}\}$ is the set of vectors generated by the online algorithm when it is applied to S. Now, let f be the classifier defined by $\{\mathbf{w}^v\}_{v\in\mathcal{Y}}$. In words, we have defined the prototype for phoneme or phoneme group v to be the average over all prototypes generated by the online algorithm for v. For a general discussion on taking the average online hypothesis see [15].

5   Experiments

We begin this section with a comparison of the online algorithm and batch algorithm with standard multiclass classifiers which are oblivious to the hierarchical structure of the phoneme set. We conducted experiments with a synthetic dataset and a data set of phonemes extracted from continuous natural speech.

The synthetic data was generated as follows: we constructed a symmetric trinary tree of depth 4 and used it as the hierarchical structure. This tree contains 121 vertices which are the "phonemes" of our multiclass problem. We then set $\mathbf{w}^0,\ldots,\mathbf{w}^{120}$ to be some orthonormal set in $\mathbb{R}^{121}$, and defined the 121 prototypes to be $\mathbf{W}^v = \sum_{u\in\mathcal{P}(v)}\mathbf{w}^u$. We generated 100 train vectors and 50 test vectors for each "phoneme". Each example was generated by setting $(\mathbf{x}, y) = (\mathbf{W}^y + \boldsymbol{\eta}, y)$, where $\boldsymbol{\eta}$ is a vector of Gaussian noise generated by randomly drawing each of its coordinates from a Gaussian distribution with expectation 0 and variance 0.16. This dataset is referred to as *synthetic* in the figures and tables appearing in this section. We didn't use any kernel on this dataset in any of the experiments.

The second dataset used in our experiments is a corpus of continuous natural speech for the task of phoneme classification. The data we used is a subset of the TIMIT acoustic-phonetic dataset, which is a phonetically transcribed corpus of high quality continuous speech spoken by North American speakers [18]. Mel-frequency cepstrum coefficients (MFCC) along with their first and the second derivatives were extracted from the speech in a standard way, based on the ETSI standard for distributed speech recognition [19] and each feature vector was generated from 5 adjacent MFCC vectors (with overlap). The TIMIT corpus is divided into a training set and a test set in such a way that no speakers from the training set appear in the test set (speaker independent). We randomly selected 2000 training features vectors and 500 test feature vectors per each of the 40 phonemes. We normalized the data to have zero mean and unit variance and used an RBF kernel with $\sigma = 0.5$ in all the experiment with this dataset.

We trained and tested the online and batch versions of our algorithm on the two datasets. To demonstrate the benefits of exploiting the hierarchal structure, we also trained and evaluated standard multiclass predictors which ignore the structure. These classifiers were trained using the algorithm but with a "flattened" version of the phoneme hierarchy. The (normalized) cumulative tree-induced error and the percentage of multiclass errors for each experiment are summarized in Table 1 (online experiments) and Table 2 (batch experiments). Rows marked by *tree* refer to the performance of the algorithm train with knowledge of the hierarchical structure, while rows marked by *flat* refer to the performance of the classifier trained without knowledge of the hierarchy. The results clearly indicate that exploiting the hierarchical structure is beneficial in achieving low tree-induced errors. In all experiments, both online and batch, the hierarchical phoneme classifier achieved lower tree-induced error than its "flattened" counterpart. Furthermore, in most of the experiments the multiclass error of the algorithm is also lower than the error of the corresponding multiclass predictor, although the latter was explicitly trained to minimize the error. This behavior exemplifies that employing a hierarchical phoneme structure may prove useful even when the goal is not necessarily the minimization of some tree-based error.

Further examination of results demonstrates that the hierarchical phoneme classifier tends to tolerate small tree-induced errors while avoiding large ones. In Fig. 4 we depict the differences between the error rate of the batch algorithm and the error rate of a standard multiclass predictor. Each bar corresponds to a different value of $\gamma(y, \hat{y})$, starting from the left with a value of 1 and ending on the right with the largest possible value of $\gamma(y, \hat{y})$. It is clear from the figure that the batch algorithm tends to make "small" errors by predicting the parent or a sibling of the correct phoneme. On the other hand the algorithm seldom

Table 1. Online algorithm results

DATA SET	TREE INDUCED ERROR	MULTICLASS ERROR
SYNTHETIC DATA (TREE)	**0.83**	**44.5**
SYNTHETIC DATA (FLAT)	1.35	51.1
PHONEMES (TREE)	**1.64**	40.0
PHONEMES (FLAT)	1.72	**39.7**

Table 2. Batch algorithm results

DATA SET	TREE INDUCED LAST	TREE INDUCED BATCH	MULTICLASS LAST	MULTICLASS BATCH
SYNTHETIC DATA (TREE)	**0.04**	**0.05**	**4.1**	**5.0**
SYNTHETIC DATA (FLAT)	0.14	0.11	10.8	8.6
SYNTHETIC DATA (GREEDY)	0.57	0.52	37.4	34.9
PHONEMES (TREE)	**1.88**	**1.30**	48.0	**40.6**
PHONEMES (FLAT)	2.01	1.41	48.8	41.8
PHONEMES (GREEDY)	3.22	2.48	73.9	58.2

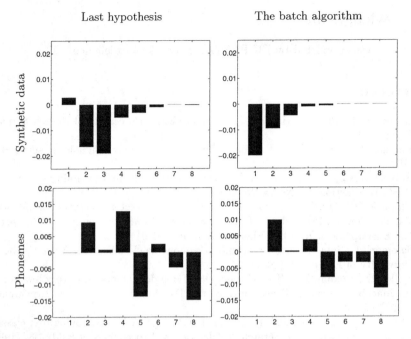

Fig. 4. The distribution of the tree induced-error for each dataset used in the experiments. Each bar corresponds to the difference between the error of the batch algorithm minus the error of a multiclass predictor

chooses a phoneme or a phoneme group which is in an entirely different part of the tree, thus avoiding large tree induced errors. In the phoneme classification task, the algorithm seldom extends a prediction $\hat{y}$ such that $\gamma(y, \hat{y}) = 9$ while the errors of the multiclass predictor are uniformly distributed.

We conclude the experiments with a comparison of the hierarchical algorithm with a common construction of hierarchical classifiers (see for instance [6]), where separate classifiers are learned and applied at each internal vertex of the hierarchy independently. To compare the two approaches, we learned a multiclass predictor at each internal vertex of the tree hierarchy. Each such classifier routes an input feature vector to one of its children. Formally, for each internal vertex v of $\mathcal{T}$ we trained a classifier f_v using the training set $S_v = \{(\mathbf{x}_i, u_i) | u_i \in \mathcal{P}(y_i), v = \mathcal{A}(u_i), (\mathbf{x}_i, y_i) \in S\}$. Given a test feature vector $\mathbf{x}$, its predicted phoneme is the leaf $\hat{y}$ such that for each $u \in \mathcal{P}(\hat{y})$ and its parent v we have $f_v(\mathbf{x}) = u$. In other words, to cast a prediction we start with the root vertex and move towards one of the leaves by progressing from a vertex v to $f_v(\mathbf{x})$. We refer to this hierarchical classification model in Table 2 simply as *greedy*. In all of the experiments, the batch algorithm clearly outperforms greedy. This experiment underscores the usefulness of our approach which makes global decisions in contrast to the local decisions of the greedy construction. Indeed, any single prediction error at any of the vertices along the path to the correct phoneme will impose a global prediction error.

Acknowledgment

This work was supported by EU PASCAL network of excellence.

References

1. Deller, J., Proakis, J., Hansen, J.: Discrete-Time Processing of Speech Signals. Prentice-Hall (1987)
2. Rabiner, L.R., Schafer, R.W.: Digital Processing of Speech Signals. Prentice-Hall (1978)
3. Robinson, A.J.: An application of recurrent nets to phone probability estimation. IEEE Transactions on Neural Networks 5 (1994) 298–305
4. Clarkson, P., Moreno, P.: On the use of support vector machines for phonetic classification. In: Proceedings of the International Conference on Acoustics, Speech and Signal Processing 1999, Phoenix, Arizona (1999)
5. Salomon, J.: Support vector machines for phoneme classification. Master's thesis, University of Edinburgh (2001)
6. Koller, D., Sahami, M.: Hierarchically classifying docuemnts using very few words. In: Machine Learning: Proceedings of the Fourteenth International Conference. (1997) 171–178
7. McCallum, A.K., Rosenfeld, R., Mitchell, T.M., Ng, A.Y.: Improving text classification by shrinkage in a hierarchy of classes. In: Proceedings of ICML-98. (1998) 359–367
8. Weigend, A.S., Wiener, E.D., Pedersen, J.O.: Exploiting hierarchy in text categorization. Information Retrieval 1 (1999) 193–216
9. Dumais, S.T., Chen, H.: Hierarchical classification of Web content. In: Proceedings of SIGIR-00. (2000) 256–263
10. Katz, S.: Estimation of probabilities from sparsedata for the language model component of a speech recognizer. IEEE Transactions on Acoustics, Speech and Signal Processing (ASSP) 35 (1987) 400–40
11. Vapnik, V.N.: Statistical Learning Theory. Wiley (1998)
12. Crammer, K., Dekel, O., Shalev-Shwartz, S., Singer, Y.: Online passive aggressive algorithms. In: Advances in Neural Information Processing Systems 16. (2003)
13. Herbster, M.: Learning additive models online with fast evaluating kernels. In: Proceedings of the Fourteenth Annual Conference on Computational Learning Theory. (2001) 444–460
14. Kivinen, J., Warmuth, M.K.: Exponentiated gradient versus gradient descent for linear predictors. Information and Computation 132 (1997) 1–64
15. Cesa-Bianchi, N., Conconi, A., C.Gentile: On the generalization ability of on-line learning algorithms. IEEE Transactions on Information Theory (2004) (to appear).
16. Weston, J., Watkins, C.: Support vector machines for multi-class pattern recognition. In: Proceedings of the Seventh European Symposium on Artificial Neural Networks. (1999)
17. Censor, Y., Zenios, S.: Parallel Optimization: Theory, Algorithms, and Applications. Oxford University Press, New York, NY, USA (1997)
18. Lemel, L., Kassel, R., Seneff, S.: Speech database development: Design and analysis . Report no. SAIC-86/1546, Proc. DARPA Speech Recognition Workshop (1986)
19. : ETSI Standard, ETSI ES 201 108 (2000)

Towards Predicting Optimal Fusion Candidates: A Case Study on Biometric Authentication Tasks

Norman Poh and Samy Bengio

IDIAP Research Institute, Rue du Simplon 4, CH-1920 Martigny, Switzerland
{norman, bengio}@idiap.ch

Abstract. Combining multiple information sources, typically from several data streams is a very promising approach, both in experiments and to some extend in various real-life applications. However, combining too many systems (base-experts) will also increase both hardware and computation costs. One way to selecting a subset of optimal base-experts out of N is to carry out the experiments explicitly. There are $2^N - 1$ possible combinations. In this paper, we propose an analytical solution to this task when weighted sum fusion mechanism is used. The proposed approach is at least valid in the domain of person authentication. It has a complexity that is additive between the number of examples and the number of possible combinations while the conventional approach, using brute-force experimenting, is multiplicative between these two terms. Hence, our approach will scale better with large fusion problems. Experiments on the BANCA multi-modal database verified our approach. While we will consider here fusion in the context of identity verification via biometrics, or simply biometric authentication, it can also have an important impact in meetings because this *a priori* information can assist in retrieving highlights in meeting analysis as in "who said what". Furthermore, automatic meeting analysis also requires many systems working together and involves possibly many audio-visual media streams. Development in fusion of identity verification will provide insights into how fusion in meetings can be done. The ability to predict fusion performance is another important step towards understanding the fusion problem.

1 Introduction

Combining multiple systems, or base-experts, to boost performance is a very promising approach. In [1], for instance, as many as 14 experts were fused and tested on the XM2VTS database. This study concluded that by adding more experts, the performance of the fused system will not be degraded. While this is true, in practice, fusion leads to added hardware and computational cost. Hence, it is often desirable to select an optimal subset of experts for fusion.

If there are N base-experts, a brute-force experimenting will require $2^N - 1$ fusion experiments to select the smallest optimal subset of base-expert candidates for fusion. Here, in the context of biometric authentication (BA), we attempt to *reduce* the overhead computation cost *without compromising* the effectiveness. The overhead cost is avoided by evaluating the F-ratio criterion $2^N - 1$ times instead of carrying out $2^N - 1$ experiments. F-ratio is a term that is non-linearly proportional of Equal Error Rate (EER).

S. Bengio and H. Bourlard (Eds.): MLMI 2004, LNCS 3361, pp. 159–172, 2005.

F-ratio arises naturally when assuming that the client and impostor scores are normally distributed. The accuracy of this criterion depends only on how accurately one can estimate the parameters in the VR-EER analysis. The first part of this analysis is Variance Reduction (VR) and the second part is Equal Error Rate (EER) analysis. In short, it has been shown [2] that fusion in BA using multiple experts result in reduced variance, which in turns, results in reduced EER. EER is a commonly used error measure in BA. One specificity about this analysis is that the correlation among experts are explicitly considered and can be described by a class-dependent full covariance matrix.

In this work, we will consider a subtask in meeting analysis: identity verification via biometrics, or simply biometric authentication. Knowing the identity in meeting has an important impact in meetings because this *a priori* information can assist in retrieving highlights in meetings as in "who said what". Biometric authentication also shares another similarity with meeting analysis; in biometric authentication, users (or participants) are often known and only a few biometric examples (e.g. face with different orientations, speech samples, etc) per user are available to the system. The system is then required to verify the identity. In meetings, the participants are usually known and thus tracking of the person becomes a matter of identity verification. Furthermore, automatic meeting analysis also requires many systems working together and involves possibly many audio-visual media streams, e.g., the speech signal and the facial features. Development in fusion of biometric authentication will provide insights into how fusion in meeting can be done.

In the following, by using weighted sum fusion, we show that the VR-EER analysis can be used to predict optimal fusion candidates if the development set matches the evaluation set. In the presence of slight mismatch between development and evaluation sets, such is the case of the BANCA database, the predicted subset is still acceptable.

Section 2 presents two methods to choosing optimal fusion candidates: the brute-force approach and our proposed analytical approach. Section 3 presents briefly the BANCA experiment setup whereby 70 fusion experiments will be conducted. Sections 4 verifies experimentally that F-ratio calculated from a development set matches its counterpart on an evaluation set. Section 5 further examines the predictability of fusion candidates based on F-ratio calculated from the development set. The complexity of the proposed technique is evaluated in Section 6. This is followed by conclusions in Section 7.

2   Brute-Force Experimenting Versus Analytical Solution to Predicting Optimal Fusion Candidates

This section presents a conventional approach followed by our proposed approach to predicting a subset of candidates (base-experts or systems) that will be optimised in terms of performance when combined. The first approach is termed brute-force experimenting while the second is our proposal using an analytical solution. Note that this analytical solution is only possible when the fusion model is a linear combination of a subset of (the output of) N base-experts from all the available M base-experts.

Let us introduce the following notations. Let y_i^k be the output of system i indicating how probable a given input stimulus (biometric trait) is a client when the actual class label (target class) is $k \in \{C, I\}$, i.e., either a client or an impostor. Here, the expected value of client is always greater than that of impostor, i.e., $E[y_i^{k=C}] > E[y_i^{k=I}]$, where $E[z]$ is the expectation of z. Furthermore, let us assume that the combined model is of the form:

$$y_{GEN}^k \equiv \sum_{i=1}^{N} y_i^k \alpha_i, \tag{1}$$

where N is the chosen chosen number of experts and $\alpha_i | \forall_i$ weigh the output of each base-expert.

2.1   The Brute-Force Approach

Suppose there are two sets of data containing scores of M base-experts: development and evaluation data sets. The goal is to identify among all the M, which combination of at most N base-experts will give an optimal performance. In the brute-force approach, to choose from at most N out of M base-experts, there are altogether

$$^M C_1 + {}^M C_2 + \ldots + {}^M C_N = \sum_{i=1}^{N} {}^M C_i \tag{2}$$

possibilities, where $^m C_k$ is "m choose k" or $\frac{m!}{k!(m-k)!}$ by definition. To choose from all possible combinations, the total number is $2^M - 1$. The reason for minus one is that we do not consider the solution containing 0 base-expert. The brute-force approach will perform the following:

1. For each of the possible combinations:
   - estimate the best weights in the linear combination (1) from the development set according to a criterion (such as Mean Squared Error)
   - use the weights to evaluate the performance on the development set
2. Choose the best fusion candidate based on the criterion
3. Evaluate the chosen model on the evaluation set

In practice, before the linear combination, the output y_i^k of each expert should be normalised so that none of the base-expert score y_i^k will dominate the combination just because it has large values. Let $y_i^{norm,k}$ be the normalised value of y_i^k. The most common way to normalise the score is as follows:

$$y_i^{norm,k} \equiv \frac{y_i^k - \mu_i^{all}}{\sigma_i^{all}}, i = 1 \ldots, N. \tag{3}$$

The normalizing parameters μ_i^{all} and σ_i^{all} are mean and standard deviation calculated from the development set. These parameters are then applied on both the development and evaluation sets. In this way, the procedure of linear combination actually works on *normalised score space*. The linear combination is thus performed as follows:

$$y_{GEN}^{norm,k} \equiv \sum_{i=1}^{N} y_i^{norm,k} \alpha_i, \tag{4}$$

where $\alpha_{i=1...,N}$ are weights associated to each base-expert i and $y_{GEN}^{norm,k}$ is the fused score. The weights can be found using different methods, such as least-square minimisation or Fisher's linear discriminant [3–Chap. 3]. Two sets of $\left\{ y_{GEN}^{norm,k} | k = \{C, I\} \right\}$ are thus obtained, one from the development set and the other from the evaluation set. Note that $y_{GEN}^{norm,k}$ is one-dimensional (after fusion) and $y_i^{norm,k} | \forall_i$, as well as $y_i^k | \forall_i$ are N-dimensional data (of scores). The final decision function $F(\mathbf{x})$ (given a biometric sample $\mathbf{x}$, which is implicit in all variables $y_i^k, \forall_{i=1,...,N}$), accepts or rejects an access claim by comparing $y_{GEN}^{norm,k}$ with a threshold, as follows:

$$F(\mathbf{x}) = \begin{cases} accept & \text{if } y_{GEN}^{norm} > \Delta \\ reject & \text{otherwise.} \end{cases} \qquad (5)$$

This threshold should be calculated from the development set and then applied to the evaluation set.

The above procedure is then repeated for $\sum_{i=1}^{N} {}^M C_i$ combinations. The combination or fusion candidate that gives the lowest Equal Error Rate (EER) on the evaluation set is the so-called "optimal" fusion candidate. EER is defined as the point where False Acceptance Rate (FAR) equals False Rejection Rate (FRR). They are defined as:

$$\text{FAR}(\Delta) = \frac{\text{number of FAs}(\Delta)}{\text{number of impostor accesses}}, \qquad (6)$$

$$\text{FRR}(\Delta) = \frac{\text{number of FRs}(\Delta)}{\text{number of client accesses}}. \qquad (7)$$

Note that FA and FR are functions of a pre-determined threshold Δ. The empirical procedure to find Δ that satisfies the EER criterion (on the development set) is:

$$\Delta^* = \arg \min_{\Delta} |\text{FAR}(\Delta) - \text{FRR}(\Delta)|. \qquad (8)$$

The *empirical* EER value found this way is often reported as a single value called Half Total Error Rate (HTER). It is defined as the average of FAR and FRR:

$$\text{HTER}(\Delta^*) = \frac{\text{FAR}(\Delta^*) + \text{FRR}(\Delta^*)}{2}. \qquad (9)$$

The fusion candidate with minimum HTER on the development set is considered the optimal solution. Taking normalisation step into account, for each fusion candidate the brute-force approach thus needs to loop through the data:

- once to obtained normalise scores on the development and evaluation data sets;
- at least once to calculate the weights[1] on the development data set,
- once to apply the weights on the development and evaluation data sets, and
- once to evaluate the EER criterion on the development and evaluation data sets

The optimal fusion candidate found on the evaluation set is considered the "ground-truth". When there is no mismatch between development and evaluation data sets, we expect that the optimal fusion candidate found using this procedure to be similar.

---

[1] An iterative solution may require more passes, e.g. a single-layer Perceptron.

2.2   The Analytical Solution

The proposed approach assumes that all y_i^k's are Gaussian distributed. It has the advantage that there is no need to loop through the data set $\sum_{i=1}^{N} {}^{M}C_i$ times but only once. To quickly give an intuitive picture, in a two-dimensional case (i.e., fusing only two experts), data points of one of the experiments (to be discussed in Section 3) are plotted in Figure 1. Superimposed on the data points are two full-covariance Gaussians, one for

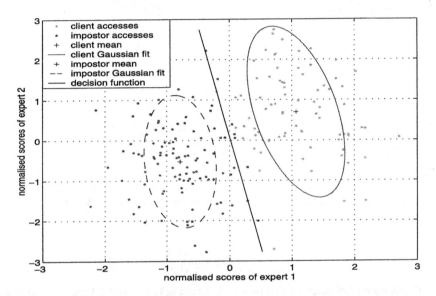

Fig. 1. A geometric interpretation of the proposed approach. Expert 1 is IDIAP's voice system and expert 2 is Surrey's automatic face authentication system, applied on the Ud-g1 BANCA data set

the client scores and the other for the impostor scores.

The technical challenge of the proposed method is to estimate the EER of the fused score $y_{GEN}^{norm,k}$. This can be done as follows: first estimate the normalising parameters μ_i^{all} and σ_i^{all} from the development set. Then, estimate the class-dependent Gaussian parameters $\Phi \equiv \{\boldsymbol{\mu}^k, \boldsymbol{\Sigma}^k\}$. $\boldsymbol{\mu}^k$ is a vector containing the class-dependent mean score of experts μ_i^k for $i = 1, \dots, N$ and $\boldsymbol{\Sigma}^k$ is the class-dependent covariance matrix whose elements are $\Sigma_{i,j}^k \equiv E[W_i^k, W_j^k]$, where W_i^k is the noise distribution associated to expert i (see also the appendix). Note that $\Sigma_{i,i}^k$ is simply the variance of scores of expert i.

From these parameters, it is possible to calculate the weights α_i and EER using an intermediate variable called F-ratio. The technical details of deriving F-ratio is beyond the scope of this study. They can be found in [2]. The calculation of weights can be found in classical references such as [3–Chap. 3]. Here, we present how the theoretical EER can be calculated. Let EER_{GEN}^{norm} be the EER of the normalised fused score. Its solution is:

$$\text{EER}_{GEN}^{norm} = \frac{1}{2} - \frac{1}{2}\text{erf}\left(\frac{\text{F-ratio}_{GEN}^{norm}}{\sqrt{2}}\right), \tag{10}$$

where

$$\text{F-ratio}_{GEN}^{norm} = \frac{\mu_{GEN}^{norm,C} - \mu_{GEN}^{norm,I}}{\sigma_{GEN}^{norm,C} + \sigma_{GEN}^{norm,I}}, \tag{11}$$

and

$$\text{erf}(z) = \frac{2}{\sqrt{\pi}} \int_0^z \exp\left[-t^2\right] dt. \tag{12}$$

$\mu_{GEN}^{norm,k}$ and $\sigma_{GEN}^{norm,k}$ are mean and standard deviation of the fused and normalised score $y_{GEN}^{norm,k}$. Their solutions are:

$$\mu_{GEN}^{norm,k} = \sum_{i=1}^{N} \frac{\alpha_i}{\sigma_i^{all}} \left(\mu_i^k - \mu_i^{all}\right) \tag{13}$$

and

$$\left(\sigma_{GEN}^{norm,k}\right)^2 = \sum_{m=1}^{N} \sum_{n=1}^{N} \frac{\alpha_m \alpha_n}{\sigma_m^{all} \sigma_n^{all}} E\left[W_m^k W_n^k\right] \tag{14}$$

respectively, for any $k \in \{C, I\}$. The derivation of Eqns. (13 and 14) can be shown in the appendix. As can be seen, all calculations can be solved analytically, including the optimal decision threshold Δ in the final decision function $F(\mathbf{x})$, as defined in Eqn. (5). The solution of Δ is:

$$\Delta = \frac{\mu_{GEN}^{norm,I} \sigma_{GEN}^{norm,C} + \mu_{GEN}^{norm,C} \sigma_{GEN}^{norm,I}}{\sigma_{GEN}^{norm,I} + \sigma_{GEN}^{norm,C}}. \tag{15}$$

The decision boundary in Figure 1 was indeed obtained using Eqn. (15). This analytical solution is actually derived from what is called VR-EER analysis due to our preceding work [2]. This analysis links the well-known variance reduction (VR) phenomenon due to committee of classifiers (as discussed in [3–Chap. 9] and elsewhere in the literature) to reduced EER. The parameters are thus called VR-EER parameters.

The next section will present the experiment setup that will be used to test our proposed approach.

3   Experiment Setup

The BANCA database [4] is the principal database used in this paper. It has a collection of face and voice prints of up to 260 persons in 5 different languages. In this paper, we only used the English subset. Hence only 52 people are used here; 26 are males and 26 are females. There are altogether 7 protocols, namely, Mc, Ma, Md, Ua, Ud, P and G, simulating matched control, matched adverse, matched degraded, uncontrolled adverse, uncontrolled degraded, pooled and grant test, respectively. For protocols P and G, there are 312 client accesses and 234 impostor accesses. For all other protocols, there are 78 client accesses and 104 impostor accesses. A set of face and speaker authentication experiments were carried out by University of Surrey (2 face experiments), IDIAP (speaker), UC3M (speaker) and UCL (face)[2]. Hence, there are 5 baseline experiments per protocol, making a total of 35 baseline experiments. Details of these experiments can be found in [5]. For each protocol, we used the following score files:

- IDIAP_voice_gmm_auto_scale_33_200
- SURREY_face_svm_auto
- SURREY_face_svm_man
- UC3M_voice_gmm_auto_scale_34_500
- UCL_face_lda_man

Moreover, for each protocol, there are two subgroups, called g1 and g2. In this paper, g1 is used as a *development* set while g2 is used as an *evaluation* set. The test set is considered the "ground-truth" data set and is used exclusively for *testing* only. It is particularly useful to determine generalisation performance, i.e., how well a classifier performs on unseen data sets. For each protocol, by combining each time two baseline experts, one can obtain 10 fusion experiments, given by $^5C_2$. This results in a total of 70 experiments for all protocols. Similarly by combining each time three baseline experts, one will have a total of $7 \times {}^5C_3 = 70$ experiments.

4   Generalisation Using Weighted-Sum Fusion

In [6], it was shown that given full knowledge about VR-EER parameters, F-ratio of fused score using the *mean* operator can be estimated accurately. Furthermore EER can be predicted fairly accurately, by assuming that the client and impostor scores are drawn from Gaussian distributions. There are two issues to be examined here. The first issue is, given full knowledge about the VR-EER parameters (typically on a development set), would theoretical F-ratios match empirical F-ratios[3]? The second issue is, would it be possible to predict F-ratio on *unseen* data. This is the issue of generalisation. In this case, F-ratio from the development set is compared to F-ratio from the evaluation sets of BANCA protocols (see Section 3) . Note that each of these tests will be repeated $2^5 - 1 = 31$ times for each of the 7 protocols, each time using a different combination of 1–5 base-experts. Hence, there are altogether 217 experiments.

These two issues are detailed below:

1. **Posterior test**. One knows all the VR-EER parameters. This is typically the case for the development set. The empirical F-ratio of each fusion candidate is compared with its theoretical counterpart, with the weights estimated from the same set. This test is called posterior because one has all the information about the data set.
2. **Evaluation test**. Having all the information about the development set, the goal here is to test if one can extrapolate this information on an (unseen) evaluation set. This

---

[2] Available at "ftp://ftp.idiap.ch/pub/bengio/banca/banca_scores"

[3] *Empirical* F-ratio means that the F-ratio is obtained by actually carrying out a complete experiment, whereas *theoretical* F-ratio means that the F-ratio is estimated analytically. Hence, evaluation of empirical F-ratio requires a pass through the data while its theoretical counterpart requires only direct applications of Eqns. (11), (13) and (14).

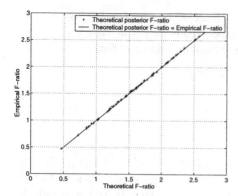

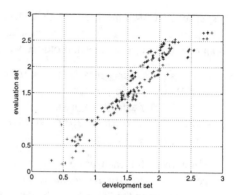

Fig. 2. Comparison of a theoretical prior F-ratio and empirical F-ratio, based on BANCA development set, over all possible combinations and all protocols, i.e., 217 data points

Fig. 3. F-ratios of combined scores of the development set versus those of the evaluation set, over all possible combinations and all protocols, i.e., 217 data points

tests how closely the development set corresponds to the evaluation set. Empirical F-ratio of evaluation set is plotted against its development set counterpart.

The results are shown in Figure 2 for the first test and Figure 3 for the second test. As can be seen, the posterior test shows that, given full knowledge about the VR-EER parameters, each data point (which corresponds to each fusion experiment) can be predicted accurately. The evaluation test shows that F-ratios of the development set is correlated to that of the evaluation set. Hence, prediction is possible. The inaccuracy is due to the inherent mismatch between the development and the evaluation sets.

5   Predicting Optimal Subsets of Base-Expert Candidates

In the previous evaluation test, it was shown that the F-ratios between the development and the evaluation sets due to fusion are correlated. This implies that good candidates for fusion in a development set would also be good candidates in the corresponding evaluation set. The next experiment is to examine how accurate the prediction of the best fusion candidate can be if we were to choose *from all* M base-experts. Note that we could have also conducted a series of experiments to find out the accuracy of predicting *at most* the N best fusion candidates from all M base-experts for different values of $N \leq M$. Since choosing from all is a more difficult task than choosing at most N, we will only illustrate the former problem. Before doing so, let us label some of the combinations as listed in Table 1. The numbers 1–5 correspond to the five base-experts discussed in Section 3. Figure 4 shows the top five fusion candidates due to choosing from all 31 fusion candidates. There are 7 sub-figures, each corresponding to a BANCA protocol. The EERs of the candidates are sorted from the smallest to the biggest in the x-axis. Hence the first item in the x-axis is the best candidate fusion candidate. For example, the best candidate according to protocol G, as shown in Figure 4, is z (1-2-3-4), according to the development set but is A (1-2-3-5) according to the evaluation set. Since

Table 1. Labels of corresponding fusion experiments using 1, 2, 3 and 4 base-experts. The numbers 1–5 in the right columns of each table correspond to the five base-experts discussed in Section 3. The letter "E" is assigned to fusion of all experts

(a) base-expert

labels	experts
a	1
b	2
c	3
d	4
e	5

(b) 2-expert fusion

labels	experts
f	1 2
g	1 3
h	1 4
i	1 5
j	2 3
k	2 4
l	2 5
m	3 4
n	3 5
o	4 5

(c) 3-expert fusion

labels	experts
p	1 2 3
q	1 2 4
r	1 2 5
s	1 3 4
t	1 3 5
u	1 4 5
v	2 3 4
w	2 3 5
x	2 4 5
y	3 4 5

(d) 4-expert fusion

labels	experts
z	1 2 3 4
A	1 2 3 5
B	1 2 4 5
C	1 3 4 5
D	2 3 4 5

the evaluation set is taken as the "ground-truth", i.e, A is the correct answer, we need to consider the top 3 candidates in order to "remedy" this error. For the protocol Mc as well as Md and Ua , it takes the top two candidates to remedy this error. Ideally, it is desirable that the top candidate as proposed by the development and evaluation set to be the same. Such is the case for protocols P, Ma and Ud. By varying the top-k candidates where $k = 1, 2, 3$ and applying the analysis for other protocols, we obtain Table 2. As can be observed, most of the errors committed by choosing the top fusion candidate can be rectified when choosing the top-2 fusion candidates. Note that even though some proposed optimal fusion candidates are not coherent with the evaluation set, the proposed optimal fusion candidates are not very far off from their follow-up candidates in terms of EER, across different protocols, i.e., top few optimal candidates have very similar EERs. As a result, even if the proposed candidate according to the development set might be incorrect, the increase of EER error due to this wrong selection is not big.

6   Analysis of Complexity

We now analyse the complexity of our proposed approach and compare it with the brute-force approach. Let the number of development examples and evaluation examples be

Table 2. Mistakes committed by choosing the top-k fusion candidate(s) by choosing from all 31 fusion candidates, over all 7 protocols, for $k = 1, 2, 3$. As k increases, errors will decrease

Top k	Errors committed over 7 protocols
1	4
2	1
3	0

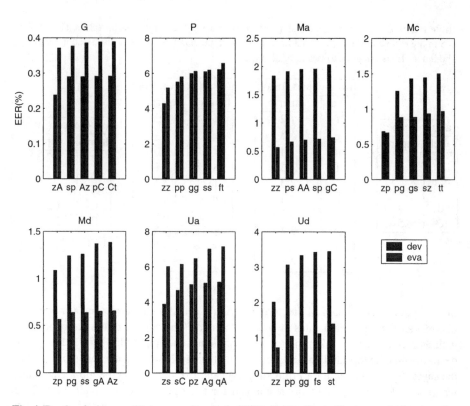

Fig. 4. Top five fusion candidates according to the EER criterion (sorted in the x-axis) by choosing from all 31 fusion candidates for each of the 7 protocols. The alphabets "XY" represent the fusion candidate X proposed by the development set and Y by the evaluation set. Tables 1(a)–(d) show the corresponding base-experts with E denoting fusing all the experts

l_{dev} and l_{eva} In the brute-force approach, to choose one best fusion candidate from all possible M base-experts, one would have to carry out the experiment $2^M - 1$ times. Furthermore, in each experiment, one has to loop through $l_{dev} + l_{eva}$ examples. The complexity is thus:

$$O\left((l_{dev} + l_{eva}) \times (2^M - 1)\right). \qquad (16)$$

In the proposed approach, one only has to loop through the both development and evaluation sets once to derive all the VR-EER parameters (i.e., class-dependent mean and covariance matrix plus the global mean and standard deviations) and then to evaluate the F-ratio criterion $2^N - 1$ times on the test set. Hence, the complexity is thus:

$$O\left(l_{dev} + l_{eva}\right) + 2^M - 1). \qquad (17)$$

In the brute-force approach, the $2^M - 1$ is multiplicative with the number of development and evaluation examples whereas in the proposed approach, these two terms are additive. Therefore, our approach is scalable to larger fusion problems with significant reduction of computation cost. It should be noted that the computation involved even in the brute-force approach in this case is simple ($M = 5$). However, for large problems, this benefit will be more obvious.

7   Conclusion

In this paper, using a Gaussian model with full covariance matrix to model the client and impostor distributions, on the zero-mean unit-variance normalised score space, we showed how to predict theoretically the performance of an authentication system based on Equal Error Rate (EER) using weighted sum fusion. This approach is based on VR-EER analysis due to [2]. The advantage of the proposed approach is that one does not have to make the assumption that the base-experts are independent and that their scores are not correlated, as frequently done in the literature. In fact, the dependency is already captured by the covariance matrix. Although a single full covariance matrix seems to be overly simple (as compared to mixture of Gaussians with diagonal covariance matrix), we have shown that it is adequate to model EER [6] as a function of *F-ratio*, a quantity that measures how separable the client distribution is from the its impostor counterpart.

The central idea of this work is to use F-ratio as a criterion to search for an optimal subset of base-experts for fusion in an efficient way. Although F-ratio was previously established in [2], this study demonstrates a way to predict the performance of fusion analytically, without compromising the effectiveness when one actually carries out the fusion experiments. Hence the proposed technique allows us to select an optimal subset of base-experts for fusion in an efficient way. To choose one optimal fusion candidate from M base-experts, the brute-force approach needs to carry out $2^M - 1$ experiments and for each experiment, this approach will need to cycle through the data set several times. The proposed approach needs only to loop through the development and test set once and to evaluate the F-ratio criterion $2^M - 1$ times. Hence, our approach has only a fixed computation cost with respect to the size of the available data set and will scale well with large fusion problems.

We tested our approach on the BANCA database and showed that F-ratio can be predicted accurately if one has the full knowledge about the data distribution (e.g. development data set). The prediction degrades when one knows less and less about the data (e.g. the test data set). In fact, by actually carrying out 217 fusion experiments on the BANCA database, we showed that the F-ratio on the development set (g1) is correlated to that of the test set (g2), despite their mismatch. Exploiting this ability, we were able to predict an optimal subset of fusion (base-expert) candidates fairly accurately on the 7 BANCA protocols. The accuracy cannot be 100% since there exists an intrinsic mismatch between the development and evaluation sets.

Acknowledgment

This work was supported in part by the IST Program of the European Community, under the PASCAL Network of Excellence, IST-2002-506778, funded in part by the Swiss Federal Office for Education and Science (OFES) and the Swiss NSF through the NCCR on IM2. The authors also thank the anonymous reviewers for detailed comments and suggestions. This publication only reflects the authors' views.

A   Derivation of Solutions

Suppose $y_{i,j}^k$ is the j-th observed sample of the i-th response of class k, recalling that $i = 1, \ldots, N$ and $k = \{C, I\}$. We assume that this observed variable has a deterministic component and a noise component and that their relation is additive. The deterministic component is due to the fact that the class is discrete in nature, i.e., during authentication, we know that a user in *either* a client or an impostor. The noise component is due to some random processes during biometric acquisition (e.g. degraded situation due to light change, miss-alignment, etc) which in turns affect the quality of extracted features. Indeed, it has a distribution governed by the extracted feature set x often in a non-linear way. By ignoring the source of distortion in extracted biometric features, we actually assume the noise component to be random (while in fact they may be not if we were able to systematically incorporate all possible variations into the base-expert model).

   Let μ_i^k be the deterministic component. Note that its value is *only dependent on* the class $k = \{C, I\}$ and independent of j. We can now model $y_{i,j}^k$ as a sum of this deterministic value plus the noise term $w_{i,j}^k$, as follows:

$$y_{i,j}^k = \mu_i^k + w_{i,j}^k, \tag{18}$$

for $k \in \{C, I\}$ where $w_{i,j}^k$ follows an unknown distribution W_i^k with zero mean and $(\sigma_i^k)^2$ variance, i.e., $w_{i,j}^k \sim W_i^k\left(0, (\sigma_i^k)^2\right)$. By adopting such a simple model, from the fusion point of view, we effectively encode the i-th expert score as the sum of a deterministic value and another random variable, in a class-dependent way. Following Eqn. (18), we can deduce that $y_{i,j}^k \sim Y_i^k \equiv W_i^k\left(\mu_i^k, (\sigma_i^k)^2\right)$. We can then write:

$$Y_i^k = \mu_i^k + W_i^k, \tag{19}$$

The expectation of Y_i^k (over different j samples) is:

$$E[Y_i^k] = E[\mu_i^k] + E[W_i^k] = \mu_i^k. \tag{20}$$

Let $\Sigma_{i,j}^k$ be the i-th and j-th element of the covariance matrix of $Y_i^k | \forall_i$, i.e., $\boldsymbol{\Sigma}^k$. It can be calculated as:

$$\Sigma_{i,j}^k \equiv E\left[(Y_i^k - \mu_i^k)(Y_j^k - \mu_j^k)\right]$$
$$= E[W_i^k W_j^k] \tag{21}$$

where $\Sigma_{i,j}^k$ is the covariance between two distributions Y_i^k and Y_j^k. When $i = j$, we have the definition of variance of Y_i^k, i.e.,

$$\Sigma_{i,i}^k \equiv (\sigma_i^k)^2 = E[W_i^k W_i^k]. \tag{22}$$

Let $\mu_{GEN}^{norm,k}$ and $\sigma_{GEN}^{norm,k}$ be the mean and standard deviation of combined scores derived from y_i^k for $i = 1, \ldots, N$ (see Eqn. (4)). Let $Y_{GEN}^{norm,k}$ be the distribution from which $y_{GEN}^{norm,k}$ is drawn. Note that μ_{GEN}^k and σ_{GEN}^k can be defined by Eqn. (20) and Eqn. (22)

by replacing the index i by GEN and similarly for $\mu_{GEN}^{norm,k}$ and $\sigma_{GEN}^{norm,k}$. The expected value of $Y_{GEN}^{norm,k}$, for $k = \{C, I\}$, is:

$$
\begin{aligned}
\mu_{GEN}^{norm,k} &\equiv E[Y_{GEN}^{norm,k}] \\
&= \sum_{i=1}^{N} \alpha_i E[Y_i^{norm,k}] \\
&= \sum_{i=1}^{N} \frac{\alpha_i}{\sigma_i^{all}} \left(E[Y_i^k] - \mu_i^{all} \right) \\
&= \sum_{i=1}^{N} \frac{\alpha_i}{\sigma_i^{all}} \left(\mu_i^k - \mu_i^{all} \right)
\end{aligned}
\tag{23}
$$

The variance of $Y_{GEN}^{norm,k}$ is:

$$
\begin{aligned}
(\sigma_{GEN}^{norm,k})^2 &= Cov(Y_{GEN}^{norm,k}, Y_{GEN}^{norm,k}) \\
&= E\left[\left(Y_{GEN}^{norm,k} - E[Y_{GEN}^{norm,k}] \right)^2 \right] \\
&= E\left[\left(\sum_{i=1}^{N} \frac{\alpha_i(Y_i^k - \mu_i^{all})}{\sigma_i^{all}} - \sum_{i=1}^{N} \frac{\alpha_i(\mu_i^k - \mu_i^{all})}{\sigma_i^{all}} \right)^2 \right] \\
&= E\left[\left(\sum_{i=1}^{N} \frac{\alpha_i(Y_i^k - \mu_i^k)}{\sigma_i^{all}} \right)^2 \right] \\
&= E\left[\left(\sum_{i=1}^{N} \frac{\alpha_i W_i^k}{\sigma_i^{all}} \right)^2 \right]
\end{aligned}
\tag{24}
$$

To expand Eqn. (24), one should take care of possible correlation between different W_m^k and W_n^k, as follows:

$$
\begin{aligned}
(\sigma_{GEN}^{norm,k})^2 &= E\left[\left(\sum_{m=1}^{N} \sum_{n=1}^{N} \frac{\alpha_m W_m^k \alpha_n W_n^k}{\sigma_m^{all} \sigma_n^{all}} \right) \right] \\
&= \sum_{m=1}^{N} \sum_{n=1}^{N} \frac{\alpha_m \alpha_n}{\sigma_m^{all} \sigma_n^{all}} E\left[W_m^k W_n^k \right]
\end{aligned}
\tag{25}
$$

for any $k \in \{C, I\}$.

References

1. J. Kittler, K. Messer, and J. Czyz, "Fusion of Intramodal and Multimodal Experts in Personal Identity Authentication Systems," in *Proc. Cost 275 Workshop*, Rome, 2002, pp. 17–24.

2. N. Poh and S. Bengio, "Why Do Multi-Stream, Multi-Band and Multi-Modal Approaches Work on Biometric User Authentication Tasks?," in *IEEE Int'l Conf. Acoustics, Speech, and Signal Processing (ICASSP)*, Montreal, 2004, pp. vol. V, 893–896.

3. C. Bishop, *Neural Networks for Pattern Recognition*, Oxford University Press, 1999.

4. E. Bailly-Baillière, S. Bengio, F. Bimbot, M. Hamouz, J. Kittler, J. Mariéthoz, J. Matas, K. Messer, V. Popovici, F. Porée, B. Ruiz, and J.-P. Thiran, "The BANCA Database and Evaluation Protocol," in *Springer LNCS-2688, 4th Int. Conf. Audio- and Video-Based Biometric Person Authentication, AVBPA'03*. 2003, Springer-Verlag.

5. Christine Marcel, "Multimodal Identity Verification at IDIAP," Communication Report 03-04, IDIAP, Martigny, Switzerland, 2003.

6. N. Poh and S. Bengio, "How Do Correlation and Variance of Base Classifiers Affect Fusion in Biometric Authentication Tasks?," Research Report 04-18, IDIAP, Martigny, Switzerland, 2004.

Mixture of SVMs for Face Class Modeling

Julien Meynet[1], Vlad Popovici, and Jean-Philippe Thiran

Signal Processing Institute, Swiss Federal Institute of Technology Lausanne,
CH-1015 Lausanne, Switzerland
http://itswww.epfl.ch

Abstract. We[1] present a method for face detection which uses a new SVM structure trained in an expert manner in the eigenface space. This robust method has been introduced as a post processing step in a real-time face detection system. The principle is to train several parallel SVMs on subsets of some initial training set and then train a second layer SVM on the margins of the first layer of SVMs. This approach presents a number of advantages over the classical SVM: firstly the training time is considerably reduced and secondly the classification performance is improved, we will present some comparisions with the single SVM approach for the case of human face class modeling.

1 Introduction

Human face detection is one of the most important tasks of the face analysis and can be viewed as a pre-processing step for face recognition systems. It is always important to find a precise localization of faces in order to be able to later recognize them. The difficulty resides in the fact that the face object is highly deformable and its aspect is also influenced by the environmental conditions. On the other hand, the class of objects which do not belong to the face class is large and can not be modeled. Thus finding a model for the face class is a challenging task. In the last years, many methods have been proposed, we give a brief overview of the most significant of them.

A fast face detection alorithm has been proposed by Viola and Jones[1] , it uses simple rectangular Haar-Like features boosted in a cascade structure. We have used this fast approach as a pre-processing step in order to obtain a fast and robust face detection system.

Then, one of the most representative approaches for the class of neural networks–based face detectors is the work reported by Rowley et. al. in [2]. Their system has two major components: a face detector made of a scanning window at each scale and position, and a final decision module whose role is to arbitrate multiple detections.

---

[1] The authors thank the Swiss National Science Foundation for supporting this work through the National Center of Competence in Research on "Interactive Multimodal Information Management (IM2)".

S. Bengio and H. Bourlard (Eds.): MLMI 2004, LNCS 3361, pp. 173–181, 2005.

Sung and Poggio have developed a clustering and distri-bution-based system for face detection [3]. There are two main components in their system: a model of the face/non–face patterns distribution and a decision making module. The two class distributions are each approximated by six Gaussian clusters.

A naive Bayes classifier based on local appearance and position of the face pattern at different resolutions is described by Schneiderman and Kanade in [4]. The face samples are decomposed in four rectangular subregions which are then projected to a lower dimensional space using PCA and quantized into a finite set of patterns.

Osuna et. al. developed a face detector based on SVM that worked directly on the intensity patterns [5]. A brief description of the SVM is given in this paper also. The large scale tests they performed showed a slightly lower error rate than the system of Sung and Poggio, while running approximately 30 times faster.

In [6], Popovici and Thiran proposed to model the face class using a SVM trained in eigenfaces space. They showed that even a very low dimensional space (compared with the original input space) suffices to capture the relevant information when used in conjunction with a powerful classifier, like a non linear SVM. We propose here an extension of these ideas that employs a mixture of SVMs (MSVM in the following) for better capturing the face class variability. We use the analysis from [6] for choosing the input space of our classifier, but we will also extend the feature vector by adding a new term that accounts for the information lost through the PCA process. The idea of using mixture of experts (in our case SVMs) is not new, but we will use a slightly different approach: the final decision is taken by a SVM that is trained using the margins output by the first layer of SVMs. In training this final SVM we penalize more the false negative type of errors (missed faces) to favor the detection of faces. Other ways of combining the experts can be used: for example, in [7] the EM algorithm was used to train the experts. Later [8] replaced neural network experts by SVMs but still trained each expert on the whole dataset. The use of parallel SVMs trained on subsets of large scale problem has been studied in 2002 in [9]. However, the second layer remained a neural network.

We will introduce the MSVM and we will justify its use both from a theoretical perspective and a more practical one. In section 2 we will briefly review the SVM theory and then we will describe the MSVM approach. The MSVM will be trained on face and non face examples pre-processed by PCA, as described on section 2.3. Finally, in sections 3 and 4 we present some experiments and comparisons with classical SVM and we draw some conclusions.

2   Mixtures of SVMs

2.1   An Overview of Classical SVM

Let us begin with a brief overview of the classical SVM algorithm. More information about SVM can be found in [10], [11].

Let $\{(\mathbf{x}_i, y_i) | i = 1, \ldots, l\} \subset \mathbb{R}^n \times \{-1, +1\}$ be a set of examples. From a practical point of view, the problem to be solved is to find that hyperplane that correctly separates the data while maximizing the sum of distances to the closest positive and negative points (i.e. *the margin*). The hyperplane is given by[2]:

$$h_{\mathbf{w},b}(\mathbf{x}) = \langle \mathbf{w}, \mathbf{x} \rangle + b = 0 \tag{1}$$

and the decision function is

$$f(\mathbf{x}) = \mathrm{sgn}(h_{\mathbf{w},b}(\mathbf{x})) = \mathrm{sgn}\left(\langle \mathbf{w}, \mathbf{x} \rangle + b\right) \tag{2}$$

In the case of linearly separable data, maximizing the margins means to maximize $\frac{2}{\|\mathbf{w}\|}$ or, equivalently, to minimize $\|\mathbf{w}\|^2$, subject to $y_i(\langle \mathbf{w}, \mathbf{x} \rangle + b) \geq 1$. Suppose now that the two classes overlap in feature space. One way to find the optimal plane is to relax the above constraints by introducing the *slack variables* ξ_i and solving the following problem (using 2-norm for the slack variables):

$$\min_{\xi, \mathbf{w}, b} \|\mathbf{w}\|^2 + C \sum_{i=1}^{l} \xi_i^2 \tag{3}$$

$$\text{subject to} \qquad y_i(\langle \mathbf{w}, \mathbf{x}_i \rangle + b) \geq 1 - \xi_i \quad \forall i = 1, \ldots, l \tag{4}$$

where C controls the weight of the classification errors ($C = \infty$ in the separable case).

This problem is solved by means of Lagrange multipliers method. Let $\alpha_i \geq 0$ be the Lagrange multipliers solving the problem above, then the separating hyperplane, as a function of α_i, is given by

$$h_{\alpha_i,b}(\mathbf{x}) = \sum_{i,\alpha_i > 0} y_i \alpha_i \langle \mathbf{x}_i, \mathbf{x} \rangle + b \tag{5}$$

Note that usually only a small proportion of α_i are non-zero. The training vectors $\mathbf{x}_i$ corresponding to $\alpha_i > 0$ are called *support vectors* and are the only training vectors influencing the separating boundary.

In practice however, a linear separating plane is seldom sufficient. To generalize the linear case one can project the input space into a higher–dimensional space in the hope of a better training–class separation. In the case of SVM this is achieved by using the so–called "kernel trick". Basically, it replaces the inner product $\langle \mathbf{x}_i, \mathbf{x}_j \rangle$ with a kernel function $K(\mathbf{x}_i, \mathbf{x}_j)$. As the data vectors are involved only in this inner products, the optimization process can be carried out in the feature space directly. Some of the most used kernel functions are:

$$\text{the polynomial kernel} \qquad K(\mathbf{x}, \mathbf{z}) = (\langle \mathbf{x}, \mathbf{z} \rangle + 1)^d \tag{6}$$

$$\text{the RBF kernel} \qquad K(\mathbf{x}, \mathbf{z}) = \exp(-\gamma \|\mathbf{x} - \mathbf{z}\|^2) \tag{7}$$

---

[2] We use $\langle \cdot, \cdot \rangle$ to denote the inner product operator

2.2   Mixture of SVMs (MSVM)

SVM techniques are well known since a few years for many reasons, among them their generalization capabilities. However, as explained in the previous subsection, training a SVM usually requires solving a quadratic optimization problem, which means it also varies quadratically with the number of training examples. We know by experience that because of the large variability of both face and non face classes, building a face detection system requires a large amount of examples. So in order to make easier the training of the SVM (in term of training time) we use a parallel structure of SVMs similar to the one introduced in [9]. A first part of the dataset is splitted and clustered and each cluster is used to train each SVM of the first layer. And then the remaining example are used to train a second layer SVM, based on the margins of the first layer SVMs. Basically, the input space for the 2nd layer SVM is the space of margins generated by the 1st layer SVMs. We can represent the output of such a mixture of $M+1$ experts as follows:

$$h_{\alpha_i,b}(\mathbf{x}) = \sum_{i,\alpha_i>0} y_i\alpha_i K(\mathbf{m}_i(x_i), \mathbf{m}(x)) + b \qquad (8)$$

where $\mathbf{m}(\mathbf{x})$ is the vector of margins output by the M SVMs in the first layer given the input $\mathbf{x}$.

Assuming that we want to train M SVMs in the first layer, we will need $M+1$ training sets (an additional one is used to train the second layer SVM) - see figures 1. We use two different approaches for generating the $M+1$ subsets. One consists of a random partitioning of the original training set. The second one is more elaborated: we first randomly draw a sample that will be used for training the second layer and then we use a clustering algorithm, like k-Means[12] , for building the M subsets needed for training the first layer SVM.

In both cases we train each SVM-L1-i using a cross-validation process to select the best parameters then we use the $M+1$-th dataset for training the second layer SVM (SVM-L2): we let each of SVM-L1-i to classify the examples from this dataset and we take the margins output by the SVM-L1-i as input for SVM-L2. The margin can be seen as a measure of confidence in classifying an example, so, in some sense, the second layer SVM learns a non linear function that depends on the input vector and which assembles the confidences of each individual expert.

From a practical point of view, we have decomposed a problem of $O(N^2)$ complexity in $M+1$ problems of $O(\lceil\frac{N}{M+1}\rceil^2)$ complexity. As $N >> M$ this decomposition is clearly advantageous, and has the potential of being implemented in parallel, reducing even more the training time. Another issue that should be mentionned here is related to the robustness of the final classifier. In the case of a single SVM, if the training set contains outliers or some examples heavily affected by noise, its performance can be degraded. However, the chances of suffering from such examples are less important in the case of MSVM.

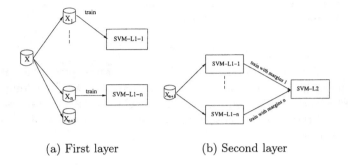

(a) First layer   (b) Second layer

Fig. 1. Training of the SVMs of the first ans second layer

2.3   Construction of the Eigenfaces

As we use a large number of examples, we use Principal Component Analysis(PCA) to decrease the dimensionality of the image space. We first recall the definition of PCA and then we will discuss some possible improvements.

Principal Component Analysis (PCA) and Eigenfaces. Let $x_1, \ldots, x_l \in \mathbb{R}^n$ be a set of n-dimensional vectors and consider the following linear model for representing them

$$\mathbf{x} = W_{(k)}\mathbf{z} + \mu \tag{9}$$

where $W_{(k)}$ is a $n \times k$ matrix, $\mathbf{z} \in \mathbb{R}^k$ and $\mu \in \mathbb{R}^n$. For a given $k < n$, the PCA can be defined ([13]) as the transformation $W_{(k)}$ whose column vectors $\mathbf{w}_j$, called *principal axes*, are those orthonormal axes onto which the retained variance under projection is maximal. It can be shown that the vectors $\mathbf{w}_j$ are given by the dominant k eigenvectors of the sample covariance matrix[3] $S = \frac{1}{l}\sum_l (\mathbf{x}_i - \mu)(\mathbf{x}_i - \mu)'$ such that $S\mathbf{w}_j = \lambda\mathbf{w}_j$ and where μ is the sample mean. The vector $\mathbf{z}_i = W'_{(k)}(\mathbf{x}_i - \mu)$ is the k-dimensional representation of the observed vector $\mathbf{x}_i$. The projection defined by PCA is optimal in the sense that amongst the k-dimensional subspaces, the one defined by the columns of $W_{(k)}$ minimizes the reconstruction error $\sum_i \|\mathbf{x}_i - \hat{\mathbf{x}}_i\|^2$ where $\hat{\mathbf{x}}_i = W_{(k)}\mathbf{z}_i + \mu$.

Now let us view an image as a vector in $\mathbb{R}^n$ space by considering its pixels in lexicographic order. Then the PCA method can be applied to images as well, and in the case of face images the principal directions are called *eigenfaces* [14],[15]. Some details about the estimation of the eigenfaces space dimensionality such as classification in eigenfaces space using SVMs are shown in [6].

Distance from Feature Space (DFFS). Traditionally, the distance between a given image and the class of faces has been decomposed in two orthogonal components: the *distance in feature space* (corresponding to the projection onto

---

[3] We denote with a prime symbol the transpose of a matrix or a vector.

the lower dimensional space) and the *distance from feature space (DFFS)* (accounting for the reconstruction error).

$$DFFS = \sqrt{\|\mathbf{x} - \mu\|^2 - \|\mathbf{z}\|^2} \tag{10}$$

Given this and considering that the DFFS still contains some useful information for classification, we can improve the discrimination power by adding the value of the DFFS to the projection vector. Thus considering that we keep 85% of total variance with the k first eigenvectors, we use the following vectors to perform the classification.

$$X = (x_1, \ldots, x_k, x_{k+1}), \tag{11}$$

where $x_1, \ldots, x_k$ represent the projection onto the $k-$ dimensional eigenfaces space and x_{k+1} the DFFS.

3   Experiments and Results

Our experiments have been based on images from the BANCA [16] and the XM2VTS[17] databases for the faces whereas the non faces examples were chosen by bootstrapping on randomly selected images. In order to test the accuracy and the validity of the method, we have used a dataset as follows: A training set made of 8256 faces and 14000 non face examples, all images with the fixed size 20×15 pixels. The validation set had 7822 faces and 900000 non faces of the same size. We first tried to find a coherent PCA decomposition before training the SVMs. The PCA reduces the dimensionality of the input space but also the eigenfaces proved to be more robust features in real-world applications than the raw pixel values.

We first estimated the dimensionality of the eigenfaces space that we need to keep 85% of total variation. For this we have estimated the number of examples from which the eigenfaces space has a stable dimensionality for keeping 85% of total variation. So we performed the PCA decomposition on a randomly selected part of the training set and from the 300-dimensional input space we kept only 17 eigenfaces. As explained earlier, the vector used for the classification task is made by adding the DFFS value to the projection onto the eigenfaces space.

Then, the face training set has been splitted into 2 subsets. The first part, containing 5000 examples, has been splitted into 5 subsets, either by clustering or by random sampling. We trained the SVM-L1-i on these 5 subsets, each combined with 2000 negative examples and the remaining subset (3000 faces and 4000 non faces) was passed through all the trained SVM-L1-i.The output margins were used to train the second layer SVM. Table 1 shows the classification results on the validation set for each SVM.

Using the random sampling for generating the training sets for the first layer has the advantage of reducing the importance of outliers or unusual examples, but leads to SVMs that need more support vectors for good performances. On the other hand, using k-Means clustering leads to SVMs that perform like experts on their own domain, but whose common expertise should cover the full domain.

Table 1. Performances on the validation set for both random sampling (r.s.) and k-Means clustering (k-m)

Classifier	Faces(%)		NonFaces(%)	
	r.s.	k-m	r.s.	k-m
SVM-L1-1	86.23	76.47	99.00	98.86
SVM-L1-2	84.91	82.32	99.00	97.68
SVM-L1-3	85.13	81.23	99.02	98.77
SVM-L1-4	84.64	77.12	99.13	99.12
SVM-L1-4	85.66	74.29	99.12	99.12
SVM-L2	93.60	95.37	98.14	96.43

Table 2. Comparison between MSVM with random sampling (MSVM,r.s), MSVM with k-Means clustering (MSVM,k-m) and a single SVM trained on the complete training set

Classifier	Faces(%)	Non Faces(%)	Total N° SV
MSVM,r.s	93.60	98.14	1673
MSVM,k-m	95.37	96.43	1420
Single SVM	92.8	99.52	2504

It is interesting to see that the MSVM has better generalization capabilities than a single SVM trained on the initial dataset. This result shows that as explained in section 2, MSVM does not only give improvements in term of training time but also in term of classification performances. We can also notice the importance of the SVM-L2: The TER (Total error rate) has been improved from a single SVM but it is really more interesting for face detection as it improves the true positive rate (even if the false positive rate is degraded). Just recall that in the face detection world, we often want to detect a maximum number of faces even if some non face examples are misclassified. Another advantage of this method compadred to the single SVM trained on the complete dataset is that the total number of support vectors (last column in table2) is radically inferior in the case of MSVM. This emphasizes the gain of time and computation complexity given by the MSVM.

This approach has also been implemented and tested as a face detector on real world images. Some examples from the BANCA [16] database are shown in Figure 2 For this implementation, we used a pre-processing using the face detector proposed in [1].

4   Conclusions

In this paper we presented a method for face class modeling using mixtures of SVMs. This approach presents an extension to the SVM technique which allows a better use of particularly large datasets. We have used this mixture of experts approach in the context of face detection using a PCA decomposition

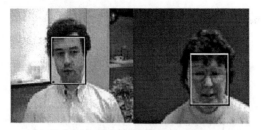

Fig. 2. Face detection on BANCA [16] examples

and then adding the DFFS to the features in order to decrease the information loss through the PCA process. We have proposed here a mixture of SVMs made of several SVMs in a first layer trained on independent subsets of the initial dataset and a second layer trained on the margins predicted by the first layer SVMs given another independent subset. It has been shown that this structure allowed a significant improvement from the single SVM trained on the complete database. On the first hand, the training time is largely reduced because of the parallel structure and the splitting of the original subset, and on the other hand, the discrimination capabilities are improved because of the possible presence of noise and outliers in the dataset. In order to have a structure more adapted to the datasets, we are now working on more specialized experts, for example by using a clustering in eigenfaces space based on a more appropriated metrics.

References

1. Viola, P., Jones, M.: Rapid object detection using a boosted cascade of simple features. In: Proceedings IEEE Conf. on Computer Vision and Pattern Recognition. (2001)
2. Rowley, H.A., Baluja, S., Kanade, T.: Human face detection in visual scenes. In Touretzky, D.S., Mozer, M.C., Hasselmo, M.E., eds.: Advances in Neural Information Processing Systems. Volume 8., The MIT Press (1996) 875–881
3. Sung, K., Poggio, T.: Example-based learning for view-based human face detection. IEEE Transaction on Pattern Analysis and Machine Intelligence **20** (1998) 39–51
4. Schneiderman, H., Kanade, T.: Probabilistic modeling of local appearance and spatial relationship for object recognition. In: Proceedings of Computer Vision and Pattern Recognition. (1998) 45–51
5. Osuna, E., Freund, R., Girosi, F.: Training support vector machines: an application to face detection. In: Proceedings of Computer Vision and Pattern Recognition. (1997)
6. V. Popovici and J.-P. Thiran: Face Detection using SVM Trained in Eigenfaces space. In: Proceedings of the 4th International Conference on Audio- and Video-Based Biometric Person Authentication. (2003) 925–928
7. Nowlan, R.A.J.M.I.J.S.J., rey E. Hinton, G.: Adaptive mixtures of local experts. In: Neural Computation 3(1), 1991. (1991) 79–87

8. Kwok, J.T.: Support vector mixture for classification and regression problems. In: Proceedings of the International Conference on Pattern Recognition (ICPR). (1998) 255–258
9. Collobert, R., Bengio, S., Bengio, Y.: A parallel mixture of svms for very large scale problems (2002)
10. Vapnik, V.: The Nature of Statistical Learning Theory. Springer Verlag (1995)
11. Cristianini, N., Shawe-Taylor, J.: An Introduction to Support Vector Machines and Other Kernel-Based Learning Methods. Cambridge University Press (2000)
12. Darken, C., and Moody, J.: Fast adaptive k-means clustering: Some empirical results (1990)
13. Hotteling, H.: Analysis of a complex of statistical variables into principal components. Journal of Educational Psychology (1933) 417–441, 498–520
14. Sirovich, L., Kirby, M.: Low-dimensional procedure for the characterization of human faces. Journal of the Optical Society of America A 4 (1987) 519–524
15. Turk, M., Pentland, A.: Eigenfaces for recognition. Journal of Cognitive Neuroscience 3 (1991) 71–86
16. Bengio, S., Bimbot, F., Mariéthoz, J., Popovici, V., Porée, F., Bailly-Baillière, E., Matas, G., Ruiz, B.: Experimental protocol on the BANCA database. IDIAP-RR 05, IDIAP (2002)
17. K Messer and J Matas and J Kittler and J Luettin and G Maitre: XM2VTSDB: The Extended M2VTS Database. In: Second International Conference on Audio and Video-based Biometric Person Authentication. (1999)

AV16.3: An Audio-Visual Corpus for Speaker Localization and Tracking

Guillaume Lathoud[1,2], Jean-Marc Odobez[1], and Daniel Gatica-Perez[1]

[1] IDIAP Research Institute, CH-1920 Martigny, Switzerland
[2] EPFL, CH-1015 Lausanne, Switzerland
{lathoud, odobez, gatica}@idiap.ch

Abstract. Assessing the quality of a speaker localization or tracking algorithm on a few short examples is difficult, especially when the ground-truth is absent or not well defined. One step towards systematic performance evaluation of such algorithms is to provide time-continuous speaker location annotation over a series of real recordings, covering various test cases. Areas of interest include audio, video and audio-visual speaker localization and tracking. The desired location annotation can be either 2-dimensional (image plane) or 3-dimensional (physical space). This paper motivates and describes a corpus of audio-visual data called "AV16.3", along with a method for 3-D location annotation based on calibrated cameras. "16.3" stands for 16 microphones and 3 cameras, recorded in a fully synchronized manner, in a meeting room. Part of this corpus has already been successfully used to report research results.

1 Introduction

This paper describes a corpus of audio-visual data called "AV16.3", recorded in a meeting room context. "16.3" stands for 16 microphones and 3 cameras, recorded in a fully synchronized manner. The central idea is to use calibrated cameras to provide continuous 3-dimensional (3-D) speaker location annotation for testing audio localization and tracking algorithms. Particular attention is given to overlapped speech, i.e. when several speakers are simultaneously speaking. Overlap is indeed an important issue in multi-party spontaneous speech, as found in meetings [9]. Since visual recordings are available, video and audio-visual tracking algorithms can also be tested. We therefore defined and recorded a series of scenarios so as to cover a variety of research areas, namely audio, video and audio-visual localization and tracking of people in a meeting room. Possible applications range from automatic analysis of meetings to robust speech acquisition and video surveillance, to name a few.

In order to allow for such a broad range of research topics, "meeting room context" is defined here in a wide way. This includes a high variety of situations, from "meeting situations" where speakers are seated most of the time, to "motion situations" where speakers are moving most of the time. This departs from existing, related databases: for example the ICSI database [4] contains audio-only recordings of natural meetings, the CUAVE database [7] does contain audio-visual recordings (close-ups) but focuses on multimodal speech recognition. The CIPIC [1] database focuses on Head-Related Transfer Functions. Instead of focusing the entire database on one research topic, we chose to have a single, generic setup, allowing very different scenarios for different recordings. The goal is to provide annotation both in terms of "true" 3-D speaker location in the microphone arrays' referent, and "true" 2-D head/face location in the image plane of each camera. Such annotation permits systematic evaluation of localization and tracking algorithms, as opposed to subjective evaluation on a few short examples without annotation. To the best of our knowledge, there is no such audio-visual database publicly available. The dataset we present here has begun to be used: two recordings with static speakers have already been successfully used to report results on real multi-source speech recordings [5].

While investigating for existing solutions for speaker location annotation, we found various solutions with devices to be worn by each person and a base device that locates each personal device. However, these solutions were either very costly and extremely performant (high precision and sampling rate, no tether between the base and the personal devices), or cheap but with poor precision and/or high constraints (e.g. personal devices tethered to the base). We therefore opted for using calibrated cameras for reconstructing 3-D location of the speakers. It is important to note that this solution is potentially non-intrusive, which is indeed the case on part of the corpus presented here: on some recordings no particular marker is worn by the actors.

In the design of the corpus, two contradicting constraints needed to be fulfilled: 1) the area occupied by speakers should be large enough to cover both "meeting situations" and "motion situations", 2) this area should be entirely visible by all cameras. The latter allows systematic optimization of the camera placement. It also leads to robust reconstruction of 3-D location information, since information from all cameras can be used.

The rest of this paper is organized as follows: Section 2 describes the physical setup and the camera calibration process used to provide 3-D mouth location annotation. Section 3 describes and motivates a set of sequences publicly available via Internet. Section 4 discusses the annotation protocol, and reports the current status of the annotation effort.

2   Physical Setup and Camera Calibration

For possible speakers' locations, we selected a L-shaped area around the tables in a meeting room, as depicted in Fig. 1. A general description of the meeting room can be found in [6]. The L-shaped area is a 3 m-long and 2 m-wide rectangle, minus a 0.6 m-wide portion taken by the tables. This choice is a compromise to fulfill the two constraints mentioned in the Introduction. Views taken with the different cameras can be seen in Fig. 2. The data itself is described in Sect. 3.

The choice of hardware is described and motivated in Sect. 2.1. We adopted a 2-step strategy for placing the cameras and calibrating them. First, camera

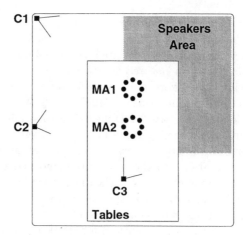

Fig. 1. Physical setup: three cameras C1, C2 and C3 and two 8-microphone circular arrays MA1 and MA2. The gray area is in the field of view of all three cameras. The L-shaped area is a 3 m-long by 2 m-wide rectangle, minus a 0.6 m-wide portion taken by the tables

placement (location, orientation, zoom) is optimized, using a looping process including sub-optimal calibration of the cameras with 2-D information only (Sect. 2.2). Second, each camera is calibrated in a precise manner, using both 2-D measurements and 3-D measurements in the referent of the microphone arrays (Sect. 2.3).

The idea behind this process is that if we can track the mouth of a person in each camera's image plane, then we can reconstruct the 3-D trajectory of the mouth using the cameras' calibration parameters. This can be useful as audio annotation, provided the 3-D trajectory is defined in the referent of the microphone arrays. We show that the 3-D reconstruction error is within a very acceptable range.

2.1   Hardware

We used 3 cameras and two 10 cm-radius, 8-microphone arrays from an instrumented meeting room [6]. The two microphone arrays are placed 0.8 m apart. The motivation behind this choice is threefold:

- Recordings made with two microphone arrays provide test cases for 3-D audio source localization and tracking, as each microphone array can be used to provide an (azimuth, elevation) location estimate of each audio source.
- Recordings made with several cameras generate many interesting, realistic cases of visual occlusion, viewing each person from several viewpoints.
- At least two cameras are necessary for computing the 3-D coordinates of an object from the 2-D coordinates in cameras' image planes. The use of three cameras allows to reconstruct the 3-D coordinates of an object in a robust

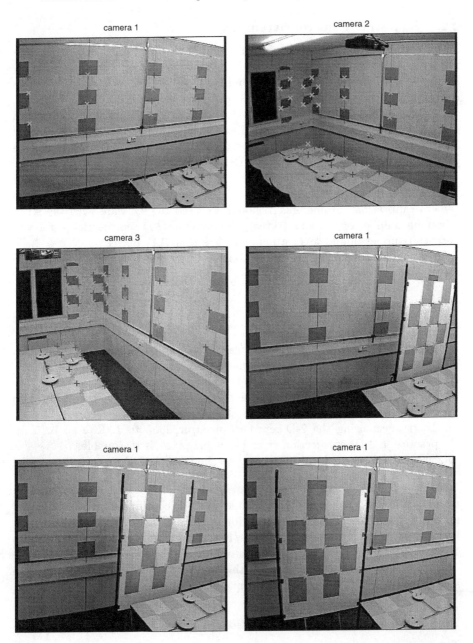

Fig. 2. Snapshots from the cameras at their final positions. Red "+" designate points in the calibration training set Ω_{train}, green "x" designate points in the calibration test set Ω_{test}

manner. Indeed, in most cases, visual occlusion occurs in one camera only; the head of the person remains visible from the two other cameras.

2.2   Step One: Camera Placement

This Section describes the looping process used to optimize cameras placement (location, orientation, zoom) using 2-D information only. We used a freely available Multi-Camera Self-Calibration (MultiCamSelfCal) software [10]. "Self-calibration" means that 3-D locations of the calibration points are unknown. The MultiCamSelfCal uses only the 2-D coordinates in the image plane of each camera. It *jointly* produces a set of calibration parameters[1] for each camera and 3-D location estimates of the calibration points, by optimizing the **"2-D reprojection error"**. For each camera, **"2-D reprojection error"** is defined as the distance in pixels between the recorded 2-D points and the projection of their 3-D location estimates back onto the camera image plane, using the estimated camera calibration parameters. Although we used the software with the strict minimum number of cameras (three), the obtained 2-D reprojection error was decent: its upper bound was estimated as less than 0.17 pixels.

The camera placement procedure consists in an iterative process with three steps: Place, Record and Calibrate:

1. *Place* the three cameras (location, orientation, zoom) based on experience in prior iterations. In practice the various cameras should give views that are as different as possible.
2. *Record* synchronously with the 3 cameras a set of calibration points, i.e. 2-D coordinates in the image plane of each camera. As explained in [10], waving a laser beamer in darkness is sufficient.
3. *Calibrate* the 3 cameras by running MultiCamSelfCal on the calibration points. MultiCamSelfCal optimizes the 2-D reprojection error.
4. To try decreasing the 2-D reprojection error, loop to 1. Else go to 5. In practice, a 2-D reprojection error below 0.2 pixels is reasonable.
5. Select the camera placement that gave the smallest 2-D reprojection error.

Multi-camera self-calibration is generally known to provide less precision than manual calibration using an object with known 3-D coordinates. The motivation for using it was ease of use: the calibration points can be quickly recorded with a laser beamer. One iteration of the Place/Record/Calibrate loop thus takes about 1h30. This process converged to the positioning of the camera depicted in Fig. 1.

For detailed information, including the multi-camera self-calibration problem statement, the reader is invited to refer to the documentation in [10].

2.3   Step Two: Camera Calibration

This Section describes precise calibration of each camera, assuming the cameras' placement fixed (location, orientation, zoom). This is done by selecting and optimizing the calibration parameters for each camera, on a calibration object. For each point of the calibration object, both true 3-D coordinates **in the microphone arrays' referent** and true 2-D coordinates in each camera's image

---

[1] For a description of camera calibration parameters see [2].

plane are known. 3-D coordinates were obtained on-site with a measuring tape (measurement error estimated below 0.005 m). Crosses in Fig. 2 show the 3-D calibration points. These points were split in two sets: Ω_{train} (36 points) and Ω_{test} (39 points).

Particular mention must be made of the model selection issue, i.e. how we chose to model non-linear distortions produced by each camera's optics. An iterative process that evaluates adequacy of the calibration parameters of all three cameras in terms of **"3-D reconstruction error"** was adopted: the Euclidean distance between 3-D location estimates of points visible from at least 2 cameras, and their true 3-D location. The camera calibration procedure can be detailed as follows:

1. *Model selection*: for each camera, select the set of calibration parameters based on experience in prior iterations.
2. *Model training*: for each camera, estimate the selected calibration parameters on Ω_{train} using the software available in [2].
3. *3-D error*: for each point in Ω_{train}, compute the Euclidean distance between true 3-D coordinates and 3-D coordinates reconstructed using the trained calibration parameters and the 2-D coordinates in each camera's image plane.
4. *Evaluation*: estimate the "training" maximum 3-D reconstruction error as $\mu + 3\sigma$, where μ and σ respectively stand for mean and standard deviation of the 3-D error, across all points in Ω_{train}.
5. To try decreasing the maximum 3-D reconstruction error, loop to 1. Else go to 6.
6. Select the set of calibration parameters and their estimated values, that gave the smallest maximum 3-D reconstruction error.

The result of this process is a set of calibration parameters and their values for each camera. For all cameras the best set of parameters were focal center, focal lengths, r^2 radial and tangential distortion coefficients.

Once the training was over, we evaluated the 3-D error on the unseen test set Ω_{test}. The maximum 3-D reconstruction error on this set was 0.012 m. This maximum error was deemed decent, as compared to the diameter of an open mouth (about 0.05 m).

3   Online Corpus

This Section first motivates and describes the variety of sequences recorded, and then describes in more details the annotated sequences. "Sequence" means:

- 3 video DIVX AVI files (resolution 288x360), one for each camera, sampled at 25 Hz. It includes also one audio signal.
- 16 audio WAV files recorded from the two circular 8-microphone arrays, sampled at 16 kHz.
- When possible, more audio WAV files recorded from lapels worn by the speakers, sampled at 16 kHz.

All files were recorded in a synchronous manner: video files carry a time-stamp embedded in the upper rows of each image, and audio files always start at video time stamp 00:00:10.00. Complete details about the hardware implementation of a unique clock across all sensors can be found in [6]. Although only 8 sequences have been annotated, many other sequences are also available. The whole corpus, along with annotation files, camera calibration parameters and additional documentation is accessible[2] at: http://mmm.idiap.ch/Lathoud/av16.3_v6. It was recorded over a period of 5 days, and includes 42 sequences overall, with sequence duration ranging from 14 seconds to 9 minutes (total 1h25). 12 different actors were recorded. Although the authors of the present paper were recorded, many of the actors don't have any particular expertise in the fields of audio and video localization and tracking.

3.1   Motivations

The main objective is to study several localization/tracking phenomena. A non-limiting list includes:

- Overlapped speech.
- Close and far locations, small and large angular separations.
- Object initialization.
- Variable number of objects.
- Partial and total occlusion.
- "Natural" changes of illumination.

Accordingly, we defined and recorded a set of sequences that contains a high variety of test cases: from short, very constrained, specific cases (e.g. visual occlusion), for each modality (audio or video), to natural spontaneous speech and/or motion in much less constrained context.

Each sequence is useful for at least one of three fields of research: analysis of audio, video or audio-visual data. Up to three people are allowed in each sequence. Human motion can be static (e.g. seated persons), dynamic (e.g. walking persons) or a mix of both across persons (some seated, some walking) and time (e.g. meeting preceded and followed by people standing and moving).

3.2   Contents

As mentioned above, the online corpus comprises of 8 annotated sequences plus many more unannotated sequences. These 8 sequences were selected for the initial annotation effort. This choice is a compromise between having a small number of sequences for annotation, and covering a large variety of situations to fulfill interests from various areas of research. It constitutes a minimal set of sequences covering as much variety as possible across modalities and speaker behaviors. The process of annotation is described in Sect. 4.

The name of each sequence is unique. Table 1 gives a synthetic overview. A more detailed description of each sequence follows.

---

[2] both HTTP or FTP protocols can be used to browse and download the data.

Table 1. List of the annotated sequences. Tags mean: [A]udio, [V]ideo, predominant [ov]erlapped speech, at least one visual [occ]lusion, [S]tatic speakers, [D]ynamic speakers, [U]nconstrained motion, [M]outh, [F]ace, [H]ead, speech/silence [seg]mentation

Sequence name	Duration (seconds)	Modalities of interest	Nb. of speakers	Speaker(s) behavior	Desired annotation
seq01-1p-0000	217	A	1	S	M, seg
seq11-1p-0100	30	A, V, AV	1	D	M, F, seg
seq15-1p-0100	35	AV	1	S,D(U)	M, F, seg
seq18-2p-0101	56	A(ov)	2	S,D	M, seg
seq24-2p-0111	48	A(ov), V(occ)	2	D	M, F
seq37-3p-0001	511	A(ov)	3	S	M, seg
seq40-3p-0111	50	A(ov), AV	3	S,D	M, F
seq45-3p-1111	43	A(ov), V(occ), AV	3	D(U)	H

seq01-1p-0000 A single speaker, static while speaking, at each of 16 locations covering the shaded area in Fig. 1. The speaker is facing the microphone arrays. The purpose of this sequence is to evaluate audio source localization on a single speaker case.

seq11-1p-0100 One speaker, mostly moving while speaking. The only constraint on the speaker's motion is to face the microphone arrays. The motivation is to test audio, video or audio-visual (AV) speaker tracking on difficult motion cases. The speaker is talking most of the time.

seq15-1p-0100 One moving speaker, walking around while alternating speech and long silences. The purpose of this sequence is to 1) show that audio tracking alone cannot recover from unpredictable trajectories during silence, 2) provide an initial test case for AV tracking.

seq18-2p-0101 Two speakers, speaking and facing the microphone arrays all the time, slowly getting as close as possible to each other, then slowly parting. The purpose is to test multi-source localization, tracking and separation algorithms.

seq24-2p-0111 Two moving speakers, crossing the field of view twice and occluding each other twice. The two speakers are talking most of the time. The motivation is to test both audio and video occlusions.

seq37-3p-0001 Three speakers, static while speaking. Two speakers remain seated all the time and the third one is standing. Overall five locations are covered. Most of the time 2 or 3 speakers are speaking concurrently. (For this particular sequence only snapshot image files are available, no AVI files.) The purpose of this sequence is to evaluate multi-source localization and beamforming algorithms.

seq40-3p-0111 Three speakers, two seated and one standing, all speaking continuously, facing the arrays, the standing speaker walks back and forth once behind the seated speakers. The motivation is both to test multi-source localization, tracking and separation algorithms, and to highlight complementarity between audio and video modalities.

seq45-3p-1111 Three moving speakers, entering and leaving the scene, all speaking continuously, occluding each other many times. Speakers' motion is unconstrained. This is a very difficult case of overlapped speech and visual occlusions. Its goal is to highlight the complementarity between audio and video modalities.

3.3   Sequence Names

A systematic coding was defined, such that the name of each sequence (1) is unique, and (2) contains a compact description of its content. For example "seq40-3p-0111" has three parts:

- "seq40" is the unique identifier of this sequence.
- "3p" means that overall 3 different persons were recorded – but not necessarily all visible simultaneously.
- "0111" are four binary flags giving a quick overview of the content of this recording. From left to right:
  bit 1: 0 means "very constrained", 1 means "mostly unconstrained" (general behavior: although most recordings follow some sort of scenario, some include very strong constraints such as the speaker facing the microphone arrays at all times).
  bit 2: 0 means "static motion" (e.g. mostly seated), 1 means "dynamic motion". (e.g. continuous motion).
  bit 3: 0 means "minor occlusion(s)", 1 means "at least one major occlusion", involving at least one array or camera: whenever somebody passes in front of or behind somebody else.
  bit 4: 0 means "little overlap", 1 means "significant overlap". This involves audio only: it indicates whether there is a significant proportion of overlap between speakers and/or noise sources.

4   Annotation

Two types of annotations can be created: in space (e.g. speaker trajectory) or time (e.g. speech/silence segmentation). The definition of annotation intrinsically defines the performance metrics that will be used to evaluate localization and tracking algorithms. How annotation should be defined is therefore debatable. Moreover, we note that different modalities (audio, video) might require very different annotations (e.g. 3-D mouth location vs 2-D head bounding box). Sections 4.1 and 4.2 report the initial annotation effort done on the AV16.3 corpus. Sections 4.3, 4.4 and 4.5 detail some examples of application of the available annotation. Section 4.6 discusses future directions for annotation.

4.1   Initial Effort

The two sequences with static speakers only have already been fully annotated: "seq01-1p-0000" and "seq37-3p-0001". The annotation includes, for each

Fig. 3. Snapshots of the two windows of the Head Annotation Interface

speaker, 3-D mouth location and speech/silence segmentation. 3-D mouth location is defined relative to the microphone arrays' referent. The origin of this referent is in the middle of the two microphone arrays. This annotation is also accessible online. It has already been successfully used to evaluate recent work [5]. Moreover, a simple example of use of this annotation is available whithin the online corpus, as described in Sect. 4.3.

As for sequences with moving speakers and occlusion cases, three Matlab graphical interfaces were written and used to annotate location of the head, of the mouth and of an optional marker (colored ball) on the persons' heads:

BAI: the Ball Annotation Interface, to mark the location of a colored ball on the head of a person, as an ellipse. Occlusions can be marked, i.e. when the ball is not visible. The BAI includes a simple tracker to interpolate between manual measurements.

HAI: the Head Annotation Interface, to mark the location of the head of a person, as a rectangular bounding box. Partial or complete occlusions can be marked.

MAI: the Mouth Annotation Interface, to mark the location of the mouth of a person as a point. Occlusions can be marked, i.e. when the mouth is not visible.

All three interfaces share very similar features, including two windows: one for the interface itself, and a second one for the image currently being annotated. An example of snapshot of the HAI can be seen in Fig. 3. All annotation files are simple matrices stored in ASCII format.

All three interfaces are available and documented online, within the corpus itself. We have already used them to produce continuous 3-D mouth location annotation from sparse manual measurements, as described in Sect. 4.5.

4.2   Current State

The annotation effort is constantly progressing over time, and Table 2 details what is already available online as of August 31st, 2004.

Table 2. Annotation available online as of August 31st, 2004. "C" means continuous annotation, i.e. all frames of the 25 Hz video are annotated. "S" means sparse annotation, i.e. the annotation is done at a rate less than 25 Hz (given in parenthesis)

Sequence	ball 2-D 3-D	mouth 2-D	3-D	head 2-D	speech/silence segmentation
seq01-1p-0000		C	C		precise
seq11-1p-0100	C C	C	C		
seq15-1p-0100		S(2 Hz)	S(2 Hz)		
seq18-2p-0101	C C	C	C		
seq24-2p-0111	C C	C	C	S(2 Hz)	
seq37-3p-0001		C	C		undersegmented
seq40-3p-0111		S(2 Hz)	S(2 Hz)		
seq45-3p-1111		S(2 Hz)	S(2 Hz)	S(2 Hz)	

4.3   Example 1: Audio Source Localization Evaluation

The online corpus includes a complete example (Matlab files) of single source localization followed by comparison with the annotation, for "seq01-1p-0000". It is based on a parametric method called SRP-PHAT [3]. All necessary Matlab code to run the example is available online[3]. The comparison shows that the SRP-PHAT localization method provides a precision between -5 and +5 degrees in azimuth.

4.4   Example 2: Multi-object Video Tracking

As an example, the results of applying three independent, appearance-based particle filters on 200 frames of the "seq45-3p-1111" sequence, using only one of the cameras, are shown in Fig. 4, and in a video[4]. The sequence depicts three people moving around the room while speaking, and includes multiple instances of object occlusion. Each tracker has been initialized by hand, and uses 500 particles. Object appearance is modeled by a color distribution [8] in RGB space.

   In this particular example we have not done any performance evaluation yet. We plan to define precision and recall based on the intersecting surface between the annotation bounding box and the result bounding box.

4.5   Example 3: 3-D Mouth Annotation

From sparse 2-D mouth annotation on each camera we propose to (1) reconstruct 3-D mouth location using camera calibration parameters estimated as explained in Sect. 2.3, (2) interpolate 3-D mouth location using the ball location as origin of the 3-D referent. The 3-D ball location itself is provided by

---

[3] http://mmm.idiap.ch/Lathoud/av16.3_v6/EXAMPLES/AUDIO/README
[4] http://mmm.idiap.ch/Lathoud/av16.3_v6/EXAMPLES/VIDEO/av-video.mpeg

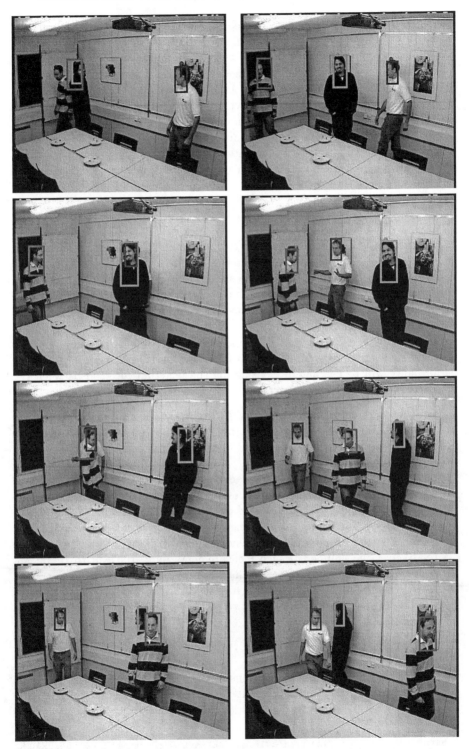

Fig. 4. Snapshots from visual tracking on 200 frames of "seq45-3p-1111". 200 frames (initial timecode: 00:00:41.17). Tracking results are shown every 25 frames

the 2-D tracker in the BAI interface (see Sect. 4.1) and 3-D reconstruction. The motivation of this choice was twofold: first of all, using simple (e.g. polynomial) interpolation on mouth measurements was not enough in practice, since human motion contains many complex non-linearities (sharp turns and accelerations). Second, visual tracking of the mouth is a hard task in itself. We found that interpolating measurements in the moving referent of an automatically tracked ball marker is effective even at low annotation rates (e.g 2 Hz = 1 video frame out of 12), which is particularly important since the goal is to save on time spent doing manual measurements. A complete example with all necessary Matlab implementation can be found online[5]. This implementation was used to create all 3-D files available within the corpus.

4.6   Future Directions

Difficulties arise mostly in two cases: 1) predominance of overlapped speech, and 2) highly dynamic situations, in terms of motions and occlusions. 1) can be addressed by undersegmenting the speech and defining proper metrics for evaluation. By "undersegmenting" we mean that less segments are defined, each segment comprising some silence and speech which is too weak to be localized. An example is given in [5].

2) is more difficult to address. It is intrinsically linked to the minimum interval at which annotation measurements are taken, and therefore the interval at which performance will be evaluated. Considering the fact that location between two measurements can be interpolated, two attitudes can be envisaged:

1. On short sequences, with very specific test cases, the interval can be chosen very small, in order to obtain fine-grained, precise spatial annotation. Even with interpolation, this would require independent observer(s) to give many true location measurements.
2. On long sequences, the interval can be chosen larger. If the interpolated annotation is used for performance evaluation, slight imprecision can be tolerated, as compensated by the size of the data ("continuous" annotation). If the manual annotation measurements only are used for performance evaluation ("sparse" annotation), the evaluation will be more precise, and the relatively large number of such measurements may still lead to significant results. By "significant" we mean that the standard deviation of the error is small enough for the average error to be meaningful.

5   Conclusion

This paper presented the AV16.3 corpus for speaker localization and tracking. AV16.3 focuses mostly on the context of meeting room data, acquired synchronously by 3 cameras, 16 far-distance microphones, and lapels. It targets

---

[5] http://mmm.idiap.ch/Lathoud/av16.3_v6/EXAMPLES/3D-RECONSTRUCTION/README

various areas of research: audio, visual and audio-visual speaker tracking. In order to provide audio annotation, camera calibration is used to generate "true" 3-D speaker mouth location, using freely available software. To the best of our knowledge, this is the first attempt to provide synchronized audio-visual data for extensive testing on a variety of test cases, along with spatial annotation. AV16.3 is intended as a step towards systematic evaluation of localization and tracking algorithms on real recordings. Future work includes completion of the annotation process, and possibly data acquisition with different setups.

Acknowledgments

The authors acknowledge the support of the European Union through the AMI, M4, HOARSE and IM2.SA.MUCATAR projects. The authors wish to thank all actors recorded in this corpus, Olivier Masson for help with the physical setup, and Mathew Magimai.-Doss for valuable comments.

References

1. Algazi, V., Duda, R., Thompson, D.: The CIPIC HRTF Database. Proceedings of WASPAA (2001).
2. Bouguet, J.Y.: Camera Calibration Toolbox for Matlab (01/2004). http://www.vision.caltech.edu/bouguetj/calib_doc/
3. DiBiase, J., Silverman, H., Brandstein, M.: Robust Localization in Reverberant Rooms. Microphone Arrays, Eds. Brandstein, M., Ward, D., Springer (2001), 157–180.
4. Janin, A., Baron, D., Edwards, J., Ellis, D., Gelbart, D., Morgan, N., Peskin, B., Pfau, T., Shriberg, E., Stolcke, A., Wooters, C.: The ICSI Meeting Corpus. Proceedings of ICASSP (2003).
5. Lathoud, G., McCowan, I.A.: A Sector-Based Approach for Localization of Multiple Speakers with Microphone Arrays. To appear in Proceedings of SAPA (2004).
6. Moore, D.: The IDIAP Smart Meeting Room. IDIAP Communication COM-02-07 (2002).
7. Patterson, E., Gurbuz, S., Tufekci, Z., Gowdy, J.: Moving Talker, Speaker-Independent Feature Study and Baseline Results Using the CUAVE Multimodal Speech Corpus. Eurasip Journal on Applied Signal Processing (2002), vol. 11, 1189–1201.
8. Perez, P., Hue, C., Vermaak, J., Gangnet, M.: Color-based Probabilistic Tracking. Proceedings of ECCV (2002).
9. Shriberg, E., Stolcke, A., Baron, D.: Observations on Overlap: Findings and Implications for Automatic Processing of Multi-Party Conversation. Proceedings of Eurospeech (2001) vol. 2, 1359–1362.
10. Svoboda, T.: Multi-Camera Self-Calibration (08/2003).http://cmp.felk.cvut.cz/svoboda/SelfCal/index.html

The 2004 ICSI-SRI-UW Meeting Recognition System

Chuck Wooters[1], Nikki Mirghafori[1], Andreas Stolcke[1,2], Tuomo Pirinen[1,5],
Ivan Bulyko[3], Dave Gelbart[1,4], Martin Graciarena[2], Scott Otterson[3],
Barbara Peskin[1], and Mari Ostendorf[3]

[1] International Computer Science Institute, Berkeley, California, USA
[2] SRI International, Menlo Park, California, USA
[3] University of Washington, Seattle, Washington, USA
[4] University of California at Berkeley, Berkeley, California, USA
[5] Tampere University of Technology, Tampere, Finland
{wooters, nikki, stolcke}@icsi.berkeley.edu

Abstract. The paper describes our system devised for recognizing speech
in meetings, which was an entry in the NIST Spring 2004 Meeting Recognition Evaluation. This system was developed as a collaborative effort
between ICSI, SRI, and UW and was based on SRI's 5xRT Conversational Telephone Speech (CTS) recognizer. The CTS system was adapted
to the Meetings domain by adapting the CTS acoustic and language
models to the Meeting domain, adding noise reduction and delay-sum
array processing for far-field recognition, and adding postprocessing for
cross-talk suppression for close-talking microphones. A modified MAP
adaptation procedure was developed to make best use of discriminatively
trained (MMIE) prior models. These meeting-specific changes yielded an
overall 9% and 22% relative improvement as compared to the original
CTS system, and 16% and 29% relative improvement as compared to our
2002 Meeting Evaluation system, for the *individual-headset* and *multiple-
distant* microphones conditions, respectively.

1   Introduction

Recognizing speech in meetings provides numerous interesting challenges for the
research community, ranging from teasing apart and recognizing highly interactive and often overlapping speech to providing robustness to distant microphones
recording multiple talkers. Data collected from meeting rooms provide an ideal
testbed for such work, supporting research in robust speech recognition, speaker
segmentation and tracking, discourse modeling, spoken language understanding,
and more.

In recognition of this, NIST began its Meeting Room project [1], hosting a
workshop in Fall 2001 to share information on resources and plans with other
involved parties (including data providers CMU, ICSI, and LDC) and sponsoring
its first Meeting Recognition evaluation in spring 2002 as part of the Rich Transcription evaluation series (RT-02) [2]. At that time, meeting room resources

S. Bengio and H. Bourlard (Eds.): MLMI 2004, LNCS 3361, pp. 196–208, 2005.

were extremely limited (as was participation in the eval!) and so the evaluation was essentially an exercise simply in benchmarking systems trained for other domains, such as conversational telephone speech and broadcast news. Our work on this task, as well as related meetings research from that period, is reported in [9].

The next Meeting Recognition evaluation, RT-04S, was held in March 2004. In the intervening two years, there has been an explosion of interest in the Meetings domain, with a number of new projects focusing on the Meeting Room task and substantial amounts of meeting room data becoming available.

The 75-meeting ICSI Meeting Corpus [6] was released by the LDC at the start of 2004 and several other collections, such as data recorded by CMU [14] and by NIST itself, are being readied for public release. It has thus become possible to conduct true Meetings-centric research, focusing development on the particular problems presented by the Meetings task, such as the acoustics of tabletop microphones and the specialized but varying topical content.

In March 2004 NIST conducted an evaluation of speech recognition systems for meetings (RT-04S), following on its initial Meetings evaluation two years prior (RT-02) [2]. Our team had participated in RT-02 with an only slightly modified CTS recognition system, providing little more than a baseline for future work. For RT-04 our goal was to assemble a system specifically for meeting recognition, although the limited amounts of meeting-specific training data dictated that such a system would still be substantially based on our CTS system. This paper describes and evaluates the design decisions made in the process.

The evaluation task and data are described in Section 2. Section 3 includes the system description, followed by results and discussion in Section 4. Conclusions and future work are presented in Section 5.

2   Task and Data

2.1   Test Data

Evaluation Data. The RT-04S evaluation data consisted of two 1-hour meetings from each of the recording sites CMU, ICSI, LDC, and NIST. Systems were required to recognize a specific 11-minute segment from each meeting; however, data from the entire meeting was allowed for purposes of adaptation, etc. Separate evaluations were conducted in three conditions:

MDM Multiple distant microphones (primary)
IHM Individual headset microphones (required contrast)
SDM Single distant microphone (optional)

The CMU meetings came with only one distant mic; for the other meetings between 4 and 7 distant mics were available. The IHM systems were allowed to use all mics (distant or individual). For MDM and SDM conditions, NIST only evaluated regions of speech with a single talker, thus eliminating overlapping speech. Unlike recent CTS evaluations, the Meetings evaluation included non-

Table 1. RT-04 training and test data differences per source

	ICSI	CMU	LDC	NIST
Evaluation Data				
Num distant mics	6	1	4	7
Development Data				
Individual mics	Head	Lapel	Lapel	Head
Training Data				
Total available	74 hrs	11 hrs	None	14 hrs
% Failed alignment	0.1%	10%	N/A	0.1%
Recording Condition	Head+ Distant	Lapel only	N/A	Head+ Distant

native speakers of English. Table 1 summarizes the differences among the sources for training and test data.

Development Data. The RT-02 evaluation data (another 8 meetings from the same sources) served as the development test set for RT-04. However, this set was somewhat mismatched to the RT-04 evaluation data in that CMU and LDC used lapel[1] instead of head-mounted microphones. An additional 5 meetings (2 ICSI, 2 CMU, 1 LDC) were available from the RT-02 devtest set.

2.2   Training Data

Training data was available from CMU (17 meetings, 11 hours of speech after segmentation), ICSI (73 meetings, 74 hours), and NIST (15 meetings, 14 hours). No data from LDC was available. The CMU data was problematic in that only lapel and no distant microphone recordings were available.

We excluded any data which failed to force-align with the released transcriptions. This eliminated 0.1% of the data from each of ICSI and NIST, and 11% from CMU. For acoustic training of the distant mic systems, we also excluded regions with overlapped speech, based on forced alignments of the individual mic signals.

3   System Description

In this section we describe our meeting recognition system. Our system was based on a fast (5 times real-time) version of SRI's CTS recognizer. Figure 1 shows the key aspects of the system and highlights the adaptations we made to the baseline CTS system.

The top section of the diagram (denoted by "Training") shows meeting specific adaptations performed in the training phase of the system. Specifically, the

---

[1] Throughout the text, *individual mic* subsumes both individual lapel and individual head-set mic conditions.

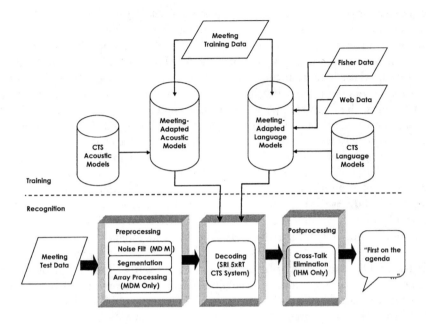

Fig. 1. The overall system architecture

CTS acoustic and language models were adapted with meeting-related acoustic and textual data to create better matched models. These adaptations are discussed in Sections 3.2 and 3.3, respectively. The bottom portion of the diagram (denoted by "Recognition") shows modifications to the recognition processing of the baseline CTS, namely, the addition of pre- and post-processing steps. The pre-processing steps of signal processing, segmentation, and array processing are discussed in Sections 3.1, 3.1, and 3.1, respectively. The post-processing step is discussed in Section 3.5.

3.1 Signal Processing and Segmentation

Noise Reduction of the Far-Field Microphone Signals. The distant mic signals are filtered using a batch version of the noise reduction algorithm developed for the Aurora 2 front-end proposed by ICSI, OGI, and Qualcomm [3]. The algorithm performs Wiener filtering with typical engineering modifications, such as a noise over-estimation factor, smoothing of the filter response, and a spectral floor. We modified the algorithm to use a single noise spectral estimate for each meeting waveform. This was calculated over all the frames judged to be nonspeech by the voice-activity detection component of the Qualcomm-ICSI-OGI front end. We applied it independently for each meeting waveform and used overlap-add resynthesis to create noise-reduced output waveforms, which then served as the basis of all further processing.

Segmentation. To identify regions of speech activity and segment them into suitable chunks for further processing, a recognizer with two phones (speech and nonspeech) was used to decode the signal. The phone models impose minimum duration constraints and the language model (LM) penalizes switches between the two models. The resulting segments were postprocessed to satisfy length constraints, and to pad speech boundaries with a few frames of nonspeech. For distant mics, the algorithm performs acoustic clustering to keep different speakers in separate segments, and to group same or similar speakers into clusters that can subsequently be used for feature normalization and acoustic adaptation.

For the headset mics condition, the segmentation models were trained on ICSI and NIST headset mics training data, using forced alignments against the references. For the distant mic conditions, two sets of models were trained: ICSI and NIST data were used to train models for those two sources; the RT-02 devtest data (which included some CMU and LDC far-field data) were used to train models for segmenting the CMU and LDC meetings.

Multiple Distant Microphone Array Processing. For MDM processing, segmentation was performed on a single, central mic. Array processing was then performed separately on each speech region of the noise-reduced signals according to the common segmentation. The waveform segments from the various distant microphones were aligned to compensate for time skew and sound travel delays. Finally the aligned signals were summed to yield a single new segmented waveform.

The rationale behind this processing is that speech will be summed in-phase and amplified, whereas noise components are summed out of phase and will be dampened. Delays for time alignment were estimated using maximal cross-correlation, in which the central mic channel was used as the reference. Since the microphone and speaker locations were unknown, the same search interval was used for all microphone pairs at a given site; an educated guess as to the possible delay ranges was made based on available documentation of the recording room configurations. Note that the method assumes that each waveform segment contains only one speaker and thus that the alignment delays would not vary within a segment (hence the segmentation step had to precede the array processing).

3.2   Acoustic Modeling and Adaptation

Gender-dependent recognition models were derived from CTS models trained on 420 hours of telephone speech from the Switchboard and CallHome English collections. The MFCC models used 12 cepstral coefficients, energy, 1st, 2nd and 3rd order difference features, as well as 2x5 voicing features over a 5-frame window [5]. The 62-component raw feature vector was reduced to 39 dimensions using heteroscedastic linear discriminant analysis [8]. PLP models used a similar configuration, except that no voicing features were included and a two-stage transform, consisting of standard LDA followed by a diagonalizing transform [12] were used to map the feature space from 52 to 39 dimensions. Also, the PLP models were trained with feature-space speaker adaptive training [7].

The CTS models were adapted to the meeting domain using ICSI and NIST training data (the CMU meetings were deemed to be mismatched to the eval data, as discussed in Section 2.2). Since the prior models had been trained with the maximum mutual information criterion (MMIE) [11] we developed a version of the standard maximum a-posteriori (MAP) adaptation algorithm that preserves the models' discriminative properties. CTS MMIE models were used to collect numerator and denominator counts on the meeting data (downsampled to 8kHz). These counts were combined with CTS numerator and denominator counts, respectively. Finally, new Gaussian parameters were estimated from the combined counts (mixture weights and HMM parameters were left unchanged in the process).

Experiments showed that an adaptation weight near 20 for the numerator and 5 for the denominator was optimal. Furthermore, as reported in Section 4, most of the improvement can be achieved by only adapting the numerator counts; this could be convenient for some applications since denominator training requires lattices to be generated for the adaptation data.

Feature Mapping. We also experimented with the probabilistic optimum filtering (POF) [10] approach to cope with the mismatch between far-field signals and our CTS-based recognition models. In this approach a probabilistic mapping of noisy (distant mic) to clean (headset mic) features is trained based on stereo recordings. However, the method is complicated by time skew between channels, changing speakers, and location-specific background noise. We obtained an error reduction with a feature mapping trained on test data, but were not able to obtain an improvement when using only training data, and therefore did not include this method in our final system.

3.3   Language Model and Vocabulary

Our CTS language model is a mixture LM with 4M words of Switchboard-1 and 2, and 150M words of Broadcast News, and it includes 191M words of web data chosen for style and content [4]. It was adapted for meeting recognition by adding two meeting-specific mixture components: Meetings transcripts from ICSI, CMU, and NIST (1.7M words), and newly collected web data (150M words) related to the topics discussed in the meetings and also aimed at covering new vocabulary items. Also, 5.3M words from the CTS Fisher collection were added for coverage of current topics. The mixture was adapted by minimizing perplexity on a held-out set consisting of approximately equal amounts of transcripts from the four sources. We also experimented with source-specific LMs, but found that the available tuning data was insufficient to estimate source-specific mixture weights robustly.

Figure 2 show the language model perplexities for different sources. We see that the lowest perplexities are those of the ICSI data. This might be because the discussion topics are consistent throughout these recording sessions and there is a relatively small set of common speakers. Additionally, we observe that the ICSI subset benefits the most reduction in perplexity from the addition of meetings-

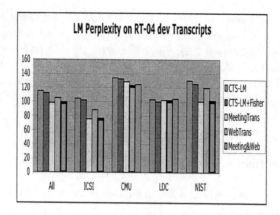

Fig. 2. The language model perplexities for different sources

specific data, given the reasonable explanation that the majority of the meetings text data comes from this source. The perplexities of the CMU set are the highest. Also, the CMU subset benefits the most from the addition of web data and the least (degrades slightly, in fact) from the addition of meetings data. These trends are probably due to the wide range and variety of topics discussed in the CMU meetings.

The vocabulary was extended (relative to the baseline CTS system) to include all non-singleton words from Fisher and Meetings transcripts. The vocabulary size was close to 50,000, and yielded a 0.9% out-of-vocabulary rate on the development test transcripts. The pronunciation dictionary was inherited from the CTS system and was based on the CMU dictionary, with added phones for filled pauses and laughter.

3.4   Decoding

The recognition search was structured as in the SRI "fast" (5xRT) CTS system. Within-word MFCC models were adapted with phone-loop MLLR and used to generate bigram lattices. The lattices were then rescored with a 4-gram LM and consensus-decoded to obtain preliminary hypotheses. These were then used to estimate speaker-adaptive feature transforms and MLLR model transforms for the cross-word PLP models, which were employed to generate 2000-best lists from trigram-expanded lattices. The N-best lists were then rescored with a 4-gram LM, pronunciation, pause, and duration models [13], and combined into final confusion networks, from which 1-best hypotheses and confidence values were extracted.

3.5   Cross-Talk Suppression

The decoded word hypotheses from the IHM system were postprocessed in an attempt to eliminate cross-talk. We assumed that when cross-talk was sufficiently

Table 2. Improvement of the new baseline CTS system as compared to the system used in the RT-02 evaluation, reported on RT-02 eval set

	All	ICSI	CMU	LDC	NIST
Individual Mics					
RT-02 System	36.0	25.9	47.9	36.8	35.2
RT-04 CTS Base	32.8	24.0	44.3	33.2	31.5
Single Distant Mic					
RT-02 System	61.6	53.6	64.5	69.7	61.6
RT-04 CTS Base	56.6	48.8	61.9	60.5	60.3

loud, recognized words with low confidence would be produced, and that most speech was not overlapped. Therefore, we time-aligned the words on all channels, and deleted those words which had confidence score below a given threshold, and overlapped, by at least 50%, with a word on another channel.

4 Results and Discussion

4.1 Improvements to the Baseline System

Since both the old RT-02 system and this year's baseline system were developed for the CTS domain, we were interested to see how much of the improvements made on the CTS recognition task would carry over to the Meeting task. Using RT-02 system components comparable to the current 5xRT system, the WER on the 2002 CTS task reduced from 29.4% to 23.6%, a 20% relative reduction. As shown in Table 2, the same system achieved relative improvements of 8% and 9% on the RT-02 meeting evaluation data, in the individual and distant mic conditions, respectively.

In the following sections, we report results on the official RT-04S development test, whose references differed somewhat from the RT-02 evaluation set. We present experiments in cumulative fashion, so that each improvement is the baseline for the following experiment. To be consistent with RT-02, unless otherwise noted, individual mic recognition uses reference segmentations, while distant mic experiments use automatic segmentation, plus noise filtering.

4.2 Language Model Adaptation

First we examine the effect of LM adaptation (see Section 3.3), shown in Table 3. The improvement is roughly 5% overall and appears to be more substantial for ICSI and NIST, and less so for CMU and LDC data. Besides the lack of training data for LDC meetings, the observed difference could be due to the consistency of meeting topics in the ICSI and NIST data, and their relative variability in the CMU meetings.

Table 3. Effect of language model adaptation on RT-04 devtest data

	All	ICSI	CMU	LDC	NIST
Individual Mics					
Baseline	33.3	23.5	44.6	34.2	32.0
Adapted LM	31.5	20.9	43.6	33.7	28.5
Single Distant Mic					
Baseline	56.2	45.9	61.0	63.7	59.9
Adapted LM	53.6	43.0	60.8	62.9	52.3

Table 4. Effect of different acoustic adaptation algorithms on the IHM condition (RT-04 dev). The source of the adaptation data is matched to the test data (except for LDC, where ICSI data was used in adaptation)

	All	ICSI	CMU	LDC	NIST
Unadapted	31.5	20.9	43.6	33.7	28.5
MLE-MAP	30.4	18.4	42.8	33.2	28.0
NUM-MAP	30.0	18.3	42.0	33.0	**27.3**
MMIE-MAP	**29.8**	**17.9**	**41.4**	**32.9**	27.6

4.3   Acoustic Model Adaptation

Next we tested the MMIE-MAP acoustic adaptation approach described in Section 3.2. Table 4 shows small, yet consistent, improvements over the standard MLE-MAP approach. MMIE adaptation was effective even if only the numerator counts were updated ("NUM-MAP").

For the IHM condition, models were adapted on training data recorded with head-mounted microphones; for the MDM and SDM conditions, training data recorded with distant microphones were used. For the latter conditions, experiments showed that adapting models to duplicate versions of the data from different microphones decreased the WER by 35-63% more than when models were adapted to data from the central microphone only.

Table 5 shows the improvement of adapted versus unadapted models. Acoustic adaptation provided an impressive improvement of 12.5% for the SDM condition (12.6% for delay-summed MDM) and 5.3% for the individual mic condition. For the distant mic conditions, combining the ICSI and NIST data for adaptation proved to be more effective than source-matched adaptation. Also for the distant mic condition, the best results for CMU were produced by using ICSI-only adapted models. Acoustic adaptation was most effective for ICSI data. One reason is surely that ICSI was the source with by far the most adaptation data. Another likely reason is that ICSI meetings are dominated by speakers that recur throughout the entire corpus, including in the test sets.

Table 5. Effect of acoustic adaptation on RT-04 devset. "SM Adapted" means *source-matched*: the source of the adaptation data is matched to the test. "I+N adapted" means adapted to *ICSI+NIST* training data. +: there was no training data for LDC, so ICSI data was used. *: recognition on CMU was best with models adapted to ICSI-only, and SDM and MDM results are identical since only 1 microphone was available. Since the CMU and LDC dev data were mismatched to the eval data for IHM (lapel vs. headset), they were given less consideration in making the overall design decisions

	All	ICSI	CMU	LDC	NIST
Individual Mics					
		Headset	Lapel	Lapel	Headset
Unadapted	31.5	20.9	43.6	33.7	28.5
SM Adapted	29.8	17.9	41.4	32.9+	27.6
I+N Adapted	30.3	17.4	43.0	34.0	27.5
Single Distant Mic					
Unadapted	53.6	43.0	60.8	62.9	52.3
SM Adapted	48.5	35.5	60.6	56.0	49.0
I+N Adapted	46.9	34.3	59.0*	54.3	46.9
Multiple Distant Mics (Delay-Summed)					
Unadapted	50.1	35.2	60.7	61.5	49.9
I+N Adapted	43.8	28.4	59.0*	52.3	44.0

4.4   Array Processing

The acoustic front-end processing of delay-summing the test signal (as discussed in Section 3.1) produced a further improvement of 6.6%. The delay-summing technique was also most effective for ICSI data, possibly because we had more information about ICSI's meeting room configuration than for the other sources. Delay-summing the adaptation data proved to be not as effective as using acoustic models that were adapted to multiple versions of the signal from all microphones (by 5% relative). This may be because in the latter case channel variability is better represented in the adaptation data.

4.5   Segmentation

Table 6 shows WERs with different segmentations. For individual mics, the automatic segmentation increases the WER significantly compared to using reference segmentations. Research on speaker diarization techniques could be a solution in recognizing cross-talk and producing a better segmentation.

4.6   Cross-Talk Supression

The cross-talk suppression technique described in Section 3.5 led to a 2% WER reduction (see Table 7). The improvement was largest for the lapel recordings (CMU and LDC); postprocessing was not done for NIST meetings, which seemed to have very little cross-talk.

Table 6. The table shows WERs with different segmentations. TC stands for True Clustering, and AC for Automatic Clustering

	All	ICSI	CMU	LDC	NIST
Individual Mics					
Ref seg	30.3	17.4	43.0	34.0	27.5
Auto seg	36.8	20.8	51.1	45.7	29.8
Multiple Distant Mics (Delay-Summed)					
Ref seg (TC)	42.9	25.8	58.2	53.2	43.6
Ref seg (AC)	44.1	27.8	56.9	55.9	43.8
Auto seg	43.8	28.4	59.1	52.3	44.0

Table 7. The table shows the effect of cross-talk removal postprocessing on WER

	All	ICSI	CMU	LDC	NIST
Individual Mics					
Auto seg	36.8	20.8	51.1	45.7	29.8
Auto+Postproc	36.1	20.5	50.2	43.8	30.1

Table 8. Results on the RT-04 evaluation set. "H" marks headset, "L" lapel mic conditions

	All	ICSI	CMU	LDC	NIST
Individual Mics					
Dev IHM	36.1	20.5	50.2 L	43.8 L	30.1
RT-04s IHM	34.8	24.2	40.3 H	44.7 H	27.1
Distant Mics					
Dev MDM	43.8	28.4	59.1	52.3	44.0
RT-04s MDM	46.7	27.6	56.4	51.2	41.5
RT-04s SDM	50.7	34.6	56.4	52.2	56.2

4.7   2004 Evaluations Results

Finally, Table 8 shows the results on the RT-04 evaluation set, which turned out remarkably similar to the devtest overall. The CMU individual mic recognition is much improved, presumably as a result of the switch to headset mics, though this doesn't seem to be true for LDC. Note that, for the MDM condition, even though the per-source WERs are all lower, the overall WER is not, due to the fact that the more difficult sources (CMU and LDC) contribute a larger portion of the test set.

4.8   The "Fast" Versus the "Full" System

After having developed and tuned the system based on our 5xRT recognition architecture, we ported our current full (20xRT) CTS evaluation system to the

Table 9. Results with full recognition system on RT-04 evaluation set

System	MDM	IHM	CTS
5xRT	46.7	34.8	24.1
Full	44.5	32.7	22.2

Meeting domain. The full system adds a second decoding path using within-word PLP and cross-word MFCC models, lattice regeneration and model readaptation, and a final system combination of three different acoustic models. Table 9 shows overall results for IHM, MDM, and, for reference, 2003 CTS recognition. We see almost identical absolute error reductions on the three test sets, although the relative improvement is somewhat smaller on Meetings (around 5%, compared to 8% for CTS).

5   Conclusions and Future Work

We have shown how a combination of model adaptation, pre- and post-processing techniques can be effective in retargeting a conversational telephone speech recognizer to the meeting recognition task. The severe acoustic mismatch for distant microphones especially was alleviated by a combination of discriminative model adaptation and signal enhancement through noise filtering and array processing. Combined with LM adaptation, we achieved relative improvements of 9% and 22%, respectively, for individual and distant mic conditions. The system gave excellent results in the Spring 2004 NIST evaluation.

Still, many challenges remain. Automatic speech segmentation remains a problem, leading to significant degradation compared to a manual segmentation, which we hope to remedy with the use of novel acoustic features. Meetings also provide fertile ground for future work in areas such as acoustic robustness, speaker-dependent modeling, and language and dialog modeling.

Acknowledgments

This work was partly supported by the European Union 6th FWP IST Integrated Project AMI (Augmented Multi-party Interaction, FP6-506811, publication AMI-15), and by the Swiss National Science Foundation (through NCCR's IM2 project). We also thank Ramana Gadde, Jing Zheng, and Wen Wang at SRI for advice and assistance.

References

1. http://www.nist.gov/speech/test_beds/mr_proj/
2. http://nist.gov/speech/tests/rt/

3. A. Adami, L. Burget, S. Dupont, H. Garudadri, F. Grezl, H. Hermansky, P. Jain, S. Kajarekar, N. Morgan, and S. Sivadas, Qualcomm-ICSI-OGI features for ASR, ICSLP 2002.

4. I. Bulyko, M. Ostendorf, and A. Stolcke, Getting More Mileage from Web Text Sources for Conversational Speech Language Modeling using Class-Dependent Mixtures, HLT 2003, pp. 7-9.

5. M. Graciarena, H. Franco, J. Zheng, D. Vergyri, and A. Stolcke, Voicing Feature Integration in SRI's Decipher LVCSR System. ICASSP 2004, Montreal. To appear.

6. A. Janin, D. Baron, J. Edwards, D. Ellis, D. Gelbart, N. Morgan, B. Peskin, T. Pfau, E. Shriberg, A. Stolcke, and C. Wooters, The ICSI Meeting Corpus, ICASSP 2003, Hong Kong.

7. H. Jin, S. Matsoukas, R. Schwartz and F. Kubala, Fast Robust Inverse Transform SAT and Multi-stage Adaptation, Proc. DARPA Broadcast News Transcription and Understanding Workshop, pp. 105-109, Lansdowne, VA, 1998.

8. N. Kumar, Investigation of Silicon-Auditory Models and Generalisation of Linear Discriminant Analysis for Improved Speech Recognition. PhD thesis, John Hopkins University, 1997.

9. N. Morgan, D. Baron, S. Bhagat, H. Carvey, R. Dhillon, J. Edwards, D. Gelbart, A. Janin, A. Krupski, B. Peskin, T. Pfau, E. Shriberg, A. Stolcke, and C. Wooters, Meetings about Meetings: Research at ICSI on Speech in Multiparty Conversations, ICASSP 2003, Hong Kong.

10. L. Neumeyer and M. Weintraub, Probabilistic Optimum Filtering for Robust Speech Recognition, Proc. ICASSP, Adelaide, Australia, pp. I417-I420, 1994.

11. D. Povey and P. C. Woodland, Large-scale MMIE Training for Conversational Telephone Speech Recongition, Proc. NIST Speech Transcription Workshop, College Park, MD, 2000.

12. G. Saon, M. Padmanabhan, R. Gopinath and S. Chen, Maximum Likelihood Discriminant Feature Spaces. ICASSP 2000, pp. 1747-1750.

13. D. Vergyri, A. Stolcke, V. R. R. Gadde, L. Ferrer, and E. Shriberg, Prosodic Knowledge Sources for Automatic Speech Recognition. ICASSP 2003, pp. 208-211, Hong Kong.

14. A. Waibel, M. Bett, F. Metze, K. Reis, T. Schaaf, T. Schultz, H. Soltau, H. Yu, and K. Zechner, Advances in Automatic Meeting Record Creation and Access, ICASSP 2001.

On the Adequacy of Baseform Pronunciations and Pronunciation Variants

Mathew Magimai-Doss[1,2] and Hervé Bourlard[1,2]

[1] IDIAP Research Institute, CH-1920 Martigny, Switzerland
[2] Swiss Federal Institute of Technology (EPFL), CH-1015 Lausanne, Switzerland
{mathew, bourlard}@idiap.ch

Abstract. This paper presents an approach to automatically extract and evaluate the "stability" of pronunciation variants (i.e., adequacy of the model to accommodate this variability), based on multiple pronunciations of each lexicon words and the knowledge of a reference baseform pronunciation. Most approaches toward modelling pronunciation variability in speech recognition are based on the inference (through an ergodic HMM model) of a pronunciation graph (including all pronunciation variants), usually followed by a smoothing (e.g., Bayesian) of the resulting graph. Compared to these approaches, the approach presented here differs by (1) the way the models are inferred and (2) the way the smoothing (i.e., keeping the best ones) is done. In our case, indeed, inference of the pronunciation variants is obtained by slowly "relaxing" a (usually left-to-right) baseform model towards a fully ergodic model. In this case, the more stable the model is, the less the inferred model will diverge from it. Hence, for each pronunciation model so generated, we evaluate their adequacy by calculating the Levenshtein distance of the the new model with respect to the baseform, as well as their confidence measure (based on some posterior estimation), and models with the lowest Levenshtein distance and highest confidence are preserved. On a large telephone speech database (Phonebook), we show the relationship between this "stability" measure and recognition performance, and we finally show that automatically adding a few pronunciation variants to the less stable words is enough to significantly improve recognition rates.

1   Introduction

In standard automatic speech recognition (ASR) systems during recognition, for each acoustic observation x_n at time frame n, the acoustic model outputs the likelihoods of each subword unit e.g. phoneme, which is used by the subsequent decoding step. The decoding step uses the acoustic probabilities /likelihoods, the pronunciation model of the words present in the lexicon, and the language model (grammar) to output the most probable sequence of words that could have generated the acoustic observation sequence $X = \{x_1, \cdots, x_n, \cdots, x_N\}$ [1].

The lexicon of an ASR system contains the words and their standard pronunciations i.e. a sequence of subword units [2]. We refer to this sequence of

S. Bengio and H. Bourlard (Eds.): MLMI 2004, LNCS 3361, pp. 209–222, 2005.
© Springer-Verlag Berlin Heidelberg 2005

subword units of a word as baseform pronunciation of the word. The baseform pronunciation of each word is generally obtained from a standard lexical dictionary which contains both the meaning of the word and the way the word is to be pronounced. This could be further enriched by phonological rules. In standard hidden Markov model (HMM) based ASR during decoding, it is a stochastic pattern matching problem where given the acoustic models of subword units, we have to match the acoustic observation sequence X and pronunciation model (sequence of subword units). In speech recognition systems, it is generally expected that speaker(s) pronounce the words according to the phonetic transcription given in the lexicon; but speaker(s) do introduce pronunciation variation which leads to a mismatch between the acoustic observation and pronunciation model. The pronunciation variation can occur at the [3]

1. Acoustic characteristic level due to speaking style, speaking rate, different accent, pitch, differences in the length of the vocal tract, background noise (Lombard effect), emotion or stress.
2. Lexical characteristic level due to phonological processes such as assimilation, co-articulation, reduction, deletion and insertion, accent or "liaisons" in French.

For the reasons described above, the baseform pronunciation cannot properly model the pronunciation variation. Sometimes even with high frame/phoneme level performance the word performance can still be poor because the lexical constraints are not correct.

There are different ways to improve the match between acoustic parameters and pronunciation models, such as,

1. Adapting or enriching the pronunciation models. For example, generating new pronunciation variants and adding them to the lexicon or creating pronunciation lattices [3].
2. Adapting the acoustic model, such as iterative training [3], sharing the parameters of the phoneme models in baseform pronunciation with parameters of the phonemes in alternate realization(s) [4].
3. Extracting subword units and word pronunciations automatically from the data [5].

The most common practice is to generate new pronunciation variants. The approaches used for generating new pronunciation variants can be broadly classified as, (a) knowledge-based (b) data-driven approaches, or (c) a mix of both [3]. The generated pronunciations are kept separate [3] or merged into a single (more complex) HMM [6]. These pronunciation variants can also be pruned/smoothed to keep only the most representative ones. However, while this improves the matching properties of each of the words individually, the way these multiple pronunciations are defined is also known to increase the confusion between words.

In this paper, we take an alternate approach where:

− The adequacy of the baseform pronunciation of words in the lexicon is evaluated [7] i.e. how stable the baseform pronunciation is to acoustic variability.

– When the baseform pronunciation is inadequate for a given word, pronunciation variants that are as stable as possible to acoustic variability and at the same time not too dissimilar to the baseform pronunciation are extracted and added to the lexicon.

The adequacy of a given baseform pronunciation model is evaluated by (1) relaxing the lexical constraints of the baseform pronunciation and (2) measuring the confidence level of the acoustic match for the inferred pronunciation variants:

1. Inference of pronunciation variants: as is usually done, this is achieved by phonetically decoding each training utterance through an ergodic HMM. However, in our case, this ergodic HMM is initialized to only allow the generation of a first order approximation of the baseform pronunciation, and is later relaxed iteratively to converge towards a fully ergodic HMM. For each of these HMM configurations, a phonetic transcription is generated (pronunciation variant) and evaluated.
2. Evaluation of each of the inferred phonetic transcriptions through the use of a confidence measure and the Levenshtein distance between the inferred phonetic sequence and the associated baseform pronunciation. Here, we basically assess the "stability" of the baseform pronunciation to perturbations through the confidence measure and Levenshtein distance obtained.

As a by product, this evaluation procedure provides a framework to extract new pronunciation variants which are reliable and closer to the baseform pronunciation. Investigation of the proposed approach on a task-independent speaker-independent isolated word recognition task has yielded significant improvement in the performance of the system.

In addition to this, we show that the proposed evaluation procedure can be used to evaluate different acoustic models. For example in this study, we use acoustic models that are trained with standard Mel frequency cepstral coefficients (MFCCs) acoustic features and acoustic models that are trained with both MFCCs and auxiliary features [8,9]. We observe that modelling standard acoustic features along with auxiliary features such as pitch frequency and short-term energy improves the stability of the baseform pronunciation of words.

The paper is organized as follows. Section 2 describes the pronunciation model evaluation procedure. Section 3 describes briefly the measures used in our studies to assess the adequacy of pronunciation. Section 4 and Section 5 present the experimental setup and analytical studies, respectively. Section 6 presents the pronunciation variants extracting procedure and the results of the recognition studies. Finally, Section 7 concludes with discussion and future directions of work.

2   Evaluation of Pronunciation Models

HMM inference is a technique to infer the "best" HMM model associated with a given set of utterances [10]. This inference is done by performing subword-unit level decoding of the utterance, matching the acoustic sequence X on an *ergodic* HMM model [1]. For our studies, we use hybrid hidden Markov model/artificial neural network (HMM/ANN) systems [1] and each HMM state q_k corresponds to a context-independent phoneme which is associated with a particular ANN output. A fully ergodic HMM model contains a set of fully-connected phonetic states with uniform transition probabilities. Figure 1 shows a 3-state ergodic HMM model, including the non-emitting initial and final states I and F.

A fully ergodic HMM is capable of producing any state sequence (since there is no grammar or lexical constraint in it), as opposed to a left-to-right HMM which can only produce constrained state sequences. An ergodic HMM is obviously too general to model lexical constraints. In current ASR systems, the words are usually represented as left-to-right sequences of subword-units. For example, Figure 2 illustrates a word represented by pronunciation $\{q_2, q_1, q_2\}$.

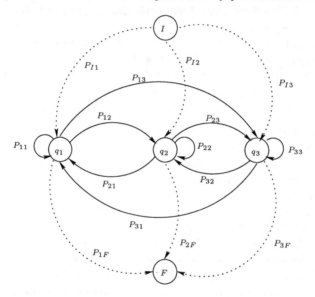

Fig. 1. 3-state Ergodic HMM

The transition probability matrix for the fully ergodic HMM is

$$T = \begin{bmatrix} P_{II} & P_{I1} & P_{I2} & P_{I3} & P_{IF} \\ P_{1I} & P_{11} & P_{12} & P_{13} & P_{1F} \\ P_{2I} & P_{21} & P_{22} & P_{23} & P_{2F} \\ P_{3I} & P_{31} & P_{32} & P_{33} & P_{3F} \\ P_{FI} & P_{F1} & P_{F2} & P_{F3} & P_{FF} \end{bmatrix} = \begin{bmatrix} 0.00 & 0.33 & 0.33 & 0.33 & 0.00 \\ 0.00 & 0.25 & 0.25 & 0.25 & 0.25 \\ 0.00 & 0.25 & 0.25 & 0.25 & 0.25 \\ 0.00 & 0.25 & 0.25 & 0.25 & 0.25 \\ 0.00 & 0.00 & 0.00 & 0.00 & 1.00 \end{bmatrix} \quad (1)$$

---

[1] an ergodic HMM contains a set of fully-connected phonetic states with arbitrary transition probability matrix.

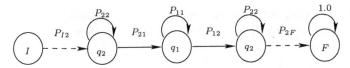

Fig. 2. Left-to-Right HMM

In pronunciation modelling literature, the HMM inference approach is used to generate pronunciation variants [10], by performing phonetic decoding (inference) of several utterances of the same/different words through the fully ergodic HMM which doesnot encode any lexical constraints. The proposed pronunciation model evaluation approach is based on a HMM inference mechanism which uses the prior knowledge of baseform pronunciation. For each lexicon word, and given its baseform pronunciation,

1. We first start from a transition matrix representing a first-order approximation of the baseform pronunciation (thus only allowing the transitions present in the left-to-right HMM). This is done by taking the transition probability of a fully ergodic HMM, say (1), adding an ϵ to the transitions present in the baseform pronunciation (for e.g. Figure 2) followed by a re-normalization, and thus yielding a transition matrix such as in (2). This ergodic model is referred to here as a *constrained ergodic model*.

$$T = \begin{bmatrix} 0.0 & \frac{1}{3+3\epsilon} & \frac{1+3\epsilon}{3+3\epsilon} & \frac{1}{3+3\epsilon} & 0.0 \\ 0.0 & \frac{1}{4+4\epsilon} & \frac{1+4\epsilon}{4+4\epsilon} & \frac{1}{4+4\epsilon} & \frac{1}{4+4\epsilon} \\ 0.0 & \frac{1+4\epsilon}{4+8\epsilon} & \frac{1}{4+8\epsilon} & \frac{1}{4+8\epsilon} & \frac{1+4\epsilon}{4+8\epsilon} \\ 0.0 & \frac{1}{4} & \frac{1}{4} & \frac{1}{4} & \frac{1}{4} \\ 0.0 & 0.0 & 0.0 & 0.0 & 1.0 \end{bmatrix} \quad (2)$$

For a large value of ϵ, this *constrained ergodic model* is a first order approximation of baseform pronunciation

2. This *constrained ergodic model* is then slowly relaxed by decreasing the value of ϵ. For $\epsilon = 0.0$, this model is then equivalent to a fully ergodic HMM.

We note here that when a constrained ergodic HMM is used for inference, it can still recognize state sequences other than the baseform pronunciation because of first order Markov assumption. For example, the above example of a constrained ergodic HMM can recognize state sequences such as $\{q_2, q_1, q_2, q_1, q_2\}$ or just q_2 apart from the intended state sequence $\{q_2, q_1, q_2\}$.

A constrained ergodic HMM encodes the lexical constraint information through the transitional probability matrix. But when the ϵ value is decreased, the lexical constraint is relaxed such that the transition probability matrix starts allowing transitions which are not present in the baseform pronunciation. The fully ergodic HMM is a special case of constrained ergodic HMM which does not have any lexical constraint information.

The underlying idea exploited in the present paper thus consists of generating for each utterance of a given lexicon word several pronunciation variants through successive relaxation of the transition matrix, i.e. decreasing the value of ϵ. The quality of these inferred pronunciation variants are then assessed in terms of different measures, including:

1. Confidence measure: measuring the confidence level (based on posterior probabilities or likelihood ratio) between the acoustic sequence and the different inferred pronunciation variants, as already proposed in [11].
2. Levenshtein distance [12] between the inferred pronunciation variants and the baseform pronunciation.
3. "Speed of divergence": if the inferred pronunciation variants do not diverge too quickly from the baseform pronunciation when relaxing the transition probability matrix, it is indeed a sign that the baseform pronunciation is quite "stable", and thus adequate.

3   Measures

Hybrid HMM/ANN based systems are capable of estimating the posterior probability $P(M|X)$ of model M given the acoustic observations, X [1]. In literature, different confidence measures that can be derived from a hybrid HMM/ANN system based on local phone posterior probabilities, $P(q_k|x_n)$ have been suggested [11, 7], where x_n is the feature vector at time frame n and q_k is the state hypothesis.

In this paper, we use the posterior probability based confidence measure. The posterior based confidence measure is defined as the normalized logarithm of the segment-based accumulated posterior probabilities.

3.1   Confidence Measure

For a given segmentation (resulting in our case from a Viterbi algorithm using local posterior probabilites), we define the accumulated posteriors for all the acoustic vectors observed on state q_k as:

$$CM_{post}(q_k) = \prod_{n=b_k}^{n=e_k} P(q_k|x_n), \tag{3}$$

where b_k and e_k are the begin and end frames of a state hypothesis q_k. Defining minus log of $CM_{post}(q_k)$ as the state-based confidence measure

$$\mathcal{CM}_{post}(q_k) = - \sum_{n=b_k}^{n=e_k} \log P(q_k|x_n) \tag{4}$$

the *normalized word-level posterior probability based confidence measure* is then defined as:

$$\mathcal{CM}_{wpost} = \frac{1}{K} \sum_{k=1}^{k=K} \frac{\mathcal{CM}_{post}(q_k)}{e_k - b_k + 1}, \tag{5}$$

Where K is the number of constituent phonemes in the inferred model. *The lower the value* $\mathcal{CM}_{wpost}$, *the higher the confidence level is.* The average posterior probability can then be computed as $exp(-\mathcal{CM}_{wpost})$.

3.2   Levenshtein Distance

When HMM inference is performed, we obtain the phonetic decoding from the best path. The confidence measures are computed using the best path as described earlier in this section. In our case apart from confidence measures, measuring the difference between the inferred pronunciations and the baseform pronunciation is of equal interest because it is possible to infer a pronunciation with high confidence level that is completely different from the baseform pronunciation. We measure the difference between the inferred pronunciation and the baseform pronunciation in terms of Levenshtein distance (LD).

Given two strings, the Levenshtein distance is defined as the minimum number of changes that has to be made in one string to convert it into another string [12]. Consider two strings /c/ /a/ /t/ and /a/ /c/ /t/, in this case the Levenshtein score is two as a minimum of two changes have to be made to convert any one of the strings into another.

4   Experimental Setup

We use the PhoneBook speech corpus for our studies [13]. There are 42 context-independent phonemes including silence, each modelled by a single emitting state. The standard acoustic vector x_n is the MFCCs extracted from the speech signal using an analysis window of 25 ms with a shift of 8.3 ms. Cepstral mean subtraction and energy normalization are performed. Ten Mel frequency cepstral coefficients (MFCCs), the first-order derivatives (delta) of the ten MFCCs and the c_0 (energy coefficient) are extracted for each time frame, resulting in a 21 dimensional acoustic vector. The auxiliary features used in this study are pitch frequency and short-term energy.

We use the following trained systems for our studies:

1. Hybrid HMM/ANN baseline system trained with standard features (system-base).
2. Hybrid HMM/ANN systems trained with standard features and auxiliary features. These systems have been shown to improve the performance of ASR systems [8, 9]. The auxiliary features are used in two different ways
   (a) Concatenated to the standard feature to get an augmented feature vector with which hybrid HMM/ANN system is trained. The system trained with pitch frequency as auxiliary feature is denoted as system-app-p, and the system trained with short-term energy as auxiliary feature is denoted system-app-e.
   (b) Auxiliary features conditioning the emission distribution similar to gender modelling. The system trained with pitch frequency as the auxiliary

feature is denoted as system-cond-p, and the system trained with short-term energy as the auxiliary feature is denoted system-cond-e.
For further details about how these systems can be implemented, refer to [8, 9].

These systems were trained with a training set consisting of 19420 utterances and a validation set consisting of 7290 utterances. All the systems have the same number of parameters. The test set consists of 8 different sets of 75 word lexicon amounting 6598 utterances. These systems were trained for speaker-independent task-independent, small vocabulary (75 words) isolated word recognition. The words and speakers present in the training set, validation set and test set do not overlap.

5   Analytical Studies

We performed analytical studies using the acoustic models of system-base, system-app-p and system-cond-e. In our studies, system-app-p and system-cond-e perform significantly better than system-base [8]. We used a part of the validation set, 75 words, each spoken on average by 12 different speakers. We performed evaluation of baseform pronunciations in the following manner:

1. For a given word utterance X, and given its known baseform pronunciation, initialize the $K \times K$ transition probability matrix (where $K = 44$ in our case, corresponding to the 42 phonemes, plus initial and final states) with a very large ϵ value (10^{10}), to constrain the ergodic model to be equivalent to a first-order approximation of the baseform pronunciation of the word.
2. Perform forced Viterbi decoding based on that model using local posterior probabilities $P(q_k|x_n)$.
3. From the resulting best path, extract the phonetic level decoding and compute $\mathcal{CM}_{wpost}$.
4. Compute Levenshtein distance LD between the phonetic sequence obtained from step 3 and the baseform pronunciation.
5. Relax the underlying model towards a fully ergodic model by decreasing the ϵ value, and repeat steps 2-4 to infer new phonetic transcription and compute their associated $\mathcal{CM}_{wpost}$ and LD.

The ideal case suitable for automatic speech recognition would be something like shown in Figure 3, where

1. When the inference is performed on a constrained ergodic HMM the Levenshtein distance is zero.
2. As the constrained ergodic HMM is relaxed to fully ergodic HMM the inferred pronunciations diverge less from the baseform pronunciation.

But in practice, we observe the following (see Figure 4)

1. When the inference is performed on a constrained ergodic HMM (i.e. large value for ϵ) the confidence level is low and the Levenshtein distance is low.

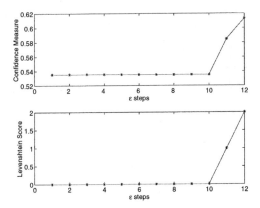

Fig. 3. A case where the baseform pronunciation of word keeble uttered by a female speaker matches well with the acoustic observation. The inference was done with acoustic models of system-app-p. For the sake of clarity, the confidence level is plotted as $exp(-\mathcal{CM}_{wpost})$

2. As the constrained ergodic HMM is relaxed to fully ergodic HMM the confidence level increases and the Levenshtein distance also increases.

As can observed from the Figures 3 and 4 with posterior-based confidence and Levenshtein distance together we can analyze the stability of the baseform pronunciation; but it is difficult to make conclusions about the adequacy of the baseform pronunciation based on the evaluation of a single utterance. So, to make a decision about the adequacy of a baseform pronunciation and to extract pronunciation variants we will need more than one utterance.

We evaluated the baseform pronunciation of all the 75 words using their multiple utterances with the procedure described earlier in this section. We did the same evaluation with acoustic models of system-base, system-app-p and system-cond-e. The main outcomes of this analytical study are the following:

1. When the baseform pronunciation of a word matches acoustic observations well, the evaluation across different speakers mostly yields a behavior similar to Figure 3 i.e confidence level is high and when the lexical constraints are relaxed the speed of divergence is slow.
2. When a baseform pronunciation is inadequate, the confidence level is low and the speed of divergence is fast for most of the utterances of the word.
3. When comparing across the acoustic models system-base, system-app-p and system-cond-e, none of the models are totally superior over others. Most of the time the acoustic models trained with MFCCs and auxiliary features match the baseform pronunciation well. In order to visualize it, at each inference step (i.e. for each value of ϵ) we combined the posterior-based confidence measure and the levenshtein score in the following way

$$comb = \mathcal{CM}_{wpost} + \log(1 + LD)$$

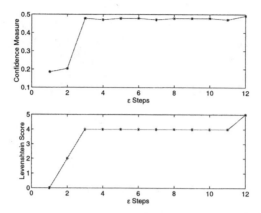

Fig. 4. A case where the baseform pronunciation of word keeble uttered by a female speaker doesnot match well with the acoustic observation. The inference was done with acoustic models of system-app-p. For the sake of clarity, the confidence level is plotted as $exp(-\mathcal{CM}_{wpost})$

Taking $\log(1 + LD)$ is appropriate as LD is an integer and has a wide dynamic range compared to $\mathcal{CM}_{wpost}$. Also, we are interested in changes in LD at lower levels (i.e. the deviations that are not too far from the baseform pronunciation) which the log function represents well. A high *comb* value means low confidence i.e $\mathcal{CM}_{wpost}$ and/or LD are high. We observed that for the majority of the utterances it is low for the acoustic models trained with both MFCCs and auxiliary features when compared to acoustic models just trained on MFCCs. This is illustrated in Figure 5.

This is an interesting outcome i.e., the baseform evaluation procedure can be used to evaluate different acoustic models by fixing the pronunciation models. Also, an alternate approach to model pronunciation variation would be to fix the baseform pronunciations and optimizing acoustic parameters so as to maximize their matching and discriminating properties.

6   Extraction of Pronunciation Variants and Speech Recognition Studies

We perform recognition studies by:

1. First evaluating the baseform pronunciations of the test lexicon words (these words are neither present in the training set or validation set) using the pronunciation evaluation procedure described in the last section.
2. For the words for which the baseform pronunciation are inadequate, pronunciation variants are extracted from the evaluation procedure itself and added to the lexicon.
3. Then, recognition studies are performed with the updated lexicon.

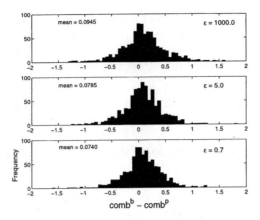

Fig. 5. Histogram of difference between the $comb^b$ value (obtained by using acoustic models of system-base) and $comb^p$ value (obtained by using acoustic models of system-app-p) for different values of ϵ, for all the utterances

In order to do this study, we split the test set randomly (keeping the gender balance) into two parts: (a) "*H-set*", used for baseform pronunciation evaluation and pronunciation variant extraction (45% of the original test set). (b) "*T-set*", used for recognition studies (55% of the original test set). Since, each speaker has spoken each word only once, the speakers present in the *H-set* of any word are not present in the *T-set* of that word.

The recognition performance of different systems on *T-set* for 8 different sets of 75 words lexicon and one set of 602 words lexicon are given in Table 1. The performance of the 75 word lexicon is the average of the 8 word error rates (obtained for the 8 different sets of 75 words lexicon)..

Table 1. Recognition studies performed on 8 different sets of 75 words lexicon and one set of 602 words lexicon with single pronunciation for each word. Performance is measured in terms of word error rate (WER), expressed in %. Notations: O: Auxiliary feature observed, H: Auxiliary feature hidden (i.e. integrated over all possible values of auxiliary feature)

Systems		Performance 75 words	Performance 602 words
system-base		4.2	11.0
system-app-p	O	2.5	7.3
system-cond-p	O	3.5	9.9
	H	4.0	11.3
system-app-e	O	5.3	13.3
system-cond-e	O	2.9	8.3
	H	3.5	10.2

We extracted the pronunciation variants using the acoustic models of system-app-p for this study, as this system performs better than all the systems and also it better matches the acoustic observation and baseform pronunciation (as observed in last section). For the utterances of each word in *H-set*, we ran the evaluation procedure

1. If it is found that for the majority ($\geq 50\%$) of utterances of the word the baseform pronunciation is adequate. Then, no pronunciation variants are included.

2. If the above condition is not satisfied, we look for the most frequently inferred pronunciation variant (not diverging far from the baseform) across different utterances, during evaluation. We add it to the lexicon. If there is no commonly inferred pronunciation (it mostly happens for short words.), we extract variants from each utterance such that the confidence level is high (average posterior $exp(-\mathcal{CM}_{wpost})$ close to 0.5 or above) and at the same time LD is low (≤ 2).

In the present study, we have done this manually. In future, we would like to automate it using a combined measure such as *comb* described in the last section. The statistics of the test lexicon after adding the pronunciation variants is given in Table 2 (combining all the words in the lexicons of the 8 different test sets).

Table 2. Statistics of test lexicon. The first column mentions the number of pronunciations and the second column gives the number of words with that number of pronunciations

# of resulting Pronunciation models	Number of words
1	441
2	106
3	48
4	7

We performed recognition studies with the updated lexicon(s). The results of the recognition studies performed on 8 different sets of 75 words lexicon and one set of 602 words lexicon are given in Table 3.

Comparing the performances of the respective systems in Tables 1 and 3, we observe that by adding new pronunciation variants we improve the performance of the 75 words lexicon system significantly. Improvements are also obtained in the case of one set of 602 words lexicon (in some cases an absolute improvement of 1%). This indicates that the addition of new pronunciation variants in the lexicon does not increases the confusion between the words. The interesting point to observe here is that the pronunciation variants were extracted using acoustic models of system-app-p; it could be expected that the extracted pronunciation variants are more suitable for system-app-p as opposed to all the systems. On the contrary, we can see that the addition of pronunciation variants improve the performance of all systems.

Table 3. Recognition studies performed on 8 different sets of 75 words lexicon and one set of 602 words lexicon with multiple pronunciations . Performance is measured in terms of WER (expressed in %). Notations: O: Auxiliary feature observed, H: Auxiliary feature hidden. † improvement in the performance is significant (McNemar's test) compared to the results in Table 1 (with 95% confidence or above)

Systems		Performance 75 words	Performance 602 words
system-base		$3.0^\dagger$	$10.1^\dagger$
system-app-p	O	$1.7^\dagger$	$6.4^\dagger$
system-cond-p	O	$2.8^\dagger$	$9.2^\dagger$
	H	3.3	$10.7^\dagger$
system-app-e	O	$4.3^\dagger$	$12.0^\dagger$
system-cond-e	O	$2.3^\dagger$	7.9
	H	$2.7^\dagger$	$9.2^\dagger$

7   Summary and Conclusions

In this paper, we proposed an approach based on HMM inference to evaluate the adequacy of pronunciation models. For each lexicon word, the general idea is to start from a *constrained ergodic model*, corresponding to the first-order approximation of the baseform pronunciation and thus only allowing the generation of phonetic sequences basically identical to the baseform pronunciation. This *constrained ergodic model* is then iteratively relaxed to converge towards a fully ergodic HMM, thus allowing all possible phonetic sequences. For each configuration of this relaxed ergodic HMM, the optimal phonetic sequence is extracted and its relevance is estimated in terms of (1) a confidence measure (based on posterior probabilities) and (2) the Levenshtein distance with respect to the baseform pronunciation. A good pronunication model should result in a high confidence level and a good stability when relaxing the ergodic HMM. This approach was used to evaluate baseform pronunciation of the words in the lexicon and, extract new pronunciation for the words whose baseform pronunciation were not stable. Recognition studies performed on task-independent speaker-independent isolated word recognition task yielded significant improvement.

In addition to this, in our analytical studies we showed that the proposed pronunciation model evaluation approach can be used to evaluate different acoustic models. When comparing across different acoustic models, we observed that acoustic models trained with both standard features and auxiliary features could improve the stability of the baseform pronunciation of words. This suggests an alternate approach to model pronunciation variation, where the baseform pronunciations can be fixed and the acoustic models are enriched so as to maximize their matching and discrimination properties. This has to be studied further.

In future, we would like to investigate measures to combine the confidence score, Levenshtein distance and "speed of divergence" in order to automatically evaluate the baseform pronunciations and extract pronunciation variants. We would also like to study different relaxation schemes (such as exponential, logarithmic etc.) and their effect on pronunciation variant extraction.

Acknowledgements

This work was supported by the Swiss National Science Foundation (NSF) under grant MULTI (2000-068231.02/1) and Swiss National Center of Competence in Research (NCCR) on Interactive Multimodal Information Management (IM)2. The NCCR is managed by the Swiss NSF on behalf of the federal authorities. This paper has benefitted from the work of Ait-Aissa Hassou done at IDIAP. The authors would like to thank Guillaume Lathoud and Joanne Moore for their valuable comments and suggestions.

References

1. Bourlard, H., Morgan, N.: Connectionist Speech Recognition - A Hybrid Approach. Kluwer Academic Publishers (1994)
2. Ostendorf, M.: Moving beyond the 'Beads-on-a-String' model of speech. In: Proc. IEEE ASRU Workshop. (1999)
3. Strik, H., Cucchiarini, C.: Modeling pronunciation variation for ASR: A survey of the literature. Speech Communication **29** (1999) 225–246
4. Sarclar, M.: Pronunciation modeling for conversational speech recognition. PhD dissertation, CSLU, Johns Hopkins University, Baltimore, USA (2000)
5. Bacchiani, M., Ostendorf, M.: Joint lexicon, acoustic unit inventory and model design. Speech Communication **29** (1999) 99–114
6. Stolcke, A., Omohundro, S.M.: Best-first model merging for hidden Markov models. Technical Report tr-94-003, ICSI, Berkeley, Califronia, USA (1994)
7. Magimai-Doss, M., Bourlard, H.: Pronunciation models and their evaluation using confidence measures. Technical Report RR-01-29, IDIAP, Martigny, Switzerland (2001)
8. Magimai.-Doss, M., Stephenson, T.A., Bourlard, H.: Using pitch frequency information in speech recognition. In: Eurospeech. (2003) 2525–2528
9. Stephenson, T.A., Magimai.-Doss, M., Bourlard, H.: Speech recognition with auxiliary information. IEEE Trans. Speech and Audio Processing **4** (2004) 189–203
10. Mokbel, H., Jouvet, D.: Derivation of the optimal phonetic transcription set for a word from its acoustic realisation. In: Proceedings of Workshop on Modeling Pronunciation Variation for Automatic Speech Recognition. (1998) 73–78
11. Williams, G., Renals, S.: Confidence measures from local posterior probability estimates. Computer Speech and Language **13** (1999) 395–411
12. Sankoff, D., Kruskal, J.: Time Warps, String Edits and Macromolecules: The theory and practise of sequence comparison. CSLI Publications, Leland Stanford Junior University (1999)
13. Pitrelli, J.F., Fong, C., Wong, S.H., Spitz, J.R., Leung, H.C.: PhoneBook: A phonetically-rich isolated-word telephone-speech database. In: ICASSP. (1995) 1767–1770

Tandem Connectionist Feature Extraction for Conversational Speech Recognition

Qifeng Zhu[1], Barry Chen[1,2], Nelson Morgan[1,2], and Andreas Stolcke[1,3]

[1] International Computer Science Institute
[2] University of California, Berkeley
[3] SRI International
{qifeng, byc, morgan, stolcke}@icsi.berkeley.edu

Abstract. Multi-Layer Perceptrons (MLPs) can be used in automatic speech recognition in many ways. A particular application of this tool over the last few years has been the Tandem approach, as described in [7] and other more recent publications. Here we discuss the characteristics of the MLP-based features used for the Tandem approach, and conclude with a report on their application to conversational speech recognition. The paper shows that MLP transformations yield variables that have regular distributions, which can be further modified by using logarithm to make the distribution easier to model by a Gaussian-HMM. Two or more vectors of these features can easily be combined without increasing the feature dimension. We also report recognition results that show that MLP features can significantly improve recognition performance for the NIST 2001 Hub-5 evaluation set with models trained on the Switchboard Corpus, even for complex systems incorporating MMIE training and other enhancements.

1 Introduction

As described in [3] and many other sources, with large enough training data and a large enough MLP, and using 1-of-c binary coded class targets, an MLP can learn the posterior probability of a class given an observation, $P(c|o)$. This was effectively used in *acoustic modeling* in hybrid MLP-HMM systems [10] , where the scaled likelihood of a frame given a phone state in an HMM is computed by the posterior probability, $P(c|o)$, scaled by the phone prior probability, $P(c)$. This inherently discriminant approach worked well for many tasks, and was particularly useful for combinations of features with different statistical properties (e.g., continuous and binary features) [13].

On the other hand, over the last decade the dominant paradigm for speech recognition has incorporated mixtures of Gaussians to represent emission distributions for HMMs. Within this framework, many performance-enhancing refinements have been developed, such as feature adaptation, mean and variance adaptation, discriminative training, etc.. To benefit from the strengths of both MLP-HMM and Gaussian-HMM techniques, the Tandem solution was proposed in 2001, using modified MLP outputs as observations for a Gaussian-HMM [7]. An error analysis of Tandem MLP-based features [12] showed significant differences from the errors of a system using cepstral features. This suggested that a combination of both fea-

S. Bengio and H. Bourlard (Eds.): MLMI 2004, LNCS 3361, pp. 223–231, 2005.
© Springer-Verlag Berlin Heidelberg 2005

ture styles might be even better. This was applied to the Aurora distributed speech recognition task [2], and later to the EARS conversational telephone recognition task [11]. Here we continue this work, applying the combination techniques to increasingly more complex systems, and noting the properties of the features that might be responsible for the virtues of the MLP-based features.

In Section 2.1 properties of MLP features are discussed. Section 2.2 shows some technical details on how to combine MLP features with PLP features to achieve good ASR results. Section 2.3 presents results with systems incorporating other techniques that provide error reduction that could be redundant with that provided by MLP features, in the sense that both approaches could potentially eliminate similar errors. In particular, we have started using HMM-based systems incorporating discriminative training (via MMIE), better language model rescoring, and system combination (ROVER).

2   Using MLP-Based Features in LVCSR

2.1   Properties of MLP-Based Features

Currently, short-term spectral-based (typically cepstral) features are used in ASR, (MFCC or PLP). These features are typically non-Gaussian, and are most often modeled by mixtures of Gaussians. When diagonal covariance matrices are used, many Gaussian mixtures are required to effectively model the feature distributions for conversational speech.

MLPs are effective at modeling unknown distributions. Cepstral features can be used as inputs to train an MLP with phoneme classes as targets. The MLP outputs, which are approximations to phone posterior probabilities given input features, can also be used as features for HMM. This MLP can then also be regarded as a nonlinear feature transform. There have been many kinds of linear feature transforms, such as LDA or HLDA [5], that make the transformed feature better for modeling by Gaussian mixtures for an HMM. This then suggests a question: when an MLP is used as a feature transform, i.e., when posterior approximations are used as features, what properties of this approach make it useful?

For the work reported here, the MLPs are trained using 46 mono-phones as targets. Thus, the MLP outputs have 46 components. For each phone class, one out of the 46 components corresponds to the underlying phone class. In this paper we call this component the "in-line" component for the class, and the rest are "off-line" components.

Figure 1 shows the feature distribution of three phone classes /ah/(triangle), /ao/ (star), and /aw/ (circle) in feature space spanned by the first three components of PLP feature. Figure 2 shows the feature space of the three MLP outputs corresponding to the same three phone classes, trained using PLP feature. The feature distributions for the three classes are more regular in the MLP feature space than PLP feature space. This is because the MLP is able to discriminatively learn the irregular class boundaries and transform the features within the boundary close to their class target used in training, and transform the irregular class boundaries to equal posterior hyper-planes in the feature space of posteriors. The outputs are not always good estimates of the class posteriors. Errors occur, as shown in the figures, and the frame accuracy derived from choosing the class with the highest posterior is about 70%. However, since the outputs are complemented by PLP features, they are rarely altogether bad.

While the distributions of MLP outputs shown in Figure 2 are regular, they are difficult to model using a few Gaussian mixtures due to the sharpness of the distribution. In-line components distribute roughly uniformly between 0 and 1 and taper away near 0, and off-line components distribute very narrowly around 0. To Gaussianize the feature distributions, a simple approach is to take the log of the MLP outputs. Figure 3 shows the feature distributions of the log MLP outputs for the same three classes of the same three MLP output components.

The typical distribution of the "in-line" (correct class) component of the (log) MLP-based features is concentrated close to 0 and tapers away gradually, which is due to the compression of the high posteriors close to 1 and the expansion of low posteriors by the logarithm. The typical distribution of an "off-line" (incorrect class) component is close to a single Gaussian centered at a high negative number, which is expanded by the logarithm from the narrow posterior distribution close to zero. Two typical distributions of the log in-line and off-line components are shown in Figure 4. These distributions in Figures 3 and 4 should be easier to model with Gaussian mixture models.

While making the feature space more regular, these MLP-based features can also reduce the variation among speakers. Speaker differences are major sources of within-class variance that can increase the overlap between acoustic models. We compute PLP features with per-speaker (in practice, per-conversation-side) vocal tract length normalization (VTLN), where piece-wise linear frequency warping for each speaker

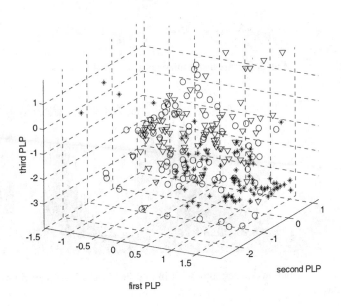

Fig. 1. Feature distributions of the first three PLP components for three classes, /ah/(triangle), /ao/ (star), and /aw/ (circle)

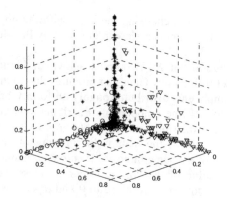

Fig. 2. Feature distributions of the three MLP outputs corresponding to the three classes, /ah/(triangle), /ao/ (star), and /aw/ (circle)

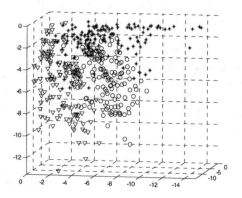

Fig. 3. Feature distributions of the log MLP outputs

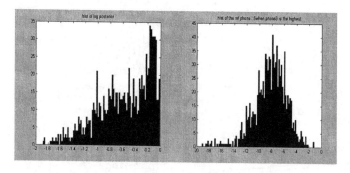

Fig. 4. Typical distributions (histogram) of an in-line (left) and an off-line (right) MLP-based feature component

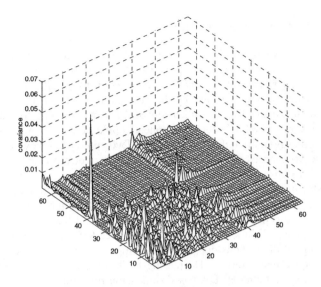

Fig. 5. Variances of all elements in the SAT transform among different speakers

is used to reduce speaker variation [1]. This VTLN is important but still leaves much speaker variability due to factors other than frequency warping. MLP-based features, trained with different speakers for the same target, can decrease this. A way to show this is by looking at the variances of speaker adaptive training (SAT) transforms among speakers, since differences on SAT transform could be used to represent speaker differences [6]. An SAT adaptation matrix was computed for each speaker on the concatenation of PLP features of 39 dimensions (13 static and their first and second derivatives) and MLP-based features (orthogonalized and truncated) of 25 dimensions, where all the feature components are normalized to zero mean and unit variance. Without speaker variation, all the SAT transforms would be the same; otherwise, they would differ. Figure 5 shows the variances of every component of the SAT transform matrix among different speakers. The first 39 by 39 block of the SAT transform matrix has high variances, which means more variations among speakers in the PLP feature, but the next 25 by 25 block has smaller variances, which means small variation among speakers. The ratio of the average variance of the PLP block to that of the MLP-based feature block is 1.6.

While MLP-based features are being used here as HMM observations, they still have the properties of (log) phone posterior estimates. This makes it possible to combine different MLP outputs trained with same targets but different inputs to improve the features without increasing the total feature dimension. These MLPs may emphasize different aspects of the target class, so a combination may yield further improvement. In practice, we use two types of MLPs and combine MLP outputs using a weighted sum (of probabilities), where the weights are a normalized version of the inverse entropy [9]. The two types of MLP-based features are PLP-MLP and the TRAPs (or HATs) [4], which offer complementary information on the phone class. The first of these incorporates inputs from roughly 100 ms of speech (using 9 sequential PLP cepstral vectors as input), and the second uses 500 ms of input (from critical band energy trajectories).

2.2   Using MLP-Based Features with PLP

A simple way to combine PLP and MLP-based features is to concatenate them. The resulting feature vector can be as long as 39+46=85, where 39 is the dimension of PLP feature (either from PLP –12 and 2 derivatives or, as we ultimately switched to, PLP-12 and 3 derivatives followed by dimensionality reduction to 39). The MLP-based features originally have a dimension of 46, corresponding to the number of phone classes used. The 85 feature components could contain significant redundancies, and so dimensionality reduction was used. Two approaches were tried. KLT was applied to the MLP-based features and the components corresponding to the smallest eigenvalues were truncated. Another approach was to apply a more complicated linear feature transform, HLDA, to search for the best non-trivial feature mapping direction and discard the nuisance dimensions [5][14]. For KLT, the components corresponding to the highest 17 eigenvalues had 95% of the total original feature variance. Keeping the most significant 25 dimensions after KLT covered 98% of the total original variance. Including all dimensions doesn't always improve ASR, and in fact a truncated feature often gave better results. Decreasing to fewer than 15 dimensions typically hurt. In practice, we found HLDA based dimension reduction gave us no advantage over KLT when adaptation is used. Consequently in subsequent experiments we only used KLT for the MLP features.

We also found that it was important to modify scaling factors for the models, much as in previous years we had found it necessary to optimize such parameters for varying amounts of acoustic context for the hybrid HMM/ANN system. In particular, we found it useful to optimize a scale factor on the log likelihood associated with the individual Gaussians in the mixture. For a longer feature, the log likelihood has a larger dynamic range, and this Gaussian weight should be tuned to a much lower number such as 0.3 instead of 0.8, which was the best tuned value to fit PLP features with 39 dimensions. Note that for systems that don't have such tunable parameter, a more aggressive dimension reduction after KLT of the MLP feature, such as to reduce to 17, is needed as a trade-off.

When VTL-normalized PLP is used as an HMM feature, per-speaker mean and variance normalization is still helpful. We also use per-speaker mean and variance normalized PLP to train MLPs and to generate MLP features. The MLP-based features are then normalized globally to zero mean and unit variance after KLT or HLDA before being used as an observation for the HMMs.

An extra per speaker normalization after MLP transformation was still helpful, apparently reducing some speaker variation left after the mean and variance normalization before the MLP-based nonlinear transform. This is not a property of linear transforms, for which a previous per-speaker mean and variance normalized feature will still be per-speaker normalized, if the transform matrix is properly scaled.

The SRI Decipher system [14] was used to conduct recognition experiments. Table 1 shows the ASR results in word error rate on the NIST 2001 Hub-5 test set. The training set contained about 68 hours of conversational telephone speech (largely Switchboard) data. Gender dependent HMMs were trained with a maximum likelihood criterion, and a bigram language model was used in the decoding. The MLP feature dimension was reduced from 46 to 25 using KLT. The baseline is PLP with the first three derivatives followed by HLDA to reduce to 39 dimension (referred to as PLP2); previous experience had suggested that incorporating more than two derivatives without HLDA was not useful. Results show 6-9% error reduction by adding MLP-based features. First, we appended MLP features trained using 9 frames of PLP (PLPMLP) to the baseline PLP2 features. Next we appended the HATs MLP feature (HATs). These MLP features were further per-speaker mean and variance normalized after the KLT which we found to further reduce error rates. The last two rows show results from appending the inverse entropy combination of PLPMLP and HATs to the baseline feature. The first is without the extra speaker normalization of the MLP features, and this shows how this extra normalization helps. Clearly the combination of MLPs focusing on long term (~500 ms) and medium term (~100ms) gives lower WER.

The features were further tested with MLLR adaptation, where three adaptation transform matrices were computed for each speaker to reduce the difference between the testing condition of the speaker and the trained HMMs. Table 2 shows that the MLP features work well with MLLR.

Table 1. Word error rate on DARPA Eval2001NIST 2001 Hub-5 test set with PLP baseline and PLP plus different MLP features. (* PLP2 is PLP with three derivatives plus HLDA)

Feature	Word Error Rate (Relative error reduction)
PLP2 (*) baseline	37.2
PLP2+PLPMLP-KLT25-spknorm	36.1 (3.0%)
PLP2+HATs-KLT25-spknorm	36.0 (3.2%)
PLP2 + (PLPMLP,HATS)-KLT25	34.8 (6.5%)
PLP2+(PLPMLP,HATS)-KLT25-spknorm	34.0 (8.6%)

Table 2. Word error rate on NIST 2001 Hub-5 test set. MLLR adaptation is used on PLP2+MLP-based features

Feature	WER (Error reduction)
PLP2 baseline	35.8
PLP2+ (PLPMLP,HATS)-KLT25	33.4 (6.7%)
PLP2 + (PLPMLP,HATS)-KLT25-spknorm	32.6 (8.9%)

2.3 Using a Better LVCSR System

A key question is whether the front-end based techniques described here provide error reductions that are redundant or complementary with more advanced backend techniques, i.e., more powerful acoustic modeling and decoding techniques, which are used in state-of-the-art LVCSR systems. Impressive improvements provided in simple systems can often disappear with more powerful systems. We hypothesize that this could occur due to similarities between the methods being combined (e.g., using discriminative features and discriminative HMM training). Another hypothesis might be that the errors that were easier to correct would be eliminated by either of two dissimilar methods (e.g., new features or a better language model). To address these concerns, we used the new features for versions of the SRI system that included discriminative training using maximum mutual information estimation (MMIE), a 4-gram language model and duration model based rescoring (4G-LM), and system combination (ROVER) with MFCC-based ASR [14]. A related concern was whether improvements could still be observed when more training data is used.

Table 3 shows the recognition results with the improved system. To save time, the gender-dependent experiment was only conducted on male data (although spot checks with females showed similar results). A full-fledged LVCSR system was trained using 200 hours of male Switchboard data, but MLPs were trained with 128 hours of male speech. Results show that the relative error reduction due to adding MLP-based features can carry through to the improved system.

Table 3. Male WERs and relative error reductions on NIST 2001 Hub-5 set with the improved system

ASR System	PLP2	+ MLP	Error reduction
MMIE	30.8	28.6	7.1%
MMIE+ 4G-LM	25.6	23.5	8.2%
+System ROVER	24.5	23.0	6.1%

3   Summary and Conclusion

Using MLP-based features can improve ASR performance on a large conversational telephone speech recognition task, even when large amounts of training data, discriminant training (MMIE) and other system enhancements are used.

MLP-based features provide a data-driven front-end approach to feature extraction that improves discrimination and ease of modeling. They can incorporate significantly more temporal context than conventional features and are optimized to approximate phone posteriors conditioned on this context. The MLP is trained discriminatively, can reduce speaker variability that is irrelevant to word recognition, and can generate feature distributions that are easily modeled by Gaussian mixture-based HMMs.

Experiments show that MLP-based features offer unique benefits that appear to be complementary to those provided by other techniques such as MMIE and system combination. When properly used, MLP-based features can improve ASR performance in the conversational telephone LVCSR task significantly by reducing errors from 5% to 9%.

Acknowledgements

This work was made possible by funding from the DARPA EARS Novel Approaches Grant No. MDA972-02-1-0024. Thanks also to Hynek Hermansky, Ozgur Cetin, and Pratibha Jain for many relevant discussions.

References

1. Andreou, A., Kamm, T., and Cohen, J., "Experiments in Vocal Tract Normalization," *Proc. CAIP Workshop: Frontiers in Speech Recognition II*, 1994.
2. Benitez, C., Burget, L., Chen, B., Dupont, S., Garudadri, H., Hermanskey, H., Jain, P., Kajarekar, S., Morgan, N., and Sivadas, S., "Robust ASR front-end using spectral based and discriminant features: experiments on the Aurora task", *Eurospeech 2001.*
3. Bourlard, H., and Wellekens, C., "Links between Markov models and multilayer perceptrons," *IEEE Trans. Pattern Anal. Machine Intell.* **12**:1167-1178, 1990.
4. Chen, B., Zhu, Q., Morgan, N. "Learning long term temporal features in LVCSR using neural networks", *submitted to ICSLP 2004.*
5. Gales, M.J.F., "Semi-tied covariance matrices for hidden Markov models", *IEEE Trans. Speech and Audio Processing,* vol 7, pp. 272-281, 1999.
6. Gao, X., Zhu, W., and Shi, Q., "The IBM LVCSR System Used for 1998 Mandarin Broadcast News Transcription Evaluation", *Proc. DARPA Broadcast News Workshop,* 1999.
7. Hermansky, H., Ellis, D.P.W. and Sharma, S. "Tandem connectionist feature extraction for conventional HMM systems", Proc. *ICASSP 2000,* pp. 1635-1638.
8. Hermansky, H., and Sharma, S. , "TRAPS - Classifiers of Temporal Patterns", in Proc. ICSLP 1998.
9. Misra, H., Bourlard, H., and Tyagi, V., "New entropy based combination rules in HMM/ANN multi-stream ASR", in *Proc. ICASSP*, 2003.
10. Morgan, N. and Bourlard, H., "Continuous speech recognition", *IEEE Signal Processing Magazine,* vol. 12, no. 3, pp. 24, May 1995.
11. Morgan, N., Chen, B., Zhu, Q. and Stolcke, A., "TRAPping Conversational Speech: Extending TRAP/Tandem approaches to conversational telephone speech recognition", ICASSP 2004.
12. Reyes-Gomez, M. and Ellis, D.P.W, "Error visualization for Tandem acoustic modeling on the Aurora task", *ICASSP* 2002.
13. Robinson, A.J., Cook, G.D., Ellis, D.P.W., Fosler-Lussier, E., Renals, S.J., and Williams D.A.G., "Connectionist speech recognition of Broadcast News", *Speech Communication, vol. 37, no. 1-2, pp. 27-45.* 2002
14. Stolcke, A., Bratt, H., Butzberger, J., Franco, H., Rao Gadde V.R., Plauche, M., Richey, C., Shriberg, E., Sonmez, K., Weng, F., and Zheng, J., "The SRI March 2005 Hub-5 conversational speech transcription system", *Proc. NIST Transcription Workshop 2000.*

Long-Term Temporal Features for Conversational Speech Recognition

Barry Chen, Qifeng Zhu, and Nelson Morgan

International Computer Science Institute, Berkeley, CA, USA
{byc, qifeng, morgan}@icsi.berkeley.edu

Abstract. The automatic transcription of conversational speech, both from telephone and in-person interactions, is still an extremely challenging task. Our efforts to recognize speech from meetings is likely to benefit from any advances we achieve with conversational telephone speech, a topic of considerable focus for our research. Towards both of these ends, we have developed, in collaboration with our colleagues at SRI and IDIAP, techniques to incorporate long-term ($\sim$500 ms) temporal information using multi-layered perceptrons (MLPs). Much of this work is based on prior achievements in recent years at the former lab of Hynek Hermansky at the Oregon Graduate Institute (OGI), where the TempoRAl Pattern (TRAP) approach was developed. The contribution here is to present experiments showing: 1) that simply widening acoustic context by using more frames of full band speech energies as input to the MLP is suboptimal compared to a more constrained two-stage approach that first focuses on long-term temporal patterns in each critical band separately and then combines them, 2) that the best two-stage approach studied utilizes hidden activation values of MLPs trained on the log critical band energies (LCBEs) of 51 consecutive frames, and 3) that combining the best two-stage approach with conventional short-term features significantly reduces word error rates on the 2001 NIST Hub-5 conversational telephone speech (CTS) evaluation set with models trained using the Switchboard Corpus.

1   Introduction

Conversational speech recognition remains a difficult problem, both for telephone speech and for in-person meetings. Since all current state-of-the-art recognition engines rely on acoustic features computed over a short (e.g., 25 ms) analysis window, using short-term spectral or cepstral analysis, it has seemed reasonable to pursue sources of information that incorporated radically different analyses. While it is in principle true that the standard HMM/GMM models and training methods maximize criteria that in principle incorporate information across the entire training set, it is nonetheless clearly the case that measures incorporating differing amounts of time (such as LDA or delta features) have often provided significant improvements. It has been our thesis (and that of our collaborators in the EARS Novel Approaches program) that explicitly computing new and com-

S. Bengio and H. Bourlard (Eds.): MLMI 2004, LNCS 3361, pp. 232–242, 2005.
© Springer-Verlag Berlin Heidelberg 2005

plementary functions of the time frequency plane has the potential to radically change the performance of recognizers for these difficult tasks.

In particular, the arguments of researchers such as Jont Allen [1] have long suggested that constraining initial analyses to fairly narrow portions of the spectrum was both consistent with psychoacoustics and likely to be more robust to variability in spectral properties. Hynek Hermansky's group, originally at OGI, pioneered a method using processing over small parts of the spectrum, e.g., critical bands, while capturing long-term (500-1000 ms) information for phonetic classification using multi-layered perceptrons (MLP). Their approach learned temporal patterns based on consecutive frames of log critical band energies (LCBEs), and used these patterns as a basis for phonetic classification [4][7]. More specifically, they developed an MLP architecture called TRAPS, which stands for "TempoRAl PatternS". The TRAPS system consists of two stages of MLPs. In the first stage critical band MLPs learn phone probabilities posterior on the input, which is a set of consecutive frames (usually 51-100 frames) of LCBEs, or LCBE trajectory. A "merger" MLP merges the output of each of these individual critical band MLPs resulting in overall phone posteriors probabilities. This two stage architecture imposes a constraint upon the learning of temporal information from the time-frequency plane: correlations among individual frames of LCBEs from different frequency bands are not directly modeled; instead, correlation among long-term LCBE trajectories from different frequency bands are modeled.

TRAPS by themselves perform about as well as more conventional ASR systems using cepstral features derived from a short-term spectrum, and significantly improve word error rates when used in combination with these short-term features. TRAPS complement conventional systems by performing better on speech examples that are problematic for models trained on conventional features. We worked on improving the TRAPS architecture in the context of TIMIT phoneme recognition [2]. This led us to the development of Hidden Activation TRAPS (HATS), which differ from TRAPS in that HATS use the hidden activations of the critical band MLPs instead of their outputs as inputs to the "merger" MLP. Instead of using critical band level phoneme probabilities, HATS uses outputs of critical band "matched filters" for inputs to the second stage merger. We found that HATS significantly outperformed TRAPS while using many fewer parameters.

In this paper, we wanted to further explore the incorporation of long-term features for the recognition of conversational telephone speech (CTS). More specifically we want to explore two major questions: first, does the two-stage learning of HATS and TRAPS actually provide any advantage over a naive one-stage learning, where the latter consists of training an MLP to learn phone probabilities using 51 consecutive frames of LCBEs from all 15 critical bands in one step? Confirming this hypothesis would show that the temporal constraints on learning were a useful component of the new analysis, rather than just being irrelevant in contrast to the expansion to a wider analysis window. And second, are the nonlinear transformations of critical band trajectories, provided in different ways by

HATS and TRAPS, actually necessary? For this second question, we compare linear and nonlinear first stage critical band learning approaches and use these results as inputs to the second stage "merger" MLP.

We start this discussion with detailed architecture descriptions in Section 2 and experimental setup explanations in Section 3. In Section 4 frame accuracy results for each of the various long-term architectures are presented and discussed. Section 5 presents word recognition results using phone posterior features derived from the various long-term architectures, and Section 6 discusses results from using these posterior features in combination with a conventional short-term feature. Finally, Section 7 summarizes the conclusions.

2   MLP Architectures

2.1   The Big Dumb Neural Net (BDNN) Revisited: The One-Stage Approach

In earlier work, we experimented with the use of hybrid HMM/ANN systems incorporating significant amounts of temporal context for the estimation of scaled emission likelihoods [9]. Similarly, a straightforward approach to incorporating greater temporal context for feature estimation is to give an MLP more frames of short-term spectral features and simply let the MLP learn what it needs to estimate phonetic posteriors, which in turn would be processed to make them more appropriate features for a mixture-of-gaussians HMM. For our experiments, we chose this comparatively simple approach as the baseline architecture. In all of the experiments in this paper, the inputs to the MLPs are LCBEs calculated every 10 ms on 8 kHz sampled speech, yielding a total of 15 bark scale spaced LCBEs. These are then normalized over an utterance to have zero mean and unity variance. Figure 1 shows our baseline approach (henceforth referred to as "15 Bands x 51 Frames") which uses 51 frames of all 15 bands of LCBEs as inputs to an MLP. These inputs are built by stacking 25 frames before and after the current frame to the current frame, and the target phoneme comes

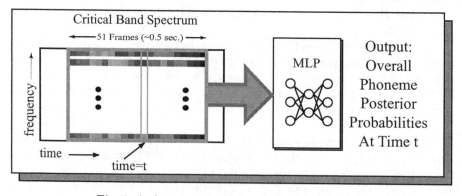

Fig. 1. Architecture for Naive One-Stage Approach

from the current frame. As is common for this type of MLP use, the network is trained with output targets that are "1.0" for the class associated with the current frame, and "0" for all others. For all of the systems described in this paper, the MLPs are trained on 46 phoneme targets obtained via forced alignment from SRI's LVCSR recognizer [11], and consist of a single hidden layer with sigmoidal nonlinearity and an output layer with softmax nonlinearity.

2.2   Two-Stage Approaches

We hypothesize that it will be useful to constrain the learning so that the MLP is forced to represent temporal structure. We investigated several architectures that partition the learning into two stages: first, learn what is important for phonetic classification given single critical band energy trajectories of 51 frames; and second, combine what was learned at each critical band to learn overall phonetic posteriors. This "divide and conquer" approach to learning splits the task into two smaller and possibly simpler sub-learning tasks.

For the first of these two stage architectures, we calculate principal component analysis (PCA) transforms for successive 51 frames of each of the 15 individual 51 frames of LCBE resulting in a 51 x 51 transform matrix for each of the 15 bands. We then use this transform to orthogonalize the temporal trajectory in each band, retaining only the top 40 features per band. Figure 2 shows how we then use these transformed (and dimensionally reduced) features as input to an MLP. In a related approach, we replaced PCA with linear discriminant analysis (LDA) "trained" on the same phoneme targets used for MLP training. This transform projects the LCBE of a single band onto vectors that maximize the between class variance and minimize the within class variance for phoneme classes. These two two stage linear approaches are henceforth denoted as "PCA40" and "LDA40" respectively.

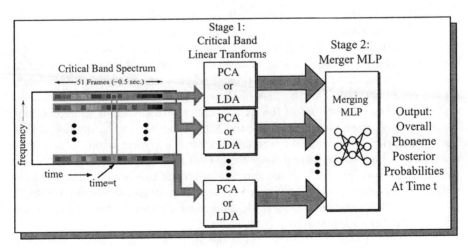

Fig. 2. Architecture for Two-Stage Linear Approaches

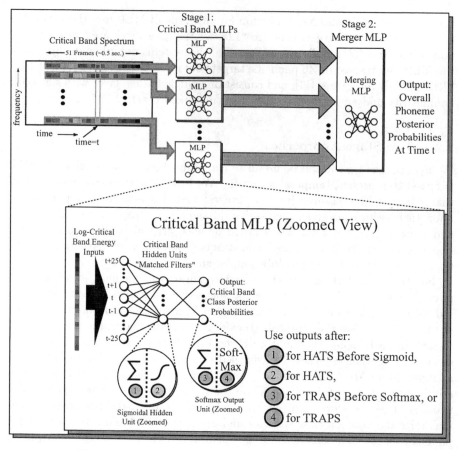

Fig. 3. Architecture for Two-Stage Nonlinear Approaches

Finally, there are four two-stage nonlinear approaches that we experimented with. In each of these, MLPs are trained on each of the 15 critical bands. The trained networks are used to nonlinearly transform critical band energy trajectories into inputs for a second stage merger MLP that combines and transforms this critical band information into estimates of phoneme posteriors conditioned on the entire spectrum. In the first of these approaches, the input to the second stage is the dot product of the LCBE inputs with the input to hidden unit weights of the corresponding critical band MLP. Another way to say this is that the values prior to the sigmoid computation for the critical band hidden units are used as inputs to the second stage merger MLP. We refer to this architecture as "HATS Before Sigmoid". While this first approach consists of a linear matrix multiply, we categorize it as nonlinear because the matrix was learned as part of a structure that included nonlinear sigmoid functions, which have a significant effect on the values learned.

The second approach, "HATS", takes the outputs of each hidden unit as the input to the merger MLP. The third approach takes the activations after the hidden to output weight matrix multiplication, but just before the final softmax nonlinearity of the critical band MLPs. This approach is denoted as "TRAPS Before Softmax", and is a modification of the more commonly used fourth approach that takes the regular activations from the critical band MLPs (that are phoneme posterior probabilities conditioned on the LCBE inputs) as inputs to the merger net. This last nonlinear approach will be denoted as "TRAPS". Figure 3 shows each of these non linear two stage architectures.

3   Experimental Setup

For all of the experiments reported in this paper, we show test results on the 2001 Hub-5 evaluation data (Eval2001), a large vocabulary conversational telephone speech test set consisting of a total of 2,255,609 frames and 62,890 words. The training set that we used for both MLP and HMM training consisted of about 68 hours of conversational telephone speech data from four sources: English CallHome, Switchboard I with transcriptions from Mississippi State, and Switchboard Cellular. This training set corresponds to the one used in [10] without Switchboard Credit Card data. Training for both MLPs and HMMs was done separately for each gender, and the test results below reflect the overall performance on both genders. We hold out 10% of the training data as a cross validation set in MLP training. For fairness in comparison, all of the long-term temporal systems had roughly the same number of total network parameters (about 500,000 weights and biases). In preliminary experiments we found that forty hidden units per critical band for HATS was sufficient for good performance, so we made sure that all the two-stage systems had forty hidden units or in the case of PCA and LDA forty dimensions at the critical band level. This restriction to forty hidden units for the TRAPS system is not what has been reported in the past when researchers refer to TRAPS, but for this study, we enforced this for fair comparison's sake. We note that this could potentially be a suboptimal decision for the TRAPS, but that nonetheless holding the number of parameters constant across the alternate methods still permits some interpretability for the results.

Once the MLPs were trained, we used them to generate posterior features for an HMM back-end recognizer in a similar manner as was done in [3]. More specifically, the back-end that we used was similar to the first pass of the system described in [11], using a bigram language model and within-word triphone acoustic models. Further details on the posterior features used will be explained in sections 5 and 6.

4   Classification Accuracy Results and Discussion

In this section we examine the frame level classification of each of the various neural net architectures on the Eval2001 test set. Frame level accuracy serves as a good preliminary indicator of performance and is the ratio of the number of

Table 1. Frame Accuracies on Eval2001. The relative improvement is not given for the last row since it uses very different features from the baseline system (PLP cepstra rather than LCBEs), though the accuracy is still given to suggest that the best of the temporal systems performs similarly

System Description (Rank)	Frames Correct (%)	Baseline Improv. (% Rel.)
Baseline: 15 Bands x 51 Frames (6)	64.73	-
PCA40 (5)	65.50	1.19
LDA40 (4)	65.52	1.22
HATS Before Sigmoid (3)	65.80	1.65
HATS (1)	**66.91**	**3.35**
TRAPS Before Softmax (2)	65.85	1.73
TRAPS (7)	63.96	-1.19
PLP 9 Frames	67.57	NA

correctly classified frames to the total number of frames, where classification is deemed correct when the highest output of the MLP corresponds to the correct phoneme label. Table 1 summarizes the frame accuracy scores, relative improvement over baseline, and rank for each of the seven temporal architectures. For reference, we have included a conventional intermediate temporal context MLP that uses 9 frames of per-side normalized (mean, variance, and vocal tract length) PLP plus deltas and double deltas as inputs ("PLP 9 Frames"). This intermediate context MLP was trained on the same training data and phonetic targets as the others.

The one-stage 15 Bands x 51 Frames system serves as our naive baseline system and gets 64.73% of all frames correct. With the exception of the TRAPS system, all of the two-stage systems did better than this. From this, we can see that simply feeding an MLP classifier more frames for temporal context is suboptimal, but using the right two-stage approach is also important. HATS outperforms all other two-stage approaches at the frame level by achieving a 66.91% accuracy. HATS Before Sigmoid and TRAPS Before Softmax perform comparably at 65.80% and 65.85% respectively, while PCA and LDA approaches perform similarly at 65.50% and 65.52% respectively. At the frame level, it seems that forcing the system to focus first on learning what it can in each of the long-term narrow frequency band inputs independently is a useful constraint, particularly in the case of HATS.

5   MLP Based Feature Recognition Results and Discussion

Frame accuracy results give a good preliminary indication of performance, but can sometimes only be moderately correlated to word error rates. We performed word recognition experiments by transforming the outputs of the various MLPs and using them as features for the SRI speech recognizer. Specifically, in each case we took the log of the outputs from the MLPs and then decorrelate the features via PCA. Then we applied per-side mean and variance normalization on these transformed outputs and use the result as the front-end features in our HMM back-end. As in the previous section, we report here the performance of the seven feature sets incorporating a long temporal input (500 ms), and include results for a moderate but more conventional input range (100ms for 9 frames of PLP). Table 2 summarizes the rank, word error rate (WER), and improvement over the one-stage baseline when appropriate.

Looking at tables 1 and 2, we can see that HATS always ranks 1 when compared to all other long temporal systems, achieving 3.35% and 7.29% relative improvement over the baseline one-stage approach in frame accuracy and WER respectively. The TRAPS (after softmax) doesn't provide an improvement over the baseline, but all of the other approaches do. This suggests that constraining the learning in the two-stage process can be helpful if the architecture is appropriate. The final softmax nonlinearity in the critical band MLPs in TRAPS is the only difference between it and TRAPS Before Softmax, so including this nonlinearity during recognition, causes significant performance degradation, though it is apparently critical to include it during training. It is likely that the softmax's output normalization is obscuring useful information that the second-stage MLP needs. Since the HATS system significantly outperforms both the HATS Before Sigmoid and TRAPS Before Softmax systems, this means that the sigmoid nonlinearity is helpful whereas the extra linear mapping from hidden units to critical band phones is not. Another way to interpret this is that when using our two-stage learning approach, the best first-stage approach is to learn "probabilities" of certain critical band energy patterns. These "probabilities" correspond to the outputs of the hidden units of the critical band MLPs, and the patterns correspond to the energy trajectories represented by the input to hidden unit weights (essentially a nonlinear form of matched filters).

6   Feature Augmentation Results and Discussion

Previous studies have shown time and again that systems learning temporal patterns perform reasonably well by themselves, but work particularly well in combination with the more conventional short-term full band features [4, 5, 6]. Our current results also corroborate this previous finding. In the following experiments, we started with SRI's EARS Rich Transcription 2003 front-end features - 12th order PLP plus first three ordered deltas, per side mean, variance, and vocal tract length normalized, all transformed by heteroskedastic linear discriminant analysis (HLDA), keeping the top 39 features. Using these baseline features (HLDA(PLP+3d)), we performed a first pass viterbi recognition on Eval2001 and achieved a 37.2% word error rate (WER).

We then appended the top 25 dimensions after PCA on each of the temporal features described in section 5 to the baseline HLDA(PLP+3d) features.

Table 2. WER of Systems Using Stand-Alone Posterior Features on Eval2001

System Description (Rank)	WER (%)	Baseline Improv. (% Rel.)
Baseline: 15 Bands x 51 Frames (6)	48.0	-
PCA40 (2)	45.3	5.63
LDA40 (3)	46.5	3.13
HATS Before Sigmoid (4)	45.9	4.38
HATS (1)	**44.5**	**7.29**
TRAPS Before Softmax (4)	45.9	4.38
TRAPS (7)	48.2	-0.42
PLP 9 Frames	41.2	NA

Table 3. WER of Systems Using Augmented Posterior Features on Eval2001

System Description (Rank)	WER (%)	Baseline Improv. (% Rel.)
Baseline: Non-Augmented HLDA(PLP+3d)	37.2	-
15 Bands x 51 Frames (6)	37.1	0.27
PCA40 (2)	36.8	1.08
LDA40 (2)	36.8	1.08
HATS Before Sigmoid (2)	36.8	1.08
HATS (1)	**36.0**	**3.23**
TRAPS Before Softmax (5)	36.9	0.81
TRAPS (7)	37.2	0.00
PLP 9 Frames	36.1	2.96
Inv Entropy Combo HATS + PLP 9 Frames	34.0	8.60

Table 3 summarizes the rank, WER, and relative improvement over the baseline HLDA(PLP+3d) features. All systems below the baseline system refer to the features that are appended to the baseline HLDA(PLP+3d) features.

When HATS features augment the conventional HLDA(PLP+3d) features, WER can be reduced by 3.23% relative, which is much better than the other long-term temporal methods tested. The one-stage approach and TRAPS lag the other two-stage approaches which perform roughly at the same level. Using the intermediate-term PLP 9 Frames system to augment HLDA(PLP+3d) features gives about the same performance as HATS. If we combine the posterior probability outputs of HATS and PLP 9 Frames systems using an inverse entropy weighting method [8], take the log followed by PCA to 25 dimension, and append to HLDA(PLP+3d) features, we get the "Inv Entropy Combo HATS+PLP 9 Frames" features. These features achieve a sizable 8.60% relative improvement over the HLDA(PLP+3d) features alone. This improvement is greater than the sum of the individual HATS augmentation and PLP 9 Frames augmentation. In combination, HATS and PLP 9 Frames features act synergistically to reduce WER.

7   Conclusions

We have compared several different approaches for incorporating long-term temporal information in MLP based front-end acoustic models and have shown that applying specific temporal constraints on the learning from time-frequency plane is important. More specifically, the one-stage approach, in which we fed 51 consecutive frames of 15 log critical band energies to the MLP, was not as good as any of the two-stage approaches in which we have constrained the learning into two stages. The first of these stages extracts relevant information for phoneme classification within each long-term critical band energy trajectory, while the second stage combines what was learned in the first stage to produce the overall phoneme probabilities. We have also observed that, under the constraints of these experiments (i.e., fixing the total number of parameters and the number of hidden units for critical band transformation), the HATS approach significantly outperformed all other long-term temporal systems, both as a standalone feature to an HMM back-end, and when it is concatenated with conventional PLP features. Finally, HATS features combines synergistically with intermediate time (100 ms rather than 500 ms) MLP-based features to achieve an 8.6% relative WER reduction on the Hub-5 2001 NIST evaluation test set for the transcription of conversational telephone speech. This degree of improvement is considered quite significant (both statistically and in terms of impact on progress in the NIST evaluations).

Acknowledgements

We want to thank Andreas Stolcke for all his support and help in running the SRI recognition system. This work is supported by the DARPA EARS Novel Approaches Grant: No. MDA972-02-1-0024.

References

1. J. B. Allen, "How do humans process and recognize speech?," *IEEE Trans. on Speech and Audio Processing*, vol. 2, no. 4, pp. 567-577, 1994.
2. B. Chen, S. Chang, and S. Sivadas, "Learning Discriminative Temporal Patterns in Speech: Development of Novel TRAPS-Like Classifiers", in Proc. Eurospeech 2003.

3. D. P. W. Ellis, R. Singh, and S. Sivadas, "Tandem Acoustic Modeling in Large-Vocabulary Recognition", in Proc. ICASSP 2001.
4. H. Hermansky, S. Sharma, "TRAPS - Classifiers of Temporal Patterns", in Proc. ICSLP 1998.
5. H. Hermansky, S. Sharma, "Temporal Patterns (TRAPs) in DSR of Noisy Speech," Proc. ICASSP, Phoenix, 1999.
6. H. Hermansky, P. Jain, "Band-independent speech-event categories for TRAP based ASR" Proc. Eurospeech, Geneva, 2003.
7. H. Hermansky, S. Sharma, and P. Jain, "Data-Derived Non-Linear Mapping for Feature Extraction in HMM", in Proc. ICASSP 2000.
8. H. Misra, H. Bourlard, and V. Tyagi, "New Entropy Based Combination Rules In HMM/ANN Multi-Stream ASR", in Proc. ICASSP 2003.
9. N. Morgan, and H. Bourlard, "Continuous Speech Recognition: An Introduction to the Hybrid HMM/Connectionist Approach." *Signal Processing Magazine*, pp 25-42, May 1995
10. N. Morgan, B. Chen, Q. Zhu, and A. Stolcke, "TRAPping Conversational Speech: Extending TRAP/Tandem approaches to conversational telephone speech recognition", in Proc. ICASSP 2004.
11. A. Stolcke, H. Bratt, J. Butzberger, H. Franco, V. R. Rao Gadde, M. Plauche, C. Richey, E. Shriberg, K. Sonmez, F. Weng, and J. Zheng, "The SRI March 2000 Hub-5 conversational speech transcription System", in Proc. NIST Speech Transcription Workshop 2000.

Speaker Indexing in Audio Archives
Using Gaussian Mixture Scoring Simulation

Hagai Aronowitz[1], David Burshtein[2], and Amihood Amir[1,3]

[1] Department of Computer Science, Bar-Ilan University, Israel
{aronowc, amir}@cs.biu.ac.il
[2] School of Electrical Engineering, Tel-Aviv University, Israel
burstyn@eng.tau.ac.il
[3] College of Computing, Georgia Tech, USA

Abstract. Speaker indexing has recently emerged as an important task due to the rapidly growing volume of audio archives. Current filtration techniques still suffer from problems both in accuracy and efficiency. In this paper an efficient method to simulate GMM scoring is presented. Simulation is done by fitting a GMM not only to every target speaker but also to every test utterance, and then computing the likelihood of the test call using these GMMs instead of using the original data. GMM simulation is used to achieve very efficient speaker indexing in terms of both search time and index size. Results on the SPIDRE and NIST-2004 speaker evaluation corpuses show that our approach maintains and sometimes exceeds the accuracy of the conventional GMM algorithm and achieves efficient indexing capabilities: 6000 times faster than a conventional GMM with 1% overhead in storage.

1 Introduction

Indexing large audio archives has emerged recently [5, 6] as an important research topic as large audio archives now exist. The goal of speaker indexing is to divide the speaker recognition process into 2 stages. The first stage is a pre-processing phase which is usually done on-line as audio is inserted into the archive. In this stage there is no knowledge about the target speakers. The goal of the pre-processing stage is to do all possible pre-calculations in order to make the search as efficient as possible when a query is presented. The second stage is activated when a target speaker query is presented. In this stage the pre-calculations of the first stage are used.

Previous research such as [7] suggests projecting each utterance into a speaker space defined by anchor models which are a set of non-target speaker models. Each utterance is represented by a vector of distances between the utterance and each anchor model. This representation is calculated in the pre-processing phase. In the query phase, the target speaker data is projected to the same speaker space and the speaker space representation of each utterance in the archive is compared to the target speaker vector using a distance measure such as Euclidean distance. The disadvantage of this approach is that it is intuitively suboptimal (otherwise, it would replace the Gaussian mixture model (GMM) [1, 2] approach and wouldn't be limited to speaker indexing). Indeed, the EER reported in [7] is almost tripled when using anchor models instead of

S. Bengio and H. Bourlard (Eds.): MLMI 2004, LNCS 3361, pp. 243–252, 2005.
© Springer-Verlag Berlin Heidelberg 2005

conventional GMM scoring. This disadvantage was handled in [7] by cascading the anchor model indexing system and the GMM recognition system thus first filtering efficiently most of the archive and then rescoring in order to improve accuracy. Nevertheless, the cascaded system described in [7] failed to obtain accurate performance for speaker misdetection probability lower than 50%. Another drawback of the cascade approach is that sometimes the archive is not accessible for the search system either because it is too expensive to access the audio archive, or because the audio itself was deleted from the archive because of lack of available storage resources (the information that a certain speaker was speaking in a certain utterance may be beneficial even if the audio no longer exists, for example for law enforcement systems). Therefore, it may be important to be able to achieve accurate search with low time and memory complexity using only an index file and not the raw audio.

Our suggested approach for speaker indexing is by harnessing the GMM to this task. GMM has been the state-of-the-art algorithm for this task for many years. The GMM algorithm calculates the log-likelihood of a test utterance given a target speaker by fitting a parametric model to the target training data and computing the average log-likelihood of the test utterance feature vectors assuming independence between frames. Analyzing the GMM algorithm shows asymmetry between the target training data and the test call. This asymmetry seems to be not optimal: if a Gaussian mixture model can model robustly the distribution of acoustic frames, why not use it to represent robustly the test utterance?

In [3] both target speakers and test utterances were treated symmetrically by being modeled by a covariance matrix. The distance between a target speaker and a test utterance was also defined as a symmetric function of the target model and the test utterance model. Unfortunately, a covariance matrix lacks the modeling power of a GMM, which results in low accuracy. In [4] cross likelihood ratio was calculated between the GMM representing a target speaker and a GMM representing a test utterance. This was done by switching the roles of the train and test utterances and averaging the likelihood of the test utterance given the GMM parameterization of the train utterance with the likelihood of the train utterance given the GMM parameterization of the test utterance, but the inherent asymmetry of the GMM scoring remained.

Therefore, the motivation for representing a test utterance by a GMM is that this representation is robust and smooth. In fact, the process of GMM fitting exploits a-priori knowledge about the test utterance - the smoothness of the distribution. Using universal background model (UBM) MAP-adaptation for fitting the GMM exploits additional a-priori knowledge. Our speaker recognition algorithm fits a GMM for every test utterance in the indexing phase (stage 1), and calculates the likelihood (stage 2) by using only the GMM of the target speaker, and the GMM of a test utterance.

The organization of this paper is as follows: the proposed speaker recognition system is presented in Section 2. Section 3 describes the experimental corpuses, the experiments and the results for the speaker recognition systems. Section 4 describes the speaker indexing algorithm and analyzes its efficiency. Finally, section 5 presents conclusions and ongoing work.

2 Simulating GMM Scoring

In this section we describe the proposed speaker recognition algorithm. Our goal is to simulate the calculation of a GMM score without using the test utterance data but using only a GMM fitted to the test utterance.

2.1 Definition of the GMM Score

The log-likelihood of a test utterance $X = x_1,...,x_n$ given a target speaker GMM Q is usually normalized by some normalization log-likelihood (UBM log-likelihood, cohort log-likelihood, etc.) and divided by the length of the utterance. This process is summarized by equation (1):

$$score(X|Q) = \frac{LL(X|Q) - LL(X|\text{norm models})}{n} \tag{1}$$

Equation (1) shows that the GMM score is composed of a target-speaker dependent component – the average log-likelihood of the utterance given the speaker model $(LL(X|Q)/n)$ and a target-speaker independent component – the average log-likelihood of the utterance given the normalization models $(LL(X|\text{norm-models})/n)$. For simplicity, the rest of this paper will focus on a single normalization model, the UBM, but the same techniques can be trivially used for other normalization models such as cohort models. The GMM model assumes independence between frames. Therefore, the log-likelihood of X given Q is calculated in equation (2):

$$\frac{1}{n}LL(X|Q) = \frac{1}{n}\sum_{i=1}^{n}\log(\Pr(x_i|Q)) \tag{2}$$

2.2 GMM Scoring Using a Model for the Test Utterance

The vectors $x_1,...,x_n$ of the test utterance are acoustic observation vectors generated by a stochastic process. Let us assume that the true distribution of which the vectors $x_1,...,x_n$ were generated by is P. The average log-likelihood of an utterance Y of asymptotically infinite length $|Y|$ generated by the distribution P is given in equation (3):

$$\frac{1}{n}LL(Y|Q) = \frac{1}{|Y|}\sum_{i=1}^{|Y|}\log(\Pr(y_i|Q)) \xrightarrow[|Y|\mapsto\infty]{} \int_x \Pr(x|P)\log(\Pr(x|Q))dx \tag{3}$$

The result of equation (3) is that the log-likelihood of a test utterance given distribution Q is a random variable that asymptotically converges to an integral of a function of distributions Q and P. In order to use equation (3) we have to know the true distribution P and we have to calculate the integral.

2.3 Estimation of Distribution P

We assume that the test utterance is generated using a true distribution P. Therefore, P should be estimated by the same methods that distribution Q is estimated from the training data of the target speaker, i.e. by fitting a GMM, though the order of the model may be tuned to the length of the test utterance.

2.4 Calculation of $\int_x \Pr(x|P)\log(\Pr(x|Q))dx$

Definitions:

w_i^P, w_j^Q :   The weight of the ith/ j[th] Gaussian of distribution P/Q.

μ_i^P, μ_j^Q :   The mean vector of the ith/ j[th] Gaussian of distribution P/Q.

$\mu_{i,d}^P, \mu_{j,d}^Q$:   The dth coordinate of the mean vector of the ith/ j[th] Gaussian of distribution P/Q.

σ_i^P, σ_j^Q :   The standard deviation vector of the ith/ j[th] Gaussian of distribution P/Q (assuming diagonal covariance matrix).

$\sigma_{i,d}^P, \sigma_{j,d}^Q$:   The dth coordinate of the standard deviation vector of the ith/ j[th] Gaussian of distribution P/Q (assuming diagonal covariance matrix).

P^i, Q^i :   The ith/ j[th] Gaussian of distribution P/Q.

$N(x|\mu,\sigma)$:   The probability density of a vector x given a normal distribution with mean vector μ and standard deviation vector σ (assuming diagonal covariance matrix).

n_g^P, n_g^Q :   The number of Gaussians of distribution P/Q.

dim: The dimension of the acoustic vector space.

Distribution P is a GMM and is defined in equation (4):

$$\Pr(x|P) = \sum_{i=1}^{n_g^P} w_i^P \Pr(x|P_i)$$ (4)

Using equation (4) and exploiting the linearity of the integral and the mixture model we get:

$$\int_x \Pr(x|P)\log(\Pr(x|Q))dx = \sum_{i=1}^{n_g^P} w_i^P \int_x \Pr(x|P_i)\log(\Pr(x|Q))dx$$ (5)

In order to get a closed form solution for the integral in equation (5) we have to use the following approximation. Note that:

$$\int_x \Pr(x|P_i)\log(\Pr(x|Q))dx =$$

$$\int_X N(x\,|\,\mu_i^P,\sigma_i^P)\log\left[\sum_{j=1}^{n_g^Q} w_j^Q \times N(x\,|\,\mu_i^Q,\sigma_j^Q)\right]dx$$

$$\geq \int_X N(x\,|\,\mu_i^P,\sigma_i^P)\log\left[w_j^Q \times N(x\,|\,\mu_j^Q,\sigma_j^Q)\right]dx \tag{6}$$

$$= \log w_j^Q - \sum_{d=1}^{\dim}\frac{(\mu_{i,d}^P-\mu_{j,d}^Q)^2}{2\sigma_{j,d}^{Q\,2}} - \sum_{d=1}^{\dim}\log\sigma_{j,d}^Q - \frac{1}{2}\sum_{d=1}^{\dim}\left(\frac{\sigma_{i,d}^P}{\sigma_{j,d}^Q}\right)^2 - \frac{\dim}{2}\log 2\pi$$

Equation (6) presents an inequality that is true for every Gaussian j therefore we have n_g^Q closed form lower bounds for the integral (for every Gaussian j we get a possibly different lower bound).

The tightest lower bound is achieved by setting j to j_opt_i which is defined in equation (7):

$$j\_opt_i = \arg\max_j\left\{\log w_j^Q - \sum_{d=1}^{\dim}\frac{(\mu_{i,d}^P-\mu_{j,d}^Q)^2}{2\sigma_{j,d}^{Q\,2}} - \sum_{d=1}^{\dim}\log\sigma_{j,d}^Q - \frac{1}{2}\sum_{d=1}^{\dim}\left(\frac{\sigma_{i,d}^P}{\sigma_{j,d}^Q}\right)^2\right\} \tag{7}$$

The approximation we use in this paper is obtained by taking the tightest lower bound defined by equations (6, 7) as an estimate to the integral $\int_x \Pr(x|P_i)\log(\Pr(x|Q))dx$.

2.5 Speeding Up Calculation of $\int_x \Pr(x|P)\log(\Pr(x|Q))dx$

Let us assume for simplicity that the same number of Gaussians (g) is used for both P and Q. The complexity of approximating the integral is $O(g^2\ dim)$: for every Gaussian of P the closest Gaussian (according to equation (7)) in Q must be found. This search can be accelerated without any notable loss in accuracy by exploiting the fact that both P and Q are adapted from the same UBM. Before the indexing phase, the asymmetric distance between each pair of Gaussians from the UBM is computed according to equation (7). For each Gaussian i, the set of distances to all other Gaussians is sorted and the closest-N Gaussians are found and stored in a Gaussian specific list L_i. In the search phase, when searching for the closest Gaussian for P^i in Q, only the Gaussians in the list L_i are examined. This suboptimal calculation of the approximation improves the time complexity to $O(Ng\ dim)$ and is empirically superior to the one used in [11].

2.6 Global Variance Models

Global variance GMM models are GMM models with the same diagonal covariance matrix shared among all Gaussians and all speakers. Using global variance GMMs has the advantages of lower time and memory complexity and also improves robustness when training data is sparse. The reduced modeling power of using a global variance can be compensated by moderately increasing the number of Gaussians. The robustness issue may be especially important when modeling short test utterances. Applying the Global variance assumption to equations (6, 7) results in much simpler equations (8, 9):

$$\int_x \Pr(x|P_i)\log(\Pr(x|Q))dx \geq \log w_j^Q - \sum_{d=1}^{\dim} \frac{\left(\mu_{i,d}^P - \mu_{j,d}^Q\right)^2}{2\sigma_d^2} + C \tag{8}$$

In (8) C is a speaker independent constant.

$$j\_opt_i = \arg\max_j \left\{ \log w_j^Q - \sum_{d=1}^{\dim} \frac{\left(\mu_{i,d}^P - \mu_{j,d}^Q\right)^2}{2\sigma_d^2} \right\} \tag{9}$$

2.7 GMM Quantization

In order to reduce the amount of storage needed for storing the GMM of each conversation in the archive, the mean vectors are stored by using a single byte for each coefficient instead of 4 bytes. The quantization is done by the following procedure: the mean of Gaussian i, μ_i is represented by first computing $\delta_i = \mu_i - ubm_i$ which is the difference vector between the mean of the ith Gaussian of the current conversation and the mean of the ith Gaussian of the UBM. δ_i is relatively easy to quantize and it is quantized linearly using Gaussian specific scaling.

3 Experimental Results

3.1 The SPIDRE Corpus

Experiments were conducted on the SPIDRE corpus [8] which is a subset of the Switchboard-I corpus. The SPIDRE corpus consists of 45 target speakers, four conversations per speaker, and 100 2-sided non-target conversations. All conversations are about 5 minutes long and are all from land-line phones with mixed handsets. The 100 non-target conversations were divided to the following subsets: fifty two-sided conversations were used as training and development data, and the other fifty two-sided conversations were used as test data. The four target conversations per speaker were divided randomly to two training conversations and two testing conversations, therefore some of the tests are in matched handset condition and some are in mismatched handset condition. The second side of the training target conversations was used as additional development data, and the second side of the testing target conversations was used as additional non-target testing data.

3.2 The NIST-2004 Corpus

After tuning the system on SPIDRE, additional experiments were done on a much larger corpus, the NIST-2004 speaker evaluation data set [10]. The primary data set was used for selecting both target speakers and test data. The data set consists of 616 1-sided single conversations for training 616 target models, and 1174 1-sided test conversations. All conversations are about 5 minutes long and originate from various channels and handset types. In order to increase the number of trials, each target model was tested against each test utterance. For the NIST-2004 experiments the SPIDRE corpus was used for training the UBM and for development data.

3.3 The Baseline GMM System

The baseline GMM system in this paper was inspired by the GMM-UBM system described in [1, 2]. The front-end of the recognizer consists of calculation of Mel-frequency cepstrum coefficients (MFCC) according to the ETSI standard [9]. An energy based voice activity detector is used to locate and remove non-speech segments and the cepstral mean of the speech segments is calculated and subtracted. The final feature set is 13 cepstral coefficients + 13 delta cepstral coefficients extracted every 10ms using a 20ms window. A gender independent UBM was trained using 100 non-target conversation sides (about 8 hours of speech + non-speech). Target speakers were trained using MAP adaptation. Several model orders were evaluated on SPIDRE– 512, 1024 and 2048 Gaussians. Both standard diagonal covariance matrix GMMs and global diagonal covariance matrix GMMs were evaluated. A fast scoring technique was used in which only the top 5 highest scoring Gaussians are rescored using the target models [2]. In the verification stage, the log likelihood of each conversation side given a target speaker is divided by the length of the conversation and normalized by the UBM score. The resulting score is then normalized using z-norm [1]. The DET curve of the global variance GMM system with 1024 Gaussians evaluated on the SPIDRE corpus is presented in Figure 1. The EER of the global variance GMM system is 9.6%.

3.4 Accuracy of the GMM Simulation System – SPIDRE Results

The DET curve of the GMM simulation system evaluated on the SPIDRE corpus is presented in Figure 1. 1024 Gaussians are used for parameterization of test utterances, and 1024 Gaussians are used for parameterization of target speakers. The pruning factor used is N=10. It is clear that the GMM simulation system performs practically the same as the GMM system. The EER of the GMM simulation system is 9.4%. Results for 512 and 2048 Gaussians show the same similarity between both systems.

3.5 NIST-2004 Results

The DET curve of the global variance GMM system with 2048 Gaussians evaluated on the NIST-2004 corpus is presented in Figure 2. The EER of the GMM system is 14.95%. Note that an equivalent standard diagonal covariance matrix GMM system achieved an EER of 15.2%.

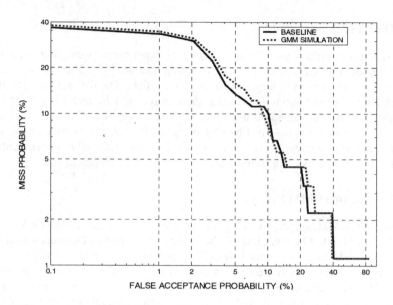

Fig. 1. DET curve comparing the baseline GMM system to the GMM simulation system on the SPIDRE corpus

The DET curve of the GMM simulation system with 2048 Gaussians (both for target speaker and for test utterance) and with a pruning factor N=10 evaluated on the NIST- 2004 corpus is presented in Figure 2. It is clear that the GMM simulation

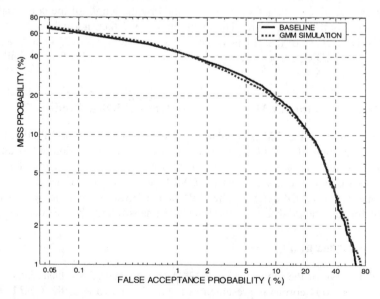

Fig. 2. DET curve comparing the baseline GMM system to the GMM simulation system on the NIST-2004 corpus

system performs practically the same as the GMM system. The EER of the GMM simulation system is 14.4%. Note that the EER is higher on NIST-2004 than on SPIDRE because each target speaker is trained from a single conversation (compared to 2) and because of the severe channel mismatch (cellular, landline, cordless, speaker-phone, etc.).

3.6 Gaussian Pruning in the GMM Simulation System

Experiments were done in order to find an optimal value for **N**. For **N**=10 no degradation in performance was found on any experiment (both SPIDRE and NIST-2004). For **N**=5 negligible degradation in performance was found on some experiments.

Table 1. EER on of Gaussian simulation system as function of pruning factor (NIST-2004)

N	EER (%)
1	14.6
5	14.5
10	14.4
no pruning	14.4

4 Speaker Indexing

A speaker indexing system can be built using the GMM simulation algorithm. The indexing system can be measured in terms of accuracy, time complexity in indexing phase, time complexity of search phase, and the size of the index. Tables 2,3 show the search phase time complexity and index size of the GMM simulation system compared to the GMM based indexing system. In tables 2,3, g is the number of Gaussians for both test and train parameterization (1024), d is the acoustic space dimension (26), s is the mean size of a test utterance (30000 frames), n is the mean size of a test utterance after silence removal (6000 frames), N is the pruning factor (10). We neglect the time complexity of the front-end used by the baseline system.

Table 2. Search phase time complexity per test utterance of the GMM and simulated GMM indexing systems

	Time complexity	Speedup factor
Baseline (GMM)	$O(gnd)$	1
GMM simulation	$O(g^2d)$	6
GMM simulation + Gaussian pruning N=10	$O(Ngd)$	600
GMM simulation + Gaussian pruning N=1	$O(Ngd)$	6000

Table 3. Index size per test utterance for the GMM and for the simulated GMM indexing systems

	Index size	Index size in KB
Baseline (GMM)	80s	2400
GMM simulation	g(d+1)	27

5 Conclusions

In this paper we have presented the GMM simulation algorithm which is a method to simulate the conventional GMM scoring algorithm in a distributed way suitable for speaker indexing. A speaker indexing system based on the GMM simulation algorithm is at least as accurate as one based on the conventional GMM algorithm and is about 6000 times faster and requires roughly 1% of the storage.

The focus of our ongoing research is reducing the size of the index and obtaining sub-linear time complexity for the search phase.

References

1. Reynolds, D. A., "Comparison of background normalization methods for text-independent speaker verification", in Proc. *Eurospeech*, pp.963-966, 1997.
2. McLaughlin, J., Reynolds, D. A., and Gleason, T., "A study of computation speed-ups of the GMM-UBM speaker recognition system", in Proc. *Eurospeech*, pp.1215-1218, 1999.
3. Schmidt M., Gish H., and Mielke A., "Covariance estimation methods for channel robust text-independent speaker identification". In Proc. *ICASSP*, pp. 333-336, 1995.
4. Tsai W. H., Chang W. W., Chu Y. C., and Huang C. S., "Explicit exploitation of stochastic characteristics of test utterance for text-independent speaker identification", in Proc. *Eurospeech*, pp. 771-774, 2001.
5. Foote J., "An overview of audio information retrieval", ACM Multimedia Systems, 7:2--10, 1999.
6. Chagolleau I. M. and Vallès N. P., "Audio indexing: What has been accomplished and the road ahead", in *JCIS*, pp. 911-914, 2002.
7. Sturim D. E., Reynolds D. A., Singer E. and Campbell, J. P., "Speaker indexing in large audio databases using anchor models", in Proc. *ICASSP*, pp. 429-432, 2001.
8. Linguistic Data Consortium, SPIDRE documentation file, http://www.ldc.upenn.edu/Catalog/readme_files/spidre.readme.html
9. "Speech processing, transmission and quality aspects (stq); distributed speech recognition; front-end feature extraction algorithm; compression algorithms," ETSI Standard: ETSI-ES-201-108-v1.1.2, 2000, http://www.etsi.org/stq.
10. "The NIST Year 2004 Speaker Recognition Evaluation Plan", http://www.nist.gov/speech/tests/spk/2004/SRE-04_evalplan-v1a.pdf.
11. Aronowitz H., Burshtein D., Amir A., "Speaker indexing in audio archives using test utterance Gaussian mixture modeling", to appear in Proc. ICSLP, 2004.

Speech Transcription and Spoken Document Retrieval in Finnish

Mikko Kurimo[1], Ville Turunen[1], and Inger Ekman[2]

[1] Helsinki University of Technology, Neural Networks Research Centre,
FI-02150 Espoo, Finland
[2] Department of Information Studies, University of Tampere, Finland
Mikko.Kurimo@hut.fi
http://www.cis.hut.fi/mikkok

Abstract. This paper presents a baseline spoken document retrieval system in Finnish that is based on unlimited vocabulary continuous speech recognition. Due to its agglutinative structure, Finnish speech can not be adequately transcribed using the standard large vocabulary continuous speech recognition approaches. The definition of a sufficient lexicon and the training of the statistical language models are difficult, because the words appear transformed by many inflections and compounds. In this work we apply the recently developed language model that enables n-gram models of morpheme-like subword units discovered in an unsupervised manner. In addition to word-based indexing, we also propose an indexing based on the subword units provided directly by our speech recognizer, and a combination of the both. In an initial evaluation of newsreading in Finnish, we obtained a fairly low recognition error rate and average document retrieval precisions close to what can be obtained from human reference transcripts.

1 Introduction

The interest in searching information spoken in different languages is growing fast, because the rapid increase of spoken information available in digital libraries and other digital audio and video archives all over the world. For English data the state-of-art of spoken document retrieval (SDR) have reached the point where even the archives of spoken audio and video without manual annotation have become valuable sources of information. Some examples of such multimodal data are broadcast news, sports videos, and recordings of meetings or even telephone conversations. In some applications such as broadcast news the accuracy of retrieval from transcripts produced by speech recognition can already be very close to that from human reference transcripts [1].

Audio indexing systems have recently been demonstrated for several other languages than English, too, but the majority of the world's languages are still lacking sufficiently accurate large-vocabulary continuous speech recognition (LVCSR). Even though substantial audio archives of such languages already exist, the portability of LVCSR systems to new languages is restricted by the

S. Bengio and H. Bourlard (Eds.): MLMI 2004, LNCS 3361, pp. 253–262, 2005.

severe structural differences of the languages. Thus, the English-driven speech technology must seek for fundamentally new solutions for success there.

This paper describes and evaluates a full text recognition based SDR system for Finnish. As far as we know this is pioneering work, not only for Finnish, but also for the other languages of similar agglutinative word structure, such as Estonian, Hungarian, and Turkish. The main difficulty in using the standard LVCSR technology is the required lexical and language modeling. Because the words commonly consist of many inflections and compounds, training the models of sufficient coverage of the language would not only require huge corpora, but the models also become unfeasible to process in close-realtime speech recognition. Finding a suitable set of subword units that could substitute words as building blocks of the lexicon and language models (LMs) is not an easy task, either. Furthermore, for a purely phonetic transcription approach without lexicon and LMs, the problem in continuous speech is that the recognition error rate rises very high [2].

The novel Finnish SDR system relies on our research group's recently developed unlimited vocabulary speech recognition system that allows the use of statistical n-gram LMs based on morpheme-like subword units discovered in an unsupervised manner [3, 4]. Related LVCSR systems that have previously been presented are, for example, the one using a more heuristically motivated unit set for Finnish [5] and the ones utilizing rule-based units for Czech [6], and Turkish [7]. These systems could be used for SDR, as well, given that the recognition performs sufficiently well for the rare but important content words which usually fall out of the reach of rule-based word splitting.

The indexing of the automatically transcribed text documents normally utilizes a traditional weighted bag-of-words approach with stopping, stemming and suitable index weighting as, for example, in [8, 9]. In this paper we evaluate two indexing methods, one that uses baseformed words as index terms and another that takes directly the morphemes produced by our speech recognizer. The retrieval is evaluated by processing the test queries into index terms, respectively, and ranking the proposed documents based on their match.

2   Automatic Speech Transcripts for Finnish

The LVCSR system utilized for transcribing the Finnish speech into text is basically the same as in [3], but with a few small improvements [10]. The goal of the system development has been to make the transcripts generally as readable as possible by minimizing the average amount of word and letter errors. The SDR precision depends most on certain semantically important content words that weigh most as the index terms for the documents. Thus, it is interesting to see how well this more general LVCSR system performs in a SDR evaluation and in this section we briefly describe its main features and discuss their implications to SDR and differences to other (English) SDR systems such as [8, 9].

2.1   Acoustic Modeling

The system applies context-independent hidden Markov models (HMMs) that are trained for 25 Finnish phonemes and 16 of their long variants. The probability density function of emitted features in each HMM state is modeled by a mixture of 10 diagonal Gaussians including a global maximum likelihood linear transformation to uncorrelate the mel-cepstral and their delta feature vector components. Because the phoneme durations are contrastive in Finnish, the HMMs are equipped by explicit duration models [10]. Most modern LVCSR systems such as the Finnish systems described in [3, 10] apply context-dependent HMMs. The main reason for deviating from this approach here, was to get a simpler and more compact system that would be easier to train, because the SDR evaluation task did not have much training data for the speaker. Our stack decoder that allows a flexible use of different LMs [3] also restricts the use of context dependent acoustic models, in practice, to within-word contexts, which somewhat decreases its benefits.

2.2   Language Modeling

The LMs in this work are back-off trigrams with Kneser-Ney smoothing trained by the SRILM toolkit [11] for a data-driven set of 65K morpheme-like units. In agglutinative languages such as Finnish, the main problem in large-vocabulary lexical and language modeling is that the conventional word-based approach does not work well enough [3]. Lexical models suffer from the vast amount of inflected word forms and n-gram LMs additionally from the virtually unlimited word order. A solution is to split the words into morpheme-like units to build the lexicon and statistical LMs. This is possible, because the set of subword units can be selected so that all the words are adequately represented and still the pronunciation of the units can be determined from simple rules. The unsupervised machine learning algorithm presented in [4] that selects such units based on a large text corpus seems to provide means to train good LMs for unlimited vocabulary, at least for Finnish [3] and Turkish [7]. The text corpus used in this work for morpheme discovery and LM training includes totally 30M words from electronic books, newspaper texts, and short news stories.

One problem with LMs of data-driven morphemes that is very relevant in SDR is the correct transcription of foreign words, especially the proper names. In our sstem the foreign words are transformed to correspond as well as possible to the Finnish pronunciation using a set of manually designed rules. However, the pronunciation of the foreign words is variable and generally quite different from Finnish. Furthermore, many foreign names that would be important for SDR occur infrequently in the Finnish text data, so the statistically formed subword units will typically represent them by splitting into short segments, which increases the changes of confusions and reduces the strength of the LMs.

A further problem for recognition based on subword units is that the recognition result comes as a sequence of morphemes, not words. To be able to segment the morpheme sequences into word sequences, a special symbol was introduced in LMs to model the word break points. The LMs including the word break symbols can then determine the word breaks even when no silence can be heard between consecutive words. However, frequent errors are made in word breaks related to compound words, which are difficult to human listeners, as well.

3   Indexing the Transcribed Documents

3.1   Word-Based Index Terms

First the obtained automatic speech transcripts must be segmented into documents which here coincides with the actual speech files. To prepare the index terms for each document, the traditional approach (in English) is to perform stopping and stemming for all the words in the transcripts. Instead of a stem, it is more convenient in Finnish to use the base form of the word that can be found by a morphological analyzer[1]. This is because the inflections may also change the root of the word so much that it would be generally difficult to define and extract unique stems. The words that the analyzer [12] could not process were used as index terms as such. For highly inflective languages like Finnish the use of baseforms as index terms is important, because all the inflected forms usually bear the same meaning as their baseform, with respect to the topic of the document. The initial experiments that we performed using the unprocessed inflected forms as index terms lead to very bad performance, which was no surprise. We also observed that the effect of stopping for this task was small, probably due to the applied index weighting that already strongly favours the rare words. The index weight of each index term in a document was the standard TFIDF, that is, the term frequency in the document divided by the frequency of documents in the whole collection, where the term occurs.

The index was prepared from the processed transcripts using the MG toolkit [13] which was also used for the retrieval experiments. In the information retrieval (IR) phase the words in the query are processed exactly like the documents to produce a list of the right kind of index terms. Each document is ranked by summing the index weights of the processed query words. Finally the ranked list is cut off at any desired level to produce the search result.

3.2   Morpheme-Based Index Terms

Whereas the first indexing method was based on word baseforming that requires several further processing steps after the speech recognition, we developed another method, as well, which is much simpler and more direct. Because the speech recognizer already knows how to split the words into morpheme-like subword units designed for obtaining better LMs, we took those units directly from the recognizer's output as the index terms for the document. Typically, these units that we call morphs perform an operation that resembles the English stemming, that is, separates a root-like morpheme that often occurs in the corpus as such from the frequently occurring prefixes and suffixes. Although the statistical

---

[1] Licensed from Lingsoft <http://www.lingsoft.fi>.

morphs are very rough approximations of stems, prefixes and suffixes, because they are only based on the available training corpus, they have also other qualities that make them highly plausible as index terms. This approach makes the transcription and indexing process very simple, because we can skip the word building and baseforming phases. Thus, it is also likely to avoid all the errors caused by the transformation of the morpheme sequences into word sequences and limitations of the morphological analyzer needed for finding the baseforms.

The MG toolkit [13] is applied as in word-based index, but directly on the speech recognizer's output corresponding to each document. IR is performed similarly as well, except that instead of processing queries by baseforming, the words are split into the morphs in exactly the same way as the texts used for training the recognizer's LMs.

3.3   Combined Index

Experiments were also performed to combine the word-based and morpheme-based indexes in the retrieval. As a simple way to obtain a combined index we concatenated both index term lists for each documents and then proceeded by MG to build the total index. The same concatenation approach was then utilized for processing the queries.

4   Experiments and Results

4.1   Goal and Measures for the SDR Evaluation

The purpose of the evaluation was twofold. First, we wanted to evaluate our recently developed Finnish LVCSR system using various metrics relevant to the intended application. Second, we wanted to check how well the new baseline SDR system performs compared to retrieval from human reference transcripts.

The most common measure of LVCSR performance is the word error rate (WER). In WER all word errors (substituted, added and deleted words) are counted equally significant. For applications where LVCSR is needed to understand the content or to perform some actions, it is natural that not all the words nor word errors are equally meaningful. A step towards document retrieval is to use the term error rate (TER) instead of WER. TER counts only errors that most likely affect the indexing, so it compares only the frequencies of words after stemming (word suffixes excluded) and stopping (common function words excluded). TER is defined as the difference of two index term histograms (the recognition result H and the correct transcription R) (summation t is over all resulting terms):

$$\text{TER} = \sum_t |R(t) - H(t)| / \sum_t R(t) * 100\% \ . \tag{1}$$

For languages like Finnish WER is sometimes quite inaccurate measure of speech recognition performance, because the words are long and constitute of a highly variable amount of morphemes. For example, a single misrecognized morpheme in the word "Tietä-isi-mme-kö-hän" leads to 100 % WER, whereas in English the corresponding WER for the translation "Would we really know" would be only 25 %. Because the exact extraction of the morphemes is often difficult, the phoneme or letter error rate (LER) has been used instead.

To evaluate the SDR performance we have adopted the measures used in the TREC-SDR evaluation [1]. The ranked list of relevant documents obtained for each test query is analyzed according to the precision at different recall levels and the total recall-precision curve for different systems is plotted (see Fig. 1, for example). Some key statistics can also be computed such as the average precision (AP) over all recall levels and the precision of the top R documents (RP), where R is the amount of documents relevant to the query. In practical IR work, the precision of the top ranked documents, the five best (P5), for example, is also quite relevant. Although it is obviously difficult to compose an exhaustive set of test queries and human relevance judgments, these recall and precision measures are expected to differentiate the performance of the LVCSR systems in a more meaningful manner than by using the direct transcription error rates.

4.2   Transcription and Retrieval Task

The speech data consists of 270 spoken news stories in Finnish. The average news story lasts one minute. The whole material is read by one single (female) speaker in a studio environment. Before reading, the stories were modified to resemble radio broadcasts. This consisted of removing or rephrasing numeral expressions, quotation and information included in braces. The news are accompanied with binary relevance judgments for 17 topics made by multiple independent judges [14]. The topics are formulated as typical test queries such as: "The decisions of OPEC concerning oil price and output."

The recognized transcripts were produced by splitting the whole material into two independent sets: One for training the acoustic models of the speech recognizer and one for evaluating the recognition accuracy and the SDR performance. To be able to evaluate on the whole material we switched the roles of the sets and trained the recognizer again from the scratch.

4.3   Results

Table 1 shows the performance of the described baseline Finnish speech recognition system. The current task seems to be more difficult than the previous book reading evaluation [3, 10]. The speech is clear and the noise level low, but there was only about two hours of suitable training data available for the speaker. Due to this lack of training data, we choose to apply context-independent phoneme models, in contrary to the earlier works [3, 10]. This reduces dramatically the amount of acoustic models to be estimated. The LM training data is the same as in the previous evaluations, but it does not necessarily match well to the spoken news that were from a different decade than the newswire texts. Given these somewhat inaccurate acoustic and language models, the obtained recognition results are not bad at all.

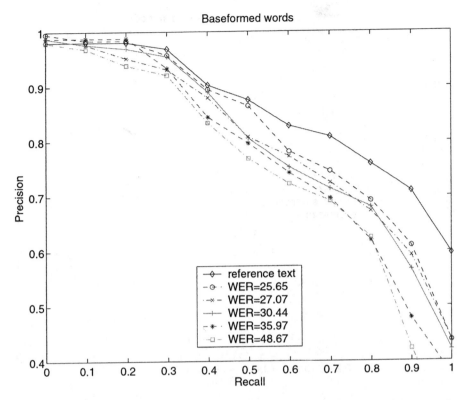

Fig. 1. The IR precision at different recall levels for the alternative ways to run the speech recognizer automatic transcripts compared to using the human reference transcripts

Table 1. The performance statistics of the speech recognizer in the transcription task. The corresponding average precision obtained from human reference transcripts was 84.1%. Beam size refers to the pruning settings of the decoder. For "Data+" we got 50 % more acoustic training data

	Beam 20	Beam 30	Beam 40	Beam 70	Data+
Real-time factor (RT)	0.7	1.3	2.4	8.1	8.1
Word error rate (WER) %	48.7	36.0	30.4	27.1	25.7
Letter error rate (LER) %	12.1	8.5	7.1	6.2	5.6
Term error rate (TER) %	44.8	31.8	26.2	22.3	20.8
Average precision (AP) %	72.9	75.9	78.0	78.0	80.4

The different transcriptions in Table 1 were obtained by changing the amount of pruning (the beam width increased from 20 to 70 hypothesis) in the decoder and finally adding 50% more acoustic training data. The results indicate that more training data and less pruning does not only decrease recognition errors,

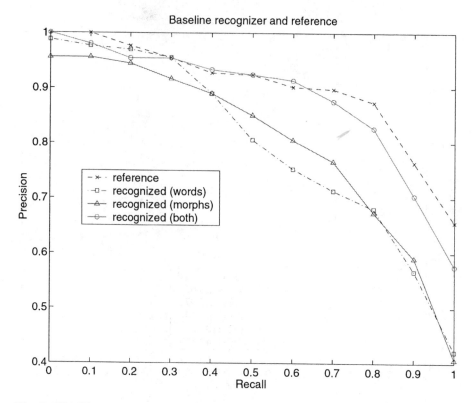

Fig. 2. The IR precision at different recall levels for the alternative ways to index the automatic transcripts. The speech recognizer is the same for all indexes (and the same as "Beam 40" in Table 1). The reference index was made as "both", but using the human reference transcripts

Table 2. Some of the key retrieval precision statistics in the SDR evaluation obtained for the alternative indexes. The speech recognizer is the same for all indexes (and the same as "Beam 40" in Table 1). The reference index was made as "Words+Morphs", but using the human reference transcripts

	Morphs	Words	Words+Morphs	Reference
R-precision (RP) %	71.6	71.2	81.3	84.9
Average precision (AP) %	79.2	78.0	87.5	89.4
Top-5 precision (P5) %	90.6	91.8	92.9	94.1

but also improves the average SDR precision. Figure 1 shows the more detailed evaluation of the SDR using the standard recall-precision curve.

Figure 2 compares the recall-precision curve of the baseline document index (baseformed words as index terms) to index prepared from the recognizer's output morphs directly. Although there are clear performance differences along the curve, the average precisions by the two indexes are almost the same. However, as Table 2 clearly demonstrates, combining the two indexes (morphs and base-form words) seems to give the best results which are already very close to the precisions obtained from the human reference transcripts.

5   Discussion

As a more meaningful evaluation of the speech recognition performance than the standard error rate analysis, the SDR recall and precision show clear improvements obtained by increasing training data and decreasing hypothesis pruning. Table 1 indicates as well that all the improvements in speech recognition, even as measured by the term error rate, do not imply a higher retrieval precision. An example of this is the increase of the decoder's beam parameter above 40 (see Table 1). Even though the best obtained speech transcripts still fail to produce as accurate an index as the reference transcripts, the performance is so close that the baseline speech recognizer seems to be good enough for this application.

Based on these experiments in Finnish we obviously cannot state, how successful would the morpheme-based speech transcription and retrieval be in other languages. The applicability of morphemes may depend on several issues: how much information can be read from the morpheme structure, how well can it be automatically revealed by the unsupervised word-splitting algorithm, and how well does the morpheme-based recognition fit to the decoder and LMs at hand. However, it seems that because some recognized documents are better retrieved by using baseformed words and some by morphs, the combination of both indexes would maximize the recall and precision of the retrieval.

6   Conclusions

We described a new spoken document indexing and retrieval system based on unlimited vocabulary speech recognition. This approach enables the use of statistical language models in the transcription and indexing for highly inflective and agglutinative languages such as Finnish. The baseline system is successively evaluated in a recently developed Finnish SDR task. The obtained recognition error rate is fairly low and the average document retrieval precision close to the one obtained from human reference transcripts.

Future work is to check how much the baseline results can be improved by more accurate speech recognition and advanced indexing methods, such as query and document expansions using suitable background texts. The creation of a larger SDR evaluation task using broadcast news and other radio and television programs is already in progress. It will also be interesting to try this approach for other languages that have either lots of inflections such as Russian or lots of compound words such as German, or both, such as Hungarian, Turkish, and Estonian.

Acknowledgements

The authors are grateful to the rest of the speech recognition team at the Helsinki University of Technology for help in developing the speech recognizer and the morpheme discovery, and to Mr. Nicholas Volk from University of Helsinki in expanding the numbers, abbreviations, and foreign words closer to the Finnish pronunciation for our LMs. The work was supported by the Academy of Finland in the projects *New information processing principles* and *New adaptive and learning methods in speech recognition.*

This work was supported in part by the IST Programme of the European Community, under the PASCAL Network of Excellence, IST-2002-506778. This publication only reflects the authors' views.

References

1. J. Garofolo, G. Auzanne, and E. Voorhees, "The TREC spoken document retrieval track: A success story," in *Proc. Content Based Multimedia Information Access Conference*, 2000.
2. I. Ekman, "Finnish speech retrieval," Master's thesis, University of Tampere, Finland, 2003, (in Finnish).
3. V. Siivola, T. Hirsimäki, M. Creutz, and M. Kurimo, "Unlimited vocabulary speech recognition based on morphs discovered in an unsupervised manner," in *Proc. Eurospeech*, 2003, pp. 2293–2296.
4. M. Creutz, "Unsupervised discovery of morphemes," in *Proc. Workshop on Morphological and Phonological Learning of ACL-02*, 2002, pp. 21–30.
5. J. Kneissler and D. Klakow, "Speech recognition for huge vocabularies by using optimized sub-word units," in *Proc. Eurospeech*, 2001, pp. 69–72.
6. W. Byrne, J. Hacič, P. Ircing, F. Jelinek, S. Khudanpur, P. Krbec, and J. Psutka, "On large vocabulary continuous speech recognition of highly inflectional language — Czech," in *Proc. Eurospeech*, 2001, pp. 487–489.
7. K. Hacioglu, B. Pellom, T. Ciloglu, O. Ozturk, M. Kurimo, and M. Creutz, "On lexicon creation for turkish LVCSR," in *Proc. Eurospeech*, 2003, pp. 1165–1168.
8. S. Renals, D. Abberley, D. Kirby, and T. Robinson, "Indexing and retrieval of broadcast news," *Speech Communication*, vol. 32, pp. 5–20, 2000.
9. B. Zhou and J. Hansen, "Speechfind: An experimental on-line spoken document retrieval system for historical audio archives," in *Proc. ICSLP*, 2002.
10. J. Pylkkönen and M. Kurimo, "Using phone durations in Finnish large vocabulary continuous speech recognition," in *Proc. Nordic Signal Processing Symposium (NORSIG)*, 2004.
11. A. Stolcke, "SRILM - an extensible language modeling toolkit," in *Proc. ICSLP*, 2002.
12. K. Koskenniemi, "Two-level morphology: A general computational model for word-form recognition and production," PhD thesis, University of Helsinki, 1983.
13. I. Witten, A. Moffat, and T. Bell, *Managing Gigabytes: Compressing and Indexing Documents and Images.* Morgan Kaufmann Publishing, 1999, 2nd edition.
14. E. Sormunen, "A method for measuring wide range performance of Boolean queries in full-text databases, " PhD thesis, University of Tampere, 2000.

A Mixed-Lingual Phonological Component Which Drives the Statistical Prosody Control of a Polyglot TTS Synthesis System

Harald Romsdorfer, Beat Pfister, and René Beutler

Speech Processing Group,
Computer Engineering and Networks Laboratory,
ETH Zurich, Switzerland
{romsdorfer, pfister, beutler}@tik.ee.ethz.ch

Abstract. A polyglot text-to-speech synthesis system which is able to read aloud mixed-lingual text has first of all to derive the correct pronunciation. This is achieved with an accurate morpho-syntactic analyzer that works simultaneously as language detector, followed by a phonological component which performs various phonological transformations. The result of these symbol processing steps is a complete phonological description of the speech to be synthesized. The subsequent processing step, i.e. prosody control, has to generate numerical values for the physical prosodic parameters from this description, a task that is very different from the former ones. This article shows appropriate solutions to both types of tasks, namely a particular rule-based approach for the phonological component and a statistical or machine learning approach to prosody control.

1 Introduction

Following the approach of generative phonology in [CH68], text-to-speech (TTS) synthesis requires the underlying syntactic structure in order to derive the correct pronunciation, as has been shown, e.g., in [Tra95] and [Spr96]. This underlying structure is even more important in the case of polyglot TTS where mixed-lingual input text has to be processed. Such texts can contain various types of inclusions from other languages.[1]

An appropriate morphological and syntactic analyzer for mixed-lingual text has been presented in [PR03]. Such an analyzer is most suitably realized with lexica and sets of grammar rules (i.e. the linguistic knowledge of the languages concerned), which are applied by means of a parser. In other words, it is obvious to use symbol processing methods here.

There are other subtasks of TTS synthesis, however, that demand for other types of solutions. Particularly, in prosody control, where linguistic knowledge is very scarce, we consider rule-based approaches inappropriate. We therefore prefer statistical models and machine learning approaches to solve the prosody control problem.

---

[1] Three major groups of foreign inclusions can be identified: mixed-lingual word forms with foreign stems, full foreign word forms that follow the foreign morphology, multi-word inclusions that are syntactically correct foreign constituents.

S. Bengio and H. Bourlard (Eds.): MLMI 2004, LNCS 3361, pp. 263–276, 2005.

In the sequel we present two components of our TTS synthesis system, one using symbol processing methods and one based on a statistical model. The structure of the article is as follows: In Sect. 2 we sketch the architecture of our polyglot TTS system with its two main parts. Subsequently, we describe in Sect. 3 the phonological component which is based on a special type of rules. The output of this component is a minimal but complete information on each sentence to be synthesized. This information is called the phonological representation. Section 4 explains our approach to statistical prosody control and shows in more details how the fundamental frequency of a sentence is generated from its phonological representation.

2   Overview of the Polyglot TTS System PolySVOX

The task of our TTS system, called polySVOX, is to produce high-quality synthetic speech from mixed-lingual text. Thereby a polyglot pronunciation is aimed at, which means that foreign inclusions are pronounced in accordance to the rules of the originating language. Assimilation to the base language is rather marginal and primarily happens close to language switching positions.

In contrast to so-called multilingual TTS systems that can be switched to operate in one of several languages modes, but that treat in general each language with an independent subsystem and synthesize it with a language-specific voice, our polyglot TTS system has to apply the knowledge of all languages concerned in parallel and obviously needs one and the same voice for all languages. These are vital prerequisites to seamlessly switch between languages within sentences and even within words.

Additionally, it is most desirable that the TTS system can easily be configured for an arbitrary set of languages. In order to achieve this, the language knowledge and the processing have strictly been separated.

Basically, polySVOX consists of two main parts, called transcription stage and phono-acoustical model (cf. Fig. 1).

The *transcription stage* is strictly voice-independent and implements the linguistic competence of the TTS process. It comprises a morphological and syntactic analyzer, realized as a bottom-up chart parser, plus a subsequent rule-based phonological component determining syllable stress levels, prosodic phrase boundaries and phone transformations. Due to the strict separation of linguistic data from the correspond-

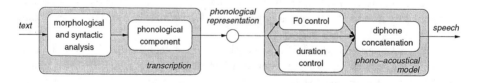

Fig. 1. Overview of the polyglot TTS system polySVOX: The voice-independent transcription stage transforms a sentence of the input text into the phonological representation of the corresponding utterance. The voice-dependent phono-acoustical model generates the sentence prosody from this phonological representation and produces the speech signal

ing algorithms the transcription stage can easily be reconfigured for a new language. Provided that some basic rules are obeyed, a mixed-lingual transcription part can be constructed by loading a set of monolingual data sets, as shown in [PR03]. The output of the transcription stage is called phonological representation.

The *phono-acoustical model* is the voice-dependent part of the TTS process that implements the linguistic performance. It generates the prosody from the phonological representation of an utterance by means of statistical models. For duration control a multivariate adaptive regression splines (MARS) model is used (see [Rie98]). Fundamental frequency (F_0) is generated by means of a recurrent neural network (RNN) which is presented in Sect. 4.2. Finally, the synthetic speech signal is generated by concatenation of diphones, as shown in [TP99].

From the sketch of these two main parts it is obvious that the two tasks are of quite a different nature. In our TTS system this is reflected by the different types of information processing methods: In the transcription stage, that transforms symbolic into symbolic information, knowledge- and rule-based methods are used. Here the main challenge to the polyglot system is the exploration of algorithms that allow a combined usage of linguistic competence of an arbitrary set of languages. The phono-acoustical model, however, maps symbolic information to physical parameters, mainly by means of statistical models (or machine learning approaches) and signal processing methods.

The fundamentally different solutions selected for the two parts are further detailed in the two following sections: Whereas in Sect. 3 the phonological component[2] is shown as an example for symbolic processing, Sect. 4 illustrates the prosody control of the polySVOX system, particularly the fundamental frequency modeling.

3   Phonological Component

In the polySVOX architecture, syllabification, stress assignment, phrasing and various phonological transformations are done in the so-called phonological component. This component processes the syntax tree from the morphological and syntactic analyzer and generates the phonological representation (cf. Fig. 2).

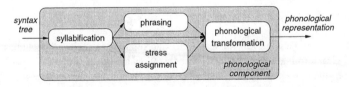

Fig. 2. Overview of the phonological component

In the following, we demonstrate the functionality of the phonological component by means of the mixed-lingual example sentence: "Anciens Amis sind keine Amis anciens." ("Ex-friends are no old friends."). This German declarative sentence contains

---

[2] The other component of the transcription stage, the morphological and syntactic analyzer for mixed-lingual text has been published in [PR03].

two incomplete French noun groups, i.e., the article is missing which corresponds to the German indefinite plural form. The syntax tree of this sentence is shown in Fig. 3. The phonological component processes it as follows:

- The phone sequence is split into phonological syllables. Such syllables may span across word boundaries, in contrast to orthographic ones. Note that the syllable structure may be changed by subsequent phonological transformations.

- Stress assignment and placement of prosodic phrase boundaries are described in [Tra95]. The conceptual ideas originate from [Kip66] and [Bie66], where algorithms for the generation of sentence stress patterns and phrase boundaries from the syntactic structures of German sentences are presented. Stress assignment and phrasing for English and French sentences are based on the same algorithms, requiring different, language specific patterns and rules, however.

- Phonological transformations for phenomena like liaison, elision, linking, aspiration, assimilation, etc. are expressed with so-called multi-context rules. More details about this rule formalism are given in Sect. 3.2.

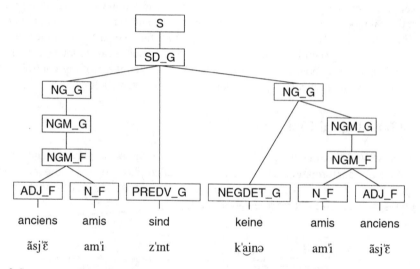

Fig. 3. Syntax tree of the sentence "Anciens Amis sind keine Amis anciens.", including graphemic and phonological terminals. The phonetic symbols follow the IPA definition. The suffixes _F and _G of the constituent identifiers indicate the languages French and German, resp

3.1   Requirements of a Mixed-Lingual Phonological Component

The requirements of a mixed-lingual phonological component are evidently determined by the kind of pronunciation wanted. For our TTS system we are aiming at a polyglot pronunciation of mixed-lingual text (cf. Sect. 2). Consequently, the phonological component of our polyglot TTS system must be able to cope with the different phonological phenomena of each language involved. These phenomena are language-specific and depend on various contexts, as illustrated by the following examples:

German Aspiration: In word-initial position, the German unvoiced plosives [p], [t] and [k] preceding a vowel are aspirated, denoted as [pʰ], [tʰ] and [kʰ], resp. They are also aspirated in word-final position before a break.

German Terminal Devoicing: All voiced plosives (obstruents) before a syllable or word boundary are devoiced.

French Liaison: In French noun groups, liaison is forbidden between a singular noun and the consecutive adjective, e.g. "un bruit effroyable" [œ̃-bʀɥi-e-fʀwa-jabl]; between a plural noun and the following adjective it is optional, e.g. "les amis agréables" [le-za-mi-(z)a-gʀe-abl]; liaison is mandatory between the preceding adjective and a noun, e.g. "un bon ami" [œ̃-bɔ-na-mi].

Liaison is generally avoided between a singular noun and the following verb, e.g. "l'étudiant entend" [le-ty-djã- ã-tã]; it is optional between a plural noun and the following verb, e.g."les étudiants entendons" [le- ze-ty-djã- (z)ã-tã-dɔ̃]; but liaison is mandatory between a clitic personal pronoun and the following verb, e.g. "on entend" [ɔ̃- nã-tã].

French Liaison Consonant Realization: The phonetic liaison consonant can be directly derived from the corresponding graphemic consonant: "s", "x" or "z" result in [z]; "c", "q" or "g" in [k], etc.

English Linking "r": Word-final "r" is usually only pronounced, if the following word begins with a vowel, e.g. "four eggs" [fɔːr- egz] but "four pounds" [fɔː- pa̰undz].

These examples show that phonological phenomena depend on various contexts: The German aspiration rule needs only phonetic context, whereas the English linking rule requires both phonetic and graphemic contexts. The French liaison rules need phonetic, graphemic and syntactic contexts. Furthermore, since all of these phonological phenomena are language-specific, language forms another context.

Additionally, cross-lingual assimilation phenomena must be considered. Even if foreign inclusions in German sentences virtually keep the pronunciation prescribed by the originating language and assimilation to the base language is very weak, it is clearly present and must be handled correctly.

In a word like e.g. "Dufourstrasse", which is composed from the French proper name "Dufour" and the German noun "Strasse" ("street"), the French [ʀ] has to be replaced by the German [r]. It would sound rather affectedly to pronounce [dʏ-fuʀ-ʃtraː-sə] instead of [dʏ-fur-ʃtraː-sə]. Such assimilations occur only near the language switching position, however, and only in short inclusions.

3.2   Phonological Transformation

The application of phonological transformations to a sentence produces the standard pronunciation of this sentence. For the example sentence of Fig. 3 this standard pronunciation is (to simplify matters, syllable stress and prosodic phrase information has been removed):

[ʔãs-jɛ̃-z a-mi- zɪnt- kʰa̰i-nə- ʔa-mi-(z) ãs-jɛ̃].

Note that phonetic symbols in parentheses are optional. The following phonological transformations have been applied in this example:

The aspiration of [kʰ] in the German word "keine" follows the German aspiration rule defined in Sect. 3.1. The plosive [t] in the word "sind" is not aspirated, however, because there is no break after this word.

The standard pronunciation of the French partial noun groups is obtained by applying the French rules for mandatory and optional liaison, resp. The first French inclusion "Anciens Amis" is pronounced [ãs-jɛ̃-za-mi]. Here the liaison consonant [z] was inserted. In the second incomplete French noun group "Amis anciens", the liaison consonant [z] is optional (as defined in Sect. 3.1) which results in [a-mi-(z)ãs-jɛ̃]. The actual realization of this optional consonant depends on the style of pronunciation wanted.

Furthermore, a cross-lingual phenomenon has to be considered which arises from the German glottal stop rule. According to this rule, potentially every initial vowel of a word or a stem morpheme is preceded by a glottal stop. A similar rule applies also for foreign inclusions, i.e., a glottal stop has to be assigned to the initial vowel of the inclusion. "Anciens Amis" therefore has to be pronounced as [ʔãs-jɛ̃-za-mi] in our example sentence.

From this example it is obvious that only the application of both the German and the French phonological transformations is able to produce the desired standard pronunciation for a German sentence with French inclusions.

Multi-context Rules: A rule formalism that is flexible enough to describe all possible context restrictions of such phonological transformations was introduced in [RP04]. This so-called multi-context rule formalism allows to define phonological transformations which are restricted by specific syntactic, graphemic and/or phonological contexts. Formally a multi-context rule consists of a subtree pattern, the separation symbol ':' and an associated phonological transformation:

$$SubtreePattern \ : \ Transformation \ ;$$

Transformations are specified in the form: $\sigma/\rho \Leftrightarrow L\_R$. These context-dependent rewrite rules are similar to the well-known two-level rules (see e.g. [Kos83]), but have been extended here to operate on all types of symbols, i.e., graphemic and phonological ones at the same time.

The subtree pattern specifies the syntactic context and defines for each constituent whether the graphemic and/or phonological terminals are subject to the phonological transformation defined by the rule. These patterns may be specified using constituent symbols plus additional wild-card symbols as listed in Table 1. The application of the associated transformation gets triggered whenever the subtree pattern can be matched with a part of the syntax tree. Examples of such subtree patterns are shown in Fig. 4.

Implementation: In the polySVOX system, the subtree patterns of multi-context rules are represented as strings. This representation includes the special symbols listed in Table 1. In the two multi-context rules for French liaison of Fig. 5, the two left syntax patterns of Fig. 4 are used. Figure 6 shows a mixed-lingual rule with the syntax pattern of Fig. 4.

Applying these multi-context rules to the syntax tree of the example sentence (cf. Fig. 3) results in following transformations: The first multi-context rule for French liaison of Fig. 5 inserts an optional [(z)]. The phonological input sequence as selected

Table 1. Wild-card and special symbols used within multi-context rules

*	any sequence (0...n) of constituents including their (possibly empty) subtrees
?	any constituent (exactly one) including its (possibly empty) subtree
(...)	syntax hierarchy marker
<...>	feature specification
[]	phonological representation operator
{}	graphemic representation operator
%id	set identifier

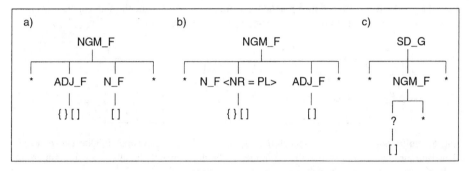

Fig. 4. Examples of subtree patterns: Pattern a) specifies the syntactic context of French mandatory liaison between a noun and a preceding adjective within a French noun group. The operator
'[ ]' selects the phonological terminals of both constituents for application by the associated
phonological rule. Analogously, the operator '{ }' selects the graphemic terminals of the first
constituent. Pattern b) specifies the syntactic context of French optional liaison between a plural
noun and a subsequent adjective. The pattern specifies the noun with an additional feature-value
pair <NR=PL>, i.e., to select only plural nouns. Pattern c) specifies a mixed-lingual syntactic
context for glottal stop assignment within French noun groups as foreign inclusions in German
declarative sentences

by the associated syntax pattern is shown on the left side and the corresponding output
sequence is shown on the right:

$$\{amis\}[ami][\tilde{a}sj\tilde{\epsilon}] \Rightarrow \{amis\}[ami(z)][\tilde{a}sj\tilde{\epsilon}]$$

The second multi-context rule for French liaison inserts a mandatory liaison [z]:

$$\{anciens\}[\tilde{a}sj\tilde{\epsilon}][ami] \Rightarrow \{anciens\}[\tilde{a}sj\tilde{\epsilon}z][ami]$$

The mixed-lingual rule of Fig. 6 which defines glottal stop insertion matches twice:

$$[\tilde{a}sj\tilde{\epsilon}z] \Rightarrow [\textipa{P}\tilde{a}sj\tilde{\epsilon}z]$$
$$[ami(z)] \Rightarrow [\textipa{P}ami(z)]$$

```
%P  set of all phone symbols
%V  set of vowel symbols

NGM_F ( * N_F <NR=PL> {}[] ADJ_F [] * ) :
              @/'(z)'  <=>  's' '}' '[' {%P} %V _ ']' '[' %V ;

NGM_F ( * ADJ_F {}[] N_F [] * ) :
              @/'z'  <=>  's' '}' '[' {%P} %V _ ']' '[' %V ;
```

Fig. 5. Multi-context rules for French liaisons: The first rule inserts an optional liaison [(z)] between French plural noun and subsequent French adjective within the nominal part of a French noun group. The second rule inserts a liaison [z] between preceding French adjective and French noun within the nominal part of a French noun group. Both rules have the same graphemic context (the grapheme "s" preceding a graphemic word boundary '}') and the same phonetic context (two neighboring vowels in front of and after a phonetic word boundary ']' '[')

```
%V  set of vowel symbols

SD_G ( * NGM_F ( ? [] * ) * ) :
              @/'?'  <=>  '[' _ %V ;
```

Fig. 6. Multi-context rule for glottal stop assignment to French inclusions in German sentences: This rule inserts a glottal stop at the beginning of the first subconstituent of French noun groups only if they are inclusions in a German declarative sentence

3.3 Phonological Representation

The output of the transcription stage (cf. Fig. 1) is called phonological representation. This representation consists of the phonetic transcription of the words of an utterance together with prosodic information such as strength and type of phrase boundaries and stress levels of syllables. In case of mixed-lingual input text, appropriately placed language tags mark the language switching positions. For the example sentence of Fig. 3, "Anciens Amis sind keine Amis anciens.", the following phonological representation is produced by the transcription stage of the polySVOX system:

#{0} (P) \F\[2]ʔãs-jɛ̃-[1]z a-mi- #{2} (T) \G\zɪnt- [2]kʰai̯-nə- \F\[3]ʔa-mi-[1](z) ãs-jɛ̃ #{0}

Besides phonetic symbols (the system-internal phonetic symbols are replaced by the corresponding IPA symbols here), phonological representations may include various special symbols which are explained in Table 2.

4 Prosody Control

In TTS synthesis, prosody control means to generate information on the following physical parameters of the speech signal to be synthesized: fundamental frequency (F_0), signal intensity and durations of phones and pauses. There are quite a number of factors

Table 2. Overview of special symbols used in the phonological representation

#{x}	phrase boundary where increasing x denotes decreasing boundary strenght:
	      #{0} sentence break before and after the sentence.
	      $\geq$ #{1} sentence-internal phrase boundaries.

(X)	phrase type mark set at the beginning of a phrase:
	   P progredient phrase Y question with rising pitch at the end
	   T terminal phrase W question with falling pitch at the end
	   S semi-terminal phrase LI, LM, LF enumeration: initial, middle and final

\X\	switch to language X, where X is e.g. E, F, G, etc. for English, French, German, resp.

[x]	syllable stress level x, where x is
	        E emphatic stress
	        1 main phrase stress
	   2, 3, 4 decreasing stress levels
	        0 completely unstressed syllable (may be omitted)

-	syllable boundary

that affect these parameters. The most important ones are syllable stress level, phrase type, position and strength of phrase boundaries, speaking style, language, etc. How all these factors in all possible combinations influence the physical parameters is virtually unknown, however. It is therefore appealing to solve the prosody control problem by means of a machine learning approach, i.e., to learn the interrelation between the influencing factors and the physical parameters of prosody (so-called prosodic parameters) from examples of natural speech.

Assuming that mutual dependency between the prosodic parameters is negligible, it is possible to model each prosodic parameter individually. Accordingly, prosody control of the polySVOX system consists of independent statistical models for F_0 and for duration control. Signal intensity is not actively controlled, since the intrinsic intensities of the diphones proved to be sufficient for the desired speaking style.

In the following we present one of the statistical prosody models, namely the F_0 model. But first it is shown how speech examples have to be prepared for the training of these independent models.

4.1   Preparation of Speech Examples for Prosody Modeling

It goes without saying, that if a natural speech example has to be used for the training of F_0 and phone duration models, F_0 and phone boundaries have to be estimated. In order to achieve independent models, however, F_0 must not be described in function of time, but e.g. per syllable.

This is achieved as follows: The speech signal of a sentence is first segmented into phones by means of an HMM-based phone recognizer. Since the speech signal generally comes from a trained speaker who has read the corresponding text, this text can be used to generate the phonological representation (using the transcription stage of the TTS system) which includes also the sequence of phone symbols that describes the standard pronunciation. It is therefore possible to estimate the phone boundaries by forced

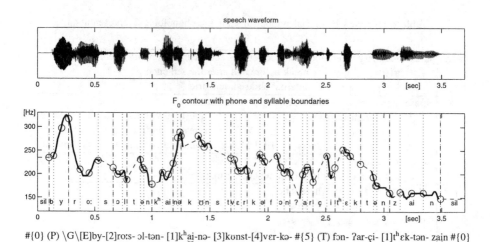

#{0} (P) \G\[E]by-[2]roːs- ɔl-tən- [1]kʰai̯-nə- [3]kʊnst-[4]vɛr-kə- #{5} (T) fɔn- ʔar-çi- [1]tʰɛk-tən- za̯in #{0}

Fig. 7. The outputs of the prosodic analysis of the sentence "Büros sollten keine Kunstwerke von Architekten sein!" ("Office buildings shouldn't be works of art of architects!") are the phone boundaries (dotted lines), the syllable boundaries (dash-dotted lines) and the F_0 contour that has been interpolated across unvoiced sections (dashed parts). The desired time-independent representation of F_0 is attained by resampling the curve at five selected points per syllable, indicated by circles. For syllables with empty onset or coda the two first or last values are coincident

alignment, which is more accurate than recognition, but still not accurate enough. Even trained speakers do not strictly speak in accordance to the standard pronunciation. In Fig. 7 it can be seen, that e.g. the words "Büros sollten" with the standard pronunciation [by-roːs- zɔl-tən] was spoken as [by-roːs- ɔl-tən]. Hence we use speaker-specific pronunciation variation rules to produce alternative pronunciations that are put together in a recognition network and the Viterbi algorithm is used to determine the best matching path through the network (see [Rom04] for more details). Thus we achieve both an adapted phonetic transcription and an accurate phonetic segmentation of the signal. Additionally, we can decide by means of the phonological description which phone boundaries are also syllable boundaries.

The F_0 detection initially produces F_0 values in function of time. As can be seen in Fig. 7, the originally piecewise F_0 curve has been linearly interpolated across unvoiced sections to get a continuous curve.[3] A syllable-wise and therefore time-independent representation of the F_0 contour can now be achieved by taking five F_0 values for each syllable, namely two at the syllable boundaries, two at the boundaries of the syllable nucleus, and the last one at the center of the nucleus. For syllables with empty onset or coda the two first or last values are coincident.

For each language concerned a collection of some 800 sentences, covering all different phrase types listed in Table 2, have been prepared as described above. All sentences

---

[3] Such continuous F_0 contours have proved to be better suited for our modeling than standard ones, where unvoiced segments are generally set to zero.

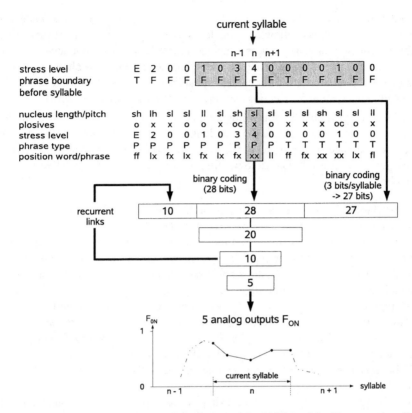

Fig. 8. Architecture plus input and output coding of the RNN used for F₀ generation: For each syllable five normalized F_{ON} values are generated using symbolic information derived from the phonological representation as input. The input information shown here has been derived from the phonological represenation of the example of Fig. 7. Concatenating the F_{ON} values of all syllables yields the complete F_{ON} contour of the utterance to be synthesized

were spoken by the same trained speaker. The resulting databases have been used for the construction of our F₀ and phone duration models.

4.2 Fundamental Frequency Control

Basically, the task of our F₀ control is to generate for each syllable five F₀ values, using the symbolic information of the phonological representation as input. Concatenating the F₀ values of all syllables yields the complete F₀ contour of the utterance to be synthesized.

The sentences of the prosody databases showed that high stress levels and strong phrase boundaries generally affect F₀ over several neighboring syllables, whereas other phonological properties affect F₀ only locally. Therefore, two syllable-aligned streams of symbols are extracted from the phonological representation and fed into the network:

- In order to consider syllable stress and phrase boundaries sufficiently, a context of three preceding and six following syllables is used to generate the F_0 values of the current syllable. For each of these syllables a three bit input is generated: two bits describing syllable stress level and one denoting the presence of a phrase boundary directly before that syllable. For context syllables beyond the start or the end of the input stream a special filler code is used (i.e. all three bits are set to zero).
- For the current syllable the following phonological properties are encoded and fed to a 28 bit input: length (short / long) and intrinsic pitch (low / high) of the syllable nucleus; presence of a plosive in the onset or coda of the syllable; the syllable stress level and prosodic phrase type; first or last position of the syllable in word and phrase.

Figure 8 shows the complete architecture of the neural network used for F_0 control: there are 65 input nodes (55 for information of the phonological representation plus 10 for recurrent links), 20 nodes in the first hidden layer, 10 nodes in the second hidden layer that are reconnected to the input layer, and five output nodes. All nodes have a sigmoidal activation function. At the start of each utterance the feedbacks are set to zero, both in training and generation mode.

The outputs of the neural network are five continuous values between 0 and 1 denoting normalized F_{0N} values. These F_{0N} values are linearly mapped onto absolute F_0 values in a voice-dependent interval, e.g. for our female voice onto the interval 120 - 420 Hz. In accordance with the training data, the five output values are positioned at the syllable boundaries, at the nucleus boundaries and in the center of the nucleus (cf. Fig. 8).

The training of the RNN was done using the back-propagation through time algorithm. This algorithm is described in [Wer90]. The 800 sentences of the prosody database were partitioned into a training set of 600 sentences and a test set of 200 sentences. As error measure we used the mean square error between the generated F_0 values and the corresponding natural F_0 values taken from the prosody database.

The mean square error proved to be no good measure for naturalness of synthetic F_0 contours. Therefore the quality of the F_0 generation model for German was finally evaluated in a listening test: 40 sentences which randomly carried either the natural or synthetic F_0 contour predicted by the RNN were presented to 12 listeners. Their task was to decide whether the F_0 contour of a heard sentence was natural or synthetic. The results showed that on average about 70 % of the decisions were correct. Note that the result of pure guessing would be 50 %. The test showed that listeners were largely unable to distinguish between synthetic and natural F_0 contours.

4.3   Prosody Control for Polyglot TTS

The approach to F_0 generation described above has shown to perform very well for TTS systems that have to synthesize speech from monolingual sentences. Our intention is to use it also for polyglot TTS synthesis, where prosody of several languages has to be considered within a single sentence.

Since prosody models are trained with an appropriately prepared prosodic database (see Sect. 4.1), this could be achieved simply by putting also a set of mixed-lingual sentences into this database. For flexibility reasons, we have decided to go another way. Our target is a polyglot TTS system that can be configured for an arbitrary set of languages. To have a prosody model for each of these possible sets would require quite a number of such models. Instead of specific models for each set of languages, we intend to combine the monolingual prosody models of those languages in some suitable manner.

Such a combination has to account for peculiarities of mixed-lingual sentences, of course. Very important is, e.g. that not only the language of a foreign inclusion, but also its length strongly influences the prosodic parameters.

5   Discussion and Conclusions

The aim of our research towards a polyglot TTS synthesis is to develop a system architecture which is as language-independent as possible and may be configured to virtually any set of languages. The configuration must completely be defined by the lingware (i.e. the language-dependent data set) that includes lexica, grammars, phonological rules, F_0 and duration model parameters, diphones, etc.

The lingware of the polyglot TTS synthesizer for a certain set of languages should primarily consist of the lingware of the individual languages and would ideally need no or only very few cross-lingual knowledge or data.

For the transcription stage of our polyglot TTS system this aim has been widely reached: the monolingual lexica, grammars and other rule sets can be combined arbitrarily and need only very small cross-lingual extensions (e.g. the inclusion grammars, see [PR03]). And given the diphones of several languages are from the same speaker, they can directly be used in the polyglot TTS synthesizer.

In the context of prosody control, however, there is still an number of remaining issues that will be subject to further research.

Acknowledgment

This work was partly supported by the Swiss National Science Foundation in the framework of NCCR IM2 and by the Swiss Commission for Technology and Innovation (CTI).

References

[Bie66]   M. Bierwisch. Regeln für die Intonation deutscher Sätze. *Studia Grammatica*, VII:99–201, 1966.

[CH68]   N. Chomsky and M. Halle. *The Sound Pattern of English*. Harper and Row, New York, 1968.

[Kip66]   P. Kiparsky. Über den deutschen Akzent. *Studia Grammatica*, VII:69–98, 1966.

[Kos83]   K. Koskenniemi. *Two-Level Morphology: A General Computational Model for Word-Form Recognition and Production*. PhD thesis, Department of General Linguistics, University of Helsinki, Finland, 1983.

[PR03]   B. Pfister and H. Romsdorfer. Mixed-lingual text analysis for polyglot TTS synthesis. In *Proceedings of the Eurospeech 2003*, pages 2037–2040, Geneva, September 2003.

[Rie98]   M. Riedi. *Controlling Segmental Duration in Speech Synthesis Systems*. PhD the-
          sis, No. 12487, Computer Engineering and Networks Laboratory, ETH Zurich (TIK-
          Schriftenreihe Nr. 26, ISBN 3-906469-05-0), February 1998.

[Rom04]   H. Romsdorfer. *An Approach to an Improved Segmentation of Speech Signals for the
          Training of Statistical Prosody Models*. Technischer Bericht Nr. 2 zum KTI-Projekt
          Nr. 6233.1 SUS-ET. Institut TIK, ETH Zürich, May 2004.

[RP04]   H. Romsdorfer and B. Pfister. Multi-context rules for phonological processing in
          polyglot TTS synthesis. In *Proceedings of the Interspeech 2004 - ICSLP*, Jeju Island
          (Korea), October 2004.

[Spr96]   R. Sproat. Multilingual text analysis for text-to-speech synthesis. In *Proceedings of
          the ICSLP'96*, Philadelphia, October 1996.

[TP99]   C. Traber, B. Pfister, et al. From multilingual to polyglot speech synthesis. In *Pro-
          ceedings of the Eurospeech*, pages 835–838, September 1999.

[Tra95]   C. Traber. *SVOX: The Implementation of a Text-to-Speech System for German*. PhD
          thesis, No. 11064, Computer Engineering and Networks Laboratory, ETH Zurich
          (TIK-Schriftenreihe Nr. 7, ISBN 3 7281 2239 4), March 1995.

[Wer90]   P. J. Werbos. Backpropagation through time: What it does and how to do it. *Proceed-
          ings of the IEEE*, 78(10):1550–1560, 1990.

Shallow Dialogue Processing Using Machine Learning Algorithms (or Not)

Andrei Popescu-Belis[1], Alexander Clark[1], Maria Georgescul[1],
Denis Lalanne[2], and Sandrine Zufferey[1]

[1] University of Geneva, School of Translation and Interpreting (ETI),
TIM/ISSCO, 40, bd. du Pont d'Arve,
CH-1211 Geneva 4, Switzerland
andrei.popescu-belis@issco.unige.ch, asc@aclark.demon.co.uk,
{maria.georgescul, sandrine.zufferey}@eti.unige.ch
[2] University of Fribourg, Faculty of Science,
DIUF/DIVA, 3, ch. du Musée,
CH-1700 Fribourg, Switzerland
denis.lalanne@unifr.ch

Abstract. This paper presents a shallow dialogue analysis model, aimed at human-human dialogues in the context of staff or business meetings. Four components of the model are defined, and several machine learning techniques are used to extract features from dialogue transcripts: maximum entropy classifiers for dialogue acts, latent semantic analysis for topic segmentation, or decision tree classifiers for discourse markers. A rule-based approach is proposed for solving cross-modal references to meeting documents. The methods are trained and evaluated thanks to a common data set and annotation format. The integration of the components into an automated shallow dialogue parser opens the way to multimodal meeting processing and retrieval applications.

1 Introduction

The design of computational methods to process dialogues between humans requires robust models and techniques for feature extraction. This paper proposes a shallow model for human dialogues that occur in meetings, along with a set of techniques for automatic detection of the features that constitute the model. The results of this *shallow dialogue analysis (SDA)* can be used in meeting processing and retrieval applications, to provide focussed accessed to the contents of the meetings [1].

The SDA approach to dialogue modelling has four major components, derived from state-of-the-art research in semantics and pragmatics: dialogue act tagging [2]; topic segmentation; detection of cross-modal references to documents [3]; and detection of discourse markers [4]. Machine learning algorithms are used to extract these features: their performances and their relevance to each task will be discussed.

S. Bengio and H. Bourlard (Eds.): MLMI 2004, LNCS 3361, pp. 277–290, 2005.

We will describe and justify the SDA model in Section 2, and provide also an annotation model and an outline of the available data. We analyse each of the four components of the SDA (cf. Sections 3, 4, 5 and 6) according to a common pattern: theoretical grounding; evaluation metric, available training data and reliability of ground truth annotation; machine learning techniques (or not) for automatic detection; performances of these techniques and discussion of their respective merits.

2   Shallow Dialogue Analysis

Modelling human dialogue is an active research area in linguistics and psychology, with applications to spoken and written language understanding by computers, and to human-computer interaction. There is, however, no generally accepted theory of human dialogue, and moreover, the various competing approaches to dialogue modelling are not quite tractable in terms of computational implementations. Our proposal of a shallow dialogue analysis model is inspired by some of the most commonly accepted hypotheses of dialogue theory, and driven by the needs of meeting processing and retrieval applications, while bearing in mind technical feasibility, robustness, and available resources.

2.1   Definition of SDA Model

Our model is composed of a set of features that combine information about the content or the state of the dialogue between two or more speakers. We consider that the dialogue unit is the *utterance*, a feature coded UT, i.e. a coherent unit of meaning that serves one function in the dialogue; the function is called *dialogue act* (DA) – another feature of our model. Although some theorists attempt to combine DA-labelled utterances into hierarchical structures, we observed that such structures are sometimes hard to annotate even for humans, and therefore do not consider them here as an SDA feature – hence the term 'shallow'.

We also consider a flat thematic structure: a dialogue is made of a series of disjoint episodes (EP), each of them dealing with a coherent topic. The extraction and resolution of references to entities is a key feature for all aspects of language understanding. We focus here on a particular type, namely the cross-modal references that are made by the speakers to documents and their sub-parts. The features are the boundaries of referring expressions (RE) as well as the links to the document elements they refer to (DE). Finally, we attempt to detect a particular class of words named *discourse markers* (DM) which play a particular role in dialogue: they can help the detection of the previous features, and can signal meta-linguistic properties of utterances, such as, here, hesitation or uncertainty.

2.2   Annotation Model

The annotation model for SDA presupposes the availability of spoken dialogue transcripts, in which the words uttered by each speaker are transcribed and timed – the other required modality being the meeting documents. Such transcripts could be generated from separate channels (recorded using individual microphones) processed by an automated speech recognizer. However, an ASR system would have a word error rate of 30% or more in such an environment [5], especially since most "individual" microphone types are still sensitive to input from other speakers too. Therefore, manually corrected transcripts are preferable, done with Transcriber [6] and exported to XML format.

For an adequate representation of the SDA features, three types of annotations must be handled: boundaries, labels on bounded segments, and links from bounded segments to other elements. Given separate transcription files per channel, annotated as XML with time stamps, we annotate intra-channel boundaries (UT, RE, DM) on the transcription, and the other elements – cross-channel boundaries (EP), labels (DA, TO), and links (DE) – as separate XML elements, grouped into annotation blocks at the end of the files [7].

2.3   Annotated Data

Complete annotation of SDA from scratch is a time consuming task. Therefore, reuse of the existing resources summarized in Table 1 is a priority. Within the (IM)2 project, three main sites provide transcribed meeting recordings, with 4–8 participants: IDIAP, Univ. of Fribourg (UniFr), and ICSI.

Table 1. Available resources for SDA research

Institute	Nb. × time	Media	Lg.	Annotation
ICSI-MR	75 × 60′	A,T	EN	UT,DA EP(30%),DM(60%)
IDIAP 1	60 × 5′	A,V,T	EN	UT, EP
ISSCO 1	8 × 30′	A,V	EN	ongoing
UniFr	22 × 15′	A,V,T,D	FR	UT,RE,DE

The first two institutions provide transcripts and UT+EP annotation for ca. 60 and ca. 20 short meetings (5′-15′), and a larger corpus is currently being recorded at IDIAP [8]. These resources consist of multimodal data (audio, video and transcription). UniFr also provides meeting documents, therefore we annotated this data with references to documents (RE, DE). The ICSI-MR project has about 75 one-hour meetings annotated with UT, DA [9], which we validated and converted to SDA format [2]. Annotation of EP boundaries on 25 ICSI-MR meetings was available from another source [10]. A series of meetings was recorded by ISSCO at IDIAP (spring 2004) and is currently being transcribed and annotated.

Stylesheets were written and conversion methods were defined for these resources, which await complete annotation of the missing SDA features. The training and test data used below makes use of all the available annotations.

3   Dialogue Acts

3.1   Dialogue Act Tagsets

An utterance is a coherent, contiguous series of words from a given speaker, which serves a precise function in the dialog. An utterance can often be equated with a proposition or a sentence, but in spoken language, utterances do not always correspond to well-formed or completed propositions. In this section, using ICSI-MR pre-segmented data (UT annotation), we will focus on the automatic assignment of dialogue functions to utterances, that is, *dialogue acts* (DA annotation).

There is little consensus on a set of DAs, since tagsets depend on the goals of their creators [11]. Among the many existing DA tagsets, the multidimensional DAMSL [12] and the one-dimensional SWBD-DAMSL [13] were used to label two-party conversations. While DAMSL offers about 4 million tag combinations, SWBD-DAMSL retains only the most frequent ones, i.e. 42 mutually exclusive tags such as 'statement', 'opinion', 'agree/accept'. SWBD-DAMSL is well adapted to automatic DA annotation and was used for language modelling in speech recognition [14].

The ICSI-MR tagset [15], used for the ICSI-MR data, extends SWBD-DAMSL, and allows one utterance to be marked with as many tags as needed. Our formalization of the ICSI-MR tagset using rewriting rules shows that the number of possible combinations of tags (DA labels) reaches several millions, which makes a huge search space for automatic DA tagging [2].

3.2   The MALTUS DA Tagset

We defined MALTUS (Multidimensional Abstract Layered Tagset for Utterances) in order to reduce the search space, by assigning exclusiveness constraints among tags, while remaining compatible with ICSI-MR. MALTUS is more abstract than ICSI-MR, but can be refined. An utterance is either marked U (undecipherable) or it has a general tag followed by zero or more specific tags. It can also bear a disruption mark. More formally:

DA → (U | (gen_tag (spc_tag)?)) (.D)?

    gen_tag → S | Q | B | H

    spc_tag → (RP | RN | RU)? RI? AT? DO? PO?

The glosses of the tags, generally inspired from ICSI-MR, are: U undecipherable, S statement, Q question, B backchannel, H hold, RP/RN/RU positive/negative/other answer, RI restated information, DO command or other performative, AT attention management (acknowledgement, tag question, etc.), PO politeness (apology, thanks, etc.), D disruption (interrupted, abandoned). There are only about 500 possible MALTUS labels (combinations of tags), but observations of the converted ICSI-MR data show that their distribution is very skewed; for instance, about 75% of the labels contain a S tag.

3.3   Automatic DA Annotation

In the experiments we present here, we focus on the multi-dimensional nature of the MALTUS tagsets, and explore the extent to which such a tagset can be predicted by classifying each dimension separately – i.e. by having a set of "orthogonal" classifiers – as opposed to classifying the entire structured object in a single step using a single multi-class classifier on a flattened representation. In prior research, some form of sequential inference algorithm has been used to combine the local decisions about the DA of each utterance into a classification of the whole utterance. The common way of doing this has been to use a hidden Markov model to model the sequence and to use a standard decoding algorithm to find either the complete sequence with maximum a posteriori (MAP) likelihood or to select for each utterance the DA with MAP likelihood. Here, we will ignore this complexity and allow our classifier access to the gold standard tags of the previous utterances - making the preliminary task substantially easier.

Since for the moment we are not using prosodic or acoustic information, but just the dialogue transcriptions, there are two sources of information that can be used to classify utterances with respect to dialogue acts: first, the sequence of words that constitutes the utterance, and second, the surrounding utterances and their classification. Hence, two sorts of features will be used here: internal lexical features derived from the words in the utterance, and contextual features derived from the surrounding utterances. We used as lexical features the 1000 most frequent words, together with additional features for these words occurring at the beginning or end of the utterance. This gives an upper bound of 3000 lexical features. We used some simple contextual features relating to basic temporal relationships between adjacent utterances such as precedence and overlap.

3.4   Results

We use a Maximum Entropy (ME) classifier which allows an efficient combination of many overlapping features. We selected 5 ICSI-MR meetings (6771 utterances) to use as our test set and 40 as our training set, leaving the others for possible later experiments. As a simple baseline we use the classifier which just guesses the most likely DA tag (S). We first performed some experiments on the original ICSI-MR tagset, to see how predictable it is. We defined a simple six-way classification task which classifies disruption forms, undecipherable forms, and the four general tags S, Q, B, H mentioned above. This is an empirically well-founded distinction: the ICSI-MR group reported inter-annotator agreement of $\kappa = 0.79$ (using the *kappa* measure [16]) for a very similar task. Our ME classifier scored 77.9% accuracy, against a baseline of 54.0%. A more relevant performance criterion for our application is the accuracy of classification into the four general tags S, Q, B, H. In this case we removed disrupted and undecipherable utterances, slightly reducing the size of the test set, and achieved a score of 84.9% (baseline 64.1%).

With regard to the MALTUS tagset, since it has some internal structure, it should accordingly be possible to identify the different parts separately, and then combine the results. We have therefore performed some preliminary experiments with classifiers that classify each level separately. We again removed the disruption tags since in our current framework we are unable to predict them accurately. The baseline for this task is again a classifier that chooses the most likely tag (S) which gives 41.9% accuracy. Using a single classifier on this complex task gave an accuracy of 73.2%.

We also trained six separate classifiers and combined the results. This complex classifier gave an accuracy of 70.5%. This mild decrease in performance is rather surprising – one would expect the performance to increase as the data sets for each distinction get larger. This can be explained by non-trivial dependencies between the classifications. There are a number of ways this could be treated, using either structured output spaces or stacked classifiers, where each classifier can use the output of the previous classifier as a feature in the next one. It is also possible that these dependencies reflect idiosyncrasies of the tagging process: tendencies of the annotators to favour or avoid certain combinations of tags. We expect the performance of a final, fully automatic classifier to be substantially higher than the results presented here, owing to the use of more powerful classifiers and, more importantly, larger and richer feature sets.

4   Topic Segmentation

4.1   Definition and Input Data

Segmentation into thematic episodes – defined as units which tend to reflect coherence around particular topics – plays an important role in automatic summarization, or in meeting indexing and retrieval. We aim here at finding the most prominent boundaries between episodes, without building a hierarchic topical structure of each meeting, hence making minimal theoretical assumptions about discourse structure. Previous studies of automatic thematic segmentation were based on various (probabilistic) lexical cohesion methods, or combined multiple features such as cue phrases and prosodic features. Their application to multi-party dialogues, as opposed to narrative or descriptive texts, remains less explored.

While focusing on multi-party dialogues, we also use narrative texts for setup and comparison purposes. We use three sets of test data, of similar length, ca. 90,000 words, without stopwords. For the ICSI-MR dialogue data, the topic boundaries for 25 meetings were defined by the consensus of at least three annotators [10]. There is an average of 7.32 episodes per one-hour meeting (test sample). Cochran's Q test showed that annotation reliability is significant at a 0.05 level. The TDT3 collection of news stories has an average of 24 segments per test sample (one news report). The subset of the Brown corpus is an artificial test set [17], where each test sample consists of ten text segments (topics). A segment contains the first n sentences ($3 \leq n \leq 11$) of a randomly selected document from the Brown corpus.

4.2   Methods for Automatic Segmentation

We investigated an approach based on Latent Semantic Analysis (LSA). LSA is generally used to induce and to represent aspects of the meaning of words reflected in their natural language usage [18], and we describe below its application to SDA annotation – first the training phase, then the test phase.

During the *learning phase*, we consider that available data is tagged at the thematic episodes level. Hence, we have the following types of segments (blocks) from the input data: a human-annotated topic segment for the ICSI-MR data; a story unit for the TDT and Brown data.

The segmented input data is first filtered to remove the most common words. Then each input block is represented in a vector space model as a n-dimensional vector, where n is the number of distinct terms in the vocabulary. So, a_{ij}, the ith element of the jth vector, is a function of the frequency of the ith vocabulary term in the corresponding block of text. Using results from information retrieval [19], this function of the frequency is expressed as: $a_{ij} = l_{ij} \cdot g_i$, where l_{ij} and g_i are local and global weights respectively. As local weightings we use: *Term Frequency (TF)*, *Binary* and *Log*. The global term weighting functions that we used are: *Normal*, *GfIdf*, *Idf*, and *Entropy*. The data matrix $A_{n \times m} = (a_{ij})_{1 \leq i \leq n, 1 \leq j \leq m}$, where m is the number of blocks of text, is called the matrix of frequencies.

After the construction of the matrix of frequencies, the method projects this matrix into an appropriate lower space dimension. This is done by performing a rank-k approximation to $A_{n \times m}$ by using its singular value decomposition [20]: $A_{n \times m} \approx \hat{A}_{n \times m} = U_{n \times k} \cdot \Sigma_{k \times k} \cdot V_{m \times k}^T$, where $k \ll \min(n, m)$ is the order of the decomposition, ^{T} denotes matrix transposition, and the diagonal matrix $\Sigma_{k \times k}$ contains the first k singular values of A in descending order. The idea behind this equation is that terms that are semantically associated are placed to some degree near one another in the subspace representation, i.e. some words that have similar co-occurrence patterns are projected into the same dimension. Finding the optimal dimensionality of the LSA reduced space is an empirical issue.

In the *test phase* of LSA, we compute the proximity between the utterances of a test sample. Given a text to be segmented, the representation of each utterance $\hat{u}$ is computed using the equation $\hat{u} = u \cdot U_{n \times k} \cdot \Sigma_{k \times k}^{-1}$ (the version without $\Sigma_{k \times k}^{-1}$ was also tested), where $U_{n \times k}$ and $\Sigma_{k \times k}$ were determined in the training phase; $u = (u_1, u_2, \ldots, u_n)$ with u_i indicating the weighted frequency of the ith vocabulary term in the utterance (using the same local and global weighting functions applied in the learning phase). The thematic distance between two utterances is then computed using the cosine metric, and topic boundaries are identified by a divisive clustering procedure [17].

4.3   Results

We evaluated mainly the relations between different factors that influence the results obtained by LSA, such as frequency matrix transformations, choice of the reduced LSA space dimensionality, choice of applying or not a ranking function on the similarity matrix before clustering. Singular value decomposition was performed using the single-vector Lanczos method implemented by Berry [20]. The baseline scores of the following simplistic algorithms are used for comparison: (1) *ALL*: considers all potential boundaries as real boundaries; (2) *NONE*: no boundary at all; (3) *RANDOM*: randomly select the boundaries. We have also experimented with the state-of-the-art algorithm developed by Choi [17], labelled C99. All the algorithms are given the correct number of segments (boundaries) in the test texts. We use the P_k error metric for evaluation [21]: P_k is the probability that a randomly chosen pair of words from a window of dimension k (k being the mean length of an episode in the reference data) is wrongly classified as being in the same segment or not.

Our findings show that the C99 algorithm has only 9% error rate on the subset of Brown corpus, but its performance decreases at 23% error rate on TDT data, and attains 37% error rate on ICSI-MR – which is even bigger than the error rate of 33.10% given by the baseline algorithm *NONE*.

In our preliminary experiments on ICSI-MR data we trained the LSA model on a dataset containing 6,124 terms. The LSA algorithm gives an error rate of about 35% when no ranking is applied. Thus the LSA results are slightly better than the C99 results, but the error rates are still higher than those given by the baseline algorithm *NONE*.

Our experiments on TDT data were done by training the LSA model on a dataset containing 63,667 terms. The error rates obtained are about 36% and we observe a slight improvement in the LSA performance (at 34%) when *Log · Entropy* was adopted instead of *TF · Idf* as initial term weighting. However, C99 performs better than LSA on TDT data. Besides, we obtained an error rate of 34.14% on the Brown data, when training was performed on a Brown subset containing 6,498 terms after the pre-processing step.

Depending on the training data, it appears that LSA applied to topic segmentation does not perform better than other, less time-consuming approaches such as C99. Our experiments show that for topic segmentation, if we interpret LSA as a mechanism for representing the terms of the collection, this technique alone is insufficient for dealing with the variability in term occurrence.

5   References to Documents

5.1   Definition of the Component

The detection of references made by the speakers to the meeting documents is an SDA component that contributes to the general understanding of a dialogue, and is related to another communication modality, namely documents (agenda, reports, memos, notes, slides, etc.). We deal here with press-review meetings that discuss the front pages of one or more newspapers.

The task requires (a) the detection of the referring expressions (REs) that make reference to the documents of the meeting, and (b) the attachment of each RE to the document element it refers to. We focus here on task (b), using REs identified by humans. Task (a) could be carried out using a repertoire of pattern matching rules.

Newspaper front pages have a hierarchical structure made of elements that can contain other elements – hence a straightforward encoding in XML. For instance, a `Newspaper` front page bears the newspaper's `Name` and `Date`, one `Master Article`, one or more `Articles`, etc. For simplicity of annotation, each content element has an ID attribute bearing a unique index. Inferring the structure of a document from its graphical aspect encoded in PDF is a task that can be automated with good performances [22]. In what follows, we use manually-generated XML representations of documents, considered 100% accurate.

In summary, the annotation task requires the construction of the correct pointers from the RE indexes to the document names and document elements, which are characterized by ID or by XPath.

5.2   Evaluation Method and Data

For evaluation, one must compare for each RE the referent (document element) found by the system with the correct one selected by the annotators. If the two are the same, the system scores 1, otherwise it scores 0. The total score is the number of correctly solved REs out of the total number of REs. The automatic evaluation measure we implemented provides two scores: (1) the number of times the document is correctly identified, and (2) the number of times the document element, characterized by its ID attribute, is correctly identified.

The annotation of the gold standard was done for 15 UniFr meetings with a total of 322 REs referring to documents, and 1 to 4 documents per meeting. Inter-annotator agreement, measured on 3 meetings with 92 REs, reaches 96% for document assignment (3 errors), and 90% on document elements (9 errors). After discussion among annotators, 100% agreement was reached on document assignment, and 97% agreement on document elements – both very high scores.

5.3   Ref2doc Algorithm Based on Anaphora Tracking

Although machine learning can be applied to coreference resolution, the scarcity of data with respect to the variety of features needed to assign a referent to an RE prompted us to define a rule-based algorithm which exploits the distinction between anaphoric and non-anaphoric REs, and the co-occurrences of words between the RE (plus context) and each document element.

The algorithm scans each meeting transcript and stores as variables the 'current document' and the 'current document element' (or article). For each RE, the algorithm determines first the document it refers to, from the list of documents associated to the meeting. REs that make use of a newspaper's name are considered to refer to the respective newspaper; the other ones are supposed to refer to the current newspaper, i.e. they are anaphors.

The algorithm then attempts to assign a document element to the current RE. First, it attempts to find out whether the RE is anaphoric or not, by matching it against a list of typical anaphors: 'it', 'the article', 'this article', 'the author'.

If the RE is anaphoric, then it is associated to the current article or document element (except for the first one, which is never anaphoric).

If the RE is not considered to be anaphoric, then the algorithm attempts to link it to a document element by comparing the content words of the RE with those of each article. The words of the RE are considered, as well as those in its left and right contexts. A match with the title of the article, or the author name, is weighted more than one with the content. Finally, the article that scores the most matches is considered to be the referent of the RE, and becomes the current document element.

5.4   Results and Observations

The baseline score for RE ↔ document association, obtained when always choosing the most frequent newspaper, is 82% accuracy (265 REs out of 322). But some meetings deal only with one document; if we look only at meetings that involve at least two newspapers, then the baseline score is 50% (46/92), a much lower value. Regarding RE ↔ document element association, if the referent is always the front page as a whole, then accuracy is 16%. If the referent is always the main article, then accuracy is 18%.

Our algorithm reaches 98% accuracy for the identification of documents referred to by REs, or 93% if we take into account only the meetings with several documents.

The accuracy for document element identification is 73% (237 REs out of 322). If we count only REs for which the document was correctly identified, the accuracy is 74% (236 REs out of 316). This score is obtained when only the right context of the RE is considered (i.e. the words after the RE), not the left one. Also, the optimal number of words to look for in the right context is about ten. Without the right context, the score drops at 40%. Finally, if anaphor tracking is disabled, the score drops at 65%, which shows the relevance of this feature.

At current levels of performance, the resolution of references to documents appears to be an efficient cross-channel process that enhances dialogue and document processing, and helps the multi-media rendering of the results.

6   Discourse Markers

6.1   Definition and Evaluation

The identification of discourse markers (DMs) – words like *actually*, *but*, *I mean*, *like*, *well* – is relevant to lower-level analysis processes such as POS tagging, parsing, or to SDA components such as DA tagging. From an SDA point of view, the detection of *like* as a DM is useful to indicate approximation, uncertainty, or fuzziness in a dialogue. As for the DM *well*, it can be used to detect topic shifts.

The present SDA component disambiguates occurrences of two important DMs, *like* and *well*, that is, separates the occurrences when they function as DMs ("pragmatic uses") from their other occurrences. For instance, *like* can be used as a preposition, adjective, conjunction, adverb, noun, verb – or as a DM, as in this example from ICSI-MR: "It took *like* twenty minutes".

The *kappa* metric [16] can be used to compare human annotations, or to score a system against a gold standard. A simpler but useful metric here is the percentage of occurrences correctly identified, or accuracy. We annotated all occurrences of *like* and *well* as DMs in 50 one-hour ICSI-MR dialogues, finding about 800 and 600 occurrences of each. When all the occurrences are classified as DMs we obtain a baseline accuracy of 37%, resp. 66%. Inter-annotator agreement reaches $\kappa = 0.65$ for the identification of the DM *like*, provided the audio is available, for prosodic cues [4]. Furthermore, to evaluate the retrieval of pragmatic uses among all uses, recall and precision are also relevant.

6.2   Automatic Detection of DMs

Three methods were tested for the detection of *like* as a DM: a simple rule-based filter, a part-of-speech tagger, and a decision-tree classifier trained on the available data. The last method, which provided the best results, was then applied to *well*.

Using first a list of collocations in order to filter out occurrences which are not DMs (e.g. *I like*, or *looks like*) we score 0.75 precision with 100% recall. A significant number of non pragmatic occurrences are thus correctly ruled out using quite a simple filter. Besides, none of the pragmatic uses was missed in the process.

Experiments with QTag, a probabilistic part-of-speech tagger [23], investigated whether the DMs could be disambiguated using POS tags, by filtering out the non-pragmatic uses, such as the cases when *like* is a verb and *well* an adverb. For the occurrences of *like*, QTag assigns mostly 'preposition' (1,412 occ.) and 'verb' (509 occ.) tags. When 'verb' is used to filter out non-DMs, recall is 0.77, precision is 0.38, accuracy 44%, and κ is only 0.02. Other interpretations of the tags do not lead to better results. The main reason that explains the failure of the tagger to detect DM uses of *like* is that it was trained only on written material.

Finally, we used the C4.5 decision tree learner (WEKA toolkit [24]) with 10-fold cross-validation of classifiers. For each occurrence of *like*, the following features were extracted automatically: (1) presence of a collocation that rules out the presence of a DM; (2) duration of the spoken word *like*; (3) duration of the pause before *like* (or initial *like*); (4) duration of the pause after *like* (or final *like*).

The best performance obtained by a C4.5 classifier is 0.95 recall and 0.68 precision for identifying DM occurrences of *like*, corresponding to 81% correctly classified instances and $\kappa = 0.63$. This is a significant performance, but it appears to be in the same range as the filter-based method. Indeed, the decision tree exhibits as the first nodes the two classes of collocation filters, thus offering a strong empirical proof of their relevance. The next feature in the tree is the duration of the pause before *like*: a relatively long pause before *like* characterizes a DM. The next features in the tree have quite a low precision, and may not generalize to other corpora.

The best classifier tends to show that apart from the collocation filters, the other features do not play an important role. Indeed, a classifier based only on the collocation filters achieves 0.96 recall and 0.67 precision for DM identification (80% correctly classified instances and $\kappa = 0.62$), which is only slightly below the best classifier. Is it that the time-based features are totally irrelevant? An experiment without the two collocation filters shows that temporal features *are* relevant, since the best classifier achieves 67% correct classification ($\kappa = 0.23$); but they are superseded by collocation-based features, when available.

The features defined for *well* are similar to those used for like: collocation-based filters and time-based features. The highest classification accuracy after training, 91% and $\kappa = 0.8$, is obtained by a decision tree combining the collocation filters and the duration of the pause after *well*. This corresponds to 91% precision and 97% recall for the DM detection task. Here again the collocation-based features provide the best classification but other time-based features alone also perform above chance.

For both DMs, the results suggest that time-based features could generalize to a whole class of DMs, though for individual DMs, such features are outperformed by collocations filters based on patterns of occurrences. Given the strong pragmatic function of DMs, it is unlikely that low-level features combined with machine learning will entirely solve the problem. However, even a partial classification could help improve SDA.

7   Conclusion and Perspectives on SDA

This paper has shown how a variety of machine learning techniques can be used to detect a set of features in dialogue transcripts. Three of the four shallow components of our model – dialogue acts, discourse markers of uncertainty, and topic segmentation – can be reliably learned from training data using statistical techniques. Two of these components are based on classifiers, but the instances to be classified are independent for DMs, and correlated for DAs. Topic segmentation requires, in a certain sense, the classification of sets of words, hence it makes use of different techniques. For one component – references to documents – machine learning did not appear, at this stage, to provide a tractable solution, since the correspondence between REs and DEs was better modelled by a set of hand-written rules. The various techniques are "shallow" as they do not build complex dialogue structures, and they process the dialogue flow quite linearly. They do not make use of complex linguistic knowledge, but of robust low-level features. Future work will study the possibility to extend the available linguistic resources without reducing coverage too much.

The components of the SDA model are in fact interdependent, which could allow for an integrated annotation mechanism. For instance, consecutive references to the same article often correspond to an episode, or episode boundaries are related to some types of dialogue acts. These relations must first be studied empirically, on manually annotated data. Then, components can be integrated using the following blackboard-style mechanism. Components can add annotations to the XML data, depending on existing annotations, but not to delete or change them, to avoid infinite loops. The SDA parser executes consecutively each component, which checks if the annotation has changed since it last processed it; if it has, then the component reprocesses the data, possibly adding new annotations. The process stops when no component is able to add new annotations.

New components should also be added to the SDA parser, based on ongoing studies of user needs and on tractability. Attention will be paid to annotations derived from other modalities, such as the use of facial expression for DA annotation.

The SDA annotations are the main features that are stored in a database of meetings, to allow meeting retrieval and browsing. Users can submit queries based on the SDA component features, to retrieve utterances from a dialogue and their context. The SDA annotations enable the production of a rich transcript of the meeting, which can be used for browsing, as a master modality that gives access to other modalities (e.g. audio and video), and in particular to the relevant meeting documents.

References

1. Armstrong, S., Clark, A., Coray, G., Georgescul, M., Pallotta, V., Popescu-Belis, A., Portabella, D., Rajman, M., Starlander, M.: Natural language queries on natural language data: a database of meeting dialogues. In: NLDB '03, Burg, Germany (2003) 14–27
2. Clark, A., Popescu-Belis, A.: Multi-level dialogue act tags. In: SIGDial '04, Cambridge, MA (2004) 163–170
3. Popescu-Belis, A., Lalanne, D.: Reference resolution over a restricted domain: References to documents. In: ACL'04 Workshop on Reference Resolution and its Applications, Barcelona (2004) 71–78
4. Zufferey, S., Popescu-Belis, A.: Towards automatic identification of discourse markers in dialogs: The case of like. In: SIGDial '04, Cambridge, MA (2004) 63–71
5. Morgan, N., Baron, D., Bhagat, S., Carvey, H., Dhillon, R., Edwards, J.A., Gelbart, D., Janin, A., Krupski, A., Peskin, B., Pfau, T., Shriberg, E., Stolcke, A., Wooters, C.: Meetings about meetings: research at ICSI on speech in multiparty conversations. In: ICASSP '03, Hong Kong, China (2003)
6. Barras, C., Geoffrois, E., Wu, Z., Liberman, M.: Transcriber: development and use of a tool for assisting speech corpora production. Speech Comm. **33** (2001) 5–22
7. Popescu-Belis, A., Georgescul, M., Clark, A., Armstrong, S.: Building and using a corpus of shallow dialogue annotated meetings. In: LREC 2004, Lisbon, Portugal (2004) 1451–1454
8. McCowan, I., Bengio, S., Gatica-Perez, D., Lathoud, G., Monay, F., Moore, D., Wellner, P., Bourlard, H.: Modeling human interaction in meetings. In: ICASSP 2003, Hong Kong, China (2003)
9. Shriberg, E., Dhillon, R., Bhagat, S., Ang, J., Carvey, H.: The ICSI meeting recorder dialog act (MRDA) corpus. In: SIGDial '04, Cambridge, MA (2004) 97–100

10. Galley, M., McKeown, K., Fosler-Lussier, E., Jing, H.: Discourse segmentation of multi-party conversation. In: ACL '03, Sapporo, Japan (2003) 562–569
11. Traum, D.R.: 20 questions for dialogue act taxonomies. Journal of Semantics **17** (2000) 7–30
12. Allen, J.F., Core, M.G.: DAMSL: Dialog act markup in several layers. Technical Report draft 2.1, Multiparty Discourse Group, Discourse Research Initiative (1997)
13. Jurafsky, D., Shriberg, E., Biasca, D.: Switchboard SWBD-DAMSL shallow discourse function annotation: Coders manual. Technical Report 97-02, draft 13, Univ. of Colorado, Inst. of Cognitive Science (1997)
14. Stolcke, A., Ries, K., Coccaro, N., Shriberg, E., Bates, R., Jurafsky, D., Taylor, P., Martin, R., Meteer, M., Van Ess-Dykema, C.: Dialogue act modeling for automatic tagging and recognition of conversational speech. Comp. Ling. **26** (2000) 339–371
15. Dhillon, R., Bhagat, S., Carvey, H., Shriberg, E.: Meeting recorder project: Dialog act labeling guide. Technical Report TR-04-002, ICSI, Berkeley, CA (2004)
16. Carletta, J., Isard, A., Isard, S., Kowtko, J.C., Doherty-Sneddon, G., Anderson, A.H.: The reliability of a dialogue structure coding scheme. Comp. Ling. **23** (1997) 13–31
17. Choi, F.Y.Y.: Advances in domain independent linear text segmentation. In: NAACL 2000, Seattle, WA, USA (2000) 26–33
18. Bellegarda, J.R.: Exploiting latent semantic information in statistical language modeling. In: Proceedings of the IEEE. Volume 88. (2000) 1279–1296
19. Dumais, S.: Improving the retrieval of information from external sources. Behavior Research Methods, Instruments and Computers **23** (1991) 229–236
20. Berry, M.W.: Large scale singular value computations. International Journal of Supercomputer Applications **6** (1992) 13–49
21. Beeferman, D., Berger, A., Lafferty, J.: Statistical models for text segmentation. Mach. Learn. **34** (1999) 177–210
22. Hadjar, K., Rigamonti, M., Lalanne, D., Ingold, R.: Xed: a new tool for extracting hidden structures from electronic documents. In: Workshop on Document Image Analysis for Libraries, Palo Alto, CA (2004)
23. Mason, O.: Programming for Corpus Linguistics: How to do Text Analysis in Java. Edinburgh University Press, Edinburgh, UK (2000)
24. Witten, I., Frank, E.: Data Mining: Practical Machine Learning Tools with Java Implementations. Morgan Kaufmann, San Francisco, CA (2000)

ARCHIVUS: A System for Accessing the Content of Recorded Multimodal Meetings

Agnes Lisowska[1], Martin Rajman[2], and Trung H. Bui[3]

[1] ISSCO/TIM/ETI, University of Geneva, 40 Bv. du Pont-d'Arve, 1211 Geneva, Switzerland
Agnes.Lisowska@issco.unige.ch
[2,3] CGC/IC, LIA/IIF/IC, Swiss Federal Institute of Technology Lausanne,
Bat. INR, 1015 Lausanne, Switzerland
{Martin.Rajman, Trung.Bui}@epfl.ch

Abstract. This paper describes a multimodal dialogue driven system, ARCHIVUS, that allows users to access and retrieve the content of recorded and annotated multimodal meetings. We describe (1) a novel approach taken in designing the system given the relative inapplicability of standard user requirements elicitation methodologies, (2) the components of ARCHIVUS, and (3) the methodologies that we plan to use to evaluate the system.

1 Introduction

In this paper we describe a multimodal system, ARCHIVUS, which allows users to access and retrieve the content of stored multimodal meetings, either through directed search or browsing. Section 2 describes our particular approach to design, including the reasoning behind the choice of elements in the system and the initial user requirements on which the design is based. Section 3 explains the input and output modalities used in the system. Section 4 explains the interaction metaphor that we have chosen for ARCHIVUS, while section 5 provides a more detailed look at how the metaphor is implemented in the system. Section 6 describes the dialogue model that will be implemented, and the ARCHIVUS dialogue management strategy. Section 7 discusses the types of data the system is capable of accessing and the data that will be used in the early stages of system development for testing purposes. Section 8 discusses how we intend to evaluate and further refine the system, while section 9 provides a brief overview of work that is planned for the near future.

2 Approach to Design

ARCHIVUS was conceived with the intent of providing users with a convenient, intuitive and multimodal means to access processed and stored recorded multimodal meetings. Currently, records of meetings are stored primarily in text format as transcripts or meeting minutes. Only occasionally can audio, and even less frequently video, records be found. Moreover, rarely are these records stored in the unified, searchable and multimedia manner proposed in the multimodal meeting domain. This fact imposes significant limitations on how the data can currently be manipulated and

S. Bengio and H. Bourlard (Eds.): MLMI 2004, LNCS 3361, pp. 291–304, 2005.

reviewed. The multimodal meeting domain strips those limitations. However, one cannot assume that all of the wide range of modalities and media made available in this domain will be useful to real users in real life situations to the same extent. Consequently, the realistic needs of the users themselves must be carefully considered and accounted for in system design from the earliest stages.

While there are several known methodologies for designing software from the human computer interaction perspective [1], they all address cases where the way in which a human performs the task that the software is intended to facilitate or replace is already well known and well defined. We believe that for the multimodal meeting domain these methodologies are to a large extent simply not applicable. Potential users of a system such as ARCHIVUS have little or no prior experience with the types of tasks that the system avails. Thus, one of the first challenges was to determine how to gather a set of valid user requirements for a system enabling a task that is unfamiliar to the user.

The approach to requirements gathering that we have taken with the preliminary design of the ARCHIVUS system is driven by informed/grounded intuition. In a first attempt at developing user requirements for the multimodal meeting domain, IM2 [2] project members developed a set of natural language 'queries', or potential questions to the system. These 'queries' were meant to be indicative, at an abstract level, of the types of functionality that the system would need to account for. The results can be found at [3]. However, the query set was both potentially biased (due to the fact that all of the participants were directly involved in the project) and hard to analyze, due to a lack of a coherent set of guidelines for outlining the context.

In order to overcome these two problems, a second, more principled study was performed where the participants included both those involved and uninvolved in the IM2 project, and included individuals coming from a wider variety of backgrounds, ranging from physicians to administrators. Additionally, to facilitate analysis of the results, the second study was structured in such a way that each participant was asked to imagine themselves in one of four potential use cases – a manager tracking project progress, a manager tracking employee performance, a new employee needing to get background on a project, and an employee who has missed a meeting about a project that they were involved in. We believe that these four use cases, in addition to that of a person wanting to verify a specific fact, are likely to be the most common cases in which users might need the ARCHIVUS system and consequently, they provide a sound framework in which to situate our work. A detailed discussion of the results of this study can be found in [4]. We believe that the user requirements that can be extrapolated from careful analysis of the queries, coupled with standard design principles and our own intuitions, serve as a sufficient starting point for the design of the preliminary version of ARCHIVUS.

Finally, the platform and environment for which we are designing the first versions of the ARCHIVUS system is that of a laptop or desktop PC used in an office environment. This decision was based on two facts. The first is that a PC environment reduces learning curves introduced by new hardware. The second is that while the use of PDAs and mobile phones is rapidly gaining popularity we are not convinced that the general population is sufficiently familiar with their use for information browsing and retrieval, nor that the devices are powerful enough to handle the information types in question. However, modification of the ARCHIVUS interface for use on handheld devices may be investigated in future work.

3 Modalities in ARCHIVUS

One of the key aims of ARCHIVUS is to provide flexible and consistent access to a variety of modalities in order to allow the user to interact with the system in the way that is most comfortable for them. This implies that all input modalities should be consistently and completely interchangeable. The user should always be able to use any of the modalities in any context and have the option of naturally changing between them if they find that communication using one of the modalities is not yielding the required results.

In the preliminary version of the system we are planning the inclusion of three active input modalities, one passive input modality, and three output modalities. The three active input modalities are voice, pointing (either through a mouse or a touch screen) and text (keyboard). The passive modality is emotion recognition, which will be used to detect the emotional state of the user and modify the dialogue strategy accordingly. The output modalities will include graphics, sound and text.

When incorporating the results of automatic speech recognition (ASR) into a system (in our case the speech input), the robustness of that system in the face of common problems encountered with ASR is called into question. In our work, we assume that the data being accessed, even if has been gathered using ASR, will have been checked and corrected by humans (at least until ASR technology provides adequate results). However, robustness of the system in the face of real ASR results can be tested using a noise generator, which simulates varying degrees of noise in text. Using the generator, we can test acceptability thresholds for ASR errors given the availability of different modality combinations. Finally, we believe that the simultaneous availability of various input modalities will also allow the user to overcome ASR problems by allowing them to actively supplement the voice modality with other modalities.

4 The ARCHIVUS Metaphor

Interaction metaphors are often used in interface design to explain to a user, in terms and concepts with which they are already familiar, how to interact with an unfamiliar application and what its functionalities might be [1]. As explained in section 2, many of the specific functionalities offered by the ARCHIVUS system will be unfamiliar to users, so it was vital to find a suitable metaphor in which to situate the system.

The metaphor that we have chosen is that of a person using an archive or library to find the information they are looking for. We believe that this metaphor will help users naturally discover and exploit the full capabilities of the system. We have found that meetings can be mapped quite easily and naturally to the content of a standard book and that a database of meetings can be mapped to the structure of a library. Moreover, we believe that the metaphor can be extended to sufficiently cover all foreseen interface functionalities.

Thus, in ARCHIVUS, the database of stored meetings is represented by a series of bookcases, each of which contains representations of meetings that are available in the database. Each individual meeting is represented as a book, and a set of related meetings as volumes of a series. The title of the book becomes the subject of a meeting, while the authors are the meeting participants. The publisher's information page can contain the time, date and location of the meeting, as well as the institutes that were involved. The table of contents corresponds to the agenda of the meeting, listing the topics of the meeting. Chapters in the book always represent individual topics in a meeting, chapter sections reflect the dialogue structure of the topic, and individual paragraphs are the specific utterances that participants make. The appendix represents a list of the documents that were used or referred to during the meeting, while the index is a list of keywords from the meeting.

Finally, while the user is interacting with the system, they will have access to an electronic notebook into which they can copy relevant sections of a meeting for future reference, or make online notes, just like the users of a regular library might have a notebook in which to write down their findings.

5   The ARCHIVUS Interface

The ARCHIVUS system has been designed as a hybrid search and browsing system. We feel that this combination of interaction paradigms is the best solution to suit the user needs for this domain and maximize the flexibility of the system in terms of the types of interactions that it allows and the level of detail of information that becomes available to the user. Moreover, searching in ARCHIVUS can be done in one of two ways. The first is through constraint satisfaction, where the user imposes constraints on the search space until the latter is sufficiently reduced to provide a single solution, or in the worst case, a small set of solutions. The other search approach uses linguistic analysis of a natural language question posed to the system to drive a keyword based search and return relevant results.

The results of either of these searches, and in many cases of the browsing as well, can be viewed on several levels. The highest, global, level is represented on the bookcase. In this case, the search has been underspecified and there remain a large number of meetings that meet the criteria. These meetings are active and visible on the bookcase. The second, local, level is the case where only a single meeting matches the search criteria. In this case, the relevant meeting is shown in the interaction area. The final case is at the target-specific level, where the search results yield a particular section of a meeting. Here, the result is that the relevant section of the meeting is shown directly.

Furthermore, while we consider our system to be dialogue based, it is not dialogue in the strictly traditional sense of the word. In the ARCHIVUS system, dialogue can also refer to an 'interactive dialogue' – a set of interactions between the user and the system that are not necessarily rooted in speech. This distinction is important since in ARCHIVUS, the user has constant access to any of the three primary modalities (voice, text and pointing) and can use any of them in any combination, or interchangeably, without affecting the interactive dialogue.

The user interface itself can be divided into seven general areas, show graphically in figure 1 and explained in detail in the following sections.

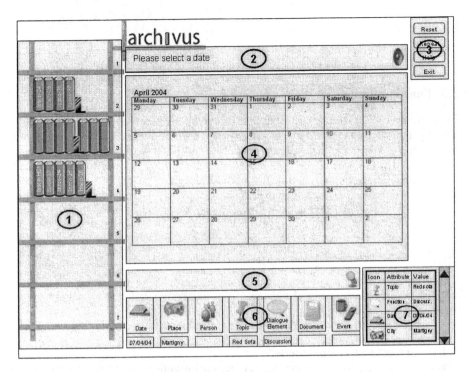

Fig. 1. The overall interface

5.1 Bookcase

The bookcase area serves two primary purposes. The first is to provide an overview of the entire database to the user. All of the meetings in the database will be represented as books on the bookcase. This global database representation gives the user constant and active feedback of the effects of their searches and criteria on the database, which can guide them in further decision-making and refinement steps. The feedback is provided through the use of shading, where brighter coloured books are those that are active (still fit the search criteria), while those that are dimmed are inactive (no longer fit the search criteria). Finally, books that are related are grouped together whenever possible, and are separated from other books by bookends.

The second purpose of the bookcase is to allow the user to browse the database without having to interact with the search/dialogue engine. It should be kept in mind that browsing can be done using any of the available modalities, including voice. When browsing, the user can select any of the meetings at any time, in which case they open in the interactive display area (5.4). Furthermore, the user can sort the meetings by changing the labels on the legs and shelves of the bookcase. The specific default settings for bookcase labels and the exact nature of the user's interaction with the bookcase will be determined over the course of the user-centered evaluation experiments described in section 8.

5.2   Prompt Bar

The prompt bar is used to visually display all prompts from the system. A "speaker" icon on the right-hand side indicates the availability of speech output.

5.3   Function Buttons

In the upper right-hand corner of the interface there are four function buttons – three directly related to the dialogue mode (*Reset, Help,* and *Repeat*), and one system button (*Exit*). When the *Reset* button is selected, all of the constraints that have been accumulated during a dialogue are erased and the system is reset to accept a new query. The *Repeat* button enables the user to hear the last prompt again, in cases where they misheard or misunderstood it. The *Help* button provides access to online help which explains the functionalities available in the interface, while the *Exit* button quits the ARCHIVUS system altogether.

5.4   Interactive Display Area

This area serves three purposes depending on the point of the interaction at which the user finds themselves; a visual display of the interactive dialogue mode, a space in which to view a meeting book, and a space in which to view multimedia elements of the database such as video and accompanying documents.

5.4.1   Interactive Dialogue Mode

When the user selects one of the criteria refinement buttons (see 5.6), the interactive dialogue mode is launched and a visual representation of the current state of the dialogue appears in the interactive display area. For example, a calendar showing possible meeting dates is displayed when the *Date* button is selected (see Fig. 1).

5.4.2   Viewing a Meeting Book

When the user has reached the book level, we expect that they will primarily be browsing the meeting. As was mentioned in section 4, a book is the representation of the meeting and consequently all aspects of the meeting should be accessible by interacting with the book. Figure 2 shows a meeting book in the ARCHIVUS system. The top line indicates the name of the meeting and the current chapter being viewed. The utterances of each participant are colour-coded to facilitate browsing. Notes in the margin indicate the name of the speaker of an utterance (much as in a play), and the presence of any accompanying documents related to an utterance or set of utterances is indicated by the document icon. The user can move through the pages of the book using the next/previous arrow buttons.

To either hear the original audio soundtrack from a part of the meeting or view the video, the user selects the appropriate audio/video icon at the bottom of the page, and then selects the utterance that they wish to hear/see. The audio/video playback will start at the selected utterance and continue until the user explicitly stops the playback.

Tabs are used to allow the user to jump to different sections of the book. The tabs on the right-hand side of the book provide links to the constant elements found in all books such as the cover, the table of contents, the index and the appendix. The tabs on the left-hand side of the book change dynamically and represent the individual 'hits' in the book that fit the current search criteria. Each of these tabs is numbered in x/y format where x is the number of the hit and y is the total number of hits in the book.

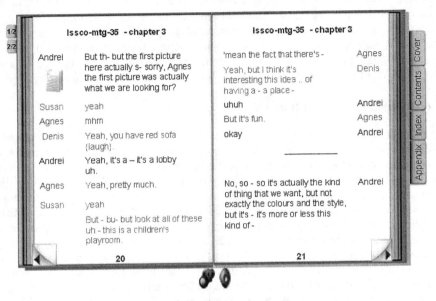

Fig. 2. An ARCHIVUS 'meeting'

Additionally, within a page, the section that is most relevant to a particular query will be 'highlighted'. Thus, if the query asks to find a discussion about some topic, the entire discussion will be highlighted, where this highlight can span several pages if the discussion happens to be long. This mechanism also allows for high level browsing of the book if the user wishes to view information at a more abstract level than that of individual utterances. The table of contents, index and appendix will be reminiscent of a web-page, where entries such as chapters, keywords and documents are clickable, and clicking on them automatically takes the user to the relevant part of the book, or opens the relevant document in the viewing area.

5.4.3 Viewing Video, Audio and Documents

The viewing area also serves to display multimedia such as video and electronic documents. Standard VCR style buttons will be used to control video and audio, while traversing documents will follow a web-like style. The viewing area, in relation to the examination of particular documents, will also allow for the incorporation of work being done by the IM2.DI group at the University of Fribourg, where they are working on interactively linking segments of documents to the part of the meeting where those segments were discussed [5]. Consequently, interacting with a document should affect the view of the book that the user has. For example, clicking on another section of the document might take the user to a different page in the book from the one from which the document was initially launched.

5.5 User Input Box

The user input box is where the user can either type an information request, or, in the case of speech input, the results of the speech recognition software appear. This area effectively allows the user to initiate a natural language driven directed search, where the user already has some idea of the information that they are seeking and poses a specific request for information to the system. Additionally, the microphone icon on the right side of the box indicates the availability of voice as an input modality.

5.6 Criteria Refinement Buttons

In order to help refine a request during the dialogue mode the interface is equipped with criteria refinement buttons. These buttons, selectable using any of the three input modalities, help the user refine a particular request. There are seven criteria refinement buttons planned for the current version of ARCHIVUS. *Place* allows the user to specify the location of a meeting. *People* shows the user the possible attributes of people that they can search on such as first name, family name, function, affiliation or photo. *Date,* allows the user to search by year, month, day and am/pm. *Topic* shows the user possible topics to search for, and indicates the keywords and meetings associated with the topic. *Dialogue Elements*, allows the user to launch a search for specific aspects of a dialogue such as discussion, argumentation, questions, decision making etc. *Events*, allows the user to search for events such as people leaving the room, mobile phones ringing, people drinking etc. *Documents* allows the user to specify the type of document to search for such as presentation slides, notes, whiteboard activity, and electronic versions of paper artifacts from the meeting.

5.7 History Area

A well-known HCI design principle is that the user should always be able to follow and backtrack along the path which they used to reach a particular point in their interaction. To this end we provide the history area, which shows the user, in iconified and textual form, the constraints that they have imposed in order to reach their goal. The content of the history will be represented in a scrollable pane in reverse chronological order.

6 Dialogue System

The multimodal dialogue system for ARCHIVUS will be based on the Rapid Dialogue Prototyping Methodology (RDPM) [6] developed at the EPFL's Artificial Intelligence Laboratory. The general idea underlying the proposed RDPM is that the dialogue model is a finite-state model that can be quite easily and systematically derived from a relational representation of the application itself, hereafter called the *task model*. More precisely, the RPDM consists of five main consecutive steps: (1) *producing a task model* for the targeted application; (2) automatically *deriving an initial dialogue model (and the associated multimodal dialogue-driven interface)* from the produced task model; (3) using the generated interface to *carry out Wizard-of-Oz experiments* (i.e. dialogue simulations) to improve the initial dialogue model; (4) *carrying out an internal field test* to further refine the dialogue model (reformulation of system messages, improved feedback, etc.), and validate the evaluation procedure (coherence, understandability); and (5) *carrying out an external field test* to evaluate the final dialogue model. In the following sub-sections, steps 1 and 2 will be described in the ARCHIVUS context. Steps 3, 4, and 5 are described in [6] and section 8.

6.1 Producing the Task Model

In the RDPM, an application is seen as a set of functions the user can invoke through the multimodal interface to perform the various functionalities provided by the application. In this perspective, an application is modeled as a set of relational tables, where the rows correspond to the possible functions (also called "solutions" or "targets") and the columns are the attributes needed to uniquely identify each of the functions, and to invoke it.

In other words, the values of the attributes in a row of the solution table (also referred to as *canonical values*) correspond to the values of the arguments of the function, the call of which results in the fulfillment of the corresponding application functionality. For example, in the IM2 domain the task model can reduce to a single generic function select_meeting(name, place, participants,…), the attributes of which identify the selection features available for the meeting search. Therefore, the task model of the IM2 project is simply a table with as many columns as there are attributes, the rows of which are the various value combinations corresponding to existing meetings. At the computational level, the calls to the select_meeting() function are implemented in the form of SQL queries to the project database containing the required information.

Notice that the current version of the RDPM presupposes that the task model consists of a single relational table, also called the *solution table*. However, in the case of more complex models consisting of several interconnected tables (for example a main table containing the acceptable value combinations of the main attributes and several additional tables relating the values present in the main table to additional attributes), standard database normalization procedures (such as join operations) can first be applied to transform the original tables into a single (eventually large) one.

6.2 Dialogue Model

In our approach, a dialogue model is defined as a set of interconnected multimodal Generic Dialogue Nodes (referred to as mGDNs, [i.e. 7]), where each of the dialogue nodes is associated with one of the attributes (also called "slots" or "fields") in the solution table. In complex applications such as ARCHIVUS, these mGDNs are divided into groups, where each group element is considered as an object and the mGDNs in the group are attributes of the object. For example, the *First Name*, *Last Name*, and *Function* mGDNs belong to the *Person* group. For any given slot, the role of the associated mGDN is to perform the simple interaction with the user that is required to obtain a valid value for the associated attribute.

In the architecture that we have selected for the implementation of our multimodal dialogue-driven interfaces, the processing of the mGDNs (i.e. the actual interaction with the user according to the specification of the mGDNs) is performed by a specific module called the *local dialogue manager*. However, this is not sufficient to carry out any real dialogue: some form of global dialogue management also has to be integrated. For example, in addition to the definition of the mGDNs and the specification of the local dialogue manager, some branching logic responsible for the management of the global dialogue flow needs to be specified. In our approach, this branching logic is hard-coded in a specific dialogue management module, called the *global dialogue manager*. The underlying assumption is that the encoded local and global dialogue flow management strategies are indeed application-independent, i.e. that, in most situations, they lead to an acceptable, though not always optimal behavior for the system. Consequently, in our approach, dialogue model design essentially reduces to the application-dependent, declarative specification of the mGDNs, the encoded dialogue management strategies being used without modification for all applications.

6.3 Multimodal GENERIC Dialogue Nodes – mGDNs

Each mGDN is designed to support three active modes - text, voice, and gesture - which are used either simultaneously or independently depending on the configuration of the mGDN. The output of an mGDN consists of semantic pairs of the form (attribute name, attribute value). Therefore, a fusion mechanism (i.e. local fusion module) needs to be used inside each mGDN to combine the specific output produced by each of the input modalities and to produce the validated output semantic pairs.

To deal with the various attributes appearing in the solution table defining the task model, we consider three main types of mGDNs: (1) Simple mGDNs (also called static mGDNs) associated with *static fields*, (2) List Processing mGDNs (also called dynamic mGDNs) associated with *dynamic fields,* and (3) Internal mGDNs, used to perform the interactions that are required by various special functions implemented in the dialogue manager (e.g. confirm a selected solution, start/reset the dialogue, etc.).

As already mentioned, the role of each mGDN is to perform a simple interaction with the user to obtain a valid value for the associated attribute. In this perspective, the difference between static and dynamic mGDNs is that the former are expecting the user to directly provide a value for the associated attribute. For example, a static mGDN associated with the "Location" attribute might ask a question such as "*What location are you looking for?*" and will be expecting an answer containing a value taken from a predefined list of values such as "*Lausanne*", "*Geneva*" or "*Martigny*". On the other hand, a dynamic mGDN will ask the user to choose from a dynamically computed list of values. For example, a dynamic mGDN associated with the "Topics" attribute will generate a list of topics and ask the user to indicate the position of their selection in the list. The List Processing mGDNs are an important component of the targeted dialogue model as they allow efficiently taking into account dynamic vocabularies that could not be reliably processed by simple mGDNs because of the limited performance of the speech recognition module in such conditions. To realize the interaction for which it is responsible, each mGDN contains two main types of components: multimedia prompts and grammars.

Multimedia prompts: Multimedia prompts contain messages and a pointing zone. The messages are visualized in the user interface and/or uttered by the mGDN during the interaction and are combined with a pointing zone (the content of which is a map, calendar or table depending on the nature of the mGDN) to allow the user to provide the desired values using keyboard, microphone or mouse click/touch screen. Several types of prompts are defined, among which are the main prompt, corresponding to the initial question asked by the mGDN, and the help prompt that is uttered/visualized if a request for help is expressed by the user. The formulation of the prompts plays an important role during the dialogue. In particular, it influences the level of *mixed initiative* (i.e. the degree of flexibility that the system allows in the interaction). For instance, a main prompt such as *"What are you looking for?"* expresses the fact that the system is ready to accept a broad range of user requests, while a more precise prompt such as *"Do you want to select a meeting, yes or no?"* implies a low level of mixed initiative as the user is only expected to answer either *yes* or *no*.

Grammars: The role of the grammars is to make the connection between the surface forms in the natural language utterances made by the users and the canonical values used in the task model (the set of values defined for the attributes associated with the mGDNs in the solution table for the application). As such, the grammars represent the main Natural Language Processing elements in the system, and might also be used in the speech recognition engine to improve recognition quality.

Finally, each mGDN is always associated with some specific global grammars such as the help and repetition grammars. These grammars correspond to *Request for Help* and *Request for Repetition* situations which are mentioned in the next section.

6.4 Local Dialogue Flow Management Strategy

Each mGDN is able to locally process five types of generic situations: (1) *OK*: the user answers the question in an acceptable way; (2) *Request for Repetition*: the user asks for repetition of the last system prompt; (3) *Request for Help*: the user does not know how to answer the question and asks for an explanation; (4) *NoInput*: the user neither produces an utterance nor uses other input modalities; and (5) *NoMatch*: the user answers but nothing useful can be extracted from any of the input modalities.

In the case of the *OK* situation, control is simply handed back to the global dialogue manager which applies the global dialogue management strategy for the activation of the next mGDN. In the other four situations, control remains at the mGDN level. In these "problematic" cases, there is, therefore, a need to repair the dialogue and the system operates in the following way: (a) *Request for Repetition*: the current mGDN is reactivated and its main prompt is played if it is the first request for repetition, otherwise a reformulated prompt is played; (b) *Request for Help*: the mGDN is reactivated and the associated help prompt is played instead of the main prompt; and (c) *NoInput/NoMatch*: the current mGDN is reactivated and the NoInput/NoMatch prompt is concatenated at the beginning of the main prompt.

6.5 Global Dialogue Flow Management Strategy

Global Dialogue Flow Management (GDFM) consists of several complementary strategies:

- a branching strategy (also called *branching logic*) defining the next mGDN to be activated;
- a dialogue dead-end management strategy to deal with dialogue situations where no solution corresponds to the request expressed by the user;

- a confirmation strategy to provide the system with validation possibilities for the values acquired during the interaction;
- a dialogue termination strategy to define when the interaction with the user should be terminated (i.e. a solution proposed); and
- a strategy to deal with incoherencies (i.e. situations where there are at least two incompatible values provided by the user).

As already mentioned, all these strategies are encoded in the global dialogue manager and are, therefore, application-independent. These strategies are explained in more detail in [6]. Additionally, our dialogue manager can work either in system-driven or mixed initiative mode. We therefore use the information from the passive modality (i.e. emotion recognition) to automatically and smoothly alternate between the two modes to enhance natural communication between the system and the user.

7 ARCHIVUS Data

The data that the ARCHIVUS system will access is expected to be stored audio, video, electronic copies of all documents used in the meetings (including presentation slides, paper artifacts, whiteboard activity and participants notes), as well as annotated transcripts of the meetings, stored in XML format. In the preliminary stages of system development and user testing, the data that we will be using is a set of four meetings recorded by members of the IM2.MDM IP [8] in the IDIAP Smart Meeting room [9]. The topic, spanning all four meetings, is the furnishing of a lounge/reading room for use by the staff of a university research group. This topic, or scenario, was chosen with the particular view of performing user-centered evaluation of the system as it is easy to relate to for most users, which will help them maintain interest in the content of the meeting. This is important in order to ensure that the evaluation reflects a true evaluation of the system and not an evaluation biased by the interestingness of the data accessed. For similar reasons, the selected meetings have been kept natural in the interactions that they include, but have at the same time been refereed in such a way that factors that might affect the evaluators' cognitive involvement in the task, such as excessive cross-talk, have been avoided.

This data will be transcribed and annotated manually. The annotations will be based on a combination of tags outlined in the MALTUS tagset [10], and additional meta-tags, indicating non-dialogue or non-textual events, such as when someone left the room, which will be determined based on the types of meta-information that were requested in the query set gathered during the user requirements elicitation study described in section 2.

8 Evaluation

As with the design and development of most software and interfaces, our evaluation process will be highly iterative. In our case this is particularly necessary since, as mentioned, determining a priori user requirements poses difficulties. Consequently, the evaluation stage will serve two purposes; 1) evaluation of the system in the traditional sense of evaluating its performance and ensuring that users can interact smoothly with it, and 2) the continued gathering and refinement of user requirements.

Given the uncertainty of the validity of the user requirements that we have gathered and the fact that the implementation of all levels of desired flexibility in the software and interface would be extremely costly, we have decided to adopt the Wizard of Oz (WOz) experiment methodology to our domain. The WOz methodology [11, 12], originally developed in the natural language processing community, is based on the notion that a user interacts with a system that has not been fully implemented. The user, however, is not aware of this fact and believes that they are interacting with a fully functional system. In reality, a human controller, known as a wizard, fills in the parts of the system that are missing.

This methodology allows both of the aforementioned evaluation goals to be met simultaneously. A user interacting with the system will be actively testing the already functional components of the system, thus satisfying the standard system evaluation aspect. At the same time, having the wizard supplement additional functionality allows the testing of design theories without having to implement them, and allows for the addition of functionalities 'on the fly'. Allowing for unforeseen actions lets developers explore new avenues of design and their feasibility in the system almost immediately, both in terms of integration into the system, and usefulness to the user. New functionalities and queries from each iteration will be integrated into the existing set of user requirements, and considered in future stages of refinement and development of the system.

Once a stable and complete ARCHIVUS system is developed, we hope to compare the performance of ARCHIVUS to other interfaces and browsers designed for the same domain, such as the Ferret Meeting Browser [13] being developed at IDIAP. In order to perform such a comparative test we plan to use the Browser Evaluation Test scheme proposed in [14].

9 Future Work

Development of the ARCHIVUS system is currently in progress. Four modules of the user interface have been partially completed (input from the keyboard, dialogue output prompt, bookcase, and pointing zone). The data described in section 8 has been transcribed and is now being annotated in detail. The immediate next steps will be completion of the implementation of the system, the development of a suitable Wizard of Oz testing environment, and an initial round of evaluation.

Acknowledgements

We would like to thank the Swiss National Science Foundation NCCR, the University of Geneva and the Ecole Polytechnique Federal de Lausanne (EPFL) for their support in funding this work, as well as Marcin Bogobowicz for his graphic arts skills.

References

1. Dix, A., J. Finlay, G. Abowd and R. Beale, *Human Computer Interaction* Second Edition, Prentice Hall, England, 1998.
2. IM2 webpage http://www.im2.ch/e/home.html
3. IM2.MDM webpage http://issco-www.unige.ch/projects/im2/mdm/
4. A. Lisowska, "Multimodal Interface Design for the Multimodal Meeting Domain: Preliminary Indications from a Query Analysis Study", Report IM2.MDM-11, Nov. 2003.
5. D. Mekhaldi, D. Lalanne and R. Ingold. "Thematic Alignment of recorded speech with documents", DocEng 2003, ACM Symposium on Document Engineering, Grenoble, 2003.
6. T. H. Bui and M. Rajman "Rapid Dialogue Prototyping Methodology", Technical Report No. 200401, Swiss Federal Institute of Technology, Lausanne (Switzerland), January, 2004.
7. E. Bilange, *Dialogue personne-machine, modélisation et réalisation informatique,* Langue, Raisonnement, Calcul, Hermès, Paris, France, 1992.
8. IM2 newsletter, May 2004.
9. D. Moore, "The IDIAP Smart Meeting Room", IDIAP-Com 02-07, 2002
10. A. Popescu-Belis, "Dialogue act tagsets for meeting understanding: an abstraction based on the DAMSL, Switchboard and ICSI-MR tagsets", Report IM2.MDM-09, September 2003.
11. N. Dahlbäck, A. Jönsson and L. Ahrenberg, "Wizard of Oz Studies – Why and How", in W.D. Gray, W.E. Helfley and Murray, D. (eds). Proceedings of the 1993 Workshop on Intelligent User Interfaces (pp. 193/200) Orlando, FL. New York, ACM Press, 1993.
12. D. Salber, and J Coutaz, "Applying the Wizard of Oz technique to the study of Multimodal Systems", 3rd International Conference EWHCI'93, East/West Human Computer Interaction, Moscow. L. Bass, J. Gornostaev, C. Unger Eds. Springer Verlag Publ. Lecture notes in Computer Science, Vol. 73. pp. 219-230. 1993.
13. Ferret Meeting Browser http://rhonedata.idiap.ch/documentation/Ferret_User_Guide/help.html
14. M. Flynn and P. Wellner, "In Search of a Good BET", IDIAP-Com 03-11, 2003.

Piecing Together the Emotion Jigsaw

Roddy Cowie[1] and Marc Schröder[2]

[1] Psychology, Queen's University,
Belfast BT7 1NN, Northern Ireland
r.cowie@qub.ac.uk
http://www.psych.qub.ac.uk/
[2] DFKI GmbH,
Language Technology Lab,
Stuhlsatzenhausweg 3,
D-66123 Saarbrücken, Germany
schroed@dfki.de
http://www.dfki.de/lt/index.html

Abstract. People are emotional, and machines are not. That constrains their communication, and defines a key challenge for the information sciences. Different groups have addressed it from different angles, trying to develop methods of detecting emotion, agents that convey emotion, systems that predict behaviour in emotional circumstances, and so on. Progress has been limited. The new network of excellence HUMAINE explores the idea that progress depends on addressing the problem as a whole, not in isolated fragments.

1 Introduction

There is a growing sense that Information Technology should be addressing various issues linked to human emotion [1]. The EC has backed that view by funding a Network of Excellence called HUMAINE, which began in January 2004 and runs until December 2007. HUMAINE is charged with laying sound foundations for emotion-sensitive computing in Europe. It is governed by a 'technical annex' agreed with the EC, and the academic sections of it are available on the HUMAINE portal [2].

One of the ideas behind HUMAINE is that the area needs to develop strategies. It is often fair to take a purely tactical approach, based on seeing opportunities to make a small advance and seizing them. Experience suggests that that approach may not work well in the area of emotion-sensitive computing. One of the reasons is the sheer range of issues that need to be handled in a co-ordinated way in order to reach first base. Another may be that people come to the field with strong preconceptions about emotion, which direct their attention away from issues that are actually vital to progress. Part of the role of strategy is to offer protection against the pull of ideas that are deeply ingrained, but misleading.

The aim of this paper is to sketch an overview of the strategic issues. It draws on the framework of the HUMAINE proposal and discussions within the project, but it is not a statement of HUMAINE's position. In effect, it is an input to the debate, within HUMAINE and beyond, that will be needed to define a strategy capable of commanding wide acceptance.

S. Bengio and H. Bourlard (Eds.): MLMI 2004, LNCS 3361, pp. 305–317, 2005.

2 Clarifying the Subject Matter

One of the strategic challenges to HUMAINE is to provide clear ways of understanding the domain to be addressed, and talking about it. The issue arises because the word 'emotion' has many senses, corresponding to a variety of concepts that people intuitively use in thinking about the domain of emotion-related phenomena [3],[4],[5]. In that kind of area, relying uncritically on everyday terms and concepts is an invitation to confusion and/or misdirection.

The network adopted a general position which is stated early in the HUMAINE Technical Annex [2]:

> 'We [will] consider emotion in an inclusive sense rather than in the narrow sense of episodes where a strong rush of feeling briefly dominates a person's awareness. ... emotion in the broad sense pervades human communication and cognition. Human beings have positive or negative feelings about most things, people, events and symbols. These feelings strongly influence the way they attend, behave, plan, learn and select.'

It is worth stressing the distinction because there are pressures that encourage research to focus on emotion in the narrow sense; and yet in the long term, it is the broad sense that is more likely to matter for technology.

Part of the response is to establish a vocabulary that makes the key distinctions easy to keep in view. Various options have been discussed in HUMAINE meetings, and the process is ongoing. Among the obvious options at this stage are terms derived directly from the passage cited above – 'episodic emotion' and 'pervasive emotion'.

'Episodic emotions' seems an appropriate way to describe states where emotion dominates people's awareness, usually for a relatively short time, by affecting their perceptions, feelings, and inclinations. The emotion may not determine the action that the person takes, but it requires effort to prevent it from doing so. Clear-cut episodic emotional states are not only relatively brief, but also relatively rare – at least among average people under average circumstances.

In contrast, 'pervasive emotion' refers to something that is an integral part of most mental states, if not all, including states where rationality seems subjectively to be firmly in control. It is integral because of the nature of a human being's subjective world: emotional overtones are part and parcel of the way people experience not only the total situation that they are in (or are imagining), but also individual agents and things in it, and the courses of action that they take or contemplate. These overtones colour experience, and incline people towards some courses of action more than others, but they are part of the background unless something triggers a kind of phase shift and propels people into a state of episodic emotion.

Practically, there would be reasonably obvious advantages if machines could register the pervasive emotion that is involved when users feel positive or negative about people or situations that they are facing or talking about, alienated or engaged by the way a person or a system is communicating, and so on; and could generate appropriately coloured responses. It is less clear how much call there would be for information technology to deal with episodic bursts of emotion – they are quite rare, and they are a sensitive area that humans might well want machines to stay out of.

In fact, one of the obvious functions of sensitivity to pervasive emotion would be to make sure that systems did not propel users into fullblown emotional episodes.

These points bear emphasis because it is easy to drift into assuming that episodic emotion has a natural priority. Some of the reasons are grounded in everyday ways of speaking and thinking. The plural form, 'emotions', almost always refers to episodic emotions; and the archetypal emotion words (fear, anger, happiness, etc) apply primarily to episodic emotions. Psychological language tends to reinforce that outlook. For instance, Scherer has proposed a definition of emotions which begins by describing them as 'episodes of massive, synchronized recruitment of mental and somatic resources ..' [6]. The description draws on good scientific evidence to sum up a particular kind of emotional phenomenon. However, it is another matter entirely whether people who are interested in what everyday language calls 'emotion' should automatically concentrate on that kind of phenomenon.

A different kind of pressure comes from the idea that being emotional consists of flicking in and out of states that are at least close to the archetypes of episodic emotion - anger, happiness, and so on. Well-known views of emotion suggest that nothing else is possible, because 'all emotions are basic emotions' [7]. People who have worked with naturalistic data have repeatedly found that it does not take that form [5], [8], [9]. It is a measure of the strength of people's preconceptions that they often respond by dismissing the data – if the data do not conform to their expectations, they conclude that the data have been poorly collected. That makes for a curious kind of empirical science.

A third kind of pressure may be inferred if not proven. Pervasive emotion, like other fundamentals of mental life such as consciousness, is frustratingly hard to pin down. It is much easier to describe episodic emotions, which contrast with other states and have a discernable structure. On the other hand, the very elusiveness of pervasive emotion may suggest that understanding it is the deeper problem.

Issues like these need to be addressed systematically. HUMAINE does so through two workpackages.

One deals with the linked tasks of conceptualizing emotion in the broad sense, and establishing terms that describe it without covertly misdirecting us. A taxonomy of 'emotion related states' is in progress: it gives recognition to multiple types of state other than the traditional archetypes, including

- Moods (e.g., cheerful, gloomy, irritable, listless, depressed, buoyant)
- Interpersonal stances (e.g., distant, cold, warm, supportive, contemptuous)
- Attitudes (e.g., liking, loving, hating, valuing, desiring)
- Affect dispositions (e.g., nervous, anxious, reckless, morose, hostile) [6]

The second strand involves the collection of data that shows how emotion features in everyday settings. More detail is given in section 5 below.

Definition, taxonomy, and the collection of specimens are not glamorous activities in a technological field. Nevertheless, to ignore them is to invite chaos or superficiality. HUMAINE tries to avoid both.

3 Foreseeing Application Areas

One of the keys to strategy is a structured view of potential applications. This section tries to provide that. It distinguishes two broad groups of three, corresponding to relatively short and relatively long term types of goal. The cutoff is associated with a watershed, which is both the single most important application and a key to other possibilities.

3.1 Trouble Shooting

Probably the most active area at present is detecting troublesome emotions - in callers using automatic exchanges, pilots, drivers, etc. [10],[11],[12],[13]. Detection of stress [14] and lying [15] are closely related. Many extensions could be imagined, e.g. detecting staff who fail to display sufficient warmth towards customers. Trouble-spotting applications as an obvious starting point; partly because it looks as if rather simple systems could achieve useful results, and partly because it fits long-established stereotypes of what emotions are (trouble!). However, the area is fraught with problems, some ethical, some to do with doubts about the level of performance that simple systems can actually achieve.

3.2 Affective Selection

Affective selection involves detecting emotion-related responses to various stimuli, and using the responses to make choices that reflect the user's preferences. For instance, our group [16] proposed to use signs of emotion to locate the types of holiday that a user might respond well to, and Aizawa [17] proposed to archive video footage of times when brain signals indicate strong emotions. There are many natural extensions, such as adjusting ambient music or colouring to suit a user's mood.

3.3 Affective Loops

Höök [18] coined this term for a type of technology that goes back at least as far as the drum. The user acts; the system reacts; the result affects the user emotionally, and encourages the user to restart the cycle. Computing offers the prospect of designing a much wider range of systems that behave in that way, most obviously for enjoyment, relaxation, or therapy (the lines are blurred). The systems need not necessarily know any more about the user's emotions than a drum does, but it opens up new possibilities if they do.

3.4 Really Natural Language Processing

This is the watershed application mentioned above. Computers would become vastly more accessible if people could use really natural language to communicate with them – that is, talk to them as they would talk to another person, and have responses of the kind another person would give. Emotion is one of the areas where progress is needed to achieve that. Emotional colouring is an integral part of person-to-person exchanges, and it is clear that people react badly to discourse that follows other rules of conversation but ignores the emotional ones. There is no generally accepted description of the emotion-related rules that people expect an interlocutor to follow, but it is easy to suggest candidates, such as

match the general emotional tone of the other speaker (emotional convergence)
pick up topics that interest the other speaker
avoid topics or styles of speech that cause the other distress or boredom
repair ill feeling

Intuitively, it seems unlikely that speech interfaces incapable of observing rules like these will be widely accepted – and hence, achieving a level of emotion-sensitivity that allows them to be observed is integral to achieving really natural language communication.

Speech interfaces that allow really natural language processing are both the single most important application of emotion sensitivity, and a prerequisite for the longer term applications.

3.5 Uncovering Feelings

This term refers to uncovering the systems of values and dispositions that surround some kind of person or object or event in a user's mind. That is very different from attaching a label to a brief emotional state, and to do it well needs sophistication about language as well as about emotion. It is an essential key to a range of services – market or political research, careers advice, politics, non-directive counselling, personalised entertainment, etc..

3.6 Facilitating Learning

This is what good teachers do – not just presenting information to a learner, but taking account of the emotional issues – boredom, excitement, pride, humiliation – that make learning likely to succeed or fail. It probably depends on a fair degree of ability to elicit feelings. It is not confined to the classroom – it applies to manuals as much as multiplication tables.

3.7 Moulding

The term is meant to convey that the system sets out to change users' outlook or values or priorities rather than simply to extend their knowledge. It is separated from facilitating learning mainly because the two are very different ethically: moulding has obvious attractions for sales or politics, but it raises major ethical concerns. Emotionally sophisticated persuaders with no conscience, but infinite patience, are a nightmare.

Two implications of this overview should be noted. First, there are rather few areas that emotion oriented technology might see as its own particular preserve (specifically the first two). More often, techniques that are specific to emotion will enhance systems with many other elements. Second, the applications that most obviously involve episodic emotions are the short term ones: emotional colouring is the key issue in the longer term.

Generally speaking, the point of introducing emotion is to rehumanise functions that for various reasons we might want machines to carry out. The level of emotionality needed to do that is not dramatic, and it probably does not need to be present all the time. Nevertheless, it seems a safe bet that systems which are able to use relevant emotional colouring will obliterate systems that are not.

4   Ethics

Ethics has already been mentioned. Whether we like it or not, it simply is a subject that arises – most obviously because people are intensely sensitive about things that touch their emotions. As a result, if research gives a hint of irresponsible invasion or manipulation, it is likely to run into serious difficulties. The risk can probably be kept low if people working in the area take the trouble to be clear and moderately sophisticated in the area of ethics – much better that than to have horror stories emerge, and severe restrictions imposed by lawyers, protestors, or both.

5   The Empirical Base: Samples of Emotional Behaviour

Samples of emotional behaviour, spontaneous or simulated, are the empirical base of the area. They provide the raw material for developing sophisticated rules, either scientifically or by automatic methods; and for templates in the various techniques that use them. There are areas where intuition and informal experience are sufficient to produce first order approximations, such as the design of basic conversational agents [19]; but long term applications clearly need a stronger empirical base. Assembling an appropriate set of samples is a major challenge.

Traditionally, the area has relied heavily on acted samples. There is growing unease with that approach [8]. Actors reproduce people's stereotypes, not the behaviour patterns that ordinary people exhibit in everyday life. One marker of the difference is that training on acted speech does not lead to good performance on spontaneous speech [10]. Another marker is the time it takes to tell whether speech is acted or spontaneous. In a recent study we found statistically significant discrimination within the shortest interval we tested, 3 seconds.

Call centre data is attracting attention as an alternative, but it has its own problems. Its main relevance is to episodic emotions that signal trouble. For that purpose, the data rate is very low: Ang studied a sample of 13,187 utterances, and found 42 that clearly qualified as irritated [11]. The data is almost always in a single modality, speech. It is also constrained in form and emotional range, making it all too likely that solutions will be tied to those features and lack generality. To illustrate the problem of emotional narrowness, Yacoub et al [20] developed a system that discriminated anger from neutral speech. However, when happy speech was introduced, it too was classified as angry – ie the discrimination produced by training on a narrow base was not actually anger/neutrality at all. To illustrate the problem of task constraints, we published evidence [21] that speakers who were deeply bored paused less (ie they ran words together). A follow-up study has since shown an exactly opposite effect. The reason is a minor change to the paradigm – the presentation created natural blocks in the first study but not the second. Experiments can expose that kind of effect: telecommunications companies do not have the same leeway.

Difficulties with other options focus attention on deliberate elicitation [5],[8]. That may involve inducing an emotional state in passive subjects or facilitating people who are actively trying to achieve it. At one extreme is subjecting people to films of surgery [22]; at the other is Picard's subject who developed mental routines for achieving specific, highly repeatable target states [23].

Developing elicitation techniques highlights the distinction between a state and the way it is expressed in a given context. The range of context effects is enormous. For instance:

- emotion driven by immediate surroundings probably differs from emotion that relates to situations that are remembered or anticipated [24];
- situations that elicit happiness do not necessarily lend themselves to establishing how it affects scripted speech, still less to establishing how it is expressed in spontaneous dialogue;
- signs may be heightened or suppressed in quite different ways according to social context [25].

Issues like these show why one of the strategic needs in the area is to stand back from the task of achieving specified emotional targets, and to define an appropriate set of targets. It is impossible to record the whole domain of emotion: research needs points of reference chosen so that given information about them, the rest of the domain can be reconstructed reasonably accurately. In the past it made sense to hope that so-called primary emotions would provide those points of reference. That carries over into a de facto tendency to concentrate on eliciting states which are at least very strongly coloured by emotion. But if the long term goal is to understand commonplace emotional colouring, those inherited tendencies need to be questioned and ideally replaced.

6   Modality and Recording

Emotion is profoundly multi-modal. It is reflected in facial expressions, gestures, body language, and actions; in the propositions expressed, the words and syntax chosen to express them, and the way they are spoken; in involuntary visceral changes, and in blood flow and electrical activity in the brain.

In an ideal world, researchers would be able to record all of the relevant modalities without compromising the essential nature of the situation. In reality, they have difficult choices to make. Introducing a camera constrains; attaching leads for psychophysiology constrains still more; brain scans can only be collected in environments that make natural expression of emotion all but impossible. That is all over and above the fact that emotion will be expressed through speech in some situations, gesture in others, and so on.

Some theoretical perspectives do suggest that certain modalities are privileged – they define 'ground truths', against which the validity of other measures has to be gauged. According to James [26], the essence of emotion was visceral response. According to Cannon [27], it was activity in specific brain centres. Recent work is more pluralist. It regards emotion as intrinsically multifaceted [28]. To attribute an emotional state is to summarise a range of objective variables. Hence, no one modality is indispensable. Equally important, there is no measure that defines unequivocally what a person's true emotional state is.

From that viewpoint, the issue is to weigh the costs and benefits of collecting particular types of measure at particular levels of resolution in a given situation. All parties need to understand how difficult the balances are. Nobody gains from studies that achieve the highest possible quality and resolution in multiple modalities at the cost of enforcing completely stilted renditions of emotion.

7   Identifying Emotional Content

One of the core tasks of research concerned with emotion is to associate emotion-related signs with labels that identify the associated emotion-related states. Databases need to present an association that can be regarded as valid; recognisers need to generate appropriate state descriptions given appropriate signs; synthesis needs to be capable of generating signs that are appropriate to a given state. Finding appropriate ways to identify emotion-related states is a substantial challenge in itself.

Central to the challenge are two groups of issues with wide-reaching implications. They involve the *form* of the description, and the *perspective* from which it is given.

The most familiar form of description is categorical. Emotions are identified by identifying verbal labels, which are either drawn directly from everyday language, or adapted from it. Typical adaptations involve distinguishing hot and cold anger, romantic and nurturant love, etc.

Episodic emotions may well have an inherently categorical structure, though note that there is little sign of convergence in attempts to define a satisfying set of categories [5]. Even if there were, it seems very unlikely that a categorical system could capture the shades of emotional colouring satisfactorily. It would involve a very large number of categories, and the categorisation would not reflect the fact that some categories are obviously very close and others very far apart.

At the opposite extreme are dimensional descriptions, which identify emotional states by associating them with points in a multidimensional space. The approach has a long history – Wundt [29] proposed it and Schlossberg [30] reintroduced in the modern era. Analyses agree that emotion concepts reflect two main dimensions, which we have called activation and evaluation [4] (though see [31] for a different approach); and a number of others which are less important, such as power or approach/avoidance.

A third option, pioneered by Ortony et al, [32], is a logical description, which identifies emotional states in relation to a series of alternatives – is the focus present or imagined? a person or a thing? and so on.

All of these options have been used in practice [8], [33],[34]. Results confirm the obvious expectations – categorical and logical descriptions raise difficult statistical problems when there is a substantial range of emotions to deal with, dimensional descriptions are more tractable but fail to make important distinctions.

The second group of issues related to identifying emotional content have been described as involving perspective. The question behind them is: whose view of an emotional episode is research concerned with?

The obvious assumption is that research should be concerned with an absolute perspective which reflects a person's state with as much scientific accuracy as possible. In some applications, that is quite reasonable: for instance, a lie detector should presumably establish whether a person is actually lying.

Equally, though, there are applications where the natural goal is to match the perspective of a representative observer. A system designed to hold relatively normal conversations does not need to penetrate deceptions that would pose problems for a person – in fact, it should be fallible in about the same way as a person would be. There are interesting questions about handling signs that different people perceive in noticeably different ways.

A third aim is to design systems that reach the same conclusions about a person's emotions as the person him- or herself. That would correspond to a kind of empathy. It is something that humans often find difficult, but it might, for instance, be important in the last three types of application outlined above.

The main point to be made here is that decisions on these issues – form of description and perspective – have a far-reaching effect on the shape of a research effort. Decisions with such strategic implications should not be made by default, on the grounds that some options come to mind more easily than others.

8   Signals to Emotion Labellings and Back

The obvious work for technologists is to construct processes that lead from an input signal to an emotion label; or from an emotion label to an output signal. The signals may be audio, visual, or physiological. The aim of this section is to illustrate the kind of challenge that arises in any of the streams. It uses speech as an example.

In speech, the signal is a fluctuating voltage. The natural image is that processing should work through a series of transformations to an identification of the emotional state in which the signal was produced – in fact two series, one dealing with the linguistic content of the signal ('what you say'), the other dealing with the paralinguistic ('how you say it'). Following through the transformations defines a useful framework.

The basics of linguistic processing are well known, and do not need to be reviewed here. However, it is worth noting two major challenges.

The first is simply to recognize words in spontaneous emotionally coloured speech. It has various properties that pose problems for standard recognition systems, including non-standard largyngeal behaviour [35], great variation in phoneme duration [36], reduced articulation, 'trailing off' rather than delivering sharp speech-silence boundaries, devoicing, intruding non-speech sounds (laughter, sniffs, sobs), or morphing speech into a cry ('noooo ...') [11].

The second challenge is to move from words to assessments of a person's emotional state. There has been related work on text, but it is impossible to judge how it transfers because the necessary samples of spontaneous emotional speech are not available.

The paralinguistic stream is less familiar. An initial set of transformations create several more useful time series. The core time series define intensity, energy in certain frequency bands, and local voice pitch; and arguably points derived from LPC or cepstral transformations, perhaps in combination with the Teager Energy Operator. With the core series may be associated derivatives and measures of local steadiness. Some teams supply these time series directly to a recognition algorithm; most insert further transformations [37].

The natural next task is segmentation – defining significant markers and the segments that lie between them. Key markers include boundaries of pauses and phrase-like units (it is debatable how closely that two are related), local maxima and points of stress in the pitch contour, and arguably boundaries of phoneme types (particularly vowels and fricatives).

Given a segmentation, processing can extract descriptors of set segment properties. These include completely standard descriptive statistics (magnitude and duration, and if a segment contains several elements, the means, ranges, etc associated with them); but also increasingly properties we have described as configurational. These include 'crescendo' (buildup of intensity over a phrase), 'topline' (the trend of pitch peaks over a phrase), and parameters of the way a phrase begins and ends; pitch peak and and trend within a vowel; prosodic similarity or contrast between successive phrases; and others. These descriptors can be related directly to measures of emotionality: it is clear that many of them correlate strongly with measures such as activation evaluation, and simple departure from neutrality [37].

Some investigators argue that a further level is needed, in which linguistic and paralinguistic streams are recombined [38],[39]. Prosody may be redescribed in systems like ToBI that are oriented to describing its linguistic significance. That allows observed prosody to be compared with the default predicted by linguistic content, and key regions (where variation is emotionally significant) to be identified. It is clear that considering linguistic issues can augment emotion recognition, but attempts to replace direct descriptors with linguistic ones have been disappointing [34].

A key reason for outlining this kind of structure is to highlight component challenges that deserve attention in their own right. For instance, really natural language processing means that people will not be constrained to ensure 'good' signals. In that context, recovering the most basic contours – intensity and pitch – is difficult. Hence, it makes sense to invest effort in developing standard methods that will deliver them reliably. The same applies to segmentation, with a qualification – the more familiar needs of linguistic processing should not be allowed to dictate the standardisation that emerges. Given that basis, teams with linguistic and psychological skills could explore the higher order issues of relationships between recovered structures and emotional expression.

Thinking at higher order makes it easy to see that a dimension has been left out in the discussion so far. It is a fundamental feature of emotion that it extends and fluctuates in time. The fundamental task is therefore not to match a set of features onto a single label, but to map structured sequences of features onto a changing emotional profile. Conceptually, that task seems easier to address from the perspective of synthesis than in the context of analysis.

In terms of synthesis, linguistics offers a natural model. Generative phonology takes speech synthesis to the point of defining sequences of tokens to be realized: generative phonetics translates that sequence into the domain of signals. Contemporary work on markup languages provides a first approximation to the kind of string that a phonology-like component might generate. There are obvious reasons to aim at convergence between the symbols used in more developed versions of that component and the properties delivered by the paralinguistic analysis, and we have shown that emotional speech synthesis can be controlled by parameters of the kind that one paralinguistic analysis system identifies as correlates of emotion [33].

Speech has been used as an example to work through, but similar issues arise in facial and gestural modalities, and to some extent in the analysis of physiological signals. In each case, the first step is to recognize the sheer scale of the task, and to find rational ways of subdividing it. It makes no sense to require every group that works in any of the areas to attempt all the tasks involved in connecting signals to states – the result is almost bound to be a proliferation of systems on too small a scale to address the basic problems in a satisfying way.

It remains to be said that issues also arise specifically from the attempt to combine different modalities. For instance, it is not at all clear whether they integrate additively; whether some have priority for some decisions (as happens with audiovisual speech reception); whether attention can determine priority; over what interval of time information from transient signals is assumed to be relevant; and much more.

9 Modelling Emotional States

To this point, the description of emotion has been considered as a process of attaching labels – whether they consist of words or sets of co-ordinates. For some short term applications, that may be enough, but it is clearly not enough to support really natural language processing. That requires ability to register what it means to be in a particular emotion-related state, in the sense of being able to gauge how people perceive their current situation, including what their priorities might be; to anticipate what a person might do next, and how they might regard alternative conceivable responses from the system; and perhaps to intuit reasons for their current state. These requirements add up to forming an internal model of the user's emotional state.

Modern theory provides a rich source of ideas about emotion models. It suggests that emotion is rooted in representations with a distinctive structure – they are selective, evaluative, link features of the situation to potential actions, and are at least not wholly propositional. Ideas like these have led to several different strands of research – traditional AI emphasizing representational power; neural nets emphasizing the subsymbolic; artificial life emphasizing the link to action and survival-related evaluation [40].

Deep progress in these areas may take a long time, but it is not difficult to envisage conversation controllers developing gradually from simple rule sets about what to say when somebody is angry, towards more general and principled solutions. Even simple rule sets open the way to systems that could sustain affective loops, and provide a context in which it is possible to begin putting together the key pieces sketched here.

10 Conclusion

HUMAINE is based on explicit recognition that achieving emotion-sensitive computing requires major empirical, theoretical, and structural issues to be addressed in a co-ordinated way. The outline given here simplifies every topic that it deals with and ignores as many others, not because they are insignificant, but because selections have to be made. Nevertheless, it may convey the daunting scale and sheer excitement of the attempt to pull such a large structure into a viable shape.

Acknowledgement

Preparation of this paper was supported EC grant IST-2002-507422, and the content is indebted to discussions with too many HUMAINE members to list.

References

1. Picard, R. W. *Affective Computing*. MIT Press, Cambridge, MA (1997)
2. HUMAINE portal   http://emotion-research.net/
3. Russell J. & Barrett-Feldman L Core affect, prototypical emotional episodes, and other things called emotion: Dissecting the elephant. *J. Pers & Soc Psychol* 76 (1999) 805-819,
4. Cowie R, Douglas-Cowie E, Tsapatsoulis N, Votsis G, Kollias S, Fellenz W, & Taylor J. Emotion recognition in human-computer interaction. *IEEE Sig Proc Magaz* 18 (2001) 32-80
5. Cowie R & Cornelius R. Describing the Emotional States that are Expressed in Speech. *Speech Comm* 40 (2003) 5-32
6. Scherer, K et al HUMAINE Deliverable D3c: Preliminary plans for exemplars: theory http://emotion-research.net/
7. Ekman P. Basic emotions. In Dalgleish, T. and Power, M. J. eds., *Handbook of Cognition & Emotion*. John Wiley, New York (1999) 301–320.
8. Douglas-Cowie E, Campbell N, Cowie R, & Roach P Emotional Speech: towards a new generation of databases. *Speech Comm* 40 (2003) 33-60
9. Kwon O, Chan K, Hao J, & Lee T-W Emotion recognition by speech signals. *Proc. Eurospeech* (2003) 125-128
10. Batliner A, Fischer K, Huber R, Spilker J & Nöth E. How to find trouble in communication. *Speech Comm* 40 (2003) 117-143
11. Ang J, Dhillon R, Krupski A, Shriberg E, & Stolcke A Prosody-based automatic detection of annoyance and frustration in human-computer dialog. *Proc. ICSLP*, Denver, Colorado (2002)
12. Hadfield P & Marks P This is your captain dozing … *New Scientist* 1682267, (2000) 21
13. McMahon E, Cowie R, Kasderidis S, Taylor J, & Kollias S What Chance that a DC Could Recognise Hazardous Mental States from Sensor Outputs? *Tales of the Disappearing Computer*, Santorini (2003)
14. Zhou G, Hansen JH, & Kaiser JF, Methods for stress classification: Nonlinear TEO and linear speech based features. *Proc. IEEE Int Conf on Acoustics, Speech,& Signal Processing*, vol. IV, (1999) 2087-2090
15. Haddad D, Ratley R , Walter S & Smith M *Investigation and Evaluation of Voice Stress Analysis Technology*. Final Report US Dept of Justice Report NCJ Number 193832 (2002)
16. ERMIS team *D03: System Architecture and Testbed Specifications* ERMIS project IST-2000-29319 (2002)
17. Aizawa K Position Statement *Proc VLBV01*, Athens (2001) 3
18. Höök K, Sengers P, & Andersson G Sense and Sensibility: Evaluation and Interactive Art *Computer Human Interaction*, Fort Lauderdale (2003)
19. Paiva A ed. *Affective Interactions: Towards a New Generation of Computer Interfaces*. Berlin: Springer-Verlag (2000)
20. Yacoub S, Simske S, Lin X, & Burns J, Recognition of emotions in interactive voice response systems. *Proc. Eurospeech*, Geneva (2003)
21. R Cowie, A McGuiggan, E McMahon, & E Douglas-Cowie Speech in the Process of Becoming Bored. *Proc. 15th ICPhS*, Barcelona (2003)
22. JJ Gross & RW Levenson. Emotion elicitation using films. *Cognition and Emotion* 9 (1995) 87-108

23. Picard RW, Vyzas E & Healey J Toward Machine Emotional Intelligence: Analysis of Affective Physiological State *IEEE Trans Patt Analysis & Machine Intell,* 23 (2001) 1175-1191

24. Stemmler G, Heldmann M, Pauls C, & Scherer T Constraints for emotion specificity in fear and anger: the context counts. *Psychophysiology* 69 (2001) 275-291

25. Parkinson B *Ideas and realities of emotion.* Routledge, New York (1995)

26. James W, What is emotion? *Mind* 9 (1884) 188-205

27. Cannon WB Against the James-Lange theory of emotion *Psych Rev* 38 (1931) 106-124

28. Cornelius R *The Science of Emotion: Research and tradition in the psychology of emotion.* Upper Saddle River: Prentice-Hall (1996)

29. Wundt W *Grundzuge der Physiologischen Psychologie* vol 2. Engelmann, Leipzig, 1903. (Original published 1874)

30. Schlosberg H, A scale for judgment of facial expressions. *Journal of Experimental Psychology* 29 (1954) 497-510

31. Watson D & Tellegen A, Toward a consensual structure of mood. *Psych Bull,* 98 (1985) 219-235

32. Ortony A, Clore G & Collins A, *The cognitive structure of emotions.* CUP, Cambridge, England (1988)

33. Schröder M Speech and Emotion Research: An overview of research frameworks and a dimensional approach to emotional speech synthesis. PhD thesis, *PHONUS 7, Research Report of the Institute of Phonetics, Saarland University* (2004)

34. Stibbard R Vocal expression of emotions in non-laboratory speech. PhD thesis, University of Reading (2001)

35. Cummings K & Clements M Analysis of glottal excitation of emotionally styled and stressed speech. *JASA* 98 (1995) 88-98

36. Williams CE & Stevens KN Emotions and speech: Some acoustical correlates. *JASA.* 52 (1972) 1238-1250

37. Cowie R, Douglas-Cowie E, Cox C, & Cemegil A T *D09: Final Version Of Non-Verbal Speech Parameter Extraction Module* ERMIS project IST-2000-29319 (2004)

38. Ladd DR, Silverman K, Tolkmitt F, Bergmann G & Scherer K Evidence for the independent function of intonation contour type, voice quality, and F0 range in signaling speaker affect. *JASA.* 78 (1985) 435-444

39. Mozziconacci S Speech variability & emotion: Production & perception. Ph. D. thesis, Technical University Eindhoven (1998)

40. Trappl R, Petta P and Payr S, eds., *Emotions in Humans and Artifacts,* Cambridge, MA: The MIT Press (2003)

Emotion Analysis in Man-Machine Interaction Systems

T. Balomenos, A. Raouzaiou, S. Ioannou, A. Drosopoulos,
K. Karpouzis, and S.Kollias

Image, Video and Multimedia Systems Laboratory
National Technical University of Athens
tmpal@mycosmos.gr, {araouz, sivann, ndroso}@image.ntua.gr,
kkarpou@softlab.ntua.gr, stefanos@cs.ntua.gr

Abstract. Facial expression and hand gesture analysis plays a fundamental part in emotionally rich man-machine interaction (MMI) systems, since it employs universally accepted non-verbal cues to estimate the users' emotional state. In this paper, we present a systematic approach to extracting expression related features from image sequences and inferring an emotional state via an intelligent rule-based system. MMI systems can benefit from these concepts by adapting their functionality and presentation with respect to user reactions or by employing agent-based interfaces to deal with specific emotional states, such as frustration or anger.

1 Introduction

Current information processing and visualization systems are capable of offering advanced and intuitive means of receiving input and communicating output to their users. As a result, Man-Machine Interaction (MMI) systems that utilize multimodal information about their users' current emotional state are presently at the forefront of interest of the computer vision and artificial intelligence communities. Such interfaces give the opportunity to less technology-aware individuals, as well as handicapped people, to use computers more efficiently and thus overcome related fears and preconceptions. Besides this, most emotion-related facial and body gestures are considered to be universal, in the sense that they are recognized along different cultures. Therefore, the introduction of an "emotional dictionary" that includes descriptions and perceived meanings of facial expressions and body gestures, so as to help infer the likely emotional state of a specific user, can enhance the affective nature [13] of MMI applications.

Despite the progress in related research, our intuition of what a human expression or emotion actually represents is still based on trying to mimic the way the human mind works while making an effort to recognize such an emotion. This means that even though image or video input are necessary to this task, this process cannot come to robust results without taking into account features like speech, hand gestures or body pose. These features provide means to convey messages in a much more expressive and definite manner than wording, which can be misleading or ambiguous. While a lot of effort has been invested in examining individually these aspects of human expression, recent research [10] has shown that even this approach can benefit from taking into account multimodal information.

S. Bengio and H. Bourlard (Eds.): MLMI 2004, LNCS 3361, pp. 318–328, 2005.

In this paper, we present a systematic approach to analyzing emotional cues from user facial expressions and hand gestures. Emotions are considered as discrete points or areas of an "emotional space" [10]. In section 2, we provide an overview of affective analysis of facial expressions and gestures. Sections 3 and 4 provide algorithms and experimental results from the analysis of facial expressions and hand gestures in video sequences. In most cases a single expression or gesture cannot help the system deduce a positive decision about the users' observed emotion. As a result, a fuzzy architecture is employed that uses the symbolic representation of the tracked features as input; this concept is described in Section 5. Results of the multimodal affective analysis system are provided in this section, while conclusions and future work concepts are included in Section 6.

2 Affective Analysis in MMI

2.1 Affective Facial Expression Analysis

There is a long history of interest in the problem of recognizing emotion from facial expressions [9], and extensive studies on face perception during the last twenty years [7], [5]. The salient issues in emotion recognition from faces are parallel in some respects to the issues associated with voices, but divergent in others.

In the context of faces, the task has almost always been to classify examples of archetypal emotions. That may well reflect the influence of Ekman and his colleagues, who have argued robustly that the facial expression of emotion is inherently categorical. More recently, morphing techniques have been used to probe states that are intermediate between archetypal expressions. They do reveal effects that are consistent with a degree of categorical structure in the domain of facial expression, but they are not particularly large, and there may be alternative ways of explaining them – notably by considering how category terms and facial parameters map onto activation-evaluation space [6].

2.2 Affective Gesture Analysis

The detection and interpretation of hand gestures has become an important part of human computer interaction (MMI) in recent years [14]. Sometimes, a simple hand action, such as placing a person's hands over his ears, can pass on the message that he has had enough of what he is hearing; this is conveyed more expressively than with any other spoken phrase. Analyzing hand gestures is a comprehensive task involving motion modeling, motion analysis, pattern recognition, machine learning, and even psycholinguistic studies.

The first phase of the recognition task is choosing a model of the gesture. The mathematical model may consider both the spatial and temporal characteristic of the hand and hand gestures [4]. The approach used for modeling plays a pivotal role in the nature and performance of gesture interpretation. Once the model is decided upon, an analysis stage is used to compute the model parameters from the image features that are extracted from single or multiple video input streams. These parameters constitute some description of the hand pose or trajectory and depend on the modeling approach used. Among the important problems involved in the analysis are those of hand localization, hand tracking [11], [12], [1] and selection of suitable image features. The computation of model parameters is followed by gesture recognition. Here, the parameters are classified and interpreted in the light of the accepted model and perhaps the rules imposed by some grammar. The grammar could reflect not only the internal syntax of gestural commands but also the possibility of interaction of gestures with other communication modes like speech, gaze, or facial expressions.

3 Facial Expression Analysis

3.1 Facial Features Extraction

Facial analysis includes a number of processing steps which attempt to detect or track the face, to locate characteristic facial regions such as eyes, mouth and nose on it, to extract and follow the movement of facial features, such as characteristic points in these regions, or model facial gestures using anatomic information about the face.

Although FAPs [8] provide all the necessary elements for MPEG-4 compatible animation, we cannot use them for the analysis of expressions from video scenes, due to the absence of a clear quantitative definition framework. In order to measure FAPs in real image sequences, we have to define a mapping between them and the movement of specific FDP feature points (FPs), which correspond to salient points on the human face [15].

The facial feature extraction scheme used in the system proposed in this paper is based on an hierarchical, robust scheme, coping with large variations in the appearance of diverse subjects, as well as of the same subject in various instances within real video sequences, we have recently developed [16]. Soft *a priori* assumptions are made on the pose of the face or the general location of the features in it. Gradual revelation of information concerning the face is supported under the scope of optimization in each step of the hierarchical scheme, producing *a posteriori* knowledge about it and leading to a step-by-step visualization of the features in search.

Face detection is performed first through detection of skin segments or blobs, merging of them based on the probability of their belonging to a facial area, and identification of the most salient skin color blob or segment. Primary facial features, such as eyes, mouth and nose, are dealt as major discontinuities on the segmented, arbitrarily rotated face. Following face detection, morphological operations, erosions and dilations, taking into account symmetries, are used to define first the most probable blobs within the facial area to include the eyes and the mouth. Searching through gradient filters over the eyes and between the eyes and mouth provide estimates of the eyebrow and nose positions. Based on the detected facial feature positions, feature points are computed and evaluated.

An efficient implementation of the scheme has been developed in the framework of the IST ERMIS project (www.image.ntua.gr/ermis).

3.2 Experimental Results

Fig. 1 shows a characteristic frame from an image sequence. After skin detection and segmentation, the primary facial features are shown in Fig. 2. Fig. 3 shows the estimates of the eyes, mouth, eyebrows and nose positions. Fig. 4 shows the initial neutral image used to calculate the FP distances.

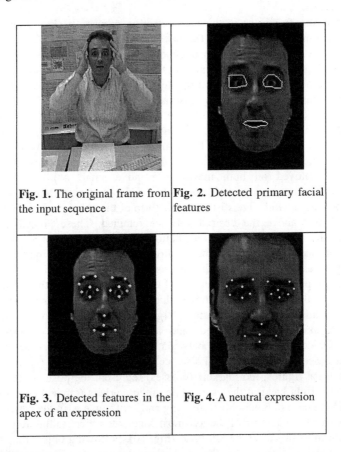

Fig. 1. The original frame from the input sequence

Fig. 2. Detected primary facial features

Fig. 3. Detected features in the apex of an expression

Fig. 4. A neutral expression

4. Gesture Analysis

4.1 Hand Detection and Tracking

In order to extract emotion-related features through hand movement, we implemented a hand-tracking system. Emphasis was on implementing a near real-time, yet robust enough system for our purposes. The general process involves the creation of *moving skin masks*, namely skin color areas which are tracked between subsequent frames. By tracking the centroid of those skin masks we produce an estimate of the user's movements.

In order to implement a computationally light system, our architecture takes into account a-priori knowledge related to the expected characteristics of the input image. Since the context is MMI applications, we expect to locate the head in the middle area of upper half of the frame and the hand segments near the respective lower corners. In addition to this, we concentrate on the motion of hand segments, given that they are the end effectors of the hand and arm chain and thus the most expressive object in tactile operations.

For each given frame, as in the face detection process, a skin color probability matrix is computed by calculating the joint probability of the Cr/Cb image values (Fig. 5). A skin color mask is then obtained from the skin probability matrix with thresholding (Fig. 6). Possible moving areas are found by thresholding the difference pixels between the current frame and the next, resulting to the possible-motion mask (Fig. 7). This mask does not contain information about the direction or the magnitude of the movement, but is only indicative of the motion and is used to accelerate the algorithm by concentrating tracking only in moving image areas. Both color (Fig. 6) and motion (Fig. 7) masks contain a large number of small objects due to the presence of noise and objects with color similar to the skin. To overcome this, morphological filtering is employed on both masks to remove small objects. All described morphological operations are carried out with a disk structuring element with a radius of 1% of the image width. The distance transform of the color mask is first calculated and only objects above the desired size are retained. These objects are used as markers for the morphological reconstruction of the initial color mask. The color mask is then closed to provide better centroid calculation. The moving skin mask (msm) is then created by fusing the processed skin and motion masks (sm, mm) through the morphological reconstruction of the color mask using the motion mask as marker. The result of this process, after excluding the head object is shown in (Fig. 8). The moving skin mask consists of many large connected areas. For the next frame a new moving skin mask is created, and a one-to-one object correspondence is performed. Object correspondence between two frames is performed on the color mask and is based on object centroid distance for objects of similar (at least 50%) area (Fig. 9). In these figures, red markers (crosses) represent the position of the centroid of the detected right hand of the user, while green markers (circles) correspond to the left hand. In the case of hand object merging and splitting, e.g. in the case of clapping, we establish a new matching of the left-most candidate object to the user's right hand and the right-most object to the left hand (Fig. 10). Following object matching in the subsequent moving skin masks, the mask flow is computed, i.e. a vector for each frame depicting the motion direction and magnitude of the frame's objects. The described algorithm is relatively lightweight, allowing a rate of several fps on a usual PC.

4.2 Gesture Classification Using HMMs

The ability of Hidden Markov Models (HMMs) to deal with time sequential data and to provide time scale invariability as well as learning capability makes them an appropriate selection for gesture classification. An excellent study on HMMs can be found in [17]. In Table 1 we present the utilized features that feed (as sequences of vectors) our HMM classifier, as well as the output classes of the HMM classifier.

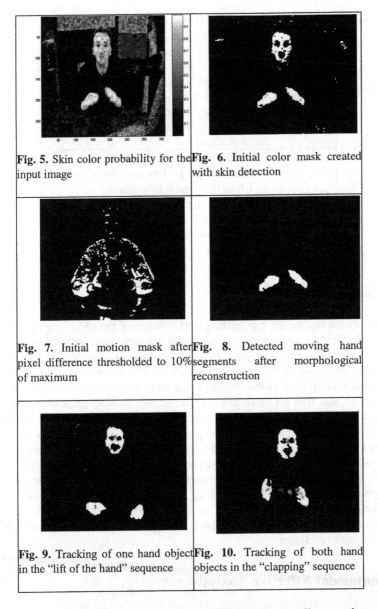

Fig. 5. Skin color probability for the input image

Fig. 6. Initial color mask created with skin detection

Fig. 7. Initial motion mask after pixel difference thresholded to 10% of maximum

Fig. 8. Detected moving hand segments after morphological reconstruction

Fig. 9. Tracking of one hand object in the "lift of the hand" sequence

Fig. 10. Tracking of both hand objects in the "clapping" sequence

The recognizer consists of M different HMMs corresponding to the modeled gesture classes. In our case, $M=7$ as it can be seen in Table 1. We use first order left-to-right models consisting of a varying number (for each one of the HMMs) of internal states $G_{k,j}$ that have been identified through the learning process. For example the third HMM which recognizes low speed on *hand lift* consists of only three states $G_{3,1}$, $G_{3,2}$ and $G_{3,3}$ while more complex gesture classes like the *hand clapping* require as much as eight states to be efficiently modeled by the corresponding HMM.

Table 1. a) Features (inputs to HMM) and **b)** Gesture Classes (outputs of HMM)

Features	$X_{lh} - X_{rh}$, $X_f - X_{rh}$, $X_f - X_{lh}$, $Y_{lh} - Y_{rh}$, $Y_f - Y_{rh}$, $Y_f - Y_{lh}$ where $C_f = (X_f, Y_f)$ the coordinates of the head centroid, $C_{rh} = (X_{rh}, Y_{rh})$ the coordinates of the right hand centroid, $C_{lh} = (X_{lh}, Y_{lh})$ the coordinates of the left hand centroid
Gesture Classes	hand clapping – high frequency hand clapping – low frequency lift of the hand – low speed lift of the hand – high speed hands over the head – gesture hands over the head – posture italianate gestures

4.3 Experimental Results

Experiments for testing the recognizing performance of the proposed algorithm were carried out. Gesture sequences of three male subjects, with maximum duration of three seconds, were captured by a typical web-camera at a rate of 10 frames per second. For each one of the gesture classes 15 sequences were acquired, three were used for the initialization of the HMM parameters, seven for training and parameters' re-estimation and five for testing. Each one of the training sequences consisted of approximately 15 frames. The selection of these frames was performed off-line so as to create characteristic examples of the gesture classes. Testing sequences were sub-sampled at a rate of 5 frames per second so as to enable substantial motion to occur. An overall recognition rate of 94.3% was achieved.

From the results obtained we observed a mutual misclassification between "Italianate Gestures" and "Hand Clapping – High Frequency"; this is mainly due to the variations on "Italianate Gestures" across different individuals. Thus, training the HMM classifier on a personalized basis is anticipated to improve the discrimination between these two classes.

5 Multimodal Affective Analysis

5.1 Facial Expression Analysis Subsystem

The facial expression analysis subsystem is the main part of the presented system; gestures are utilized to support the outcome of this subsystem.

Let us consider as input to the emotion analysis sub-system a 15 element length feature vector f that corresponds to the 15 features f_i [15]. The particular values of f can be rendered to FAP values as shown in the same table resulting in an input vector G. The elements of G express the observed values of the corresponding involved FAPs.

Let $X_{i,j}^{(k)}$ be the range of variation of FAP F_j involved in the k-*th* profile $P_i^{(k)}$ of emotion i. If $c_{i,j}^{(k)}$ and $s_{i,j}^{(k)}$ are the middle point and length of interval $X_{i,j}^{(k)}$ respectively, then we describe a fuzzy class $A_{i,j}^{(k)}$ for F_j, using the membership function $\mu_{i,j}^{(k)}$ shown in Fig. 11. Let also $\Delta_{i,j}^{(k)}$ be the set of classes $A_{i,j}^{(k)}$ that correspond to profile $P_i^{(k)}$; the beliefs $p_i^{(k)}$ and b_i that an observed, through the vector G, facial state corresponds to profile $P_i^{(k)}$ and emotion i respectively, are computed through the following equations:

$$p_i^{(k)} = \prod_{A_{i,j}^{(k)} \in \Delta_{i,j}^{(k)}} r_{i,j}^{(k)} \quad \text{and} \quad b_i = \max_k(p_i^{(k)}), \tag{1}$$

where $r_{i,j}^{(k)} = \max\{g_i \cap A_{i,j}^{(k)}\}$ expresses the *relevance* $r_{i,j}^{(k)}$ of the i-th element of the input feature vector with respect to class $A_{i,j}^{(k)}$. Actually $g = A'(G) = \{g_1, g_2, ...\}$ is the fuzzified input vector resulting from a *singleton* fuzzification procedure 3.

If a hard decision about the observed emotion has to be made then the following equation is used:

$$q = \arg\max_i b_i, \tag{2}$$

The various emotion profiles correspond to the fuzzy intersection of several sets and are implemented through a *τ-norm* of the form $t(a,b)=a \cdot b$. Similarly the belief that an observed feature vector corresponds to a particular emotion results from a fuzzy union of several sets through an *σ-norm* which is implemented as $u(a,b)=\max(a,b)$.

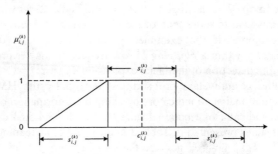

Fig. 11. The form of membership functions

An emotion analysis system has been created as part of the IST ERMIS project (www.image.ntua.gr/ermis).

5.2 Affective Gesture Analysis Subsystem

Gestures are utilized to support the outcome of the facial expression analysis subsystem, since in most cases they are too ambiguous to indicate a particular emotion. However, in a given context of interaction, some gestures are obviously associated with a particular expression –e.g. *hand clapping* of high frequency expresses *joy, satisfaction-* while others can provide indications for the kind of the emotion expressed by the user. In particular, quantitative features derived from hand tracking, like speed and amplitude of motion, fortify the position of an observed emotion; for example, *satisfaction* turns to *joy* or even to *exhilaration*, as the speed and amplitude of clapping increases. As was mentioned in Section 4, the position of the centroids of the head and the hands over time forms the feature vector sequence that feeds an HMM classifier whose outputs corresponds to particular gesture class. In the following paragraph we describe how the recognized gesture class can be used to provide indications about the occurrence of an emotional state.

Table 2 shows the correlation between some detectable gestures with the six archetypal expressions.

Table 2. Correlation between gestures and emotional states

Emotion	Gesture Class
Joy	*hand clapping-high frequency*
Sadness	*hands over the head-posture*
Anger	*lift of the hand- high speed*
	italianate gestures
Fear	*hands over the head-gesture*
	italianate gestures
Disgust	*lift of the hand- low speed*
	hand clapping-low frequency
Surprise	*hands over the head-gesture*

Given a particular context of interaction, gesture classes corresponding to the same emotional are combined in a "logical OR" form. Table 2 shows that a particular gesture may correspond to more than one gesture classes carrying different affective meaning. For example, if the examined gesture is *clapping*, detection of high frequency indicates *joy*, but a *clapping* of low frequency may express irony and can reinforce a possible detection of the facial expression *disgust*.

In practice, the gesture class probabilities derived by the HMM classifier are transformed to emotional state indicators by using the information of Table 2. Let EI_k be the emotional indicator of emotional state k ($k \in \{1,2,3,4,5,6\}$ corresponds to one of the emotional states presented in Table 2 in the order of appearance, i.e., 1->Joy, 6->Surprise), $GCS = \{gc_1, gc_2, \ldots, gc_N\}$ be the set of gesture classes recognized by the HMM Classifier ($N=7$), $GCS^k \subseteq GCS$ be the set of gesture classes related with the emotional state k, and $p(gc_i)$ be the probability of gesture class gc_i obtained from the HMM Classifier. The $EI(k)$ is computed using the following equation:

$$EI_k = \max_{gc_i \in GC^K} \{gc_i\} \qquad (3)$$

5.3 The Overall Decision System

In the final step of the proposed system, the facial expression analysis subsystem and the affective gesture analysis subsystem are integrated into a system which provides as result the possible emotions of the user, each accompanied by a degree of belief.

Although face consists the main "demonstrator" of user's emotion [9], the recognition of the accompanying gesture increases the confidence of the result of facial expression subsystem [2]. Further research is necessary to be carried out in order to define how powerful the influence of a gesture in the recognition of an emotion actually is. It would also be helpful to define which, face or gesture, is more useful for a specific application and change the impact of each subsystem on the final result.

In the current implementation the two subsystems are combined as a weighted sum: Let b_k be the degree of belief that the observed sequence presents the k-th emotional state, obtained from the facial expression analysis subsystem, and EI_k be the corresponding emotional state indicator, obtained from the affective gesture analysis subsystem, then the overall degree of belief d_k is given by:

$$d_k = w_1 \cdot b_k + w_2 \cdot EI_k \qquad (4)$$

where the weights w_1 and w_2 are used to account for the reliability of the two subsystems as far as the emotional state estimation is concerned. In this implementation we use $w_1 = 0.75$ and $w_2 = 0.25$. These values enables the affective gesture analysis subsystem to be important in cases where the facial expression analysis subsystem produces ambiguous results while at the same time leaves the latter subsystem to be the main contributing part in the overall decision system.

For the input sequence shown in Fig. 1, the affective gesture analysis subsystem consistently provided a "surprise" selection. This was used to fortify the output of the facial analysis subsystem which was around 85%.

6 Conclusions – Future Work

In this paper we described a holistic approach to emotion modeling and analysis and their applications in MMI applications. We show that it is possible to transform quantitative feature information from video sequences to an estimation of a user's emotional state. This transformation is based on a fuzzy rules architecture that takes into account knowledge of emotion representation and the intrinsic characteristics of human expression. While these features can be used for simple representation purposes, e.g. animation or task-based interfacing, our approach is closer to the target of affective computing. Thus, they are utilized to provide feedback on the users' emotional state, while in front of a computer. Possible applications include human-like agents, that assist everyday chores and react to user emotions or sensitive artificial listeners that introduce conversation topics and react themselves to specific user cues.

Future work in the affective modeling area, includes the enrichment of the gesture vocabulary with more affective gestures, as well as the relevant feature-based descriptions. With respect to the recognition part, more sophisticated methods of combination of detected expressions and gestures, mainly through a rule based system, are currently under investigation, along with algorithms that take into account general body posture information.

References

1. Wren, C., Azarbayejani, A., Darrel, T., Pentland, A.: Pfinder: Real-time tracking of the human body. IEEE Trans. Pattern Anal. Machine Intell., vol. 9, no. 7, (1997) 780-785
2. McNeill, D.: Hand and mind: what gestures reveal about thought. University of Chicago Press, Chicago, USA (1992)
3. Klir, G., Yuan, B.: Fuzzy Sets and Fuzzy Logic, Theory and Application. Prentice Hall, New Jersey (1995)
4. Lin, J., Wu, Y., Huang, T.S.: Modeling human hand constraints. In Proc. Workshop on Human Motion, (2000) 121-126
5. Scherer, K., Ekman, P.: Approaches to Emotion. Lawrence Erlbaum Associates (1984)
6. Karpouzis, K., Tsapatsoulis, N., Kollias, S.: Moving to Continuous Facial Expression Space using the MPEG-4 Facial Definition Parameter (FDP) Set. In Proc. of SPIE Electronic Imaging 2000, San Jose, CA, USA (2000)
7. Davis, M., College, H.: Recognition of Facial Expressions. Arno Press, New York (1975)
8. Tekalp, A.M., Ostermann, J.: Face and 2-D Mesh Animation in MPEG-4. Signal Processing: Image Communication, Vol. 15 (2000) 387-421
9. Ekman, P., Friesen, W.: The Facial Action Coding System. Consulting Psychologists Press, San Francisco, CA (1978)
10. Cowie, R., Douglas-Cowie, E., Tsapatsoulis, N., Votsis, G., Kollias, S., Fellenz, W., Taylor, J.: Emotion Recognition in Human-Computer Interaction. IEEE Signal Processing Magazine (2001)
11. Kjeldsen, R., Kender, J.: Finding skin in color images. In Proc. 2nd Int. Conf. Automatic Face and Gesture Recognition (1996) 312-317
12. Sharma, R., Huang, T.S., Pavlovic, V.I.: A Multimodal Framework for Interacting With Virtual Environments. Human Interaction With Complex Systems, C.A. Ntuen and E.H. Park, eds., Kluwer Academic Publishers (1996) 53-71
13. Picard, R.W.: Affective Computing. MIT Press, Cambridge, MA (2000)
14. Wu, Y., Huang, T.S.: Hand modeling, analysis, and recognition for vision-based human computer interaction. IEEE Signal Processing Magazine, vol. 18, iss. 3 (2001) 51-60
15. Raouzaiou, A., Tsapatsoulis, N., Karpouzis, K., Kollias, S.: Parameterized facial expression synthesis based on MPEG-4. EURASIP Journal on Applied Signal Processing, Vol. 2002, No. 10, 1021-1038, Hindawi Publishing Corporation (2002)
16. Votsis, G., Drosopoulos, A., Kollias, S.: A modular approach to facial feature segmentation on real sequences. Signal Processing, Image Communication, vol. 18, (2003) 67-89
17. Rabiner, L.R.: A tutorial on HMM and Selected Applications in Speech Recognition. Proceedings of the IEEE, vol.77, no. 2 (1989)

A Hierarchical System for Recognition, Tracking and Pose Estimation

Philipp Zehnder, Esther Koller-Meier, and Luc Van Gool

ETH Zurich, D-ITET, Computer Vision Laboratory,
Sternwartstr. 7, CH-8092 Zurich

Abstract. This paper presents a new system for recognition, tracking and pose estimation of people in video sequences. It is based on the wavelet transform from the upper body part and uses Support Vector Machines (SVM) for classification. Recognition is carried out hierarchically by first recognizing people and then individual characters. The characteristic features that best discriminate one person from another are learned automatically. Tracking is solved via a particle filter that utilizes the SVM output and a first order kinematic model to obtain a robust scheme that successfully handles occlusion, different poses and camera zooms. For pose estimation a collection of SVM classifiers is evaluated to detect specific, learned poses.

1 Introduction

For a semantic interpretation of films or sitcoms, we focus our research interest on the recognition, tracking and pose estimation of people. As a possible application area a virtual commentator can be used as add-on to the sound-track of programs for visually impaired people by producing a spoken description of the scenes. However, besides such an annotation tool, people recognition and tracking find applications in many areas like visual surveillance, human-computer interfaces or video indexing.

People detection is a difficult task because of the significant pattern variations that are hard to parametrize analytically. Such variations comprise different lighting conditions and the variety of appearance, face expression and structural characteristics such as clothes, glasses or mustaches. Researchers have approached the detection problem with different techniques, including SVMs [9, 13, 2, 10, 3], neural networks [11] and geometric constraints between different face features [1, 15] like eyes or lips. Some approaches rely on certain assumptions like fixed camera and a static background (e.g. [8]) which cannot be met in our case.

For our application we decided to use the combination of wavelet transform and SVMs as we want to keep the system as general as possible. We intend to build a system which is transferable and in particular can be used with other objects too. Therefore, we try to avoid explicit models, although this would probably increase the performance for a specific application. Our algorithm should be self-adapting and able to learn new objects automatically.

S. Bengio and H. Bourlard (Eds.): MLMI 2004, LNCS 3361, pp. 329–340, 2005.

A lot of research has been done which deals with performance improvement of a particular detection algorithm. In [3] different kinds of features are investigated, transformations and alternative SVM kernels are considered and methods for feature selection are analyzed. [14] presents acceleration techniques based on a special form of image representation, on a feature selection method based on AdaBoost [14] and a cascade structured search framework. It also suggests post-processing of detections to remove multiple detections in the target area. [2] combines [14] and [3] and introduces several extensions and modifications, with a special focus on dimensionality reduction at various levels of the algorithm. Our presented research results are developed on this wavelet-based classification work.

Detection methods are bottom-up approaches that scan the whole image and are therefore rather time consuming and typically not suitable for video processing. Hence, we have developed a system that combines the detection with particle filtering, resulting in a top-down approach that only evaluates the detection function at the likely new object positions. In comparison, most of the state-of-the-art approaches either recognize people at every frame or they detect them in an initial frame and then track them through the sequence. To handle cluttered backgrounds and partial occlusions, particle filters have proven sufficient as multiple hypotheses are handled simultaneously. Beside edge-based image features [5] also color distributions [7] have been used in particle filter frameworks to track people. Up to now, only a few researches have merged these two tasks [13, 4]. Verma et al. [13] describe a face detection and tracking system that uses the detection method by Schneiderman et al. [12] and combine it with a particle filter. While our first segmentation step also applies wavelets, our further processing follows a different idea. Instead of using statistics of wavelet coefficients (histograms), we utilize the output of the SVM directly. Furthermore, features are combined hierarchically to model both the upper part of a body in general and specific characteristics of an individual person. Giebel et al. [4] present also a combination between a detector and a tracker. Although they use a particle filtering framework for tracking, they detect pedestrians using a hierarchical template matching technique while the matching involves traversing a tree structure of templates.

The recognition task within this work is solved using a hierarchical approach where first people are detected in general and then specific characters. Besides the aspect of time saving, the hierarchical decision tree also reduces the rate of false positives in comparison to several independent detectors. Nakajima et al. [8] also follow the concept of a hierarchical technique. They establish a system for people recognition and pose estimation where color histograms and local features are used. SVMs are learned for all combination of classes and combined hierarchically to form a decision tree. In comparison to our approach, besides different features and using a different SVM approach, the authors in [8] employ a static background and no tracking is done. Furthermore, they assume that people do not change clothing.

The novelty of the proposed system lies in the original mixture of a hierarchical feature selection based on wavelet transforms which feeds into a SVM to classify the feature first as person and then as a specific character. This detector is combined with a particle filtering framework to yield a universal, reliable and fast system for recognition, tracking and pose estimation of people.

2 Pedestrian Detection

The following sections describe the key components of the pedestrian – or general object – detection system as presented by [2] which provides the foundation of our approach. It gives an overview of the concepts which are relevant for the presented work. For a deeper understanding the reader is referred to [2, 14, 3].

The pedestrian detector is based on the ability to classify a rectangular image patch as pedestrian or non-pedestrian. Therefore, to detect all pedestrians in an image, an exhaustive search over the whole image using various scaling levels is required.

The actual detection is split into two parts: *feature extraction* and *classification*. The former consists of a 2D wavelet transformation of the patch, where the resulting feature vector is then classified by a SVM.

This approach has been shown to deliver very good detection performance, nevertheless, it is computationally very expensive. Therefore, various techniques have been investigated to cut down processing time without sacrificing detection quality. Indeed, it was possible to make the algorithm several magnitudes faster, so that it works almost in real-time and as such is also suitable for use in video sequences instead of static images only.

2.1 Wavelet Transform

The 2D wavelet transform is used to extract a collection of features from a rectangular patch of interest in an image. There exist various other ways of transforming an image into a feature vector, but wavelets have some very attractive properties for our application. They provide basic shape information without the need for explicit models, and they can be computed very fast, especially using Haar-type wavelets.

Other feature extraction techniques typically have drawbacks in at least one of these two aspects. Either they do not provide enough shape information, or it is very expensive to extract the features. Color histograms for example are a purely global feature of the object region while raw pixel values do not include edge information. DFTs are somehow related to the wavelet transform but suffer from the trade-off between spatial or frequency resolution. Complex shape models may provide quite accurate and valuable information, but the calculation of the best matching parameters is generally expensive.

In Fig. 1 the 2D wavelet transform using Haar wavelets is depicted. Basically, it shows the decomposition of an image using the three characteristic Haar-patterns and the corresponding image representation at different scale levels.

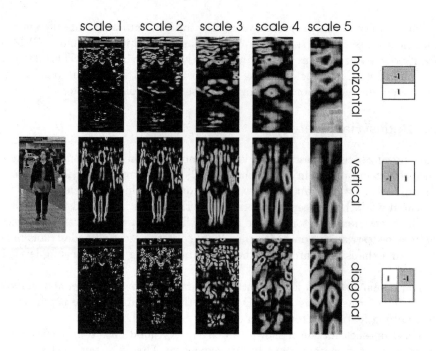

Fig. 1. Schematic representation of the 2D wavelet transform using Haar wavelets

2.2 Feature Selection

The task of feature selection is important as it determines the speed of the system. Doing a complete wavelet transform even on a small region can easily lead to very high dimensional data vectors. Sizes of hundreds or thousands of dimensions are not uncommon.

We use the AdaBoost based method as described in [14] and used in [2]. There exist various other techniques for feature selection but as shown in [2] it compares favorable to other methods. AdaBoost itself does not originate in the feature selection field. As the name suggests it is a boosting technique which has the goal to improve the accuracy of a given learning algorithm by combining several weak classifiers to build a strong classifier.

The adaptation of boosting to feature selection is based on the principle of using a separate classifier for each single feature. The algorithm then successively selects the features that perform the best. Additionally, the samples in the training set are weighted after every iteration to focus on the falsely classified ones at that point.

2.3 Support Vector Machine Classification

Support Vector Machines (SVMs) represent an algorithm that learns pattern classification from given positive and negative exemplars. The basic idea is to map the training data into a higher dimensional feature space where the two classes can be separated by a linear hyperplane. This is done in an optimal way, namely by maximizing the margin between the the hyperplane and the closest patterns of both classes. An important point to note is that the mapping is done implicitly by using a kernel function K. Such a kernel has the property that while being some – usually nonlinear – function of two vectors in the input space it corresponds to a dot product of the arguments in the mapped feature space.

After the training stage we get an evaluation function which is based on a number of kernel evaluations on support vectors $\{s_i\}_{i=1}^{N_s}$ – the patterns lying closest to the separating plane:

$$f(\boldsymbol{x}) = \sum_{i=1}^{N_s} \alpha_i y_i K(\boldsymbol{s}_i, \boldsymbol{x}) + b \tag{1}$$

where $\boldsymbol{x}$ represents the feature vector based on wavelets. $y_i \in \{-1, 1\}$ denotes the class membership of the respective support vector $\boldsymbol{s}_i$. α_i and b are coefficients and an offset determined in the training phase while searching the optimal separating plane. The class membership of $\boldsymbol{x}$ is then given by taking the sign of the evaluation function $\mathrm{sgn}(f(\boldsymbol{x}))$.

There exist various kernels that can be used for SVM classification. We extensively use a second order polynomial $(\boldsymbol{s}_i \cdot \boldsymbol{x} + 1)^2$ in our work because it delivers good classification performance at moderate computational complexity.

An important point to note at this point is that SVMs provide very good generalization performance. They have a very well developed mathematical foundation which allows them to be analyzed much easier than other algorithms like for example neural networks.

3 People Recognition

3.1 Direct Approach

Based on the pedestrian detector described above, a system for detecting and recognizing people is constructed in a straightforward manner. The idea is to use several person specific detectors instead of having just one single detector for any person. Due to the completely self-adapting nature of the pedestrian detector, it is fairly easy to construct such a specialized detector for a person. All that is required are separate training sets for each of the individuals that shall be recognized. For each individual the most important features are determined first by the method described in section 2.2. The system is then trained using a character specific set together with a set of negatives containing no people.

In this manner a set of detectors is created, one for each of the individuals. So, a single character is detected and recognized in one step. In order to find all characters on an image the detectors are applied separately on the image. Thus, the characters are located sequentially.

3.2 Hierarchical Approach

In this section we present a more elaborate technique for the detection and recognition of people that uses a hierarchical structure. Instead of doing the recognition in one step, the described algorithm contains multiple stages. Each of these stages accomplishes a specific task in the chain and is related to a certain "level of detail".

The reason for following this approach comes from experiments on recognition of people (see section 6.1) which indicate that a detector for a specific person also responds to other people. As a consequence, a hierarchical approach is proposed for the task of detection and recognition of people. The principle is shown for the case of a two stage hierarchy and two different persons. In a first step, a general people detector is used to locate people independently from their identity. In a second step, the system tries to discriminate the different characters. The advantage of this approach is that we avoid repeating the general people detection part as it would be the case when using the direct approach. So, our system can be described in the following way:

- **Stage 1: General People Detector.** To construct the general people detector two training sets are acquired, one containing exemplars of *all* the characters to be recognized, the other one containing random non-person exemplars. First, the most important features are determined using the AdaBoost technique described in section 2.2. Based on the obtained feature set, the SVM classifier is trained.
- **Stage 2: Discriminator.** To build a discriminator, a pair of training sets is needed, each containing exemplars of one specific actor. Given these training sets feature selection is carried out (section 2.2). Then, the SVM classifier is trained on those features.

The presented approach has to be extended when there are more than two individuals. A possible approach is to build additional two-class discriminators and to combine them in a multi-class discriminator. Another possibility is to extend the hierarchy further. The latter approach is more appropriate in the sense that it follows the underlying idea of hierarchy.

The advantage of using hierarchies is strongly related to the principle of information reuse. In the case of separate detectors, the information of a person being present is calculated for each character and then thrown away. With the hierarchical approach it is collected once only, which reduces computing time.

Another aspect of hierarchical recognition is its connection to the scene description. One can think of different ways of giving a description like: "There are two people in this scene". Or else a more detailed information is requested like who is in the scene and what are they doing. With the proposed hierarchical approach this is automatically available.

4   Pose Estimation

The task of pose estimation in our approach is addressed in the same way as the problem of recognizing people described above. We use a combination of the wavelet transform and SVM classification like in the pedestrian detector. Based on that technique, several pose specific detectors are created. In fact, they are discriminators each of which is responsible for separating one pair of poses. The final pose can then be inferred by combining these two-class classifiers to form a multi-class classifier.

In fact, the way of building a pose discriminator is similar to stage 1 of the hierarchical people detector (section 3.2). But instead of training sets with specific characters we use specific poses for training.

Currently, we have chosen to focus on the orientation of a person as pose. To this end separate training sets have been collected for frontal views of a person and for situations where the person is facing either to the left or to the right side.

5   Tracking

To speed up the detection, the SVM is integrated into a particle filter [5], also known as Condensation approach in the computer vision community. This has the advantage that the tracking furthermore reduces false detections which creep into the detection when no temporal knowledge is used. The Condensation algorithm can represent non-linear problems and non-Gaussian densities by propagating multiple alternate hypotheses (samples) simultaneously.

Basically, Condensation is used as the general tracking framework whereas the role of the detector is to provide a measure for each of the samples of the Condensation tracker. The physical properties of our objects are represented in a first order motion model for position and a zero order model for the size.

The weights of each sample is determined by the according output of the SVM evaluation function. Additionally, an exponential function is applied which allows to parametrize the focus of the tracker in a flexible way. It can either concentrate on the few best scoring samples only or make a more uniform selection among the samples.

6   Experimental Results

The experiments are demonstrated on sitcoms as they offer a constrained world in terms of the number of characters and the number of sets. However, they are challenging as camera movements, different non-static backgrounds and appearance changes have to be managed.

The following results are presented on an episode of "Fawlty Towers" from which training and test sets have been extracted for each of the main actors. The extraction has been done manually by specifying rectangles containing the upper part of the body of a specific actor.

That way a total of roughly 1000 exemplars per character have been collected from one half of an episode to serve as training set. The other half of the same episode has been used to create the test set. The individual sets have also been split up into pose specific sets containing *left*, *right* and *frontal* views. Additionally, for all sets a corresponding subset has been created consisting only of images that differ substantially in their background. These have been used for feature selection because otherwise a lot of non-person areas would have been considered important. All the following results were produced by processing grey scale images, as the use of color information brings only minor improvements [2].

6.1   People Recognition

Figure 2 shows a result for the direct approach to people detection and recognition applied to a test image. The rectangles indicate the regions where the algorithm has detected the character Basil. As it can be seen there are several detections that are correct, varying slightly in scale and position [1].

Fig. 2. Basil detector using the direct approach

There are some false detections however, of which some point to another character of the series named Manuel. This indicates that a recognizer for a particular person also responds to other people.

A comparison of the direct approach for people recognition with the hierarchical approach is presented in Fig. 3 in terms of ROC curves. They show the recognition performance for the character Basil.

The two direct detectors as well as the hierarchical approach are trained using the 80 most important features. This facilitates the determination of the computational complexity because it results in a comparison of the total number of support vectors.

---

[1] By post-processing the results, it is possible to combine several overlapping regions into one single region.

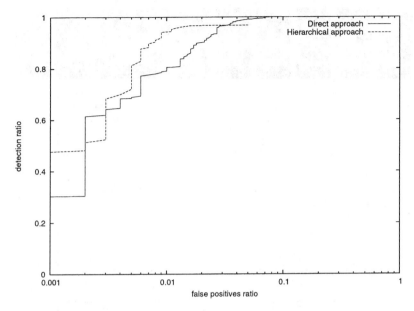

Fig. 3. Comparison of the direct and the hierarchical approach for recognition, ROC curves are shown for Basil

Table 1. Number of support vectors for the direct recognition and the hierarchical approach

Direct:	Basil	110 ⟩ 180
	Manuel	70
Hierarchical:	Basil/Manuel combined	157 ⟩ 187
	Basil vs Manuel	30

Table 1 shows the exact number of support vectors computed for the chosen setup. The total effort needed is about the same for both approaches. In detail it depends on the probability of a frame to contain Basil, Manuel or neither of them. Under the assumption that only a fraction of all frames contains a person the hierarchical scheme is faster as it only needs to evaluate one SVM in most cases.

Comparing the two approaches, the ROC curves show that the hierarchical approach is superior in the range of 70-95% recognition rate. An important property of both methods is that the percentage of false positives increases quickly when going towards very high detection rates. To avoid the undesirable effect of too many false positives one can reduce the detection rate slightly below the achievable maximum. Interestingly, at this point the hierarchical approach turns out to be much better in the sense that it shows a very low ratio of false positives. Looking at the horizontal distance of the two curves and considering the logarithmic scale of the abscissa, the amount of false positives is several times higher for the direct approach.

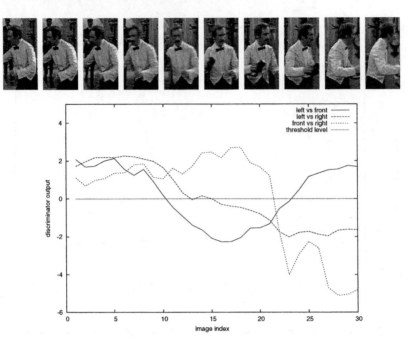

Fig. 4. Response of the 2 class pose estimators on a characteristic sequence

In the context of video analysis the loss of detections can be compensated by the fact that a single shot tends to be represented by several key frames, thereby giving the detectors repeated chances to detect the actor. On the other hand, an avalanche of false positives renders automated retrieval tools like these close to useless.

6.2 Pose Estimation

For pose estimation the following three discriminator have been trained: $left \Leftrightarrow front$, $left \Leftrightarrow right$ and $front \Leftrightarrow right$. In the feature selection step the 40 most important features have been selected. This is less compared to the detection and recognition task. Our experiments have shown that it is much easier to determine poses than to detect people.

An example for pose estimation is shown in Fig. 4, on a sequence of images where Manuel is performing a turn. The curve shows the corresponding outputs of the pose discriminators over time. Combining them results in the interpretation $left \rightarrow front \rightarrow right$ with transition indices around frames 10 and 21. This quite accurately corresponds to the true evolution of the pose.

6.3 Tracking

Figure 5 shows an example of our proposed tracking algorithm. The individual particles are shown as rectangles to bring out the characteristics of the processing. The first thing to note is that the actual tracking succeeds although the sequence offers some challenges. In the middle of the sequence the person is partially occluded, which is typically not handled very well in other approaches. In our example we see that for a short interval the tracking becomes inaccurate, but after becoming completely visible again the correct focus is regained. Clearly, this shows the robustness of our method against partial occlusion.

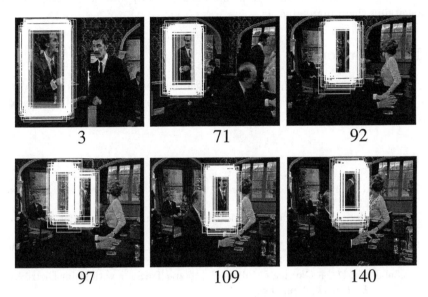

Fig. 5. Tracking Basil

For comparison, we also tested a gradient method combined with a Kalman filter. The prediction of the Kalman filter provides a rough state estimation while this initial result is then optimized along the gradient of the SVM function. However, we noticed that this tracking approach can easily get stuck in local minima while particle filters recover due to the multiple hypotheses.

7   Summary and Conclusions

We have presented an approach for recognition, tracking and pose estimation of people in video sequences. Results have been shown for analyzing sitcoms, but further applications like surveillance, human-computer interfaces etc. can be envisioned. The new contributions of our approach are

- combining a wavelet and SVM based detector with particle filtering,
- using a hierarchical recognition scheme to first detect people and then discriminate between different individuals, whereby all the parameters are learned automatically,
- using our combined approach for pose estimation.

Indeed, our system relies on sufficient discriminative data. Also it has not yet been tested with a large number of object classes expressing higher overall variance. Especially it is not obvious how to structure the problem and build a hierarchy in that case.

Future work may include integration of the tracker with the pose estimator. Pose recognition could be extended to gesture recognition. Finally, it would be very interesting to find an algorithm that automatically finds hierarchies instead of specifying them manually.

Acknowledgments

The authors would like to thank the European project CogViSys for supporting this work and IM2 and the PASCAL network for providing an inspiring research environment.

References

1. M. C. Burl, T. K. Leung and P. Perona, "Face Localization via Shape Statistics", *FG'95*, pp. 154-159.
2. V. Depoortere et al., "Efficient pedestrian detection: a test case for SVM based categorization", *DAGM'02, Cognitive Vision workshop*
3. T. Evgeniou, M. Pontil, C. Papageorgiou and T. Poggio, "Image representations for object detection using kernel classifiers" *ACCV'2000*, pp. 687-692.
4. J. Giebel and D. M. Gavrila, "Multimodal Shape Tracking with Point Distribution Models", *DAGM'2002*, pp. 1-8.
5. M. Isard and A. Blake, "CONDENSATION – Conditional Density Propagation for Visual Tracking", *IJCV'98*, Vol. 1, No. 29, pp. 5-28.
6. M. Isard and A. Blake, "A Mixed-state Condensation Tracker with Automatic Model-switching", *ICCV'98*, pp. 107-112.
7. M. Isard and J. MacCormick, "BraMBLe: A Bayesian Multiple-Blob Tracker", *International Conference on Computer Vision*, pp. 34-41, 2001.
8. C. Nakajima, M. Pontil and T. Poggio, "People Recognition and Pose Estimation in Image Sequences", *IJCNN'2000*.
9. M. Oren, C. Papageorgiou, P. Sinha, E. Osuna and T. Poggio, "Pedestrian detection using wavelet templates" *CVPR'97*, pp. 193-199.
10. E. Osuna, R. Freund and F. Girosi, "Training Support Vector Machines: an Application to Face Detection", *ICCV'97*, pp. 130-136.
11. H. A. Rowley, S. Buluja and T. Kande, "Neural Networks Based Face Detection", *PAMI'98*, Vol. 20, No. 1, pp. 22-38.
12. H. Schneiderman and T. Kanade, "A Statistic Method for 3D Object Detection Applied to Faces and Cars", *CVPR'2000*, Vol. I, pp. 746-751,.
13. R. Verma, C. Schmid and K. Mikolajczyk, "Face Detection and Tracking in a Video By Propagating Detection Probabilities", *PAMI'2003*, Vol. 25, No. 10, Oct., pp. 1215-1227.
14. P. Viola and M. Jones, "Robust Real-time Object Detection." *SCTV'2001*.
15. G. Yang and T. Huang, "Human Face Detection in a Complex Background", *Pattern Recognition*, Vol. 27, pp. 53-63, 1994.

Automatic Pedestrian Tracking Using Discrete Choice Models and Image Correlation Techniques

Santiago Venegas-Martinez[1], Gianluca Antonini[1,2], Jean Philippe Thiran[1], and Michel Bierlaire[2]

[1] Signal Processing Institute (ITS), Swiss Federal Institute of Technology (EPFL), CH-1015 Lausanne, Switzerland
{santiago.venegas,Gianluca.Antonini,JP.Thiran}@epfl.ch
http://itswww.epfl.ch
[2] Michel Bierlaire, Operation Research Group ROSO, Swiss Federal Institute of Technology (EPFL), CH-1015 Lausanne, Switzerland
http://roso.epfl.ch
michel.bierlaire@epfl.ch

Abstract. In this paper we deal with the multi-object tracking problem, with specific reference to the visual tracking of pedestrians, assuming that the pedestrian-detection step is already done. We use a Bayesian framework to combine the visual information provided by a simple image correlation algorithm with a behavioral model (discrete choice model) for pedestrian dynamic, calibrated on real data. We aim to show how the combination of the image information with a model of pedestrian behavior can provide appreciable results in real and complex scenarios.

1 Introduction

Springer In the last years the problem of the automatic multi-object detection and tracking in video sequences has found a wide range of applications. Computer vision, military and automatic surveillance systems, among the others, need reliable object tracking algorithms. In the literature we can find two main approaches. The first one is based on the target detection, where an *a-priori* knowledge of the object is necessary, for example in terms of shape, color, or texture cues. For each frame a predefined class of objects has to be detected and the tracking is performed by linking the candidates between consecutive frames [1]. In the second approach, the objects are encoded in a state-space representation [2], [3], where the state vectors (a feature-based representation of the targets) evolve over time driven by a dynamic model. Information from the propagation model and observations of the state variables are combined in a more informative posterior distribution, under a more general Bayesian framework. Different hypothesis on the noise term, gaussian/non-gaussian, and on the dynamic model equations, linear/non-linear, give rise to different and well known tracking algorithms, e.g. Kalman filter, particle filtering. In this direction many efforts have been done to improve the definition of the state-space variables and theirs dynamics, increasing the complexity of the image processing algorithms. Unfortunately, the propagation model is often defined on the image plan. This implies that the reproduced object dynamic is not always meaningful and reliable, being an image-plan

S. Bengio and H. Bourlard (Eds.): MLMI 2004, LNCS 3361, pp. 341–348, 2005.

projection of the 3D real world version. The main contribution of this paper is the combination of a proposed behavioral model for pedestrian dynamic, calibrated on real data, with a standard image processing technique, as image correlation, to approach the pedestrian tracking problem in real and complex scenarios. We assume to use a calibrated camera in such a way to know the camera parameters to have a unique correspondence between the image plan and the Top-View plan, i.e. the plane obtained with the camera ideally placed at the top of the scene to avoid projection and occlusion between objects [4] The paper is structured as follow: in section 2 we present the problem definition from a Bayesian point of view, in section 3 and 4 we explain how we get the two different source of information from image and from the behavioral model, in section 5 we combine them. We conclude presenting our results and final remarks in section 6.

2 The Bayesian Framework

The Bayesian theorem represents a natural theoretical framework to combine different sources of information, described by different probability distributions. In its more general formulation, the Bayes's low is described by the well known equation:

$$P(M|D) \; \alpha \; P(D|M) \cdot P(M) \tag{1}$$

where the left side represents the posterior distribution as the result of the combination of the information coming from the data D, observations, and from a model M describing the underlying process. In our approach we identify the $P(D|M)$ term with an image correlation matrix, opportunely normalized, and the $P(M)$ term with the probabilities given by our discrete choice model for pedestrian behavior.

3 Normalized Correlation Matrix

We compute the image correlation working on a foreground mask (obtained by background subtraction) for each frame. A detailed description of the pre-processing tasks we use can be found in [5]. Let be tr_t^i the i-th detected pedestrian position at frame t and let be r_t^i and $\hat{r}_{t+1}^i$, respectively, the image search region centered around tr_t^i and the image region centered around the same position as tr_t^i but at frame $t+1$. We compute the correlation matrix by Fast Fourier transforms to have better computational performances. The use of this method is justified, apart from its simplicity, by the assumption of the existence of a maximum displacement covered by a pedestrian over the time interval $[t, t+1]$. As a consequence, it is reasonable to assume that the true pedestrian position at frame $t+1$ stays inside the $\hat{r}_{t+1}^i$ region. In order to look at the correlation matrix as a matrix of probabilities and in order to use it in a Bayesian context, we normalize it as follow:

$$NC_{t,t+1}^i(h,k) = \frac{C_{t,t+1}^i(h,k)}{\sum_l \sum_m C_{t,t+1}^i(l,m)} \tag{2}$$

where $C_{t,t+1}^i(h,k)$ represents (h,k)-element of the correlation matrix between r_t^i and $\hat{r}_{t+1}^i$ for the i-th pedestrian and the denominator is the sum of all the elements of the matrix. This normalization implies the assumption that the probability of finding the pedestrian i in a certain position, inside the $\hat{r}_{t+1}^i$ region, is proportional to the corresponding correlation value.

3.1 Estimation of the Region Size

Normally, in correlation methods, the size of the search region represents a critical point. Assuming it as fixed is surely a coarse approximation while the attempts to take into account the geometric perspective results in quite complicated deformation models, with consequent increasing in the computational cost. In our case, we use the *a-priori* information about the target object to solve this tedious problem. We assume an averaged height of pedestrians equal to 160 cm, ignoring the error introduced by this approximation. As shown in Fig. 1, we estimate the size of the target by projecting its Top-View position on the image plan [5]. The search region is then proportional to the target size.

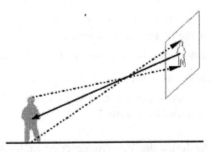

Fig. 1. Using the *a-priori* knowledge on the averaged pedestrian height it is easy to have adaptive search regions on the image plan

4   A Discrete Choice Model for Pedestrian Dynamic

The $P(M)$ term of equation 1 is provided by the discrete choice model probabilities [6], [7]. Without go into the model specification details (see [5] and [8]), we describe here the basic concepts:

- a pedestrian is a *decision maker* who has a finite set of alternative top-view positions, the so called *choice set*. These alternatives represent all the possible spatial positions where the current pedestrian can put the next step. The size and orientation of the choice set depend on the current pedestrian speed module and direction (see Fig. 2);

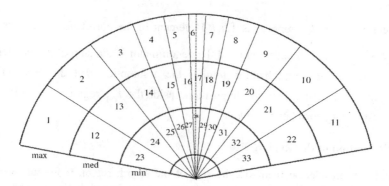

Fig. 2. The choice set is composed by 33 spatial alternatives. It is the result of 11 radial directions and 3 speed regimes (accelerated, constant speed and decelerated)

- for each alternative position j the decision maker i perceives an utility value U_{ij} which is a random variable. It is composed by a deterministic term V_{ij} function of a set of attributes describing the alternatives and a set of socio-economic attributes describing the decision maker and a random term ε that captures the correlation between alternatives;

- the output of a discrete choice model is a set of probabilities, P_j representing the probability of alternative j to be chosen by pedestrian i in a *random utility maximization* decision process. Outside the choice set, the model probability is assumed to be zero.

The attributes used to define the V_{ij} term describe each alternative in terms of the costs the decision maker should meet to move the next step on that alternative. They derive from the empirical knowledge we have about the pedestrian behavior, summerized in the following points: tendency to keep the current speed value; tendency to keep the current direction; tendency to move, if it is possible, directly towards the fixed destination; tendency to avoid collisions with other pedestrians; tendency to avoid positions that represent crossing points among many other pedestrian's trajectories; tendency to avoid positions with many other pedestrians. These empirics are formalized in the following expression:

$$V_{ij} = L_j + S_j \tag{3}$$

where the linear term L_j is defined as:

$$L_j = \sum_{k=1}^{K} \beta_k \cdot X_{jk} \tag{4}$$

and the non-linear speed term S_j as:

$$S_j = \beta_{acc} \cdot v_{dm}^{\lambda acc} + \beta_{dec} \cdot v_{dm}^{\lambda dec} \tag{5}$$

The elements X_{jk} are the K attributes used to describe the alternative j. They are: occupation, crossing, direction, destination, collision, acceleration, deceleration. We can think about the attributes in term of costs with their weights (β's. The cost related to move towards alternatives with a high occupation value (presence of other pedestrians, β_1), the cost of an alternative with many intersection points with other pedestrian's trajectories (β_2), the cost due to a change in direction (β_3), an angular displacement from an established destination (β_4) and the cost of alternatives that cause collisions (β_5). The β_{acc} and β_{dec} coefficients of the speed term refer to accelerated and decelerated alternatives (see Fig. 3) and λ_{acc} and λ_{dec} represent *elasticity* parameters, expressing how responsive is the speed term to changes in the decision maker current speed value (v_{dm}). The β's and λ's coefficients are unknown and have to be estimated. We use the Biogeme[1], based on a maximum likelihood estimation procedure. The data for the training process, Top-View pedestrian trajectories, are collected manually using 36 pedestrians from a test sequence. The nature of the correlation between alternatives is double (see Fig. 3). On one side we have the direction that plays an important role, in fact seems reasonable to consider as correlated those alternatives oriented along the same radial direction. On the other side there are the speed regimes in such a way the accelerated, decelerated and constant speed alternatives are, respectively, correlated. To capture this correlation structure we use a mixed nested logit formulation, where we model the correlation due to speed with the usual Gumbel disturbance term and the correlation due to direction with an error structure formulation [9]. The mixed formulation allows to keep a closed-form solution for the choice probabilities P_j.

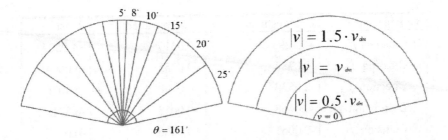

Fig. 3. The double nature of the correlation. The speed regimes and the radial directions make the alternatives to be correlated. This correlation has captured with specific hypothesis on the disturbance terms of the utility function

[1] Michel Bierlaire. An introduction to BIOGEME Version 0.6, February 2003. http://roso.epfl.ch/mbi/

5 The Posterior Distribution

We have defined the two sources of information. The first is related to the image correlation matrix, so it is defined on the image itself. The second is represented by the model probabilities, so it is referred to the probability of each position to become the next position of the current pedestrian. This source of information is therefore defined on the top-view plan (the horizontal plane where actually pedestrians move). To use the Bayes theorem, we need to project each element of the normalized correlation matrix $NC_{t,t+1}^i$, whose indexes define a position in the $\hat{r}_{t,t+1}^i$ image region, on the top-view plan and multiply it for the corresponding probability value that has given, for the same projected position, by the discrete choice model. As a result we obtain a new probability matrix, the posterior, whose maximum point indexes define a position in $\hat{r}_{t,t+1}^i$ having the maximum probability to be the next position chosen by the current pedestrian.

6 Results and Conclusions

We have shown an integration of a discrete choice pedestrian behavioral model and image correlation techniques under a Bayesian framework. The integration of the model allows us to avoid some classical problems in multi-tracking algorithms, as the jump of the trackers from one target to a close other one. Adaptive systems, where a behavioral model is computed for each object in the scene, are an useful tool when we have an *a-priori* knowledge about the objects that have to be tracked. We report in Table 1 the model estimation results. We can see how the estimated coefficient are statistically significant and the initial and final likelihood values show that the model matches quite good the available data. In Fig. 4 we show some frames from a test

Table 1. Estimation of the utility parameters. Summary statistics : Init log-likelihood = -4863.819, and Final log-likelihood = -3586.05

Variable name	Coeff estimate	Asympt std err	t-test
Occupation β_1	+0.1293	+0.0319	+4.0507
Crossing β_2	-0.0782	+0.0255	-3.0604
Direction β_3	-0.0530	+0.0098	-5.4026
Destination β_4	-0.0468	+0.0053	-8.8315
Collision β_5	-0.0061	+0.0066	-0.9165
Acceleration β_{acc}	-27.642	+5.4661	-5.0570
Deceleration β_{dec}	-0.8230	+0.1305	-6.3061
λ_{acc}	+1.5264	+0.1303	+11.709
λ_{dec}	-0.7138	+0.0879	-8.1157

sequence. Finally, in Fig. 5, we report two examples of tracked pedestrians[2]. Although the complexity of the scene is high and the camera field is quite large (implying a consistent perspective deformation of targets), our algorithm arrives to track several pedestrians. Multiple detection is the drawback in our system. The incorporation of shape cues and the study of trajectory similarity measures to merge trackers that belong to the same target are works in progress in our group.

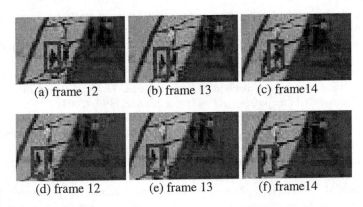

(a) frame 12   (b) frame 13   (c) frame 14

(d) frame 12   (e) frame 13   (f) frame 14

Fig. 4. Pure correlation tracking (a,b,c). At frame 14 the track on the left pedestrian jumps on the right one. Integration of the model (d,e,f). We have no tracker's jump

(a)   (b)

Fig. 5. Two examples of pedestrian tracking from real complex scenarios

Acknowledgment. This work is supported by the Swiss National Science Fundation under the NCCR-IM2 project and by the Swiss CTI under project Nr. 6067.1 KTS, in collaboration with VisioWave SA, Ecublens, Switzerland. Some of the original video sequences are courtesy of The Maia Institute, Monaco.

---

[2] The interested reader can find the elaborated video sequences at http://ltswww.epfl.ch/ltsftp/Venegas and http://ltswww.epfl.ch/ltsftp/antonini

References

1. Senior, A.W.: Tracking with Probabilistic Appearance Models, in proceedings ECCV workshop on Performance Evaluation of Tracking and Surveillance Systems, June (2002) 48-55
2. Bierlaire, M., Antonini, G., Weber, M.: Behavioural Dynamics for Pedestrians, in K. Axhausen (Ed.), Moving through nets: the physical and social dimensions of travel, Elsevier (2003) 1-18
3. Isard, M., Blake, A.: Condensation –conditional density propagation for visual tracking. International Journal on Computer Vision (1998) I(29):5-28
4. Venegas-Martinez, S., Knebel, J.F., Thiran, J.P.: Multi-Object Tracking using the Particle Filter Algorithm on the Top-View Plan, EUSIPCO (2004)
5. Antonini, G., Venegas-Martinez, S, Thiran, J.P., Bierlaire, M.: Behavioral filtering of human trajectories for automatic-multi-track initiation. Technical Report //ltswww.epfl.ch/ltsftp/Venegas/BeFilter.pdf, Signal Processing Institute, EPFL (2004)
6. Ben-Akiva, M., Bierlaire, M.: Discrete choice methods and their applications to short-term travel decisions. In Randolph Hall, (eds): Handbook of Transportation Science, Kluwer (1999) 5-34
7. Bierlaire, M.: A theoretical analysis of the cross-nested logit model. Accepted for publication in Annals of Operations Researchs.
8. Bierlaire, M., Antonini, G, Weber, M.: Behavioral dynamics for pedestrians. In K. Axhausen, (eds): Moving through nets: the physical and social dimensions of travel, Elsevier (2003) 1-18
9. Walker, J.L.: Extended Discrete Choise Models, Integrated Framework, Flexible Error Structures, and Latent Variables, PhD thesis, Massachusetts Institute of Technology (2001)

A Shape Based, Viewpoint Invariant Local Descriptor

Mihai Osian[1], Tinne Tuytelaars[1], and Luc Van Gool[1,2]

[1] Katholieke Universiteit Leuven, ESAT/PSI,
Kasteelpark Arenberg 10, Leuven 3001, Belgium
[2] Computer Vision Laboratory, BIWI, ETH Zurich,
Gloriastrasse 35, ETH-Zentrum,
CH - 8092 Zurich, Switzerland

Abstract. Affine invariant regions have proved a powerful feature for object recognition and categorization. These features heavily rely on object textures rather than shapes, however. Typically, their shapes have been fixed to ellipses or parallelograms. The paper proposes a novel affine invariant region type, that is built up from a combination of fitted superellipses. These novel features have the advantage of offering a much wider range of shapes through the addition of a very limited number of shape parameters, with the traditional ellipses and parallelograms as subsets. The paper offers a solution for the robust fitting of superellipses to partial contours, which is a crucial step towards the implementation of the novel features.

1   Introduction

Quite recently, affine invariant regions have made a rather impressive entrance into computer vision (e.g. [1, 9, 12, 16, 18]). Soon, these features have shown to have great potential for some of the long-standing problems in computer vision such as viewpoint-independent object recognition (e.g. [15]),wide baseline matching (e.g. [17]), object categorization (e.g. [2, 3]) and texture classification (e.g. [8]).

Affine invariant regions in a way ran contrary to what had been the dominant credo in the recognition literature up to that point, namely that shapes, parts, and contours were the crucial features, not texture. Yet, none of the shape related strategies had ever been able to reach the same level of performance. Intuitively, it is difficult to accept that shape shouldn't play a bigger role. Also, strategies based on affine invariant regions have not been demonstrated to recognize untextured objects and therefore offer only a partial solution. Previous attempts to construct invariant shape based features are usually limited to scale invariance and stick to circular shapes [7, 6], or try to find geometrically consistent constellations of other local simple features [10], which brings additional computational burdain. We propose a generalization of affine invariant regions. In contrast to those proposed in literature, these regions do adapt their shapes to that of the local object contours. They are based on the fitting of affinely deformed superellipses to contour segments. By combining several, partial superellipses a wide variety of region shapes can be generated with the addition of only few parameters.

The paper is structured as follows: Section 2 introduces the family of shapes called "affine superellipses". Section 3 presents our approach to fitting affine superellipses to

S. Bengio and H. Bourlard (Eds.): MLMI 2004, LNCS 3361, pp. 349–359, 2005.

partial contours. Section 4 shows some preliminary results that we obtained. Conclusions are drawn in Section 5.

2   Affine Superellipses

Ellipses and parallelograms are ideal shapes to build affine invariant regions from, because both families of shapes are closed under affine transformations. On the other hand, they are quite restrictive in terms of the possible shapes. There is a family of curves, however, that takes one additional parameter, and generates a much wider class of shapes. These are the so-called 'superellipses'. Superellipses were introduced in 1818 by the French mathematician Gabriel Lamé. Their Cartesian equation is [19]:

$$\left|\frac{x}{a}\right|^r + \left|\frac{y}{b}\right|^r = 1$$

To avoid the modulus, the above formula can be written as a function of x^2, y^2 and an exponent ϵ [5]. We first consider the particular case when the scaling coefficients a and b are both 1. We call this initial family of shapes "supercircle" of unit radius (see Fig. 1):

$$\left(x^2\right)^\epsilon + \left(y^2\right)^\epsilon = 1 \qquad (1)$$

The addition of the single parameter ϵ yields an interesting variety of shapes. Next we generalize this shape family to one that is closed under affine transformations, more precisely shapes that can be reduced to a supercircle via an affine transformation. The rationale is that as in the case of existing affine invariant regions, we want to find corresponding regions under variable viewpoints. These changes can be represented well by affine transformations. Hence, points x_e on these shapes are found as:

$$x_e = A x_c \qquad (2)$$

where x_c verifies the supercircle equation (1) and A is shorthand for the 3×3 affine transformation matrix. This family of shapes is wider than that of the original superellipses. Not only does it allow for rigid motions of the superellipses, but it also includes skewed versions, as exemplified in fig. 2. Applying affine transformations to superellipses rather than supercircles leads to exactly the same family, but with an over-parameterized representation.

We refer to the family as *affine superellipses* or *ASEs* for short. The parameter ϵ provides a viewpoint independent shape parameter. If we can compose curves with a

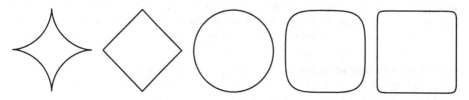

Fig. 1. "Supercircles" for different values of ϵ: 0.3, 0.5, 1, 2, 8

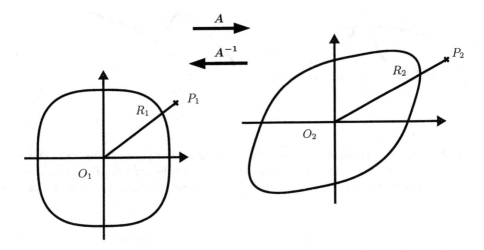

Fig. 2. Result of applying an affine transformation A to a supercircle

small set of well fitting ASEs, the corresponding ϵs and the ASEs' configuration provide compact and viewpoint independent shape information. Fitting ASEs is the subject of the next section.

3   ASE Fitting

The problem of fitting superellipses is not entirely new. Rosin [14] has compared several objective functions to be minimized. These functions represent summed distances between the data points and selected points on the model curve. It proved difficult to choose one that would perform best in all cases. An important limitation was that contours were supposed to be closed. Fitting of an initial bounding box allowed him to immediately get rid of the translation and rotation components in the optimization. In a subsequent paper Zhang and Rosin [21] generalized the optimization to partial contours. They also mapped shapes back to the circle, as a normalization step prior to the evaluation of the objective function. The latter consisted of a sum of algebraic distances between the normalized contour and the circle, taking the local contour gradient and curvature into account.

In our work, we have to deal with partial contours. We also add the skew parameter in order to deal with the full set of ASEs. Moreover, using the algebraic distance depends exponentially on ϵ. For example, considering the point (x, y) on the unit radius supercircle, the point $(x + d, y)$ yields the error $(x + d)^{2\epsilon} - x^{2\epsilon}$. This means that rectangular shapes ($\epsilon \gg 1$) are more sensitive to outliers. Therefore, we use the Euclidean distance between contour points and the intersection of the ASE with the join through the point and the ASE's center. Notice that this procedure does not normalize the ASE to a supercircle and, hence, the fitting procedure is not strictly affine invariant. We have found that prior normalization yields fitting results that are less robust, however. Some examples illustrating this are shown in fig. 3. We still need to study the precise causes

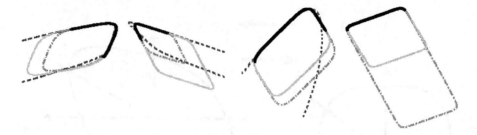

Fig. 3. Fitting superellipses to partial data. The red dashed lines represent the results of fitting using normalized distance, dotted green lines represent fitting using image distance. The original contours are gray. The segments used for fitting are drawn in black. In the last case the normalized version failed to converge

in more depth. It should be noted that the Zhang and Rosin approach is also not affine invariant, even if they normalize, as they evenly sample the image contour before normalizing. Affine invariance wasn't part of their goals. This sampling problem is shared by the PCA-based methods proposed by Pilu et al. [13], which deal with larger sets of deformations than affine, but only for closed contours.

With the notations from fig. 2, we minimize the sum of all squared Euclidean distances $P_2 R_2$, where P_2 represents a data point and R_2 is the intersection between the ASE and the line passing through P_2 and O_2 - the ASE's center:

$$D = \sum_{P_2 \in data} |P_2 - R_2|^2 \tag{3}$$

The location of R_2 is computed as follows:

$$R_2 = A R_1 \tag{4}$$

where A is an affine matrix expressing the translation T, rotation R, scale S and skew K of the ASE:

$$A = TRSK \tag{5}$$

$$T = \begin{bmatrix} 1 & 0 & t_x \\ 0 & 1 & t_y \\ 0 & 0 & 1 \end{bmatrix} \; ; \; R = \begin{bmatrix} \cos\theta & \sin\theta & 0 \\ -\sin\theta & \cos\theta & 0 \\ 0 & 0 & 1 \end{bmatrix}$$

$$S = \begin{bmatrix} s_x & 0 & 0 \\ 0 & s_y & 0 \\ 0 & 0 & 1 \end{bmatrix} \; ; \; K = \begin{bmatrix} 1 & k & 0 \\ 0 & 1 & 0 \\ 0 & 0 & 1 \end{bmatrix}$$

Switching to polar coordinates, R_1 becomes:

$$R_1(\rho, \theta) : \begin{cases} x_{R_1} = \rho_{R_1} \cos\theta_{R_1} \\ y_{R_1} = \rho_{R_1} \sin\theta_{R_1} \end{cases} \tag{6}$$

R_1 verifies the supercircle equation (1):

$$\left(\rho_{R_1}^2\right)^\epsilon \left(\left(\cos^2\theta_{R_1}\right)^\epsilon + \left(\sin^2\theta_{R_1}\right)^\epsilon\right) = 1 \tag{7}$$

$$\Leftrightarrow \rho_{R_1} = \left(\left(\cos^2 \theta_{R_1} \right)^{\epsilon} + \left(\sin^2 \theta_{R_1} \right)^{\epsilon} \right)^{\frac{-1}{2\epsilon}} \tag{8}$$

P_1 and R_1 are colinear, so by replacing

$$\begin{cases} \cos \theta_{R_1} = \dfrac{x_{P_1}}{\rho_{P_1}} \\ \sin \theta_{R_1} = \dfrac{y_{P_1}}{\rho_{P_1}} \end{cases}$$

in equations (6) and (8), R_1 can be written as a function of P_1 and ϵ:

$$R_1 = f(P_1, \epsilon) \Leftrightarrow \begin{cases} x_{R_1} = x_{P1} \left(\left(x_{P_1}^2 \right)^{\epsilon} + \left(y_{P_1}^2 \right)^{\epsilon} \right)^{\frac{-1}{2\epsilon}} \\ y_{R_1} = y_{P1} \left(\left(x_{P_1}^2 \right)^{\epsilon} + \left(y_{P_1}^2 \right)^{\epsilon} \right)^{\frac{-1}{2\epsilon}} \end{cases} \tag{9}$$

Also, $P_1 = A^{-1} P_2$, so the expression of R_2 is:

$$R_2 = A f(A^{-1} P_2, \epsilon) \tag{10}$$

Finally, the objective function has the following expression:

$$D = \sum_{P_2 \in data} |P_2 - A f(A^{-1} P_2, \epsilon)|^2 \tag{11}$$

This being a nonlinear least-squares minimization problem, we applied the Levenberg-Marquardt algorithm [20], a very effective and popular method for this category. The Levenberg-Marquardt algorithm requires an initial estimate of the objective function's parameters, then proceeds iteratively towards the minimum. At each iteration it needs to evaluate the residual error and the function's Jacobian matrix. The Jacobian has a quite complicated form, but the computations are straightforward so we omit them here.

The ϵ parameter is initialized to 2 and the skew to 0, while the other coefficients of the matrix A are initialized by an ellipse fitting algorithm [4]. The condition set for stopping the Levenberg-Marquardt algorithm is that for all of the 7 parameters the difference between successive iterations is less than 10^{-8}. On average less than 20 iterations are required for convergence.

3.1   Contour Extraction

An important issue is how the contours are extracted from natural images. Good contours are rather difficult to find, due to textures, occlusions, shadows, etc. For testing our algorithm we used a method introduced by Tuytelaars et al. [18]. Starting from a local extremum in the intensity $K(x, y)$, rays are shot under different angles. The intensity pattern along each ray emanating from the extremum is studied by evaluating the function

$$f_K(t) = \frac{|K(t) - K_0|}{max \left(d, \frac{1}{t} \int_0^t |K(\tau) - K_0| d\tau \right)}$$

with t being the Euclidean arc length along the ray, $K(t)$ the intensity at position t, K_0 the intensity extremum and d a small number added to prevent division by zero.

The point at which this function reaches an extremum is invariant under the affine geometric and photometric transformations (given the ray). All points corresponding to an extremum of f_K along the rays are linked to form a closed contour. These are the contours from which we select affine invariant segments and then fit ASEs against.

3.2   Selection of Invariant Contour Segments

When fitting to partial contours, there is a further issue that corresponding segments should be selected independent of viewpoint. This can be achieved by using simple, affine invariant criteria. One is illustrated in fig. 4. Starting from a point K, one can select a segment such that the chords from the point to each of the endpoints enclose the same area between them and the contour, i.e. $A_1 = A_2$ in fig. 4. There typically is an infinite number of such segments still. Demanding that the white triangle $\triangle KLM$ in the figure has the two areas summed ($A_1 + A_2 = 2A_1 = 2A_2$) reduces the number of such segments to a finite set of possibilities. These segments M - K - L are the ones we have fitted the ASEs to.

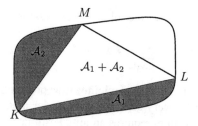

Fig. 4. Automatic selection of a partial contour: Starting from K, the chords KL and KM are drawn such that the areas A_1 and A_2 are equal and the area of the KLM triangle is equal to $A_1 + A_2$. The partial contour excludes the LM arc

When fitting we also look at the error. Local minima are of particular importance, as they suggest segments out of which the complete contour can be composed in a highly compact way. This point will be illustrated in the next section, where we show ASE-fits to contours extracted from real images.

4   Experimental Results

4.1   Synthetic Data

For testing the accuracy of the fitting module we generated noisy superellipses with different rotation, scaling, skew and epsilon coefficients. We fixed the horizontal scaling factor to 100, and modified the other parameters as follows: vertical scaling from 50 to 150 in 6 steps, rotation angle from 0 to $\pi/2$ in 30 steps, skew factor from -50 to 50 in 6 steps. For each combination we modified the value of ϵ from 1 to 30 in increments of 1 and verified the absolute error of the recovered ϵ for different noise levels. The noise was generated from a uniform distribution, having a spread of 0, 1, 2 and 4 pixels.

Fitting was done using only half of the full contour. The coordinates of the generated points were rounded to integer coordinates. The plot of the standard deviation of the estimated ϵ from the true value is shown in fig. 5. As can be seen, rectangular shapes ($\epsilon \gg 1$) are the worst affected by noise and rounding. This result is not surprising, since sharp corners become less clear as the noise increases.

In the absence of noise and without rounding the coordinates to integers, the fitting procedure can recover the original ϵ up to the fifth decimal.

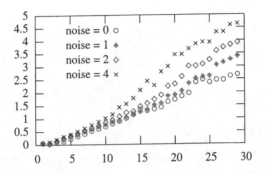

Fig. 5. Plot of the error of ϵ: The horizontal axis represents the ground truth ϵ. The vertical axis shows the standard deviation of the recovered ϵ

Fig. 6. A combination of two ASEs can approximate the rear window of a car

4.2   Natural Image Contours

Fig. 6 shows the back windows of a car, viewed from two directions. We show two types of ASEs that yield local minima for the fitting error. As can be seen, these correspond quite well, both between the mirror symmetric window pairs within each image, but also between the images. The overall shape can be represented efficiently as a combination of the two ASE types, as can be seen in the right column. The epsilon values are added in the figure and can be seen to be quite clustered. The difference in the values of ϵ is caused by non-zero mean errors during the contour extraction. Similar examples can be seen in fig. 7, 8.

Fig. 7. Car headlights represented with ASE combinations

Fig. 8. Viewpoint invariance. Note that the bottom-right image is affected by projective errors, thus the rectangular window must be approximated by two ASEs

Fig. 7 and 9 show ASEs fitted to the headlights of different cars. Again, as few as two ASEs manage to form a good approximation of these shapes. As one can see, in contrast to e.g. wheels, which always are elliptical with $\epsilon = 1$, head-lights are parts with a much wider variation in their shapes.

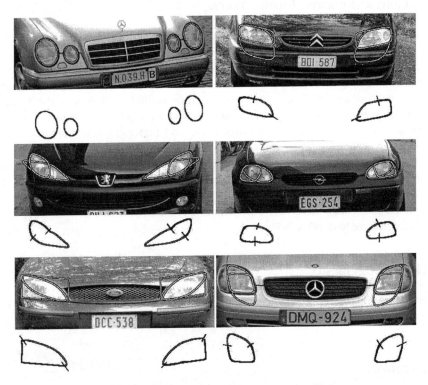

Fig. 9. Other ASE combinations fitted to car headlights

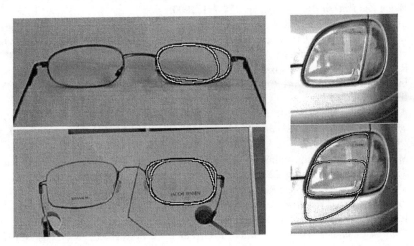

Fig. 10. Left: two pairs of glasses. Right: Detail of the headlight of a Mercedes

As can also be seen from these examples, the pairs of head-lights are approximated by ASEs with similar epsilon values. Other examples are presented in fig. 10.

5   Conclusions and Future Work

Currently, we are working on affine invariant descriptions of such ASE configurations, both in terms of their overall shape, as the texture content within their approximated contour. For the latter, already extensive sets of measures exist. Moment invariants would be one option [11]. As to the shape features, the ratio of areas of the different ASEs in the final configuration would be one simple, additional example. Other features should describe their relative positions, skews, and orientations. These can be quantified by normalizing one of the ASEs to a supercircle, and expressing these parameters with respect to the reference frame thus created.

The results seem to corroborate the viability of the ASE approach. In its full-fledged form it will not only include several of the affine invariant region types already in use, but will also provide a link between the texture based methods that these basically are, and shape-based approaches. Indeed, it stands to reason that a truly generic recognition system will have to draw on both.

Acknowledgements

The authors gratefully ackowledge support from EC Cognitive Systems project CogViSys and the fund for Scientific Research Flanders.

References

1. A. Baumberg: "Reliable feature matching across widely separated views", *IEEE Computer Vision and Pattern Recognition*, pp. 774-781, 2000.
2. M.C. Burl, M. Weber, T.K. Leung and P. Perona: "Recognition of Visual Object Classes", Chapter to appear in: *From Segmentation to Interpretation and Back: Mathematical Methods in Computer Vision*, Springer Verlag.
3. R. Fergus, P. Perona, A. Zisserman: "Object Class Recognition by Unsupervised Scale-Invariant Learning", *Proc. Conf. on Computer Vision and Pattern Recognition - CVPR*, IEEE, 2003.
4. A. Fitzgibbon, M. Pilu, R.B. Fisher: "Direct least squares fitting of ellipses", *IEEE Transactions on Pattern Analysis and Machine Intelligence*, Vol 21, Issue 5, pp. 476-480, May 1999.
5. M. Gardiner: "The superellipse: a curve that lies between the ellipse and the rectangle", *Scientific American* 21, pp. 222-234, 1965.
6. S.Helmer, D.Lowe: "Object Recognition with Many Local Features.", *to appear at Generative Model Based Vision Workshop (CVPR 2004)*
7. F.Jurie, C.Schmid: "Scale-Invariant Features for Recognition of Object Categories.", *Proc. Conf on Computer Vision and Pattern Recognition - CVPR*, IEEE, June 2004, Vol II, pp. 90-96.

8. S. Lazebnik, C. Schmid, J. Ponce: "Affine-Invariant Local Descriptors and Neighborhood Statistics for Texture Recognition", *Proc. Conf. on Computer Vision, Nice, France* - CVPR, IEEE, October 2003, pp. 649-655.
9. K. Mikolajczyk, C. Schmid: "An affine invariant interest point detector", *European Conference on Computer Vision*, Vol. 1, pp. 128-142, 2002.
10. K. Mikolajczyk, A. Zisserman, C. Schmid: "Shape recognition with edge-based features", *Proc. of the British Machine Vision Conference* - BMVC 2003
11. F. Mindru, T. Moons, L. Van Gool: "Recognizing color patterns irrespective of viewpoint and illumination", *Proc. Conference on Computer Vision and Pattern Recognition* - CVPR, IEEE, pp. 368-373, June 1999.
12. S. Obdzalek, J.Matas: "Object recognition using Local Affine Frames on Distinguished Regions", *British Machine Vision Conference*, pp. 414-431, 2002.
13. M. Pilu, A.W. Fitzgibbon, R.B. Fisher: "Training PDM on models: The case of deformable superellipses", *In Proceedings of the British Machine Vision Conference*, Edinburgh, pp. 373-382, September 1996.
14. P. Rosin: "Fitting Superellipses", *IEEE Transactions on Pattern Analysis and Machine Intelligence*, Vol 22, No. 7, July 2000.
15. F. Rothganger, S. Lazebnik, C. Schmid, J. Ponce: "3D Object Modeling and Recognition Using Affine-Invariant Patches and Multi-View Spatial Constraints", *Proc. Conf on Computer Vision and Pattern Recognition* - CVPR, IEEE, June 2003, Vol. II, pp. 272-277.
16. C. Schmid, R. Mohr: "Local Grayvalue Invariants for Image Retrieval", *IEEE Transactions on Pattern Analysis and Machine Intelligence*, 19(5), pp. 530-535, 1997.
17. D. Tell, S. Carlsson: "Wide baseline point matching using affine invariants computed from intensity profiles", *ECCV*, Vol. 1, pp. 814-828, 2000.
18. T. Tuytelaars, L.Van Gool: "Wide baseline stereo matching based on local affinely invariant regions", *Proceedings British Machine Vision Conference*, Sept.2000, pp. 412-422.
19. Eric W. Weisstein. "Superellipse." From MathWorld A Wolfram Web Resource. http://mathworld.wolfram.com/Superellipse.html
20. Eric W. Weisstein. "Levenberg-Marquardt Method." From MathWorld - A Wolfram Web Resource. http://mathworld.wolfram.com/LevenbergMarquardt Method.html
21. X. Zhang, P. Rosin: "Superellipse fitting to partial data", *Pattern Recognition*, No. 36, pp. 743-752, 2003.

Author Index

Lecture Notes in Computer Science

For information about Vols. 1–3287

please contact your bookseller or Springer